Clearly written and comprehensive in scope, this is an essential guide to syntax in the Hungarian language. It describes the key grammatical features of the language, focussing on the phenomena that have proved to be theoretically the most relevant and that have attracted the most attention. The analysis of Hungarian in the generative framework since the late 1970s has helped to bring phenomena which are non-overt in the English language into the focus of syntactic research. As Katalin É. Kiss shows, its results have been built into the hypotheses that currently make up Universal Grammar. The textbook explores issues currently at the center of theoretical debates, including the syntax and semantics of focus, the analysis of quantifier scope, and negative concord. This useful guide will be welcomed by students and researchers working on syntax and those interested in Finno-Ugric languages.

KATALIN É. KISS is Research Professor at the Institute for Linguistics, Hungarian Academy of Sciences. She is author of *Configurationality in Hungarian* (1987), co-editor (with F. Kiefer) of *The Syntactic Structure of Hungarian* (1994), and editor of *Discourse Configurational Languages* (1995).

CAMBRIDGE SYNTAX GUIDES
General editors:
S. R. Anderson, J. Bresnan, D. Lightfoot, I. Roberts, N. V. Smith, N. Vincent

Responding to the increasing interest in comparative syntax, the goal of the Cambridge Syntax Guides is to make available to all linguists major findings, both descriptive and theoretical, which have emerged from the study of particular languages. The series is not committed to working in any particular framework, but rather seeks to make language-specific research available to theoreticians and practitioners of all persuasions.

Written by leading figures in the field, these guides will each include an overview of the grammatical structures of the language concerned. For the descriptivist, the books will provide an accessible introduction to the methods and results of the theoretical literature; for the theoretician, they will show how constructions that have achieved theoretical notoriety fit into the structure of the language as a whole; for everyone, they will promote cross-theoretical and cross-linguistic comparison with respect to a well-defined body of data.

The Syntax of Early English by Olga Fischer, Ans van Kemenade, Willem
   Koopman and Wim van der Wurff
The Syntax of Spanish by Karen Zagona
The Syntax of Hungarian by Katalin É. Kiss

The Syntax of Hungarian

KATALIN É. KISS

CAMBRIDGE UNIVERSITY PRESS
Cambridge, New York, Melbourne, Madrid, Cape Town, Singapore,
São Paulo, Delhi, Dubai, Tokyo, Mexico City

Cambridge University Press
The Edinburgh Building, Cambridge CB2 8RU, UK

Published in the United States of America by Cambridge University Press, New York

www.cambridge.org
Information on this title: www.cambridge.org/9780521660471

First published 2002

A catalogue record for this publication is available from the British Library

Library of Congress Cataloguing in Publication Data

É. Kiss, Katalin
The syntax of Hungarian / Katalin É. Kiss.
   p. cm.
Includes bibliographical references and index
1. Hungarian language - Syntax.   I. Title.
PH2361.K55   2002
494'.5115 - dc21   2001043126

ISBN 978-0-521-66047-1 Hardback
ISBN 978-0-521-66939-9 Paperback

Contents

Acknowledgments

This syntax is based primarily on the results of Hungarian generative syntactic research from the past 25 years. It is a subjective enterprise in as much as it adheres to the basic outlines of the Hungarian sentence structure that I proposed in the late 1970s, consisting of a topic and a predicate, with the predicate containing a head-initial verb phrase preceded by a focus and quantifiers – a structure which can in fact be traced back to the work of Sámuel Brassai in the middle of the nineteenth century. However, it also incorporates the work of a large community of researchers in Hungary and abroad. I have directly adopted results of Huba Bartos and Marcel den Dikken on Hungarian morphosyntax, ideas of Misi Bródy concerning the focus projection, various proposals of Genovéva Puskás and Csaba Olsvay on negation, and those of László Hunyadi on quantification. Observations of Gábor Alberti appear in several chapters of the book. Anna Szabolcsi's work has influenced my view of Hungarian syntax in basic ways, particularly her works on quantification, the structure of the noun phrase, and on the structure of the non-finite verb phrase. The chapter on non-finite verb phrases has also benefited from the work of Tibor Laczkó, Ildikó Tóth, and András Komlósy. The analysis of subordination is based mainly on the work of István Kenesei, and also includes proposals by Júlia Horváth. The chapter on the postpositional phrase incorporates observations of László Marácz and Farrel Ackerman, whereas the discussion of aspect is based on the work of Ferenc Kiefer, also adopting ideas of Christopher Piñon. While I have attempted to present the various, often conflicting theories on different issues of Hungarian syntax faithfully, I have selected from the large body of literature only what I have found most significant and most convincing. The contribution of my fellow syntacticians, among them my colleagues at the Linguistic Institute of the Hungarian Academy of Sciences, and my Ph.D. and undergraduate students at the Theoretical Linguistics Program of Eötvös Loránd University cannot always be documented by references: our discussions and debates over the years have constantly affected my views on Hungarian syntax. I also owe thanks to a very conscientious and helpful anonymous reviewer.

There is also another Hungarian syntax currently available: *The Syntactic Structure of Hungarian*, edited by F. Kiefer and K. É. Kiss (Academic Press, 1994).

However, the two books differ in their coverage. This book gives a more comprehensive view of Hungarian syntax, discussing several areas not touched upon in that book (among them the structure of PP, non-finite complementation, negation, etc.). There are also topics which are discussed in detail only in the earlier book (for example, coordination, complementation versus adjunction, or aspect). In the discussion of questions that are addressed in both books, the present volume focusses on the results of the past few years.

The coverage of Hungarian syntax resembles that of the syntax chapter of *Új magyar nyelvtan* ('New Hungarian Grammar'), by K. É. Kiss, F. Kiefer, and P. Siptár (Osiris, 1998); however, it is much more explicit and technical than its Hungarian predecessor, which was intended for teachers of Hungarian.

1

Introduction

1.1   Genealogy, areal distribution

Hungarian is a Finno-Ugric language. The Finno-Ugric languages and the practically extinct Samoyed languages of Siberia constitute the Uralic language family. Within the Finno-Ugric family, Hungarian belongs to the Ugric branch, together with Mansy, or Vogul, and Khanty, or Ostyak, spoken by a few thousand people in western Siberia. The family also has:

- a Finnic branch, including Finnish (5 million speakers) and Estonian (1 million speakers);
- a Sami or Lappish branch (35 000 speakers); as well as
- a Mordvin branch, consisting of Erzya (500 000 speakers) and Moksha (250 000 speakers);
- a Mari or Cheremis branch (550 000 speakers); and
- a Permi branch, consisting of Udmurt or Votyak (500 000 speakers) and Komi or Zuryen (350 000 speakers).

Hungarian, Finnish and Estonian are state languages; Sami is spoken in northern Norway, Sweden and Finland, whereas the Mordvin, Mari, and Permi languages are spoken in the European territories of Russia.

Hungarian is spoken in Central Europe. It is the state language of Hungary, but the area where it is a native language also extends to the neighboring countries. In Hungary it has 10 million speakers, in Romania 2 million speakers, in Slovakia 700 000 speakers, in Yugoslavia 300 000 speakers, in Ukraine 150 000 speakers. There is also a Hungarian minority in Croatia, Slovenia, and Austria, and a considerable diaspora in Western Europe, North America, South America, Israel, and Australia.

The period in which the Finno-Ugric peoples represented a kind of linguistic and areal unity is believed to have lasted until 2000 BC. On the basis of linguistic evidence – e.g. the habitat of the plants and animals whose names are shared by the Finno-Ugric languages – the Finno-Ugric homeland is located on the south-western slopes of the Ural mountains. The Hungarian language must have emerged here from among the Ugric dialects after 1000 BC. The Hungarian tribes left the Finno-Ugric homeland in the fifth century AD, and occupied the territory surrounded by the Carpathian mountains in 895. In the period of migration, the language had been subject to heavy Turkic influence. After the Hungarian tribes settled in Central Europe, the Slavic languages and German had a noticeable impact on Hungarian.

The first written Hungarian records are Hungarian fragments in a Greek and a Latin text, dating from 950 and 1055, respectively. The first two surviving coherent written Hungarian texts originated in 1192–95, and in 1300. Interestingly, they are still to a large extent comprehensible to the present-day reader. Hungarian is also fairly homogeneous areally; the only dialect displaying substantial lexical, phonological, and syntactic differences from standard Hungarian is the easternmost, archaic Csángó dialect spoken in Romania.

1.2   A general overview of the syntactic and morphosyntactic features of Hungarian

Hungarian is often referred to as a free word-order language, because the grammatical functions of subject, object, etc. are not linked to invariant structural positions in the sentence. Thus, a transitive verb and its two arguments, e.g. *keresi* 'seeks' *János* 'John' *Marit* 'Mary-ACC' can form a sentence in any of the theoretically possible SVO, SOV, OVS, OSV, VSO, and VOS combinations:

(1)   János keresi Marit.   Marit János keresi.
        János Marit keresi.   Keresi János Marit.
        Marit keresi János.   Keresi Marit János.

A closer scrutiny, however, makes it clear that the order of major sentence constituents is just as strictly constrained in Hungarian as it is, for example, in English or French – merely the functions associated with the different structural positions are logical functions instead of the grammatical functions subject, object, etc.

The Hungarian sentence can be divided primarily into a topic part and a predicate part. The topic, functioning as the logical subject of predication, names the individual that will be predicated about in the sentence. The topic role is independent of the function 'grammatical subject'; in other words, an action or state can be predicated about any of its participants. Thus, in (2a) the agent, or grammatical subject, and in (2b) the theme, or grammatical object, occupies the position associated with the topic function. (Since in English the topic and the grammatical subject roles have to coincide, (2b) is translated by a passive sentence. Hungarian (2b), however, differs from (2a) only in its word order.)

(2) a.   [$_{Top}$ János] [$_{Pred}$ fel hívta Marit][1]
        John   up called Mary-ACC[2]
        'John called up Mary.'

    b.   [$_{Top}$ Marit] [$_{Pred}$ fel hívta János]
        Mary-ACC up called John-NOM
        'Mary was called up by John.'

As for the predicate of the sentence, its central element is the verb (V). The postverbal positions are argument positions. The verb usually has a so-called verb modifier (VM), i.e., a non-referential complement incorporated into it, acting as an aspectual operator, as in (3):

(3)   [$_{Top}$ János] [$_{Pred}$ **fel** ásta a kertet]
        John   up dug the garden-ACC
        'John dug up the garden.'

The preverbal section of the predicate phrase contains operator positions. The verb may be immediately preceded by a focus constituent, expressing exhaustive identification (N.B. small capitals are used in the Hungarian text here and throughout the book to mark focus, indicating its phonological prominence):

(4) a.   [$_{Top}$ János] [$_{Pred}$ MARIT   kérte fel]
        John   Mary-ACC asked VM
        'As for John, it was Mary that he asked for a dance.'

    b.   [$_{Top}$ Marit] [$_{Pred}$ JÁNOS   kérte fel]
        Mary-ACC   John-NOM asked VM
        'As for Mary, it was John who asked her for a dance.'

The focus position is preceded by a distributive quantifier position, the locus of universal quantifiers and *is* 'also' phrases; for example:

---

[1] When the verbal prefix precedes the verb, they are traditionally spelled as one word. Nevertheless, I often spell them as two separate words in this book, in order to express the fact that they represent two separate syntactic constituents.

[2] Hungarian is an agglutinating language, in which morphosyntactic elements are right-adjoined to the lexical root. In cases when the morphosyntactic elements play no role in the discussion, the order of the stem and the suffix may be reversed in the glosses in order to facilitate understanding; i.e., example (i) may be glossed as (iii), instead of the more precise (ii).

    (i)   Siettek   iskolába.
    (ii)   hurried-they school-to
    (iii)   they.hurried to.school

(5) a.   [$_{Pred}$ **Marit is**   JÁNOS   kérte fel]
         Mary-ACC too John-NOM asked VM
         '(In the case of) Mary, too, it was John who asked her for a dance.'

   b.   [$_{Pred}$ **Mindenki** MARIT   kérte fel]
         everybody Mary-ACC asked VM
         '(For) everybody, it was Mary that he asked for a dance.'

As is clear from the examples, the preverbal operator positions, too, are filled with no regard to the grammatical function of the filler.

The preverbal operator field of the predicate phrase can also contain negation in addition to the identificational focus and the distributive quantifiers. The negative particle occupies either the immediately preverbal position or the immediately prefocus position, or both simultaneously. The lower negative particle negates the VP – i.e., essentially the propositional content of the clause – whereas the higher negative particle negates the identification expressed by the focus.

(6) a.   János nem hívta fel Marit.
         John not called up Mary-ACC
         'John did not call up Mary.'

   b.   János nem MARIT hívta fel.
         'As for John, it was not Mary that he called up.'

   c.   János nem MARIT nem hívta fel.
         'As for John, it was not Mary that he did not call up.'

The negative particle triggers negative concord among universal quantifiers and indefinites, i.e., its universally quantified clause-mates, and the indefinites in its scope have a special negative form:

(7)   János senkinek   nem mondott semmit.[3]
         John nobody-DAT not said   nothing-ACC
         'John did not say anything to anybody.'

Examples (6a) and (6b), displaying preverbal negation and prefocus negation respectively, also call attention to a very characteristic property of Hungarian: operators precede and c-command their scope, i.e., Hungarian sentences are disambiguated scopally.

In sum: the Hungarian sentence structure to be argued for in this book is a hierarchical structure falling into a topic part and a predicate part, with the predicate part containing a V-initial propositional kernel as well as preverbal operators.[4]

---

[3] For arguments that the negative particle + focus string in (6b,c) is not an instance of constituent negation, and for details of negative concord, see Chapter 6.

[4] For the first formulations of this theory, see Brassai (1860, 1863–65), and É. Kiss (1977).

Chapters 2–6 of this book are devoted to establishing the precise configuration of the structural positions illustrated above, analyzing the operations filling them: examining their trigger, the constraints they are subject to, the semantic consequences they bring about, etc. Chapter 2 discusses the topic position, the topic function, and the operation of topicalization. Chapter 3, dealing with the core of the predicate phrase, examines, on the one hand, the properties, relative order, and hierarchical relations of postverbal arguments and, on the other hand, the properties of the verb modifier, acting as an aspectual operator. Chapter 4 describes the focus position, and the syntax and semantics of focussing/exhaustive identification. Chapter 5 is devoted to questions of quantification: the position of the distributive quantifier, the operation of quantifier raising, scope interpretation, and the like. Chapter 6 discusses negation, including negative concord. Operator movement across clause boundaries is examined in Chapter 10, dealing with subordination.

Hungarian lacks well-known manifestations of the structural prominence of the subject over the object. For instance, in English a subject pronoun and the genitive specifier of the object display disjoint reference; whereas an object pronoun and the genitive specifier of the subject can also corefer, as follows from Binding Condition C applied to an asymmetrical SVO (subject–verb–object) structure. In Hungarian, we find disjoint reference in both cases; compare:

(8) a.   * He_i loves $John_i$'s mother.
    b. $John_i$'s mother loves him_i.

(9) a.   * $Ő_i$ szereti $János_i$ anyját.
          he_i loves $John_i$'s mother

    b.   * $János_i$ anyja szereti $őt_i$.
          $John_i$'s mother loves him_i

The question whether the Hungarian VP is flat, with the subject and the object being sisters, or is configurational, with the subject asymmetrically c-commanding the object, was in the focus of interest in the 1980s and inspired a large amount of literature.[5] The arguments for and against a flat VP are summarized in Chapter 3. The question will also be addressed as to whether the assumption of a flat VP is compatible with current assumptions about the possible format of syntactic structures.

The apparent freedom of Hungarian word order – i.e., the attested parallelism between the syntactic behavior of the subject, object, and other arguments – and their equal eligibility for operator movement must be related to the fact that Hungarian

---

[5] See, among others, É. Kiss (1981, 1987a, 1987b), Horvath (1986a, 1986b, 1987), Marácz (1986b, 1989).

morphology is very rich. Hungarian is a nominative–accusative language with 18 cases, all of which appear to be lexically selected. (Hungarian has no grammatical-function-changing transformations such as passivization.) There is no evidence of the assignment/licensing of particular Cases being linked to particular sentence positions. Accordingly, the lack of a thematic subject does not give rise to an expletive.

Hungarian displays agreement in several areas of grammar. The verb agrees not only with the subject, but also with the object if it is definite. In the possessive construction the head noun bears an agreement suffix reflecting the person and number of the possessor. In postpositional constructions the postposition agrees in person and number with its pronominal complement. Hungarian also has a type of inflected infinitive, agreeing with its dative-marked subject. The phrase types displaying agreement all license pro-drop. Verb morphology is discussed briefly in Chapter 3, dealing with the VP. Nominal, postpositional, and infinitival inflection are analyzed in Chapters 7, 8, and 9, respectively. Inflectional morphology is treated as part of syntax.

The chapters analyzing the inner structure of the noun phrase (NP) and the postpositional phrase (PP) will reveal a great degree of parallelism between the extended VP, and the extended noun phrase/PP. Greenbergian typologies (e.g. Greenberg 1966) categorize Hungarian as a head-final language, in part because the structures of the noun phrase, the attributive adjective phrase, and the postpositional phrase are head final on the surface. However, the VP and the CP are clearly head initial, and the predicative adjective phrase need not be head final, either. This book derives all phrase types from a head-initial base, by subjecting the post-head complement to extraposition, incorporation, or phrase-internal topicalization. For example, in the case of the noun phrase, a post-head complement must be removed because it would block the merging of the head noun with case. Hungarian postpositions are morphosyntactic suffixes, and, as such, they must be right-adjoined to their complement; that is why we attest a DP P order instead of the underlying P DP.

Although Hungarian differs from the best-known Indo-European languages, particularly English, in obvious ways, its basic syntactic properties are not at all unique. Sámuel Brassai, the first linguist to identify the outlines of Hungarian sentence structure, realized already in the middle of the nineteenth century that the topic–predicate articulation relates to the subject–predicate structure attested in some Indo-European languages as the general relates to the specific. That is, the subject–predicate articulation is a topic–predicate structure with the target of topicalization restricted to the grammatical subject (compare Brassai 1860, 1863–65). The generative framework also provides a clue as to the reason for this restriction: in subject–predicate languages the subject can assume nominative case only if it is raised to Spec,IP. In Spec,IP it is closer to the topic position than the other arguments, hence it is topicalizable more economically.[6]

The immediately preverbal identificational focus of Hungarian is also a property shared by a great many languages. For example, in an examination of 35 European languages, 27 languages were found to have an invariant structural position associated with the function of identificational focus, and in 18 of these languages the focus position was found to be immediately preverbal.[7]

The distributive quantifier position at the head of the predicate phrase may not be a feature unique to Hungarian, either. Observations concerning Arabic (compare Khalaily 1995), KiLega (Kinyalolo 1990), Chinese (Bartos 2000b), etc. suggest that universal quantifiers – irrespective of their grammatical function – gravitate to a fixed position in other languages, as well.

An interesting open question is whether there are also other languages besides Hungarian in which the subject and the object behave in a parallel way in so many areas of syntax. The possibility of a head bearing a sister relation to all of its complements is not an option directly predicted by current theoretical assumptions. According to the Linear Correspondence Axiom of Kayne (1994) the hierarchical asymmetry of structural relations ensures their unambiguous mapping onto linear order. Kayne claims that the symmetry of a structural relation, i.e., the impossibility of its linearization, leads to the crashing of the derivation. Perhaps under appropriate conditions, however, the lack of asymmetry might result in a partially linearized structure of the type represented by the Hungarian VP, in which the head – asymmetrically c-commanding its complements – occupies initial position; the post-head arguments, mutually c-commanding each other, on the other hand, can stand in any order. There may also be other ways of reconciling a flat VP with Kayne's antisymmetry theory; for example one might argue that the flat VP represents an intermediate stage of the derivation, with the traces of the initial, asymmetric stage deleted.

The description of Hungarian syntax presented in this book adopts the basic theoretical assumptions and the basic methodology of generative linguistics. However, the approach is empirical rather than technical; the goal of the analyses is to present the theoretically relevant facts of Hungarian explicitly, but without necessarily providing accounts in terms of the most recent theoretical innovations.

---

[6] The claim that the subject in a subject–predicate language is, in fact, moved to topic position can be checked by examining if subjects unsuitable for the topic role – e.g. non-specific indefinites – occupy the same position that topicalizable subjects occupy. A large amount of evidence indicates that non-specific subjects stay in a predicate-internal subject position in subject–predicate languages, as well (compare É. Kiss 1996, 1998c, Diesing 1992).

[7] The details of the investigation, performed in the framework of the EUROTYP project of the European Science Foundation, appeared in É. Kiss (1998c).

2

The topic–predicate articulation of the sentence

2.1 The topic function

Although in the Hungarian sentence the complements of the verb, including the subject, can appear in various permutations (1), the syntactic structure of the sentence is constant, with its units expressing invariant logical-semantic functions.

(1) a.　A védők　　sokáig tartották a　várat　　a　törökök ellen.
　　　　the defenders long　held　　the fort-ACC the Turks　against
　　　　'The defenders held the fort against the Turks for a long time.'
　　b.　A védők sokáig tartották a törökök ellen a várat.
　　c.　A várat sokáig tartották a védők a törökök ellen.
　　d.　A várat sokáig tartották a törökök ellen a védők.
　　e.　A törökök ellen sokáig tartották a védők a várat.
　　f.　A törökök ellen sokáig tartották a várat a védők.

The sentences in (1a–f) all express predication about the referent of their initial constituent. Although they describe the same event (the event of the defenders holding the fort against the Turks for a long time), they formulate it as statements about different participants of the event. (1a,b) make a statement about the defenders (that they held the fort against the Turks for a long time), (1c,d) make a statement about the fort (that the defenders held it against the Turks for a long time), whereas (1e,f) make a statement about the Turks (that the defenders held the fort against them for a long time). That is, the sentences all instantiate a similar predication relation, with the initial constituent functioning as the logical subject of predication, and the rest of the sentence functioning as the logical predicate. In order to avoid confusion of the notions of logical subject of predication, and grammatical subject, the logical subject of predication is referred to here by the term 'topic'. So, the Hungarian sentence primarily divides into a topic and a predicate, with the topic expressing the following function:

8

(2)   *The topic function*
The topic foregrounds an individual (a person, an object, or a group of them) from among those present in the universe of discourse as the subject of the subsequent predication.

2.2   The formal features of the topic constituent

As is clear from the examples in (1a–e), the topic role is not linked to a particular grammatical function. Subjects are in fact more frequent topics than objects – but the link between subjecthood and topichood is only indirect. We tend to describe events from a human perspective, as statements about their human participants – and subjects are more often [+human] than objects are. In the case of verbs with a [–human] subject and a [+human] accusative or oblique complement, the most common permutation is that in which the accusative or oblique complement occupies the topic position (3a,b). When the possessor is the only human involved in an action or state, the possessor is usually topicalized (3c).

(3) a.   [Topic Jánost] [Predicate elütötte egy autó]
            John-ACC   hit   a   car
            'A car hit John. [John was hit by a car.]'

  b.   [Topic Jánosból] [Predicate hiányzik   a   becsület]
            from.John   is.missing the honesty
            'Honesty is missing from John. [John lacks honesty.]'

  c.   [Topic Jánosnak] [Predicate összetörték az autóját]
            John-DAT   they.broke the car-POSS-ACC
            'They broke John's car. [John had his car broken.]'

The topic, naming a participant of the action or state to be described in the sentence, represents an argument of the verb, i.e., it binds an argument position in the predicate part. (This formal criterion helps us to distinguish topics from sentence adverbials, which are predicate-external constituents not functioning as logical subjects of predication.) Since the topic denotes an individual (a person, a thing, or a group of persons or things), it is represented by a referring expression.[1] Thus,

---

[1] The notion of referentiality must be somewhat relaxed, though, for this statement to be tenable. Thus generics can also be topicalized – see (i) and (ii) – but they can be said to refer to kinds.

(i)   A nők   szeretik megosztani a   problémáikat.
        the women like   to.share   their problems
        'Women like to share their problems.'

(ii)   Egy nő   szereti megosztani a   problémáit.
        a   woman likes   to.share   her problems

(continued overleaf)

arguments with an operator feature, e.g. quantifiers, cannot be topicalized:

(4) a. * [Topic Kik] [Predicate meg védték   a   várat   a   törökök ellen]?
           who-PL   VM defended the fort-ACC the Turks   against
           'Who defended the fort against the Turks?'

    b. * [Topic Kevés várat] [Predicate meg védtek   a   zsoldosok a   törökök ellen]
           few   fort-ACC   VM defended the mercenaries the Turks   against
           'Few forts were defended against the Turks by the mercenaries.'

The topic picks an individual as the subject of the subsequent predication from among those already present in the universe of discourse; therefore, it must be represented by a constituent associated with an existential presupposition. Thus, a proper name or a definite noun phrase (or a postpositional phrase containing a proper name or a definite noun phrase) is a possible topic; an indefinite noun phrase, however, can only be topicalized if it is specific in the sense of Enç (1991), i.e., if its referent is the subset of a referent already present in the universe of discourse. From a different perspective: a topicalized indefinite noun phrase always requires a specific (i.e., partitive) interpretation. Consequently, the topicalization of a predicate-internal indefinite noun phrase brings about an interpretational difference:

(5) a.   [Predicate Meg állt   egy autó a   házunk előtt]
                      VM stopped a   car our house before
           'A car has stopped in front of our house.'

    b.   [Predicate Egy autó állt meg a házunk előtt]
           'A car has stopped in front of our house.'

    c.   [Topic Egy autó] [Predicate meg állt a házunk előtt]
           'One of the cars has stopped in front of our house.'

In (5a,b), the predicate-internal *egy autó* 'a car' is likely to be non-specific, serving to introduce a car into the domain of discourse. The topicalized *egy autó* in (5c), on the other hand, can only be understood specifically, meaning 'one of the afore-mentioned cars'. The [+specific] feature required of topicalized indefinite noun phrases is in fact also shared by definite noun phrases. (Since a definite noun phrase is identical with a previously introduced referent, and since the identity relation is a sub-type of the subset relation, its referent always represents a subset of a

As is shown below, existential quantifiers of the *valaki, valami* 'somebody, something' type can also appear in topic position; however, they can be said to behave like indefinites, which function either as referential expressions or as bound variables. *Valaki*-type expressions are topicalizable only when used referentially. Apparently universal quantifiers can also be topicalized if they are contrasted. However, as will be argued in Section 2.7, a contrasted quantifier functions as the name of a set property.

referent already present in the domain of discourse, hence it is always specific.)
Consequently, specificity – similar to referentiality – can be regarded as a necessary
feature of topic constituents; that is:

(6)   *The formal features of topic*
       A topic constituent must be [+referential] and [+specific].

The generalization in (6) appears, at first sight, to be contradicted by the fact that
a set of so-called existential quantifiers – those involving the morpheme *vala-*
'some' – can also appear in topic position; for example:

(7) a.   [Topic Valaki] [Predicate kopog]
          somebody   knocks
          'Somebody is knocking.'

    b.   [Topic Valami] [Predicate le   esett a   tetőről]
          something   VM fell   the roof-from
          'Something has fallen from the roof.'

In fact, *valaki* 'somebody' and *valami* 'something' refer to individuals in (7a,b);
what is more, they are also specific in a certain sense. These sentences are adequate
utterances in situations in which the existence of an unidentified person or object
has been inferred – e.g. when knocking has been heard at the door, or an object
has been seen flying past the window, respectively. If 'specificity' is understood
to mean 'association with an existential presupposition', then *valaki* and *valami*
in sentences like (7a,b) count as specific, hence the generalization in (6) can be
maintained.

2.3   The marking of the topic–predicate boundary

The set of examples in (5a–c) raises the question what evidence we
have for the claim that the sentence-initial noun phrase in (5b) is inside the predicate, whereas that in (5c) is external to it, occupying the topic position. The most
obvious clue is stress: the first obligatory stress, which also represents the heav-
iest grammatical stress in the sentence, falls on the first major constituent of the
predicate.[2] (In Hungarian, phrasal stress – similar to word stress – falls on the
left edge, i.e., the Nuclear Stress Rule of Chomsky and Halle (1968) operates in
a direction opposite to that attested in English.) The topic – like noun phrases
referring to a previously introduced individual, in general – usually does not bear
a primary stress. If it denotes an individual present in the universe of discourse,

---

[2] By 'grammatical stress' I mean stress not affected by pragmatic factors.

but not mentioned in the current discussion, it does receive stress, but – since it represents a separate domain of stress assignment – its stress will never be heavier than the stress on the left edge of the predicate.

The fact that the clause-initial constituent of (5b) occupies the predicate-internal focus position is also indicated by the fact that it is adjacent to the verb. The focus can be analysed to attract the verb across the verb modifier. A topic, on the other hand, never triggers verb movement. That is, a noun phrase followed by a 'V VM' sequence is a predicate-internal focus (8a); a noun phrase followed by a 'VM V' sequence, on the other hand, is a predicate-external topic (8b).

(8) a.   [Predicate DP V VM ...]
   b.   DP [Predicate VM V ...]

When we are in doubt, e.g. when the verb has no verb modifier, and the V-movement triggered by the focus would be vacuous, therefore invisible, we can locate the topic–predicate boundary by finding the rightmost position where a sentence adverbial can be inserted. Sentence adverbials can precede or follow the topic, but cannot enter the predicate. On the basis of this generalization we predict that the predicate-internal initial constituent of (5b) cannot be followed by a sentence adverbial, but the predicate-external initial constituent of (5c) can. The prediction is borne out:

(9) a.   * Egy autó *remélhetőleg* állt   meg a   házunk előtt.
        a   car hopefully   stopped VM our house   before
        'A car has hopefully stopped in front of our house.'

   b.   Egy autó *remélhetőleg* meg állt a házunk előtt.

2.4   The topic projection

The topic constituent, representing an argument of the verb, is assumed to have been preposed from the VP, binding an argument position in it. In the generative framework, in which all syntactic categories are endocentric, the landing site of topic movement is assumed to be the specifier position of a functional projection called TopP. Its abstract head, Top, can be conceived of as an element establishing a predication relation between the constituent in its specifier position, a noun phrase of topic function, and the constituent in its complement position, a verb phrase of predicate function; for example:

(10)

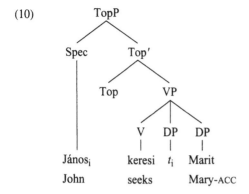

Topic movement is A-bar movement, but not operator movement. The topic is not a logical operator; e.g. it does not take scope – although, being a referential expression, it can be assigned a maximally wide scope existential quantifier.

A sentence can contain more than one topic. A sentence with two topics expresses predication about a pair of the participants of the given event or state. The two topics appear at the head of the sentence in an arbitrary order. We can assume that in such cases TopP is iterated. That is:

(11) a.

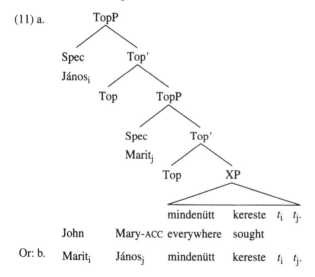

It is not clear how this type of topicalization can be fit into the Minimalist framework, where movement is always a last resort, triggered by the need for checking a morphological feature. One of the problems is that the features involved in licensing topicalization, [+referential] and [+specific], are not morphological features. The fact that not all [+referential], [+specific] constituents must move out of the VP to Spec,TopP visibly is also difficult to handle. We might assume that it is the strong [+referential], [+specific] features of the abstract Top head that need to be checked by the matching features of an argument – but then it remains unclear what causes the optional movement of a second or a third [+referential], [+specific] constituent to further Spec,TopP positions.

2.5   Apparent and real topicless sentences. The (in)definiteness effect

Examples (5a) and (5b) do not contain a visible topic, which can mean either that not all Hungarian sentences project a TopP, or that Spec,TopP is sometimes filled by an invisible element. A closer examination of possible and impossible topicless sentences will lead to the conclusion that both of these statements are true simultaneously.

Sentences with no visible topic fall into two major types. They may be sentences which describe an event as a compact unit, without predicating it of one of its participants; for example:

(12) a.   Megkezdődött a   tanév.
    began   the school-year
    'The school-year has begun.'

  b.   Emelkedik a   részvényindex.
    is.rising   the stock-index
    'The stock index is rising.'

  c.   Árulják   a   lakásukat   a   szomszédaim.
    are.selling their apartment-ACC my neighbors-NOM
    'My neighbors are selling their apartment.'

  d.   Lelőtte valaki   a   trónörököst.
    shot   somebody the heir.to.the.throne-ACC
    'Someone has shot the heir to the throne.'

A set of verbs – those expressing 'being', or 'coming into being', or 'appearing (in the domain of discourse)' – are particularly common in this construction; for example:

(13) a.   Van elég   pénz.
    is   enough money
    'There is enough money.'

  b.   Született egy gyerek.
    was.born a   child
    'A child was born.'

c. Érkezett néhány vonat.
   arrived some   train
   'Some trains arrived.'

d. Alakult két új egyesület.
   formed two new union
   'Two new unions (were) formed.'

e. Keletkezett egy tó.
   arose   a lake
   'A lake arose.'

Since these sentences assert the (coming into) being of their subject, the referent of their subject does not exist independently of the event described in the sentence. The fact that the existence of their subject cannot be presupposed means that their subject cannot be specific (see Szabolcsi 1986). Indeed, these sentences are ungrammatical with a definite subject, or with a universal quantifier (which is also claimed to be specific by Enç 1991):

(14) a. * Van minden pénz.
         is every money

b. * Született Péter.
     was.born Peter

c. * Érkezett a vonat.
     arrived the train

d. * Alakult a diákok   egyesülete.
     formed the students' union

e. * Keletkezett mindegyik tó.
     arose   every   lake

Since specificity is a necessary condition of topichood, examples (13a–e) do not have a topicalizable constituent.

What we have attested in these Hungarian sentences is in fact the well-known (in)definiteness effect.[3] Within the framework of a standard subject–predicate analysis, the reason for the (in)definiteness effect remains unclear, i.e., the necessity of keeping an indefinite subject inside the predicate and (in some languages) filling the subject position with an expletive cannot be explained (cf. Chomsky 1995: Section 4.9). From the perspective of Hungarian the English *there is* . . . construction also becomes comprehensible – provided we assume, following Brassai (1860), that the

---

[3] On the (in)definiteness/(non)specificity effect in Hungarian, see Szabolcsi (1986), É. Kiss (1995c), L. Kálmán (1995), Alberti (1997b), and Maleczki (1995, 1999).

subject–predicate structure of English is in fact a topic–predicate structure, with the set of topicalizable arguments restricted to the subject. Since in the given sentence type the existence of the subject is asserted, the subject must be a [–specific] noun phrase with no existential presupposition, therefore it cannot be topicalized, and must remain in the predicate.[4]

The question arises as to why the group of predicates allowing no specific subject appears to be larger in Hungarian than it is in English. To be able to answer this question, we have to be aware of the fact that nearly all of the Hungarian verbs triggering the indefiniteness (more precisely, the non-specificity) effect also have a counterpart containing the verb modifier *meg*, and these counterparts require a specific subject; for example:

(15) a.   Minden pénz   meg van.
          all   money VM is
          'All the money is there.'

     b.   Meg született a   baba / A baba meg született.
          VM was.born the baby
          'The baby has been born.'

     c.   Meg érkezett az Orient Expressz. / Az Orient Expressz meg érkezett.
          VM arrived the Orient Express
          'The Orient Express has arrived.'

     d.   Meg alakult a   diákok   egyesülete / A diákok egyesülete meg alakult.
          VM formed the students' union
          'The students' union has been formed.'

These verbs do not in fact tolerate a non-specific subject, e.g. a bare plural, which has no specific interpretation:[5]

(16) a.   * Meg vannak adományok.
          VM   are   donations

     b.   * Meg születtek gyerekek.
          VM   were.born children

     c.   * Meg érkeztek vonatok.
          VM arrived   trains

     d.   * Meg alakultak   egyesületek.
          VM were.formed unions

---

[4] É. Kiss (to appear) gives a more explicit formulation of this hypothesis. She argues that the regular surface position of non-specific subjects in English is Spec,IP, which is inside the predicate. Specific subjects have to move on from Spec,IP to Spec,TopP. In the *there is* ... construction the indefinite subject cannot be raised even to Spec,IP because it must be bound, hence c-commanded, by the existential quantifier implicit in *is*.

[5] Evidence for the claim that bare plurals are always non-specific is provided in É. Kiss (1995c).

Lacking a thorough semantic analysis, we can only speculate on the role that the verb modifier *meg* plays in changing the subcategorization frame of the verbs in question (i.e., in making them take a specific subject instead of a non-specific one). In the unmarked case, *meg* serves to turn a process verb into perfective; for example:

(17) a.　János fésülködött.
　　　　John　combed.himself
　　　　'John was combing himself.'

　　　b.　János meg fésülködött.
　　　　John　VM　combed.himself
　　　　'John has combed himself.'

The verbs under consideration (except *van* 'be'), however, are verbs of achievement denoting an indivisible event, which are interpreted perfectively even without *meg*. Intuitively the sentences under (13) differ from their counterparts with *meg* in what represents the main assertion in them. Whereas in the sentences without a verb modifier the lexical content of the predicate (i.e., the coming into being of an individual) is asserted, the versions containing *meg* assert primarily that this event has been completed. Since the sentences with *meg* presuppose rather than assert the (coming into) being of an individual, the presupposition of the existence of the individual does not lead to tautology any more; this is why the subjects in (15a–d) can be specific, even definite, and can also be topicalized.

The indefiniteness effect triggered by the verbs in (13) is also cancelled in the presence of an identificational focus – because then it is the exhaustive identification of a circumstance of the coming into being of an individual that represents the main assertion. This is what we attest in (18a–c):

(18) a.　Péter TAVALY született.
　　　　Peter last.year was.born
　　　　'Peter was born LAST YEAR.'

　　　b.　A　vonat KÉSŐN érkezett.
　　　　the train late　arrived
　　　　'The train arrived LATE.'

　　　c.　A tó　A　GLECCSER ALJÁBAN keletkezett.
　　　　the lake the glacier's　bottom-at arose
　　　　'The lake arose at the bottom of the glacier.'

Example (18a) asserts that the coming into being of Peter took place last year; (18b) asserts that the appearance of the train took place late, whereas (18c) asserts that the coming into being of the lake took place at the bottom of the glacier. Not only is the coming into being of an individual presupposed in each case, but the resulting individual is presupposed as well – hence the indefiniteness/non-specificity requirement on the subject is replaced by a specificity requirement. The

English equivalents of the Hungarian indefiniteness effect verbs – other than *be* – are not recognized as such, presumably because in English the sentence variants in which the lexical content of the VP is asserted are syntactically not distinguishable from the variants in which it is presupposed, neutralizing the indefiniteness effect.[6]

The topicless sentences illustrated in (12)–(13) are eventive sentences, denoting transitory stages of the universe. (In the terminology of Kratzer (1995), they are sentences with a stage-level predicate.) Non-eventive, stative sentences, or, in the terminology of Kratzer (1995), sentences with an individual-level predicate, are marked without a topic; e.g. the following sentences are only acceptable as emphatic exclamations (% indicates that the example is acceptable only in a special context):

(19) a. % Kék szeműek voltak a   gyerekek.
        blue-eyed   were   the children

   b. % Szereti János Marit.
        loves   John   Mary-ACC

Kratzer's theory of the stage-level/individual-level distinction (1995) enables us to rule out (19a,b) as neutral sentences without also ruling out the topicless (12) and (13). In Kratzer's approach the crucial difference between the stage-level (19a,b) and the individual-level (12)–(13) lies in the fact that the stage-level predicates of the former also have a spatiotemporal argument, represented by a variable, which can be associated with temporal and spatial restrictors. In the unmarked case, the temporal and spatial restrictors occupy the topic position of the sentence; for example:

(20)   [TopP Magyarországon az idén [Predicate kétszer is   megáradtak a   folyók]]
             in.Hungary   this year   twice also flooded   the rivers
        'This year in Hungary rivers have flooded twice.'

A temporal or spatial expression in Spec,TopP is interpreted as a logical subject of predication (which is especially clear if none of the obligatory arguments of the verb has also been topicalized). Intuitively, the topicless sentences in (12) and (13) also express predication about a particular spatiotemporal location: about 'here and now' in the present tense (12b,c) and (13a), and about 'there and then' in the past tense (12a,d) and (13b–e). It seems plausible to assume that these sentences also project a TopP, and have their Spec,TopP filled: they have a situationally or contextually bound empty element corresponding to 'here and now' or 'then and there' in topic position. Then, if we assume that every sentence must project a non-vacuous TopP, it will follow that the Spec,TopP position of an eventive sentence does not need a visible filler, because its event variable always licenses an invisible,

---

[6] For arguments that the non-specific subject is inside the predicate also in the English equivalents of (13a–e), see É. Kiss (1996).

situationally or contextually bound spatiotemporal element in Spec,TopP. Since stative predicates have no event variable licensing spatiotemporal expressions, the Spec,TopP position of a stative sentence must always be filled with a visible argument.

Although these assumptions enable us to derive the grammaticality difference between (19a,b) and (12)–(13), they are still not sufficient to predict the full range of facts attested. The problem is that even sentences with an individual-level predicate can be topicless if they contain a logical operator: a focus (21a), a negative particle (21b), an optative operator (21c), an interrogative operator (21d), or a universal quantifier (21e), etc.

(21) a.   KÉK SZEMŰEK a   gyerekek, nem BARNA SZEMŰEK.
          blue-eyed   the children not brown-eyed
          'The children are blue-eyed, not brown-eyed.'

     b.   Nem kék szeműek a   gyerekek
          not blue-eyed   the children
          'The children are not blue-eyed.'

     c.   Bárcsak kék szeműek lennének a   gyerekek!
          if.only blue-eyed   were   the children
          'If only the children were blue-eyed!'

     d.   Szereti János Marit?
          loves John Mary-ACC
          'Does John love Mary?'

     e.   Mindenkinek   küldött Péter egy meghívót.
          everybody-DAT sent   Peter an invitation-ACC
          'Peter sent an invitation to everybody.'

In view of the examples in (21a–e), the hypothesis that all sentences express predication about a topic is an overgeneralization. Apparently, a sentence either expresses predication or quantification (i.e., it is either of the Aristotelian or the Fregean type). A sentence expressing predication is naturally of a topic–predicate structure. A sentence expressing quantification or, more precisely, a sentence extended by one or more propositional operators, on the other hand, does not need a topic – but it can have one. A quantified expression, although viable as an independent sentence, can also be predicated of a topic – thus, in addition to (21a–e), (22a–e) are also grammatical:

(22) a.   [$_{TopP}$ A gyerekek [$_{Predicate}$ KÉK SZEMŰEK, nem BARNA SZEMŰEK]]
              the children   blue-eyed   not brown-eyed
          'The children are blue-eyed, not brown-eyed.'

     b.   [$_{TopP}$ A gyerekek [$_{Predicate}$ nem kék szeműek]]
              the children   not blue-eyed
          'The children are not blue-eyed.'

c. ? [TopP A   gyerekek [Predicate bárcsak kék szeműek lennének!]]
the children   if.only blue-eyed   were
'If only the children were blue-eyed!'

d. [TopP János [Predicate szereti Marit?]]
John   loves Mary-ACC
'Does John love Mary?'

e. [TopP Péter [Predicate mindenkinek   küldött egy meghívót]]
Peter   everybody-DAT sent   an invitation-ACC
'Peter sent an invitation to everybody.'

2.6   Sentence adverbials and the topic–predicate articulation

The topic is not the only type of predicate-phrase-external constituent; sentence adverbials must also precede the predicate. Their position relative to the topic constituents is not fixed; they can precede them, follow them, or intervene between them; for example:

(23) a.   **A várakozások ellenére/szerencsére** a várat   a törökök
the expectations despite/ luckily   the fort-ACC the Turks
[Predicate nem tudták elfoglalni]
         not could occupy
'Despite expectations/luckily, the Turks could not occupy the fort.'

b.   A várat **a várakozások ellenére/szerencsére** a törökök [Predicate nem tudták elfoglalni]

c.   A várat a törökök **a várakozások ellenére/szerencsére** [Predicate nem tudták elfoglalni]

But:

d. ?* A várat a törökök nem tudták **a várakozások ellenére/szerencsére** elfoglalni.

e. ?* A várat a törökök nem tudták elfoglalni **a várakozások ellenére/szerencsére**.

The free order of a sentence adverbial relative to the topic constituents, and its topic-like prosody might suggest at first sight that it is also a topic. However, it does not share the semantic features associated with the topic function: it is not understood as the logical subject of predication, and, accordingly, it does not have to be either referential or specific. Since it serves to modify the whole statement, the semantically most plausible position for it would be a position adjoined to the TopP projection. Such an analysis, however, would run into problems in two types of structures. In one of them, represented by (23c), the problem can be solved. Although the sentence adverbial seems to be adjoined to the predicate phrase (in this case, a NegP) instead of TopP, it fails to bear the primary stress marking the left edge of the predicate, which indicates that it is external to the predicate phrase, after all.

The decisive role of stress can be made clear by a minimal pair. A number of adverbials are ambiguous between a sentence-adverbial and a predicate-adverbial interpretation. If they are placed between the topic and the predicate, their interpretation depends on their stress. If the first primary stress of the sentence, falling on the initial constituent of the predicate, is borne by the adverbial, it is evidence of its predicate adverbial status. If the first primary stress – which is marked throughout by the symbol ′ – falls on the post-adverbial constituent, the adverbial is a predicate-external sentence adverbial; for example:

(24) a. János ′okosan meg válaszolta a   kérdést.
          John cleverly VM answered the question
          'John answered the question cleverly.'

    b. János okosan ′meg válaszolta a kérdést.
          'Cleverly, John answered the question.'

The meaning difference between (24a) and (24b) must follow from a positional difference; that is, if in (24a) *okosan* is adjoined to the predicate, in (24b) it must be dominated by a higher projection. It would be legitimate to assume that it is adjoined to a TopP projection, whose specifier (*János*) has been extracted, and has been left-adjoined to the projection dominating *okosan*. This analysis could also be extended to (23c), that is, the post-topic position of the sentence adverbial could always be derived by the leftward movement of topic constituents from behind it.

The insurmountable problem for this approach is represented by the sentence type which contains a sentence adverbial without projecting a TopP, illustrated in (25). Such sentences contain no predicate-external projection to which the sentence adverbial could be adjoined.

(25) a. A   várakozások ellenére [Predicate mindenki megjelent az ünnepélyen]
          the expectations despite   everybody appeared the ceremony-at
          'Despite expectations, everybody showed up at the ceremony.'

    b. A   várakozások ellenére [Predicate csak JÁNOS volt jelen]
          the expectations despite   only John   was present
          'Despite expectations, only John was present.'

Since the sentence adverbial has no predicate-external projection to adjoin to, the only possible solution seems to be to generate it in the specifier of a functional projection of its own (as proposed by Cinque 1997). Let us call the projection dominating the sentence adverbials in (23) and (25) Evaluative Phrase, and let us assume that it can extend a clausal projection containing minimally a predicate phrase. (Since topics are referential expressions not entering into scopal interaction with scope-bearing elements, it is immaterial whether TopP is internal or external to the Evaluative Phrase dominating the sentence adverbial.)

In view of this, e.g. (23c) has the following structure:

(26)

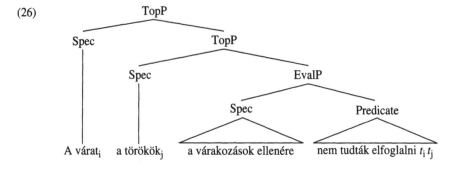

2.7   The contrastive topic[7]

In accordance with the fact that the topic serves to foreground an individual from the universe of discourse, the topic constituent is required to be [+referential] and [+specific]. Surprisingly, however, apparently non-individual-denoting elements – among them bare nouns, adverbs, and also quantifiers – can be topicalized; this is provided they are pronounced with a particular, contrastive intonation comprised of a brief fall and a long rise. With the fall on the subsequent predicate, such sentences have a 'hat' contour marked by the symbols / and \:

(27) a.   **/Biciklit**   \sok lány látott.
          bicycle-ACC many girl saw
          'Bicycle, many girls saw.'

   b.   **/Föl** \LIFTEN   megyek.
          up   elevator-on go-I
          'Up, I go by elevator.'

   c.   **/Legalább három regényt**   \kevés diák   olvasott el.
          at.least   three   novel-ACC few   student read   VM
          'At least three novels were read by few students.'

The fall–rise intonation contour of the initial constituents of (27a–c) can also be associated with a regular individual-denoting topic; for example:

(28) a.   /Jánost   \nem hívom meg.
          John-ACC not   invite-I VM
          'John, I won't invite.'

[7] Molnár (1998) provides a very detailed description of the contrastive topic phenomenon in Hungarian (and German). See also Gyuris (1999).

In this case, however, the fall–rise of the topic is merely a pragmatically motivated option; it conveys the implicature that there is also an alternative referent for whom an alternative predicate holds (i.e., there is at least one person other than János whom I will invite). In (27a–c), on the other hand, the fall–rise contour is obligatory; the sentences would be ungrammatical without it.

As a first step in the analysis of (27a–c), let us ascertain that the constituents in question are, indeed, external to the predicate part of their sentences. This is what the stress pattern of the sentences suggests: the initial constituent precedes the primary stress on the left edge of the predicate (indicated by the symbol ′). Furthermore, it can also precede sentence adverbials, which are always external to the predicate; compare:

(29) a.   **/Biciklit**   valószínűleg \sok lány látott.
          bicycle-ACC probably   many girl saw
          'Bicycle, probably many girls saw.'

   b.   **/Föl** valószínűleg \LIFTEN   megyek.
          up   probably   elevator-on go-I
          'Up, probably I go by elevator.'

   c.   **/Legalább három regényt** valószínűleg \kevés diák   olvasott el.
          at least   three novel-ACC probably   few   student read   VM
          /At least three novels were probably read by \few students.'

The next question to answer is whether the predicate-external constituent in (27a–c) is, indeed, a topic sitting in Spec,TopP, or whether a further structural position should be established for it on the left periphery of the sentence. The plausibility of the latter view is diminished by the fact that constituents with the fall–rise contour can freely mingle with topics proper.[8] Observe in (30a–c) the possible relative orders of the quantifier *minden kollégáját*, pronounced with a fall–rise, and the two regular topic noun phrases: *János* and *a születésnapjára*.

(30) a.   **/Minden kollégáját**   János a   születésnapjára [Predicate \nem szokta
          every   colleague.POSS-ACC John his birthday-on   not used
          meghívni]
          to.invite
          'Every colleague of his, John \would not invite for his birthday.'

   b.   János **/minden kollégáját** a születésnapjára [Predicate \nem szokta meghívni]
   c.   János a születésnapjára **/minden kollégáját** [Predicate \nem szokta meghívni]
          etc.

If the constituent with the fall–rise contour occupied a kind of dislocated, hanging position in the left periphery of the sentence, we would expect it to precede all

---

[8] This point was clarified by Alberti and Medve (2000).

topicalized constituents. In fact, it behaves as if it were one of the topicalized constituents – as if it were simply a contrasted/contrastive topic.

There is also evidence external to Hungarian pointing to the same conclusion: according to the Japanese grammar of Kuno (1973: 46–47), a constituent marked by the topic morpheme *wa* in the Japanese sentence is either referential/generic or contrastive. In other words, a non-referential expression can also be topicalized – but it must be assigned a contrastive intonation and interpretation. The Japanese analogy suggests that what licenses a non-individual-denoting expression in topic position in Hungarian, too, is the contrast expressed by the fall–rise contour.

The role of contrast has been clarified – in a different context – by Szabolcsi (1983a). She examined the problem of what licenses the focussing of non-individual-denoting expressions – when focussing, involving the identification of a subset of a relevant set and the exclusion of the complementary subset, is an operation which can only be performed on an unordered set of distinct individuals. She argued that non-individual-denoting expressions are focusable because they can be individuated by various means, among them by contrast. When we contrast a property denoted by a predicative bare noun with a similar property, then 'by singling them out as relevant, we actually kind of individuate those properties, that is, we disregard the fact that their extensions overlap with the extensions of other properties' (Szabolcsi 1983a: 140).

Let us adopt Szabolcsi's insight for the examples in (27) – without also employing her formal semantic apparatus. In (27a) the property *bicikli* is implicitly contrasted with a relevant property determined by the context or situation. Suppose it is contrasted with the property 'motorbike'. Theoretically it is not obvious whether the extensions of these two properties are distinct, or whether they overlap (what about a clip-on motor?), or perhaps one subsumes the other (after all, a motorbike is also a bike). Their contrast decides the issue: if they are contrasted, then they must be distinct. That is, *biciklit* denotes a distinct property, i.e., it functions practically as a [+referential] constituent. What is more, since the set of the properties *bicikli* and *motorbicikli* must already have been present in the domain of discourse (or else the listener could not reconstruct the contrast implied), *biciklit* is also [+specific], since its referent is the subset of a set of previously introduced referents. That is, the contrast supplies the bare nominal with both features required of topics. Accordingly, the bare nominal acts as a topic proper from a logical point of view; (27a) is understood as a statement about the property 'bicycle'.

In (27b) the adverb *föl* 'up' is contrasted tacitly with its counterpart *le* 'down'. The fact that it is set into contrast with an adverb denoting the opposite direction makes it clear that we use it as the name of a direction. Since it denotes a member of a set of directions present in the domain of discourse, it is not only [+referential] but also [+specific]; hence, it is a legitimate target of topicalization.

Example (27c), with a contrasted universal quantifier, represents a more complex case. According to É. Kiss (2000b), a quantifier functioning as a contrastive topic denotes a cardinality property associated with sets. In the case of (27c), *legalább három regényt* stands for the property 'subset of novels of at least three members', as opposed to the property 'subset of novels of at most two members'. It is predicated about the property 'subset of novels of at least three members' that few students read a representative of it. (An opposite statement is implied about the alternative property 'subset of novels of at most two members', namely, many students read a representative of it.) The proposed paraphrase of the meaning of (27c) also makes it clear why quantifiers in contrastive topic position give the impression of having narrow scope (apparently violating the generalization that in Hungarian the scope order of preverbal constituents corresponds to their surface order). A topicalized quantifier functions as the name of a property, and as such it has maximal scope, and is referentially invariant. The predicate, denoting a set of concrete actions, however, involves concrete realizations/representatives of this property, which do not need to coincide but can also be referentially distinct. This potential referential variance appears to be similar to the referential variance of narrow scope quantifiers; however, its source is different.

2.8   Summary

Hungarian sentence structure falls primarily into two units: one functioning as a topic and the other functioning as a predicate. The topic names an individual (a person, thing, or group) from among those present in the universe of discourse, which the predicate will make a statement about. Unlike in English, the topic does not have to coincide with the grammatical subject; it can be of any grammatical function. A topic constituent is only constrained in respect of referentiality: it must have the features [+referential] and [+specific], i.e., it must be represented by a definite noun phrase, or a specific indefinite one, or a PP dominating such a noun phrase. In fact, a non-referential phrase (e.g. a bare nominal, an adverb phrase, or a quantifier) can also assume the features [+referential] and [+specific] and be topicalized if it is contrasted, contrast being a means of individuation.

The topic is assumed to occupy the specifier position of a TopP projection, binding an argument position in the VP. A sentence can also have more than one topic, i.e., the TopP projection can be iterated. Eventive sentences having no visible topic are understood to express predication about the situationally or contextually determined spatiotemporal restriction on their event variable (referring to 'here and now', or 'there and then'). Both stative and eventive sentences can be topicless if they involve a logical propositional operator.

The facts of Hungarian also provide an insight into the motivation of the (in)definiteness/(non-)specificity effect. Predicates asserting the (coming into) being (in the domain of discourse) of their subject cannot also presuppose the existence of their subject; so their subject is necessarily non-specific, hence not topicalizable, confined to a predicate-internal position.

3

The minimal predicate

Having assigned to the Hungarian sentence a binary predication structure, and having examined the properties of the logical subject of predication, or topic, we turn to the analysis of the predicate phrase. Categorially the predicate is a VP merged with morphosyntactic elements such as tense, mood, and agreement, and either extended into an aspectual phrase, or embedded in operator projections such as a focus phrase, a distributive quantifier phrase, and/or a negative phrase. The subject of this chapter is the minimal predicate, consisting of a VP, merged with morphosyntactic heads, and extended into an AspP, but not involving a focus, a distributive quantifier, or negation.

3.1   Argument order in the VP

The lexical core of the predicate of the Hungarian sentence is a verb phrase. It is assumed to be verb initial, with the arguments following the verb in an arbitrary order – as illustrated in (1). (What motivated the assumption of a verb-initial VP in the late 1970s was that the set of possible permutations of a verb and its complements could be derived most economically from a V-initial base. Later theoretical considerations – concerning the direction of theta-role assignment and Case assignment in Universal Grammar – also confirmed this view.)

(1) a.   [$_{VP}$ Küldött Péter   egy levelet   Máriának]
              sent   PETER a   letter-ACC Mary-DAT
              'Peter sent a letter to Mary.'

   b.   [$_{VP}$ Küldött Máriának Péter egy levelet]
   c.   [$_{VP}$ Küldött egy levelet Péter Máriának]
   d.   [$_{VP}$ Küldött Péter Máriának egy levelet]

Naturally, any of the arguments can undergo topicalization, in which case it will only be represented by a trace in the VP. The different postverbal orders, although equally grammatical, are not equally unmarked. Postverbal argument order seems to depend on the same features that also play a role in topic selection. Namely, specific constituents tend to precede non-specific ones, and human constituents tend to precede non-human. Thus (1c), in which a non-specific indefinite noun phrase precedes two definite noun phrases, is slightly marked. Crucially, postverbal argument order is not determined by the grammatical functions of arguments. Consider the following minimal pairs:

(2) a. Kereste Piroskát   egy biztosítási ügynök.
        sought Piroska-ACC an insurance agent
        'An insurance agent sought Piroska.'

   b. ? Kereste egy biztosítási ügynök Piroskát.

(3) a. Keresett Piroska egy biztosítási ügynököt.
        sought Piroska an insurance agent-ACC
        'Piroska sought an insurance agent.'

   b. ? Keresett egy biztosítási ügynököt Piroska.

As (2a,b) and (3a,b) illustrate, either the VSO or the VOS order can be unmarked – provided the [+referential], [–specific] argument follows the [+referential], [+specific] one. If both arguments are [+referential] and [+specific], but they are marked for different values of the feature [+/–human], the [+human] [–human] order sounds more neutral; for example:

(4) a. El ütötte Jánost   a   Péter autója.
        VM hit   John-ACC the Peter's car-NOM
        'Peter's car hit John.'

   b. ? El ütötte a Péter autója Jánost.

(5) a. Össze törte János   a   Péter autóját.
        VM   broke John-NOM the Peter car-POSS-ACC
        'John broke Peter's car.'

   b. ? Össze törte a Péter autóját János.

Theta role seems to affect postverbal argument order only if the arguments share every other relevant feature. In that case an agent, or an experiencer (whether realized as a subject or a dative), is more likely to precede a theme than the other way round; compare:

(6) a. Meg állította János Piroskát.
        VM stopped John Piroska-ACC
        'John stopped Piroska.'

   b. ? Meg állította Piroskát János.

(7) a. Hiányzik Jánosnak Piroska.
        is-missing John-DAT Piroska
        'John is missing Piroska.'

   b. ? Hiányzik Piroska Jánosnak.

Hungarian grammars are not capable of predicting the degree of markedness of the examples in (2)–(7) – but it is not clear if they should predict it; after all, these sentences are all fully grammatical. (The symbol ? in front of the (b) examples in (4)–(7) is merely intended to express that these versions are less frequent and somewhat less natural than the (a) examples.) Perhaps it is a general perceptual strategy that we appreciate the world proceeding from familiar items to unfamiliar ones, from humans to non-humans, and from active participants of an event to passive ones.

3.2   The referentiality effect

Arguments with an operator feature (e.g. interrogative phrases or distributive quantifiers) are preposed from the VP into operator positions in the preverbal section of the predicate. The postverbal argument positions are reserved for referential expressions. An argument represented by a bare nominal must also leave the VP – see (8a) and (9a). It can only survive in a preverbal A-bar position: as an aspectual operator (8b), or a focus (9b), or – when supplied with the particle *is* 'also' – as a distributive quantifier (9c).

(8) a.   * János [$_{VP}$ táncolt keringőt]
        John   danced waltz-ACC

    b.   [János [$_{AspP}$ keringőt$_i$ táncolt t_i]]
        'John was waltzing.'

(9) a.   * [$_{TopP}$ János [$_{VP}$ táncolt kövér lánnyal]]
        John   danced fat   girl-with

    b.   [$_{TopP}$ János [$_{FP}$ KÖVÉR LÁNNYAL$_i$ táncolt t_i]]
        'It was (a) fat girl that John danced with.'

    c.   [$_{TopP}$ János [$_{DistP}$ kövér lánnyal is$_i$ táncolt t_i]]
        'John danced also with (a) fat girl.'

(The prohibition against a non-referential constituent in the VP is essentially only valid in focusless sentences – presumably because in the presence of a preverbal focus the postverbal bare nominal can always be interpreted as a focus in situ, given that a preverbal focus also licenses postverbal foci.[1])

---

[1] Another construction which licenses a postverbal bare nominal is the existential construction; for example:

(i)   János TÁNCOLT kövér lánnyal.
    John danced   fat   girl-with
    'John has danced with a fat girl (at least once).'

(continued overleaf)

Alberti (1997b) provides the following account of the distribution of grammaticality in (8)–(9). The arguments of the verb can be legitimized in one of two ways. In the unmarked case they have referential legitimacy, i.e., they serve to identify the referents that the content of the verb is predicated of. Non-referential expressions can be legitimized by obtaining predicative legitimacy in the assertive part (i.e., the operator field) of the predicate. In a neutral sentence the verb represents the (main) assertion, in other words, the new (non-presupposed) information; however, it can extend, or transfer its assertive power to elements moved to the preverbal operator field of the predicate phrase. In this field arguments assume predicative legitimacy (instead of, or in addition to, referential legitimacy).

The topic position, which, similar to the postverbal field, is only available for specific referential expressions, can also host a bare nominal if it is contrasted.

(10)   [$_{TopP}$ /Kövér lánnyal [$_{FP}$ JÁNOS [$_{VP}$ táncolt]]]
         fat   girl-with   John   danced
         'As for fat girls, it was John who danced with one/some.'

As was argued in Section 2.7, a topicalized bare nominal is individuated by being contrasted; it assumes the status of the name of a property, i.e., it obtains a kind of referential legitimacy.

3.3   The subject as an internal argument

As has been demonstrated, postverbal arguments can appear in any order. Since the different orders do not display regular semantic or phonological differences (they are essentially equivalent), they provide no evidence of an invariant underlying order, or of any movement transformation involved in their derivation. Hypotheses on Universal Grammar, among them hypotheses on theta theory, however, presuppose a hierarchical VP, in which the subject is more prominent than the object, the object being c-commanded and assigned a theta role by the V, and the subject being c-commanded and assigned a theta role by the V + object complex. The question whether facts of Hungarian concerning the configurational relation of the subject and object can be reconciled with universal assumptions, or warrant a different approach was in the focus of interest in the 1980s, and inspired a large amount of literature. Book-length contributions to the debate included:

- Horvath (1986a), who assumed a VP-external subject and a VP-internal object, with the focus in intermediate position, adjoined to the verb;

This construction may also involve a kind of focussing: V movement into the head of the focus projection.

- É. Kiss (1987a), who argued for a flat verb projection including both the subject and the object; and
- Marácz (1989), who claimed that the subject is external to the VP, but is internal to the operator projections, and ends up in postverbal position only if an operator triggers V movement across it.

Some of the issues debated in the 1980s seem to have been resolved since then. Thus, it is not an issue any more whether the subject originates in the VP or outside it. Since then it has become universally accepted that the subject is generated inside the maximal projection of the verb, and is externalized transformationally so as to obtain or check its nominative case. In Hungarian the assignment or checking of the nominative case of the subject clearly does not involve an invariant position either outside or inside the VP. When the subject is external to the extended VP, it is in topic position – which is a position that is also available for non-subjects.

Some of the subject–object asymmetries attested in English arise from the fact that the subject has been extracted from the VP into Spec,IP. If these asymmetries appear in Hungarian at all, then they appear as topic vs. internal argument asymmetries. That is, if the subject has been topicalized, then we attest the structural prominence of the subject over the object, and if the object has been topicalized, then we attest the structural prominence of the object over the subject. For example, whereas in English VP-deletion always deletes the V + object string, leaving the subject spelled out, in Hungarian it can also delete the V + subject string, leaving the object spelled out.

(11) a.   [$_{TopP}$ János [$_{VP}$ ismeri Marit]]; [$_{TopP}$ Péter viszont nem [$_{VP}$ ~~ismeri Marit~~]].
           John   knows Mary-ACC   Peter however not   knows Mary-ACC
           'John knows Mary; Peter, on the other hand, doesn't.'

   b.   [$_{TopP}$ Marit [$_{VP}$ ismeri János]]; [$_{TopP}$ Zsuzsát   viszont nem
          Mary-ACC knows John-NOM   Susan-ACC however not
          [$_{VP}$ ~~ismeri János~~]].
          knows John-NOM
          'Mary is known by John; Susan, however, isn't.'

The Superiority Condition requires that a position be filled with the closest constituent having the appropriate features. Accordingly, in English multiple questions involving a subject *wh*-pronoun and an object *wh*-pronoun, Spec,CP is filled by the subject pronoun – because the subject in Spec,IP is closer to Spec,CP than the object is. Since in Hungarian the subject does not leave the VP to assume/check nominative case, then subject and non-subject *wh*-phrases in a multiple question are predicted to be equally available for *wh*-movement. Indeed, this is what we find in both types of Hungarian multiple questions (discussed in Section 4.5.2).

(12) a. Ki melyik témáról   írt?
         who which topic-about wrote
         'Who wrote about which topic?'

    b.   Melyik témáról ki írt?

(13) a. Ki jelentett   fel kit?
         who denounced   VM whom
         'Who denounced whom?'

    b.   Kit jelentett fel ki?

A further area displaying an external argument vs. internal argument asymmetry is idiom interpretation. If the semantic composition of a verb and its arguments proceeds on phrase structure from bottom to top (a premise not accepted by e.g. Bresnan 1982), then it follows that in English idiomatic sentences containing a non-idiomatic variable, the idiomatic unit is the VP, and the non-idiomatic variable is the VP-external subject. In Hungarian idiomatic sentences containing a non-idiomatic variable, the idiomatic part is also confined to the VP, whereas the non-idiomatic variable is represented by the topic. The topicalized non-idiomatic element is usually a [+human] argument of the verb, but not necessarily its subject. It can also be, for example, an object or a goal. Topicalized possessors are particularly common; for example:

(14) a. Jánosnak [AspP ki verte az ág   a szemét]
         John-DAT   out poked the branch the eye-POSS-ACC
         'A branch has poked out John's eye. [John is run down by old age.]'

    b.   Jánost [AspP majd meg ütötte a guta]
         John-ACC   almost VM hit   the stroke
         'A stroke almost hit John. [John was upset.]'

    c.   Jánost [VP eszi a fene]
         John-ACC eats the plague-NOM
         'The plague is eating John. [John is mad (on getting something).]'

    d.   Jánost [AspP el   kapta a gépszíj]
         John-ACC   VM   caught the driving-belt-NOM
         'The driving belt has caught John. [John has been roped in.]'

    e.   Ezt a tetőt [FP csak az imádság tartja]
         this the roof-ACC only the prayer   holds
         'Only prayer holds this roof. [This roof is very shaky.]'

In sum: Hungarian does display certain symptoms of an external argument vs. internal argument asymmetry; however, the structurally prominent external argument of the Hungarian sentence is not the subject, but the topic.

Whereas the claim that Hungarian provides no empirical evidence for a VP-external subject position has become more or less generally accepted, it still remains an open question as to whether the subject is more prominent than the object inside the VP. The facts are controversial; some support the assumption of a flat VP, others argue for a hierarchical, binary branching verb projection.

3.4   The structure of the VP

3.4.1   Evidence from disjoint reference

The most transparent way of testing the VP-internal hierarchical relation of the subject and the object is the examination of Binding Condition C effects. Condition C of Binding Theory states that a referential expression cannot be bound, i.e., if it is c-commanded by a pronominal, it will be disjoint in reference. In a structure in which the subject asymmetrically c-commands the object, an object pronoun does not c-command the genitive specifier of the subject, hence Binding Condition C does not force disjoint reference on them. A subject pronoun, on the other hand, c-commands the genitive specifier of the object, and thus cannot corefer with it. This is what we attest in the following English examples:

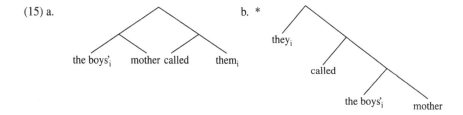

(15) a. the boys'$_i$ mother called them$_i$ b. * they$_i$ called the boys'$_i$ mother

In Hungarian coreference is impossible in both constructions. This will only follow from a symmetric structure, in which not only the subject c-commands the (genitive specifier of the) object, but also the object c-commands the (genitive specifier of the) subject; compare:

(16) a. * Fel hívta őket$_i$ a fiúk$_i$. anyja.
       VM called them the boys' mother-NOM
       'The boys' mother called them.'

  b. * Fel hívták (ők) pro$_i$ a fiúk$_i$ anyját.
       VM called they   the boys' mother-ACC
       'They called the boys' mother.'

The disjoint reference effect illustrated in (16a) cannot be 'undone' either by scrambling within the VP (17a), or by the movement of the subject into the left periphery of the sentence (17b):

(17) a. * Fel hívta a fiúk$_i$ anyja   őket$_i$.
     VM called the boys' mother-NOM them
     'The boys' mother called them.'

   b. * A fiúk$_i$ anyja fel hívta őket$_i$.
     'The boys' mother called them.'

Interestingly, as Marácz (1989) noticed, the subject–object asymmetry absent from the referential relation of a pronominal and a lexical noun phrase does show up in the relation of two lexical noun phrases:

(18) a. Fel hívta a fiúkat$_i$ a fiúk$_i$ anyja.
     VM called the boys-ACC the boys' mother-NOM
     'The boys' mother called the boys.'

   b. Fel hívta a fiúk$_i$ anyja a fiúkat$_i$.

(19) a. * Fel hívták a fiúk$_i$ a fiúk$_i$ anyját.
     VM called the boys-NOM the boys' mother-ACC
     'The boys called the boys' mother.'

   b. * Fel hívták a fiúk$_i$ anyját a fiúk$_i$.

If we adopt the hierarchical VP hypothesis, we predict the grammaticality of (18a,b), but we cannot account for the ungrammaticality of (16a) and (17a,b); we have to attribute it to some unknown reason. If we adopt the flat VP hypothesis, the ungrammaticality of (16a,b) and (17a,b) will follow; however, the grammaticality of (18a,b) cannot be predicted straightforwardly – without an auxiliary hypothesis.

   The core of the problem is the grammaticality difference between the structurally identical (16a) and (18a). As these examples demonstrate, the coreference possibilities between a pronoun and a referring expression are more strictly constrained than those between two referring expressions. If Reinhart (1983) is right in suggesting that the disjoint reference effect arising between two referring expressions falls outside the realm of the Binding Conditions,[2] then the syntactically relevant example is that in (16a), which argues for a flat VP. Then the referential relation between two referring expressions has to be accounted for by an auxiliary principle. This principle appears to be motivated thematically rather

---

[2] According to Reinhart (1983: 170) such a move would not be completely unmotivated. She claims that 'it is generally so that the reference of a full NP is more easily recoverable than the reference of a pronoun, so . . . it should be easier to identify intended coreference of two identical full NPs than of a pair of a pronoun and full NP . . .'

than structurally – e.g. whereas in (18)–(19), containing an agent subject and a theme object, the subject is more prominent than the object, in (20a,b), involving a theme subject and an experiencer object, the subject and the object are equally prominent:

(20) a. János$_i$ felesége nem érdekli Jánost$_i$.
         John's wife   not interests John-ACC
         'John's wife does not interest John.'

    b. János$_i$ feleségét nem érdekli János$_i$.
         John's wife-ACC not interests John-NOM
         'John does not interest John's wife.'

3.4.2 Evidence from anaphora

The clearest evidence for an argument hierarchy operative in Hungarian grammar is provided by facts of anaphora. Consider the binding possibilities in the following examples:

(21) a. **János** felismerte **önmagát**   a   képen.
         John   recognized himself-ACC the picture-on
         'John recognized himself in the picture.'

    b. * **Jánost**   felismerte **önmaga**   a   képen.
         John-ACC recognized himself-NOM the picture-on
         'Himself recognized John in the picture.'

(22) a. Bemutattam **a lányokat egymásnak**.
         introduced-I the girls-ACC each-other-DAT
         'I introduced the girls to each other.'

    b. ? Bemutattam **a lányoknak egymást**.
         introduced-I the girls-DAT each-other-ACC
         'I introduced each other to the girls.'

(23) a. ? Megmutattam **a gyereket önmagának** a   tükörben.
         showed-I   the child-ACC himself-DAT the mirror-in
         'I showed the child to himself in the mirror.'

    b. Megmutattam **a gyereknek önmagát**   a   tükörben.
         showed-I   the child-DAT himself-ACC the mirror-in
         'I showed the child himself in the mirror.'

(24) a. Szembesítettem **János**   **önmagával**.
         confronted-I   John-ACC himself-with
         'I confronted John with himself.'

    b. * Szembesítettem **Jánossal önmagát**.
         confronted-I   John-with himself-ACC
         'I confronted himself with John.'

(25) a. Gyakran vitatkozom **Jánossal önmagáról.**
         often   argue-I   John-with himself-about
         'I often argue with John about himself.'

   b. * Gyakran vitatkozom **Jánosról   önmagával.**
         often   argue-I   John-about himself-with
         'I often argue about John with himself.'

According to the evidence of these examples, a subject can bind an accusative object, but not vice versa. The binding relation between an accusative object and a dative is also asymmetric; it depends on the verb which can bind the other. In a sentence containing an accusative and an instrumental, only the former can bind the latter, whereas in a sentence containing an instrumental and a locative argument, the instrumental is the potential binder.

Surface order does not alter grammaticality (although the orders in which the binder precedes the anaphor may sometimes sound better). Thus, the reverse anaphor–antecedent order in (26a), derived by operator movement, and that in (26b), derived by VP-internal scrambling, are also perfectly grammatical.

(26) a. A képen   **önmagát**   ismerte   fel **János.**
         the picture-on himself-ACC recognized VM John-NOM
         'It was himself that John recognized in the picture.'

   b. Bemutattam **egymásnak**   a **lányokat.**
         introduced-I each-other-DAT the girls-ACC
         'I introduced the girls to each other.'

If our premise is Binding Condition A in its standard formulation, according to which an anaphor requires a c-commanding antecedent, the sentences in (21)–(25) provide evidence for an articulated VP-internal argument hierarchy, in which the nominative complement occupies the highest position, and the complement in a locative case occupies the lowest one. Examples (22)–(23) somewhat blur the picture though: we must conclude that in (22) the accusative c-commands the dative, whereas in (23) the dative c-commands the accusative. The different binding potentials of the two dative complements may in fact reflect a difference in their theta roles: the dative complement of *megmutat* 'show' may be an experiencer, and that of *bemutat* 'introduce' may be a goal. (Notice that the English equivalent of the dative complement in (23) can also be realized as an indirect object, whereas the English equivalent of the dative complement in (22) can only be realized as a PP. Should the possibility or impossibility of dative shift in English turn out to be thematically motivated, the English facts would also support our explanation of the distribution of grammaticality (22)–(23).)

What (22)–(23) clearly indicate is that the licensing condition of anaphoric relations cannot be morphological case. This conclusion is also confirmed by

the examination of causatives. In the case of a causative verb derived by the suffix
-tat/tet, the causee is in the instrumental case, and – despite the fact that a constituent
bearing an instrumental case and functioning as an instrument is less prominent
than an accusative object (24a,b) – the instrumental causee can bind the object,
and cannot be bound by it:

(27) a. **Jánossal és Marival** felhívattam   **egymást**.
        John-with and Mary-with call-CAUS-PAST-1SG each-other-ACC
        'I had John and Mary call each other.'

    b. * **Jánost és Marit**   felhívattam   **egymással**.
        John-ACC and Mary-ACC call-CAUS-PAST-1SG each-other-with
        'I had each other call John and Mary.'

Although the instrumental in (27a) may very well function as a subject at some
level of representation, the licensing condition of anaphora, nevertheless, cannot
be based on grammatical functions, either. Whereas in the cases discussed so far
the subject can bind the object, and not vice versa, in the case of psych verbs taking
a theme subject and an experiencer object, the binding relation between the two
arguments is more felicitous if the object binds the subject; compare:

(28) a. **Jánost önmaga**   aggasztja a legkevésbé.
        John-ACC himself-NOM worries   the least
        'Himself worries John the least.'

    b. ? **János** önmagát   aggasztja a legkevésbé.
        John   himself-ACC worries   the least
        'John worries himself the least.'

(29) a. **Jánost**   csak **önmaga**   érdekli.
        John-ACC only himself-NOM interests
        'Only himself interests John.'

    b. ? **János** csak **önmagát**   érdekli.
        John   only himself-ACC interests
        'John interests only himself.'

These examples confirm that the prominence relation licensing anaphora cannot
be determined either in terms of case, or in terms of surface grammatical functions
or surface c-command. What underlies anaphoric binding is obviously a thematic
argument hierarchy: the binder must be thematically more prominent than the
anaphor.[3] In (28)–(29) the object can bind the subject because it has an experiencer role, and an experiencer is thematically more prominent than a theme. The

---

[3] The idea that binding is thematically constrained is not new; see, for example, Williams
(1987).

(b) examples, in which the subject binds the object, are acceptable only to the extent the verb can also be associated with an agentive meaning, with the subject functioning as an agent, and the object functioning as a theme.

The crucial question is, of course, what place to attribute to the thematic argument hierarchy underlying anaphora in grammar; whether to encode it in a structural hierarchy of arguments in a VP containing multiple shells, or to encode it in the ordering of arguments in the theta-grid associated with a head in the lexicon, or perhaps simply to assume a hierarchy of the following type as a primitive of grammar:

(30)   *Thematic argument hierarchy*
        agent/experiencer > theme > goal > instrumental > locative

If we adopt the hierarchical VP approach, then we have to assign to (28a) a VP involving two VP-shells:

(31)

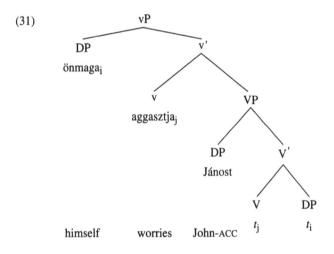

The anaphor in subject position is licensed by the fact that the object c-commands the root of the subject chain. It remains a question, however, what motivates the movement of the object of VP into the subject position of vP.

If we assume a lexically encoded thematic argument hierarchy, we can maintain the flatness of the VP. Then the primacy condition of binding will have to state that *a* can bind *b* if it both c-commands *b* or its trace, and precedes *b* in the thematic argument hierarchy. The notion of thematic prominence, however, must also be interpreted on relations between non-coarguments. The following types of antecedent–anaphor relations must be accounted for:

(32) a. Karácsonyra ajándékot   küldött **János   és   Mari   egymás**
Christmas-on present-ACC sent   John-NOM and Mary-NOM each.other's
szüleinek.
parents-DAT
'John and Mary sent presents to each other's parents for Christmas.'

b. ? Karácsonyra ajándékot küldött **egymás szüleinek János és Mari.**

c. ?? Karácsonyra ajándékot   küldtek **Jánosnak és   Marinak egymás**
Christmas-on present-ACC sent   John-DAT and Mary-DAT each.other's
szülei.
parents-NOM
'To John and Mary, each other's parents sent presents for Christmas.'

d. * Karácsonyra ajándékot küldtek **egymás szülei Jánosnak és Marinak.**

The facts that the subject can freely bind a subconstituent of the thematically less prominent object, but the object cannot, or only marginally can, bind a subconstituent of the thematically more prominent subject suggest that an argument has indirect thematic prominence also over the descendants of its thematically less prominent coarguments. Interaction with linear precedence seems to be stronger than in other cases: the lack of indirect thematic prominence can be compensated for by linear precedence.[4]

The data in (32) suggest the following generalization:

(33)   *The primacy condition of binding*
a can bind b if it c-commands b or its trace, and at least (i) or (ii) holds:
  i. a precedes b in the thematic argument hierarchy;
  ii. a precedes b in linear order.

(34)   *Thematic precedence*
a precedes b in the thematic argument hierarchy if a is ordered prior to b or to the constituent containing b in the thematic argument hierarchy.

While condition (33) correctly accounts for anaphoric relations between non-coarguments, it does not rule out constructions like (35), which are ungrammatical despite the fact that the binding relation satisfies both the c-command and the precedence conditions.

(35)   * **A   lányokban**   bíznak **önmaguk.**
the girls-INESSIVE trust   themselves-NOM
'Themselves trust in the girls.'

The ungrammaticality of (35) may follow from the assumption that binding is an asymmetric relation, which entails the following constraint:

---

[4] For further data and discussion, see Kenesei (1989) and É. Kiss (1991b, 1994b).

(36)   *The asymmetry of binding*
          If *a* can bind *b*, *b* cannot bind *a*.

In (35) the possibility of the agent binding the theme excludes the possibility of the theme binding the agent. (In (28)–(29) the different binding possibilities among the same sets of complements are associated with different theta-grids, hence (36) does not apply.) The asymmetry constraint is not relevant in cases like (32c), either, as the genitive specifier is not a potential binder of the dative argument.

3.4.3   Evidence from Weak Crossover

In English and similar languages, the asymmetric subject–object relation is also manifest in the asymmetry of the so-called Weak Crossover phenomenon. Namely, a subject operator can bind the pronominal genitive of the object; however, an object operator cannot bind the pronominal genitive of the subject:

(37) a. Who_i didn't t_i visit his_i mother?
      b. ?* $Whom_i$ didn't his_i mother visit t_i?

The most widely accepted explanation of the ungrammaticality of (37b) is that it contains a *wh*-operator which binds two variables, in violation of the bijection principle, that is:

(38)   for which x, x's mother did not visit x

In the case of (37a) this problem does not arise: the pronoun is argument-bound by the operator trace, hence the operator only has to bind a single variable:

(39)   for which x, x did not visit x's mother

In Hungarian the equivalents of both (37a) and (37b) allow the bound variable interpretation of the pronoun (represented by a pro licensed by an agreement morpheme on the possessed noun):

(40) a.   **Ki_i** látogatta meg az **pro_i** anyját?
           who visited   VM the pro's mother-ACC
           'Who visited his mother?'

      b.   **Kit_i** látogatott meg az **pro_i** anyja?
           whom visited   VM the pro's mother-NOM
           'Who did his mother visit?'

The formula in (38), from which the English Weak Crossover effect is derived, involves a subject in Spec,IP; however, the fact that the position of the subject is external to the VP is immaterial; what is crucial is that it should asymmetrically c-command the object. That is, if the explanation of the Weak Crossover effect in terms of the bijection principle is correct, it should also hold in the case of a VP-internal subject–object asymmetry. The lack of any Weak Crossover effect in the Hungarian (40b) means that in the Hungarian VP not only can the subject bind the genitive specifier of the object, but also the object can bind the genitive specifier of the subject, i.e., the subject and the object mutually c-command each other in a flat VP.[5]

In some approaches the Weak Crossover effect is derived from the Leftness Condition, which says that a variable cannot be the antecedent of a pronoun on its left (see Chomsky 1976). The Leftness Condition, too, will predict the lack of Weak Crossover effects in Hungarian only if it is interpreted on a partially ordered flat VP, in which the pronoun can be generated on the right of the variable coindexed with it, as in structure (41):

(41)   **Kit**$_i$ látogatott meg t_i az **pro**$_i$ anyja?
         whom visited   VM   the pro's mother-NOM
         'Whom did his mother visit?'

Although the core cases are symmetric, the Weak Crossover phenomenon is in fact not completely exempt from asymmetric effects in Hungarian, either; compare:

(42) a. **Minden diák**$_i$ meglátogatta az **pro**$_i$ anyját.
         every   student-NOM visited   his   mother-ACC
         'Every student visited his mother.'

    b. Az **pro**$_i$ anyját **minden diák**$_i$ meglátogatta.

    c. **Minden diákot**$_i$ meglátogatott az **pro**$_i$ anyja.
        every   student-ACC visited   his   mother-NOM
        'His mother visited every student.'

    d. ?? Az **pro**$_i$ anyja **minden diákot**$_i$ meglátogatott.

(43) a. **Mindegyik lány**$_i$ felismerte azt a   férfit, aki benyitott a **pro**$_i$ szobájába.
        every   girl recognized that the man who opened her   room-into
        'Every girl recognized the man who opened the door into her room.'

    b. Azt a férfit, aki benyitott a **pro**$_i$ szobájába, **mindegyik lány**$_i$ felismerte.

---

[5] Bródy (1995) attempts to account for the lack of the Weak Crossover effect in (40b) in the framework of a hierarchical VP. He claims that in (40b) it is not the trace of the *wh*-object that argument-binds the genitive specifier of the subject. The *wh*-object raised to Spec,FP has passed through Spec,AgrOP, and the pronominal genitive of the subject is argument-bound by the intermediate trace in Spec,AgrOP. This proposal is problematic because Hungarian displays no visible object movement to Spec,AgrOP any more than English does. If both languages display LF movement (i.e., merely feature movement) to Spec,AgrOP, then it is not clear what the source of the difference between the two languages is.

c. **Mindegyik lányt**ᵢ   felismerte az   a   férfi, aki benyitott a **pro**ᵢ szobájába.
    every   girl-ACC recognized that the man who opened her   room-into
    'The man who opened the door into her room recognized every girl.'

d. * Az a férfi, aki benyitott a **pro**ᵢ szobájába, **mindegyik lányt**ᵢ felismerte.

These examples display the same interrelation of thematic precedence, linear precedence, and grammaticality as was observed in the case of anaphoric binding between non-coarguments: the operator can bind the pronominal if it precedes the pronominal either in the thematic argument hierarchy, or in linear order, or both. If neither thematic, nor linear precedence is satisfied, binding is impossible. That is, the data attested follow from the primacy condition of binding in (33).

Notice that the grammaticality difference between (42c) and (42d), or between (43c) and (43d), is not any easier to account for in the framework of the hierarchical VP approach. If the operator is required to c-command the pronominal from its base position, then the grammatical (42c) and (43c) are predicted to be ungrammatical. If the c-command condition is allowed to be satisfied by a higher link of the operator chain as well, then the ungrammatical (42d) and (43d) are not ruled out. Furthermore, we also lose the explanation of the Weak Crossover effect in terms of the bijection principle.

3.4.4   Weighing the evidence

Binding and Weak Crossover phenomena in Hungarian display a controversial array of subject–object symmetries and asymmetries. We attest a subject–object symmetry in the case of disjoint reference between a referring expression and a c-commanding pronoun, and in the case of the core cases of Weak Crossover. Anaphora, disjoint reference between two referring expressions, and a subset of Weak Crossover cases provide evidence for a hierarchy of arguments. This argument hierarchy is not identical with the c-command hierarchy of grammatical functions in an articulated VP, but is thematically determined. In the case of certain psych verbs, for example, the object of experiencer role can bind the subject of theme role. It remains an open question if the argument hierarchy attested should be represented structurally in a VP containing multiple shells, or if it should be represented for example in the form of an ordered theta-grid in the lexicon.[6]

---

[6] For a further argument supporting a binary branching VP, see Bánréti (1994: 379).

A flat VP would, naturally, represent a problem for theories stipulating that all linguistic structures are binary branching. Kayne's theory of antisymmetry (1994) licenses only binary branching phrases composed of a head and a phrase because only the asymmetric c-command instantiated by such structures can impose a linear ordering of terminal elements. It is not inconceivable, however, that in a somewhat relaxed version of this theory the lack of asymmetry might result in a partially linearized structure of the type represented by the Hungarian VP, in which the head, asymmetrically c-commanding its complements, occupies initial position; the post-head arguments, mutually c-commanding each other, on the other hand, can stand in a random order.

3.5   Morphosyntactic projections[7]

3.5.1   Modality, tense, mood

Hungarian is an agglutinative language, i.e., the tense, mood, person, etc. morphemes appear as suffixes on the verb. These morphemes, nevertheless, are independent syntactic constituents: they either enter into agreement relations with major constituents of the VP, or act as operators taking scope over the VP. Therefore, they will be represented as heads of functional projections extending the VP.

The Hungarian verb can combine with the following types of inflectional morphemes:

i.   modality (Mod) suffix: *-hat/het* 'may', expressing either epistemic or deontic modality;[8]

ii.   tense (T) suffix: *-t/tt,* expressing past tense; null suffix, expressing present tense;

iii.   mood (M) suffix: *-na/ne*, expressing conditional; *-j*, expressing imperative/subjunctive;

iv.   object agreement (AgrO) suffix: *-ja/i*, agreeing with the definiteness feature of the object;

v.   subject agreement (AgrS) suffix: a full paradigm, agreeing with the number and person of the subject.

---

[7] This section is based mainly on Bartos (1999a), but also incorporates ideas of den Dikken (1999b). For discussions of verb–object agreement, see also Farkas (1987, 1990).

[8] Bartos (1999a) refutes the traditional view that *-hat/het* is a derivational suffix on the basis of two arguments. First, unlike derivational suffixes, *-hat/het* can be freely added to any verb stem, which is typical of inflectional suffixes. Second, it has sentential scope.

These morphemes appear affixed to the verb in the order:

V + modality + tense + mood + object agreement + subject agreement.

In observance of the mirror principle of Baker (1985), according to which morphological derivation is the mirror image of syntactic derivation, Bartos (1999a) assigns to the verb phrase the following syntactic projection:

(44)

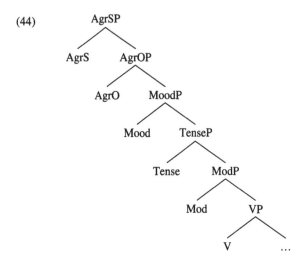

To obtain the morphophonological output of such morphosyntactic trees, we have to reverse the order of heads; for example:

(45) a.

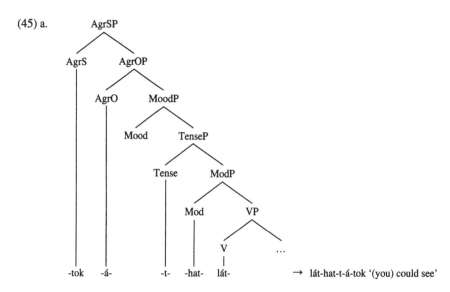

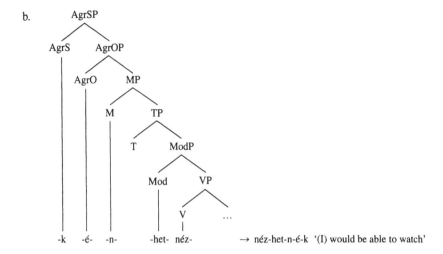

The morphosyntactic unit constituted by the verb and the inflectional suffixes attached to it can be straightforwardly derived by cyclic head movement. This is not so, however, in the case of inflected nominals, where head movement would leave intermediate specifiers stranded incorrectly behind the raised nominal; see Chapter 7. Therefore, Bartos (1999a) has proposed an alternative mechanism: he has introduced the operation of morphosyntactic merger.

(46)   *Morphosyntactic merger*
         Two structurally subjacent categories can merge into a unit constituting a single word domain if thereby one of them satisfies its morphological need (e.g. if an affix satisfies its need for a stem).

(47)   *Structural subjacency*
         X and Y are structurally subjacent if and only if
         a. X c-commands Y, and
         b. there is no Z (of the same projection level as X) such that X c-commands Z and Z c-commands Y.

Morphosyntactic merger takes place in the course of syntactic derivation. It forms a chain from the participating categories, without involving movement. Its output is a morpheme complex within which the relative order of elements is determined by their properties; for example, a morpheme marked as [+suffix] is cliticized to the right edge of the stem. The morpheme complex is pronounced in the position of the stem.

Bartos (1999a) derives the inflected verb form as follows: the verb is raised to the lowest functional head (in the above cases: to Mod(ality)) to check its [+finite] feature – but it combines with the rest of the inflectional morphemes via morphosyntactic merger. Consequently, it is pronounced in the position of its lowest inflectional ending, with all endings adjoined to its right.

The past conditional verb does not quite fit into the structure represented under (44). It is a synthetic verb form consisting of a finite past-tense lexical verb and an invariant expletive verb bearing the conditional suffix. Bartos (1999a) proposes the following analysis of this verb form: A verb in the past conditional is to be merged with a phonologically salient tense (T) morpheme and a mood (M) morpheme. The resulting [$_{word}$ V + T + M] unit constructed in syntax violates a morphophonological constraint, which rules out words containing two subsequent analytic suffixes in their inflectional domain (compare Rebrus 2000).[9] Consequently, the morphophonological component does not accept the V + T + M form, and a repair strategy is triggered. What happens is that a dummy stem (that of the copula) is inserted to pick up the M suffix; that is:

(48)

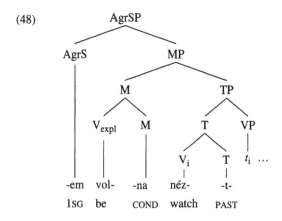

Interestingly, the singular 1st person agreement suffix (*-em*) combines with *néz-t* instead of *vol-na*, i.e., of the two available verb forms the farther one is raised to AgrS. Bartos claims that this is the more economical solution, despite appearances. Namely, if nominative case is assigned or checked by tense, and if the locus of nominative assignment/checking is the Spec,AgrSP position – as is assumed in the Minimalist framework – then T (already merged with V) has to be raised to AgrS anyway, for an independent reason. V + T movement to AgrS yields the following complex verb form:

[9] A -*hat/het* + Tense combination does not violate the constraint blocking two subsequent analytic inflectional suffixes because -*hat/het*, although morphosyntactically an inflectional suffix, is categorized from a morphophonological point of view as a derivational suffix.

(49)

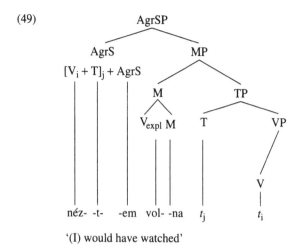

néz- -t- -em vol- -na t_j t_i

'(I) would have watched'

In Hungarian the scope principle, according to which operators have scope over the domain they c-command, is generally observed in visible syntax. Finite verb forms containing a modality suffix and a tense suffix, or a tense suffix and a mood suffix, nevertheless, appear to violate this generalization: they are ambiguous with respect to the relative scope of the two suffixes. For example, in *vár-hat-t-ak* 'wait-Mod-T-AgrS' either tense can have scope over modality (50a), or modality can have scope over tense (50b).

(50) a.   Az elítéltek csak az udvaron   vár-hat-t-ak   a   látogatóikra.
            the convicts only the courtyard-in wait-MOD-PAST-3PL their visitors-for
            'The convicts could wait for their visitors only in the courtyard.'
            T > Mod: [$_T$ were [$_{Mod}$ allowed to wait. . .]]

    b.   A vendégek talán   a   túlsó   megállóban vár-hat-t-ak,   ezért
            the guests   perhaps the opposite bus-stop-in wait-MOD-PAST-3PL therefore
            kerültük   el   egymást.
            missed-we VM each.other
            'The guests could have been waiting at the opposite bus-stop, that was why we missed each other.'
            Mod > T: [$_{Mod}$ could [$_T$ have been waiting. . .]]

V + T + M combinations, e.g. *vártak volna* 'wait-T-AgrS Expl-M' are also ambiguous scopally. The context facilitates a M > T interpretation in (51a) and a T > M reading in (51b):

(51) a.   Az őrök   vár-t-ak   vol-na,   ha szóltál   volna   nekik.
            the guards wait-PAST-3PL EXPL-COND if called-you EXPL-COND them
            'The guards would have waited if you had asked them to.'
            M > T: [$_M$ would [$_T$ have waited. . .]]

b. A vendégek szívesen vár-t-ak   vol-na   tovább, de már   nem
    the guests   gladly   wait-PAST-3PL EXPL-COND longer but already not
    lehetett.
    was.possible
    'The guests would gladly have waited longer, but it was impossible.'
    T > M: [_T it was the case that [_M they would wait]]

Interestingly, verb forms containing both a Mod(ality) and a M(ood) morpheme
are never ambiguous scopally; the scope order of the suffixes strictly corresponds
to their order of c-command; for example, *vár-hat-ná-nak* 'wait-Mod-M-AgrS'
can only mean [_M would [_Mod be possible (for them) to wait]]. That is, a modality
suffix with scope over tense is licensed by an empty mood head, and a mood suffix
with scope under tense is licensed by an empty modality head. These facts suggest
that, if only one of the Mod and M positions is filled, then a chain can be formed
between the two slots across tense. According to Bartos (1999a; 2000c), a modality
suffix can acquire scope over tense (as happens in (50b)) in the following way: the
MP projection is generated empty, as a proxy, with no feature specification, and
the V + Mod complex can be substituted into its head position, lending its feature
specification to it – as represented in (52). In the resulting chain the modality suffix
c-commands tense, and takes scope over it:

(52)   [_#P# [_TP T [_ModP [_Mod V + Mod]. . .]]] → [_ModP [_Mod V + Mod] [_TP T [_ModP t. . .]]]

In the case of (51b), the situation is somewhat different. Mood in the scope of
tense is associated with a particular modal meaning, expressing intention. Bartos
(1999a; 2000c) claims that this meaning cannot be expressed by a single morpheme
in Hungarian; instead, it is associated with a mood–modality chain, which is like
an expletive–associate chain, with the mood morpheme serving as the expletive
element, and the empty modality morpheme serving as the contentive associate.
As in expletive–associate chains in general, scope is determined by the contentive
element, which is in the c-command domain and scope of tense;[10] that is:

(53)

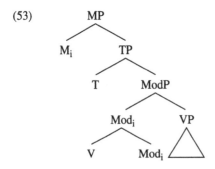

[10] For further technical details, see Bartos (1999a, 2000c).

3.5.2   Object agreement and subject agreement

The Hungarian verb is informally said to have an objective conjugation, used in the presence of a definite object, and a subjective conjugation, used
elsewhere.[11] A closer look at the morphophonological structure of the suffixes in
the objective paradigm reveals, however, that they represent the combination, or
sometimes the fusion, of a -(j)a/j(a) (in the case of a front vowel stem: an -i) suffix
and a subject agreement marker (see Rebrus 2000); compare:

(54) a. én ír-o-m a könyvet 'I write the book'   b. én ír-ok (egy könyvet) 'I write (a book)'
      te ír-o-d   te ír-sz
      ő ír-ja-0   ő ír-0
      mi ír-j-uk   mi ír-unk
      ti ír-já-tok   ti ír-tok
      ők ír-já-k   ők ír-nak

Since the two constituents of the suffixes in the objective paradigm clearly play
independent syntactic roles, they have to be analyzed as distinct functional heads.
The -j(a)/(j)a element represents the head of an object agreement phrase (AgrOP)
dominating MP, and the outermost morpheme represents the head of a subject
agreement phrase (AgrSP) dominating AgrOP.

As Bartos (1999a) demonstrated, AgrOP – i.e., the locus of agreement between
a verb and its object – cannot also be the locus of accusative assignment or checking. This conclusion is based on an argument other than the fact that accusative
assignment is not linked to an invariant Spec,AgrOP position. Bartos's point is that
infinitives do not have an object agreement suffix – still, they assign accusative
case to their object; for example:

(55) a.   Nem szép dolog becsapni   valakit.
           not   nice thing to.deceive someone-ACC
           'It is not a nice thing to deceive someone.'

     b.   Jöttünk   meglátogatni Pétert.
           came-we to.visit   Peter-ACC
           'We have come to visit Peter.'

In modal/temporal auxiliary + transitive infinitive constructions, different heads
participate in object agreement and accusative assignment: the object agreement
morpheme appears on the finite verb, whereas the source of the accusative case is
the infinitival V; compare:

---

[11] By definite object I mean an object of the category DP. NumP and NP objects trigger the
subjective conjugation. The problem of the syntactic category of noun phrases, and its
interaction with the subjective/objective conjugation are discussed in Chapter 7.

(56) a. Mikor akar-**já**-tok   meghívni Jánost?
         when want-DEF-2PL to.invite John-ACC
         'When do you want to invite John?'

   b.   Mikor akar-tok meghívni néhány kollégát?
         when want-2PL to.invite some   colleague-ACC
         'When do you want to invite some colleagues?'

In (56a) the [+definite object] feature of the AgrO suffix on the finite verb agrees
with the [+definite object] feature of the object of the infinitive.

Only transitive verbs agree with the object of their infinitive. The intransitive
verb of the following examples – taking an infinitive with a definite object in
(57a), and an infinitive with an indefinite object in (57b) – does not combine with
an object agreement suffix in either case:

(57) a. Igyekszünk   meglátogatni Pétert
         make.effort-1PL to.visit   Peter-ACC
         'We make efforts to visit Peter.'

   b.   Igyekszünk   meglátogatni néhány kollégát.
         make.effort-1PL to.visit   some   colleague-ACC
         'We make efforts to visit some colleagues.'

Den Dikken (1999b) interprets these data differently. He claims that the semi-
auxiliary-like finite verbs agreeing with the object of their infinitive participate in
clause union, that is, the AgrO projection which checks both the definiteness and
the Case of the embedded object is located in the matrix functional domain. The
verbs in (55) and (57) are incapable of clause union, hence the AgrO head checking
the definiteness and Case of the object of the infinitive must be downstairs in the
infinitival domain, represented by a phonologically null element.

In the theory of Bartos, the definite AgrO morpheme has no null allomorph.
Hence, (55a) and (57a) are regarded by him as evidence indicating that non-
finite verbs taking a definite object combine with no AgrO. Only finite transitive
verbs agree with their object, i.e., only finite transitive verbs project an AgrOP.
Naturally, if finite transitive verbs need to agree with their object – or, in Minimalist
terminology, if finite transitive verbs have an object feature to check – then they
must also agree with their indefinite object. That is, a finite verb having a [–definite]
object must also bear a phonologically null agreement suffix.

In Bartos's theory finite transitive verbs must find an object noun phrase to agree
with in the minimal finite clause containing them. In (58) the finite verb has only
the object of its infinitival complement at its disposal:

(58)   [$_{AgrSP}$ -tok [$_{AgrO}$ -já- [$_{VP}$ akar- [$_{InfP}$ -ni [$_{VP}$ lát- [$_{DP}$ Pétert]]]]]] →
                -3PL   -DEF   want-   -INF see-   Peter-ACC
         akar-já-tok lát-ni Pétert
         '(you) want to see Peter'

Pétert receives accusative case from *lát*, its V head. *Akar*, being a finite transitive verb, projects an AgrOP, and looks for an object so as to have its [+/–definite object] feature checked. The closest object it finds is the definite *Pétert*, hence AgrO will be realized as *-ja-*. If the object of *lát* were an indefinite NumP (e.g. *néhány kollégát*), AgrO would be represented by a phonologically empty suffix. The object does not move to Spec,AgrOP in visible syntax; only its definiteness feature is raised there in Logical Form (LF).

Den Dikken (1999b) has been led to the conclusion that object movement to Spec,AgrOP cannot take place in visible syntax by the following set of examples:

(59) a. Hagyok [takarítani a   szobámban]
         let-I   to.clean my room-in
         'I let my room be cleaned.'

   b. Hagyom [Jánosnak dicsérni Marit]
         let-I   John-DAT to.praise Mary-ACC
         'I let John praise Mary.'

   c. * Hagylak [Jánosnak dicsérni téged]
         let-I   John-DAT to.praise you-ACC
         'I let John praise you.'

   d. Hagylak [dicsérni téged]
         let-I   to.praise you-ACC
         'I let you be praised.'

These sentences involve a permissive construction. In (59b) and (59c) the dative permissee is also spelled out. In (59a) the matrix verb bears default indefinite object agreement – because its object, an infinitive phrase, does not count as definite. Hence, the definite object agreement suffix appearing on the verb in (59b) must be triggered by the definite object of the infinitive. In (59c–d) the matrix verb bears the *-lak/lek* object agreement suffix appearing in the presence of a 1st person subject and a 2nd person object. Den Dikken (1999b) argues that its *-l-* element is an object clitic undergoing clitic movement (an issue to be discussed more in detail below). The ungrammaticality of (59c) indicates that clitic movement is blocked by an intervening permissee, which presumably occupies an A-position, preventing A-movement across it into the matrix Spec,AgrOP – as predicted by the Relativized Minimality condition. Since agreement with a 3rd person object is not blocked by the permissee (59b), it cannot involve A-movement; the object of the infinitive must check the definiteness feature of the matrix AgrO suffix via feature movement.

Bartos's theory of verb–object agreement faces a problem. It relies on the assumption that a verb must agree with the closest object. This assumption is needed to account for example for ECM constructions like (60), in which the finite verb must agree with the definite matrix object instead of the indefinite object of the infinitive:

(60)   Nem hagy-t-uk   /*hagy-t-0-unk   a gyerekeket leckét   írni.
        not let-PAST-DEF.1PL / let-PAST-INDEF-1PL the children-ACC lesson-ACC write
        'We didn't let the children do homework.'

In the framework outlined by Bartos, an infinitive phrase is presumably also a potential object for a finite transitive verb to agree with – or else the [+/–definite object] feature of the object agreement suffix of finite transitive verbs like *akar* 'want' in constructions like *akarok úszni* 'I want to swim' remains unchecked. An infinitive phrase counts as an indefinite object, triggering a null AgrO suffix on the finite verb. The problem is how to ensure that, as long as there is a definite noun phrase inside the infinitive phrase, the verb agrees with the object of the infinitive rather than the infinitive phrase itself – while maintaining that it agrees with the closest object available.

That-clauses represent less of a problem for Bartos's approach. They are associated with a pronominal head in Hungarian, forming an appositive relation with it – see Chapter 10. The propositional content and theta role of the object are carried by the clause, whereas its categorial, case and definiteness features are carried by the pronoun. Consequently, an object clause always counts as definite, and, accordingly, it triggers the objective conjugation of the matrix verb; for example:

(61) a.   János azt   akar-**ja**-0,   hogy meghívjuk Marit.
           John it-ACC want-DEF-3SG that   invite-we   Mary-ACC
           'John wants that we invite Mary.'

     b.   János azt   akar-**ja**-0,   hogy meghívjunk valakit.
           John it-ACC want-DEF-3SG that   invite-we   someone-ACC
           'John wants that we invite someone.'

If the pronominal head of a *that*-clause is absent, the *that*-clause is transparent for long operator movement. Interestingly, when the object of an object clause undergoes long operator movement and lands for example in the focus position of the matrix clause, the matrix verb will agree with the extracted object:

(62) a.   János **Marit**   akar-**ja**-0,   hogy meghívjuk *t*.
           John Mary-ACC want-DEF-3SG that   invite-we
           'It is Mary that John wants that we should invite.'

     b.   János **kit**   akar-**0**-0,   hogy meghívjunk *t*?
           John whom want-INDEF-3SG that   invite-we
           'Whom does John want that we should invite?'

What is more, when the subject of the object clause is extracted, it can be assigned accusative case by the matrix verb, and the matrix verb will agree with this subject-turned-object:

(63) a.   János **Pétert**   akar-**ja**-0,   hogy vezesse az autóját.
           John Peter-ACC want-DEF-3SG that   drive   his car
           'It is Peter that John wants to drive his car.'

    b.   János **kit**   akar-**0**-0,   hogy vezesse az autóját?
           John whom   want-INDEF-3SG that   drive   his car
           'Whom does John want to drive his car?'

These facts can be interpreted as follows: the constituent extracted from the embedded clause moves first into the Spec,CP of the embedded sentence, which is in the local domain of both the embedded verb and the matrix verb. If the subject, which is caseless according to certain theories such as Bittner and Hale (1996), is raised into Spec,CP, then it picks up the accusative case that the matrix verb assigns to its CP object. This is what happened to *Pétert* and *kit* in (63a,b); and this is also what happens in the British English *Whom$_i$ do you suggest* [$_{CP}$ t_i [$_{IP}$ t_i *should be the chairman*]]. The extracted element first participates in subject agreement in the embedded clause, and then, upon being raised into the matrix domain, and receiving accusative case there, it participates in object agreement in the matrix clause.

In addition to the objective and subjective paradigms, there is also an isolated verb form used in the presence of a 1st person singular subject and a 2nd person object:

(64) a.   (Én) lát-lak   (téged).
           I   see-2.1SG you-ACC
           'I see you.'

    b.   (Én) hal-lak   benneteket.
           I   hear-2.1SG you.PL-ACC
           'I hear you.'

In the presence of a 3rd person subject or a 1st person plural subject, a 2nd person object triggers the indefinite conjugation, i.e., it counts as a noun phrase of the category NumP (see Chapter 7, and Bartos 1997), agreeing with a null object marker on the V;[12] compare:

---

[12] It is not clear why 1st and 2nd person objects count as indefinite NumPs, unlike 3rd person objects, which act as definite DPs. Den Dikken (1999b; 2000) has put forth an interesting, morphologically based explanation. He points out that in 1st and 2nd person accusative pronouns the pronominal stem is supplied with a 1st or 2nd person possessive agreement suffix, as follows:

       en(g)-em   mi-nk-et
       I-POSS.1SG   we-POSS.1PL-ACC
       'me'   'us'

(continued overleaf)

(65) a. Lát-**já**-k   Jánost/őt.
see-DEF-3PL John-ACC/him
'They see John/him.'

    b. Lát-**0**-nak téged/engem.
see-INDEF-3PL you/me
'They see you/me.'

Accordingly, -*lak* does not include the -*ja* object agreement morpheme. It can be decomposed into a -*k* 1st person singular agreement marker, and an -*l* 2nd person agreement marker instead. In infinitival constructions in which the infinitive has a 2nd person object, -*lak/lek* can also combine with the finite verb when it is intransitive. That is, whereas in (66a) the intransitive finite verb does not tolerate a -*ja/i* object agreement suffix despite the presence of a definite object in the infinitive phrase, in (66c) it accepts a -*lak/lek* licensed by the 2nd person object:

(66) a. * A lányok igyekez-**i**-**k**   meglátogatni **Jánost**.
the girls make.effort-DEF-3PL to.visit   John-ACC
'The girls make an effort to visit John.'

        compare:

    b. A lányok igyekez-**0**-nek   meglátogatni Jánost.
the girls make.effort-INDEF-3PL to.visit   John-ACC

    c. Igyekez-**lek**   meglátogatni (**téged**).
make.effort-2.1SG to.visit   you
'I make effort to visit you.'

A further peculiarity of -*lak/lek*, noticed by den Dikken (1999b), is that in the case of object extraction it cannot appear both in the source clause and in the target clause (68), although 3rd person objects trigger agreement in both cycles (67).

(67) a. János ÉVÁT   mond-t-**a**-0,   hogy meghív-**ja**-0.
John Eve-ACC say-PAST-DEF-3SG that   invite-DEF-3SG
'It was Eve that John said that he would invite.'

    b. Kit   mond-ott-**0**-0   János, hogy meghív-**0**-0?
whom say-PAST-INDEF-3SG John   that   invite-INDEF-3SG
'Whom did John say that he would invite?'

---

    té(g)-ed   ti-tek-et
    you-POSS.2SG   you-POSS.2PL-ACC
    'you-ACC'   'you-ACC'

Den Dikken claims that these pronominal elements form a possessive construction with an invisible clitic pronoun, i.e., a kind of clitic-doubling takes place. Clitic-doubling constructions have been argued to represent expletive–associate relations. In an expletive–associate chain the associate cannot be definite; hence, when it is coindexed with a definite argument the carrier of the definiteness feature is the expletive (i.e., in the case under discussion, the invisible clitic).

(68) a.   Azt   szeret-né-m   a legjobban, ha megismer-het-né-**lek**   **téged**.
          it-ACC like-COND-DEF.1SG the best   if learn-MOD-COND-2.1SG you-ACC
          'I would like the best if I could get to know you.'

   b.   **Téged**ᵢ szeretné-m a legjobban, ha megismerhetné-**lek** tᵢ.
        'It is you that I would like the best if I could get to know.'

   c.   * **Téged** szeretné-**lek** a legjobban, ha megismerhetné-**lek**.
   d.   * **Téged** szeretné-**lek** a legjobban, ha megismerhetné-k.

        but:

   e.   **Téged**   szeretné-**lek**   a legjobban megismerni.
        you-ACC like-COND-DEF.1SG the best   to.learn
        'It is you that I would like the best to get to know.'

Den Dikken (1999b) concludes on the basis of these facts that the -*l*- element of -*lak/lek* is, in fact, an object clitic pronoun cliticized to the subject agreement marker, and the constructions in which it occurs involve clitic-doubling. A clitic, unlike an agreement marker, cannot be iterated – that is why (68c) is ruled out. Example (68d) is ungrammatical – as opposed to (68e) – because clitic movement cannot transgress a finite clause boundary.

Subject agreement involves fewer descriptive problems. The subject agreement marker appears as the outmost inflectional suffix on the verb, hence it is placed in the head position of the highest morphosyntactic projection subsuming the VP. The number and person features of the agreement morpheme have to match those of the subject. In view of the claim that AgrO does not participate in accusative assignment, it is questionable whether Spec,AgrSP plays a role in nominative assignment/checking. Certain facts of Hungarian suggest a link only between nominative assignment/checking and TenseP. Thus, although a type of infinitive can bear an AgrS marker in Hungarian (see Section 9.4), it cannot have a nominative subject. The adverbial participial phrases -*ván/vén* – the only type of non-finite verb projections that allow a nominative subject – appear to have a tense projection, but no AgrSP (see Section 9.5). So, let us conclude tentatively that the nominative case of the subject is checked in Spec,TenseP – but only invisibly, at LF, without the phonological content of the subject also moving up there.

3.6   The verbal prefix

3.6.1   Its category and structural position

Verbs very often have a particle-like adverbial complement (in traditional Hungarian linguistic terminology: a verbal prefix), which is not only categorially selected, but is also lexically identified. The verbal prefix represents a notoriously difficult problem of describing Hungarian syntax. Native speakers' intuition is that it forms a compound with the verb selecting it. This intuition, which is reflected in traditional Hungarian grammars, and is also expressed by the spelling convention which requires the prefix + verb unit to be spelled as one word, is based on the following facts. First, prefix + verb combinations are listed in the lexicon as lexical units; for example:

(69)   *olvas* 'read'
      elolvas 'read, finish reading'
      átolvas 'read through, skim'
      felolvas 'read aloud'
      megolvas 'count (money)'
      beolvas 'tell off'
      ráolvas 'heal by words'
      etc.

These prefix + verb combinations differ not only in their meaning, but also in their argument structures. Thus, *olvas* and *felolvas* can be transitive or intransitive; *elolvas*, *átolvas*, *megolvas* are obligatorily transitive, *beolvas* takes a dative argument, whereas *ráolvas* takes an object bearing a sublative case. The meaning of the prefix + verb combination can also be completely non-compositional – e.g. *be-rúg* literally 'in-kick' means 'get drunk'. It also supports the compound analysis that in sentences containing no logical operator the verbal prefix immediately precedes the verb, and forms a phonological word with it:

(70)   János fel olvasta a   verseit.
      John up read   his poems
      'John read out his poems.'

If prefix + verb combinations were treated as compounds, these facts could easily be derived. At the same time, however, phrases may also share these properties. For example, elements of a phrasal idiom also form a single lexical unit. The subcategorization properties of the idiom can be different from those of the base verb, and the idiom can also be semantically non-compositional. The phonological evidence is not decisive, either: a verb following a prefix loses its stress to the same extent as a verb following a focus constituent does; still, the 'focus + verb' string is clearly not a compound. At the same time, the verbal prefix has syntactic properties which are only characteristic of independent syntactic units. Thus, in the presence of a focus or a negative particle the prefix stays behind the verb, and it need not even be adjacent to it; compare:

(71) a.   János tegnap   **olvasta fel** a   verseit.
      John yesterday read   up his poems
      'It was yesterday that John read out his poems.'

b.   Péter nem **olvasta** őket **fel**.
     Peter not read   them up
     'Peter did not read them out.'

The prefix and the verb can also be separated by a particle:

(72)   János fel akarta olvasni a   verseit, és **fel** is   **olvasta** őket.
        John up wanted to.read his poems and up also read   them
        'John wanted to read out his poems, and out he read them.'

The prefix can be raised into a position non-adjacent to the verb; e.g. it can undergo contrastive topicalization (73a). What is more, it can also be raised into a
superordinate clause (73b,c).

(73) a.   **Fel** csak János **olvasta** a   verseit.
          out only John read   his poems
          'Out loud, only John read his poems.'

     b.   János **fel** szeretné   **olvasni** a   verseit.
          John up would.like to.read his poems
          'John would like to read out his poems.'

     c.   **Fel** akarom, hogy **olvasd** a   verseidet.
          up I.want   that you.read your poems
          'I want that you should read out your poems.'

These facts cannot be derived if the prefix + verb complex is inserted into the
syntactic structure as a compound with deleted inner brackets. Therefore, we have
no choice but to insert the prefix as an independent syntactic unit, a lexically
selected complement of the verb.

There are also further difficult questions to answer. Namely, should the prefix be
inserted in a postverbal argument position, or in a preverbal modifier position? And,
crucially, should it be analyzed as a phrase or as a head? Certain considerations
support the base-generation of the verbal prefix in postverbal argument position.
Namely, the prefix occupies the same preverbal position in (70), where it is selected
by the verb adjacent to it, as in (73b,c), where it has nothing to do lexically–
semantically with the verb immediately following it. According to the evidence
of (73b,c) the preverbal prefix position must be a derived position for the verbal
prefix, the landing site of prefix movement. Furthermore, as is argued in Section
3.6.3, the verbal prefix represents only a subtype of a larger functional class of verb
modifiers displaying similar syntactic properties. This larger class also includes
bare nominal complements, among them objects, oblique complements expressing
a goal, and non-agentive subjects; for example:

(74) a.   János újságot   olvas.
          John newspaper-ACC reads
          'John is engaged in newspaper-reading.'

b. János iskolába ment.   c. Víz szivárog a falból.
    John to.school went   water oozes   the wall-from
    'John went to school.'   'Water is oozing from the wall.'

Although these types of verb modifiers do not refer to concrete participants of the action denoted by the VP, they bear case, and seem to be associated with a theta role. If theta-role assignment and (at least some cases of) case-assignment presuppose a verb–argument relation, then the verb modifier must be generated in postverbal position, among the arguments of the verb.

The subtype of verb modifiers called verbal prefix is constituted by a bare adverb, but, since adverbs usually have no specifier or complement, it can, in principle, also be analyzed as an AdvP consisting of a mere head. The crucial question is whether it moves like a phrase, landing in a specifier position, or moves like a head, landing in a position adjoined to another head. Head movement is local, so if prefix movement were found to be non-local, it would be evidence of the phrasal status of the prefix. In fact, long prefix movement is possible; modal and temporal auxiliaries can attract a prefix not only across an infinitive phrase boundary but also across a CP boundary:

(75) a. János **fel** akarja **olvasni** a   verseit.
         John up wants read-INF his poems
         'John wants to read out his poems.'

   b. Jánosnak **fel** kell   **olvasnia**   a   verseit.
       John-DAT up needs read-INF-3SG his poems
       'John needs to read out his poems.'

   c. János **fel** szeretném, hogy **olvassa**   a   verseit.
       John up I.would.like that read-SUBJ-3SG his poems
       'I would like that John read out his poems.'

   d. János **fel** kell, hogy **olvassa**   a   verseit.[13,14]
       John up needs that read-SUBJ-3SG his poems
       'It is necessary that John read out his poems.'

[13] Long prefix movement sounds acceptable only if the section of the embedded clause crossed by the raised prefix contains nothing but a complementizer – and perhaps a topic. Compare the distribution of grammaticality in the following set of examples.

   a. Fel kellene,   hogy olvasd   a   verseidet.
       up need-COND that you.read your poems
   b. János fel kellene,   hogy olvassa a   verseit.
       John up need-COND that read   his poems
   c. ? Fel kellene,   hogy János olvassa a   verseit.
       up need-COND that John read   his poems
   d. * Fel kellene,   hogy csak nekem olvassa János a   verseit.
       up need-COND that only to.me read   John his poems
   e. * Fel kellene,   hogy minden este olvassa János a   verseit.
       up need-COND that every night read   John his poems

There are also further powerful arguments for the phrasal status of the prefix: it can undergo topicalization and focussing, which are phrasal movement transformations:

(76) a.   [_TopP **Fel** [_FP János olvasta a   verseit]]
           up   John read   his poems
           'Loudly, JOHN read his poems.'

   b.   [_TopP János [_NegP nem [_FP **fel** ment a   lépcsőn]]], hanem **le**   ment.
         John   not   up went the stairs   but   down went
         'It was not up the stairs but down that John went.'

The prefix can constitute an elliptic sentence in itself, which, again, is a phrasal property; compare:

(77)   **Fel** olvasta János a verseit?
        'Did John read out his poems?'
        Fel.
        'He did.'

Jakab (1998) claims that in such sentences the lower verb and the complementizer merge into a single head, i.e., prefix movement is local, after all. However, sentences (c–e) might be marginal or ungrammatical for a semantic reason. Namely, as is argued in Section 3.6.2., the verbal prefix functions as an aspectual operator, and moves to Spec,AspP in order to assume scope over the VP. The focus in (d) and the quantifier in (e), on the other hand, are propositional operators, which have scope over AspP. Long prefix movement takes place when the matrix verb is an auxiliary-like modal forming a single semantic domain together with the complement clause, i.e., when the scope of the aspect marker also has to be extended over the matrix clause. The problem with (d,e) is that the aspectual operator has scope over the matrix VP, whereas the focus and the universal quantifier, which are propositional operators, only have scope over the embedded clause – although propositional operators should have wider scope than AspP.

[14] Den Dikken (1999b, footnote 28) calls attention to the fact that prefix movement across a finite clause boundary – unlike local prefix movement – is never obligatory; furthermore, it is only felicitous if the prefix has an independent semantic content. The prefix of a semantically non-compositional prefix + verb complex can only marginally be extracted; compare with (75c,d):

(i)   ?* Be szeretném,   ha olvasnál a   főnöknek.
       in I.would.like if you.read the boss-DAT
       'I would like it if you told off [scolded] the boss.'

(ii)   ? Be kell,   hogy olvassak neked.
        in needs that I.read   you-DAT
        'It is necessary that I tell you off [scold you].'

Den Dikken concludes on the basis of these facts and those discussed in footnote 13 that this type of long prefix movement is different from local prefix movement, or prefix movement across an infinitival boundary: it is an A-bar movement.

These facts appear to suggest that the verbal prefix is an AdvP consisting of a mere head, base-generated in postverbal position among the complements of the V. A preverbal prefix occupies the specifier position of a functional projection. That is, the predicate phrase of for example (70) has the following structure:

(78)

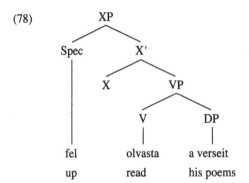

The correctness of structure (78) can be checked for example by testing if the VP can pass the usual constituency tests; for instance, if it can be coordinated with another VP. Surprisingly, it cannot:

(79) a.   János [fel [hívta Marit]] és [fel [olvasta neki a   versét]] →
           John up called Mary and up read   her his poem

     b. * János [fel [hívta Marit] és [olvasta neki a versét]]

Example (79b) is ungrammatical under the reading in which the two coordinated VPs share the same *fel* suffix; it can only be accepted if the second verb is interpreted prefixless. Its ungrammaticality can only be derived from a structure in which the last two elements of the 'prefix V object' string do not form a constituent; i.e., if the phrase is structured as follows:

(80)

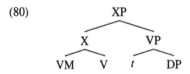

If this is the right structure of the predicate of (70), then not only the ungrammaticality of (79) follows, but also the grammaticality of the coordinate structure in (81) is predicted:

(81)   János [[le   írta] és [fel olvasta]] a   verset.
        John down put and up read   the poem
        'John wrote down and read out the poem.'

However, the grammaticality of (81) provides no evidence for structure (80); it could also be derived from (78) by right node raising.[15]

The contradictory evidence indicating the phrasal nature of prefix movement, and the incorporated head status of the prefix in surface structure can be resolved if we analyze the prefix as a projection both minimal and maximal, capable of acting either as a phrase or as a head. Suppose that the verbal prefix is generated in postverbal position as an AdvP complement of the V; then it undergoes phrasal movement into the specifier position of a functional projection dominating the finite VP, e.g. into Spec,AspP; and eventually it cliticizes to the adjacent verb.[16]

As a summary, consider the steps of the derivation of the sentence *János fel olvasta a verseit* 'John read out his poems'. For clarity's sake the morphosyntactic projections extending the VP are omitted.

(82)   a.

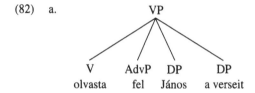

b.

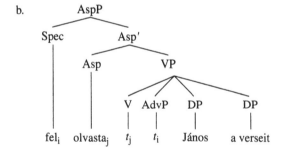

---

[15] The head versus phrasal status of the verbal prefix has been a matter of controversy for decades. Until the possibility of head movement was accepted in generative theory, prefix movement could only be analyzed as phrasal movement – compare É. Kiss (1981, 1987a) – at least within the Chomskian framework. Lexical-functionalists were the first to argue for the head properties of the verbal prefix (see Ackerman 1984, Komlósy 1985). Noticing the argument against the phrasal analysis of the prefix that (79) represents, É. Kiss (1998d) analyzes prefix movement as incorporation into the verb. Koopman and Szabolcsi (2000) argue for the phrasal status of verb modifiers.

[16] The process of merger taking place between two adjacent heads in the functional domain was observed by Dobrovie-Sorin (1993), who listed various Romanian and French examples of it. Following a suggestion of Cardinaletti and Starke (1999), Bródy (1999) argues (in connection with the cliticization of the negative particle to the verb) that a specifier can be spelled out in the adjacent head of the projection based on the full matching of its features with the feature of the head.

c.

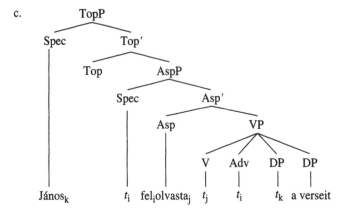

The next question to answer is what triggers the movement of the prefix into preverbal position. We have already discussed one reason why the prefix could not stay in the VP: it would violate the referentiality constraint, which forbids non-referential expressions in postverbal position. The prefix also has another reason to leave the VP: as is discussed in the next section, it plays a perfectivizing role, hence it must move into the specifier of an aspect projection.

3.6.2   The AspP projection

In the most common case, the verbal prefix complements a process verb, and in addition to modifying its lexical meaning also turns it into a verb of accomplishment, to be used perfectively (see Kiefer 1992a, 1994a, 1994b). This is what happens if *olvas* is supplied with *el, át, meg, rá,* or *be*. The difference in the aspectual potential of *olvas* and for example *átolvas* can be pointed out by showing that the former cannot be combined with a temporal adverb specifying the endpoint of a period within which the action has been performed (e.g. with a *by* phrase or an *in* phrase), whereas the latter cannot be combined with a temporal adverb specifying an interval.[17]

(83) a.   * János hétfőre   olvasta a   regényt.
            John by.Monday read   the novel
            'John read the novel by Monday.'

     b.   János egész este   olvasta a   regényt.
            John whole evening read   the novel
            'John read the novel the whole evening.'

---

[17] These tests and many others were proposed by Kiefer (1992a, 1994a, 1994b) in his detailed studies of aspect in Hungarian.

(84) a.   János hétfőre   **el**   olvasta a   regényt.
John by.Monday VM read   the novel
'John read the novel by Monday.'

   b. * János egész este   **el**   olvasta a   regényt.
John whole evening VM read   the novel
'John read the novel the whole evening.'

Felolvas, which can retain the process meaning of *olvas*, is exceptional in this respect – it is marginally also acceptable with an adverb denoting an interval:

(85) a.   János nyolc órára /egy fél   óra   alatt **fel** olvasta a   verseit.
John by   eight /a   half hour in   up read   his poems
'John read out his poems by eight/in half an hour.'

   b. ? János egész este   **fel** olvasta a   verseit.
John whole evening up read   his poems
'John read out his poems the whole evening.'

Intuitively, the prefix makes the perfective reading possible by incorporating a direction, hence a potential endpoint, into the process expressed by the base verb. Nevertheless, perfectivization is not merely a lexical process; the perfective reading only arises if the prefix immediately precedes the verb; compare:

(86) a.   **Fel mentem** a   toronyba.
up went-I   the tower-to
'I went up the tower.'

   b.   (Épp) **'mentem 'fel** a   'toronyba, amikor ki   tört   a   zivatar.
just   went-I   up the tower-to   when   out broke the thunderstorm
'I was (just) going up the tower when the thunderstorm broke out.'

   c.   **'Mentem** (már)   **fel** a   toronyba./ **'Megyek** (még) **fel** a   toronyba.
went-I   already up the tower-to   go-I   still   up the tower-to
'I have (already) been up the tower./ I will (still) go up the tower.'

The sentence in (86b) is progressive, whereas (86c) expresses an experiential reading, meaning that the event described in the VP has already taken place – or will yet take place – at indefinite times, but at least once. The two interpretations are conveyed by identical strings associated with different stress patterns. In the progressive sentence every major constituent bears a primary stress, whereas in the experiential sentence only the verb is stressed. Interestingly, in the case of the exceptional *felolvas*, the progressive reading can be expressed by the same string as the perfective one; only the experiential reading must be expressed by the reverse order of the prefix and the verb; compare:

(87) a.   **Fel olvastam** a   verseimet.
out read-I   the poems-my
'I read out my poems.'

b. (Éppen) **fel olvastam/olvastam fel** a   verseimet, amikor ki tört   a
    just   up read   read   up my poems   when   out broke the
    zivatar.
    thunderstorm
    'I was just reading out my poems when the thunderstorm broke out.'

c. **Olvastam** már   **fel** verseimet.
    read-I   already   out poems-my
    'I have already read out my poems.'

There is also a further significant fact to account for: if the VP is extended into
a focus phrase, the difference between the perfective and the progressive aspect
is neutralized; the sentences are ambiguous. Thus, the 'focus–verb–prefix' order
in the following sentence is compatible either with a time adverbial specifying a
period by the end of which the action has been performed, or with a time adverbial
specifying a point of time at which the given action was in progress.

(88) a. JÁNOS ment fel a   toronyba (éppen), amikor a   zivatar   ki tört.
         John went up the tower-to just   when   the thunderstorm out broke
         'It was John who was going up the tower when the thunderstorm broke out.'

b. JÁNOS ment fel a toronyba nyolc órára.
    'It was John who had gone up the tower by eight.'

To capture these facts, let us assume that the aspect of the VP (at the same time,
also the aspect of the sentence) is determined by an AspP subsuming the (morphosyntactically extended) VP.[18] The Asp head can have various features (according to Kiefer (1994a, 1994b) it can be [+/–eventive]; [+eventive] aspect can be
[+/–perfective]; [–perfective] can be [+/–restricted], the [+restricted] value corresponding to progressive, etc.). The prefix acts as an aspectualizer, and as such
it must be raised into Spec,AspP – to take scope over the VP, or to check the
[+perfective] feature of the Asp head, depending on our theoretical presupposi-
tions. This is what we attest in (84a), (86a), and (87a). The perfective reading
of *felolvas* in (85a) also arises in this way (I assume that the *fel* complement of
olvas is marked [+/–perfective]). Let us also make the (theoretically motivated)
assumption that the V moves to Asp, to check the aspectual feature of Asp.

If the Asp head is progressive (i.e., [–perfective]), it will not tolerate a
[+perfective] prefix in Spec,AspP (see Piñon 1995). If the prefix has no lexical meaning apart from carrying the feature [+perfective] – as is the case with *el*
in *elolvas* – it will be omitted in the progressive. In such cases it is presumably
only the verb that moves up into Asp.

---

[18] The proposed analysis is based on proposals of É. Kiss (1987a, 1992, 1994a), Kiefer
(1992a; 1994a), and Piñon (1995); it is closest to Piñon's theory.

(89)   (Éppen) olvastam (* el) a   regényt, amikor ki   tört   a   zivatar
        just   read-I   VM the novel   when out broke the thunderstorm
        'I was just reading the novel when the thunderstorm broke out.'

The same holds for durative perfectivizing prefixes. These prefixes express that
the event denoted by the VP is both indivisible as regards its temporal structure,
and simultaneously also long lasting. In the progressive the durative perfectivizing
prefix must be omitted:

(90) a.   Nagypapa **el   üldögélt** a   lócán.
          Grandpa   VM sat   the bench-on
          'Grandpa sat long on the bench.'

    b.   * Nagypapa éppen **üldögélt el** a lócán.
          'Grandpa was just sitting long on the bench.'

    c.   Nagypapa éppen **üldögélt** a lócán, amikor kitört a zivatar.
          'Grandpa was just sitting on the bench when the thunderstorm broke out.'

When the perfectivizing prefix also makes a lexical contribution, it is retained in
the progressive, as well; it is interpreted as a referential adverb with no aspectual
feature (91a). It is often replaced by a heavier version (containing the suffix *-felé*
'-wards'), which obviously serves to indicate that the adverb does not act as an
aspectual operator. A prefix denoting an endpoint or direction often goes together
with a goal complement. In that case the prefix deprived of its aspectual feature
and the goal noun phrase form an appositive construction (91b).

(91) a.   [$_{TopP}$ János$_i$[$_{AspP}$ (éppen) [$_{Asp'}$ **ment**$_j$ [$_{VP}$ t_i t_j **fel(felé)**)]]] amikor a   zivatar
          John   just   went   up(wards) when   the thunderstorm
          kitört]
          out.broke
          'John was just going up when the thunderstorm broke out.'

    b.   [$_{TopP}$ János$_i$[$_{AspP}$ (éppen) [$_{Asp'}$ **ment**$_j$ [$_{VP}$ t_i t_j [**fel** a   toronyba]]]] amikor a
          John   just   went   up the tower   when   the
          zivatar   kitört]
          thunderstorm out.broke
          'John was just going up the tower when the thunderstorm broke out.'

When interpreted as a referential argument, the prefix receives a primary stress. If
it participates in an appositive construction, the other member of the construction
will also be stressed – that is how the stress pattern associated with the progressive,
consisting of a series of heavy stresses, arises.

    A condition of the analysis of the prefix as a referential adverb is that it must
have a separate meaning component, i.e., the meaning of the prefixed verb must
be compositional – see Kiefer (1994a, 1994b) and Piñon (1995). In the case of

non-compositional verbs the failure of prefix movement into Spec,Asp will not yield a progressive interpretation; compare:

(92) a. * János (éppen) **rúgott be**, amikor haza   vitte a   felesége.
   John   just   kicked in   when   home took his wife-NOM
   'John was just getting drunk when his wife took him home.'

 b. * A   sámán   éppen **olvasott rá** a   betegre, amikor kitört   a   zivatar.
   the shaman just   read   on the sick-on when   out.broke the thunderstorm
   'The shaman was just bewitching the sick man when the thunderstorm broke out.'

For the progressive reading to arise, the verb to be raised to the progressive-marked Asp must also have an appropriate *Aktionsart* feature, i.e., it cannot denote a momentary action; it must denote a process; compare:

(93)   * János éppen **pillantott fel** az   újságból,   amikor beléptem.
   John   just   glanced   up the newspaper-from when   entered-I
   'John was just glancing up from the newspaper when I entered.'

The experiential reading illustrated in (86c) involves verb movement into a higher functional head position, presumably into F. Evidence for the fact that the verb is not in AspP is provided by the fact that it precedes the adverbs *már* 'already' and *még* 'yet', which are left-adjoined to AspP in the unmarked case; compare:

(94) a. János [$_{AspP}$ már [$_{AspP}$ **fel ment** a   toronyba]] → János **ment**$_i$ már t_i **fel** a
   John   already   up went the tower-to   toronyba.
   'John has already gone up the tower.'   'John has already been up the tower.'

 b. János [$_{AspP}$ még [$_{AspP}$ **fel megy** a   toronyba]] → János **megy**$_i$ még t_i **fel** a
   John   yet   up goes the tower-to   toronyba.
   'John will still go up the tower.'   'John will go up the tower yet (at least once).'

The assumption that the experiential verb is raised into the F head is also supported by phonological evidence. As is shown in Chapter 4, in focus constructions typically everything but the focus is presupposed, hence typically nothing but the focus is stressed. This is what we attest in experiential constructions of this type: only the focussed verb bears stress – as opposed to progressive sentences.

What is left to clarify is the case of *felolvas* under the non-perfective reading. *Fel* in its non-perfective reading resembles a class of prefixes whose lexical meaning expresses location rather than direction or goal, among them *itt* 'here', *ott* 'there', *lent* 'down', *fent* 'up', *kint* 'out(side)', *bent* 'in(side)', etc. These prefixes are used, for example, to turn a VP containing a stative (i.e., [–eventive]) verb into imperfective (i.e., [+eventive], [–restricted]). Intuitively they serve to anchor spatiotemporally the state denoted by the base verb.[19] The meaning difference between the (a) and (b) sentences in (95)–(96) is very hard to render in English:

(95) a. A taxi **állt** a   kapu előtt.
      the taxi stood the gate in.front.of
      'The taxi was standing in front of the gate.'

    b. A taxi **ott** **állt** a   kapu előtt.
       the taxi there stood the gate in.front.of
       'The taxi was standing there in front of the gate.'

(96) a. A gyerekek **alszanak** az emeleten.
      the children sleep   the second.floor-on
      'The children are sleeping on the second floor.'

    b. A gyerekek **fent alszanak** az emeleten.
       the children up sleep   the second.floor-on
       'The children are sleeping up on the second floor.'

In the following construction the location prefix is obligatory with the locative *van* 'be'. (For some reason, *van* cannot bear the phrasal stress falling on the left edge of the VP.) Compare:

(97) a. * [$_{TopP}$ Az elnök   képe [$_{VP}$ van minden kirakatban]]
         the president's portrait is   every   shop-window-in
         'The president's portrait is in every shop window.'

    b. [$_{TopP}$ Az elnök   képe [$_{AspP}$ ott/kint/bent van minden kirakatban]]
        the president's portrait   there/out/in is   every   shop-window-in
        'The president's portrait is there in every shop window.'

Although still very little is known about the semantics of the construction illustrated in (95b), (96b), and (97b), we can safely hypothesize that it involves an AspP projection with a head marked as [+eventive], [–perfective], [–restricted]. Both the prefix to be raised to Spec,AspP, and the verb to be raised to Asp must have inherent features that are compatible with the [–perfective] feature of Asp.

    Stative verbs like *imád* 'adore', *gyűlöl* 'hate', *tud* 'know' have no verb modifier. Presumably they merge with a [–eventive] Asp head, which triggers V movement but attracts nothing to Spec,AspP.

3.6.3   The class of verb modifiers

    Spec,AspP is not open only to verbal prefixes, i.e., adverbs. Non-adverbial complements can also function as aspectualizers – even if the aspectual roles of

---

[19] Compare Csirmaz and Surányi (1998).

their various types are more varied and less well understood than those of the verbal prefix.[20]

Non-adverbial complements of an aspectualizing function include bare nominal objects, bare nominal oblique complements (goals and locations), bare non-agentive subjects, predicative nouns and adjectives, as well as bare infinitives; for example:

(98) a. János **újságot**   **olvas**.
         John newspaper-ACC reads
         'John is engaged in newspaper-reading.'

   b. János **piacra**   **ment**.
       John market-to went
       'John went to the market.'

   c. János **ágyban maradt**.
       John bed-in   stayed
       'John stayed in bed.'

   d. Levél **érkezett**.
       letter arrived
       'A letter arrived.'

   e. János **orvos** **lesz**.
       John doctor becomes
       'John will become a doctor.'

   f. János **híres** **lesz**.
       John famous becomes
       'John will become famous.'

   g. Jánost   **gazdagnak tartják**.
       John-ACC rich-DAT   consider-they
       'John is considered rich.'

   h. Jánost   **boldoggá**   **tette** a hír.
       John-ACC happy-TRANSLATIVE made the news
       'The news made John happy.'

   i. János **úszni**   **fog**.
       John swim-INF will
       'John will swim.'

Similar to the verbal prefix, these types of complements are non-referential. Like the prefix, they are phrases (NPs and AdjPs) constituted by a mere head. They also share the distribution of the verbal prefix; they are alternatives to it in the sentence.

---

[20] The generalizations summarized in this section are quoted from Kiefer (1992a) and (1994a). Maleczki (1992) gives a detailed semantic analysis of bare nominal complements. On the role of bare nominals and the definiteness effect, see L. Kálmán (1995).

Thus, in neutral sentences the bare nominal immediately precedes the finite verb (99a), whereas in the presence of a focus or a negative particle the verb leaves the verb modifier behind (99b,c). The verb modifier can also be separated from the verb by the emphatic particle *is* (99d). The verb modifier can be focussed (99e), it can undergo contrastive topicalization (99f), and it can also be subject to long operator movement from an infinitive phrase (99g) or a CP (99h).

(99) a.   Mari **ebédet**   **főz**.
          Mary lunch-ACC cooks
          'Mary cooks lunch.'

     b.   Mari A KEDVÜNKÉRT **főz**   **ebédet**.
          Mary for.our.sake   cooks lunch
          'It is for our sake that Mary cooks lunch.'

     c.   Mari nem **főz**   **ebédet**.
          Mary not   cooks lunch
          'Mary doesn't cook lunch.'

     d.   Mari **ebédet**   akart   **főzni**, és   **ebédet**   is   **főzött**.
          Mary lunch-ACC wanted to.cook, and lunch-ACC also cooked
          'Mary wanted to cook lunch, and lunch she cooked.'

     e.   Mari EBÉDET   **főzött**, nem pedig   vacsorát.
          Mary lunch-ACC cooked   not   on.the.other.hand supper-ACC
          'It was lunch that Mary cooked, not supper.'

     f.   **Ebédet**   MARI **főzött**, vacsorát   pedig   PÉTER.
          lunch-ACC Mary cooked supper-ACC on.the.other.hand Peter
          'Lunch was cooked BY MARY, supper, on the other hand, BY PETER.'

     g.   Mari **ebédet**   szeretne   **főzni**.
          Mary lunch-ACC would.like to.cook
          'Mary would like to cook lunch.'

     h.   **Ebédet**   kell,   hogy **főzzek**.
          lunch-ACC needs that   I.cook
          'It is necessary that I cook lunch.'

In view of these facts there can be no doubt about it that bare nominals and verbal prefixes represent the same functional class in syntax – even if the precise semantic content of the functions of their various types (i.e., their precise contribution to the aspect of the VP, their interaction with the meaning of the verb, with its tense, with its argument structure, with the specificity/definiteness of the arguments, with the quantifiers present in the clause, with negation, etc.) is not fully understood at present.

    The aspectualizer function is clearest in the case of bare nominals of goal function (i.e., noun phrases supplied with an illative, sublative, or allative case); for example:

(100) a. János **iskolába ment**.
       John school-in went
       'John went to school.'

   b. Péter **kirándulásra ment**.
       Peter excursion-on went
       'Peter went on an excursion.'

   c. Mari **férjhez   ment**.
       Mary husband-to went
       'Mary got married.'

By imposing a limit or endpoint on the motion expressed by the verb, these complements have a perfectivizing value, similar to that of the verbal prefix.

Bare nominal complements bearing an inessive, superessive, or adessive case, on the other hand, play a role similar to verbal prefixes expressing a location; they serve to anchor stative verbs spatiotemporally; compare:

(101) a. János **iskolában marad**.
       John school-in remains
       'John remains in school.'

   b. János **kórházban tartózkodik**.
       John hospital-in stays
       'John stays in hospital.'

   c. János **meccsen van**.
       John match-on is
       'John is at a football match.'

   d. János egész délelőtt **orvosnál ült**.
       John whole morning doctor-at sat
       'John was sitting at the doctor's the whole morning.'

Resultative adjectives supplied with the -ra/re sublative suffix or the -vá/vé translative suffix also have a delimiting function in the case of certain verbs expressing a process; hence, they also act as perfectivizers; for example:

(102) a. [TopP János [AspP zöldre   festette a   kaput]]
              John   green-SUBLATIVE painted the gate-ACC
       'John painted the gate green.'

   b. [TopP A királyfi [AspP békává   vált]]
              the prince   frog-TRANSLATIVE turned
       'The prince turned into a frog.'

Sentences with a bare nominal aspectualizer are derived in the same way as sentences containing a verbal prefix. The bare nominal (an NP) is generated in postverbal argument position; however, not being referential, it cannot stay there.

It is raised to Spec,AspP, and its aspectual feature has to match that of the Asp head. The verb is raised to Asp, and eventually it merges with the bare nominal. Evidence for the bare nominal–verb merge is provided by the coordination test; compare:

(103) a. [$_{TopP}$ János [$_{AspP}$ **kezet** [$_{Asp'}$ **fogott** Péterrel]] és [$_{AspP}$ **kezet** [$_{Asp'}$ **rázott** Jánossal]]]
           John   hand-ACC took   Peter-with and   hand-ACC shook John-with
           'John clasped hands with Peter and shook hands with John.'

   b. * [$_{TopP}$ János [$_{AspP}$ **kezet** [$_{Asp'}$ [$_{Asp'}$ **fogott** Péterrel] és [$_{Asp'}$ **rázott** Jánossal]]]]

Unless the bare noun and the verb merge into a complex head, there is no obvious way to predict the ungrammaticality of (103b).[21]

3.7 The nominal predicate

Nominal and adjectival predicates were also included tentatively in the set of verb modifiers above (98e,f). Even though sentences containing a nominal or adjectival predicate have not been subject to a thorough investigation in the generative framework, there has been a consensus in the respect that the syntactic behavior of non-verbal predicates is – at least superficially – similar to that of verb modifiers. Nevertheless, they represent a more severe descriptive problem than do other types of verb modifiers – in part because the copula can also be missing under certain circumstances, in which case the bare noun or adjective acts as the lexical head of the predicate. This section aims to present some of the facts that a future analysis will have to account for.

First observe the distribution of the copula in sentences with a nominal or adjectival predicate:

(104)   Én beteg vagyok.   Mi betegek vagyunk.
        I   sick am   we sick-PL are

        Te beteg vagy.   Ti betegek vagytok.
        you sick are   you sick-PL are

        Ő beteg.   Ők betegek.
        he sick   they sick-PL

---

[21] Or perhaps the coordination of the post-VM material in (79b) and (103b) is ruled out because the coordinated strings are not maximal AspPs but merely Asp' projections. As will become clear in Chapter 4, the bare nominal verb modifier can undergo focus movement into Spec,FP. In such cases the VP, a maximal projection, can undergo coordination; for example:

(i)   János [$_{FP}$ ARCON [[$_{VP}$ vágta Pétert]   és [$_{VP}$ csókolta Marit]]], nem pedig
      John   cheek-on   hit   Peter-ACC and   kissed   Mary-ACC not however
      SZÁJON.
      lip-on
      'It was on the cheek that John hit Peter and kissed Mary, and not on the lips.'

(105) a. Ő beteg.
        he sick
        'He is sick.'

    b. Ő beteg volt.   Ő beteg lenne.
        he sick was   he sick be-COND-3SG
        'He was sick.'   'He would be sick.'

        Ő beteg lesz.   Ő legyen   beteg!
        he sick will.be   he be-IMPER-3SG sick
        'He will be sick.'   'Let him be sick!'

    c. Ő beteg akar   lenni.
        he sick wants be-INF
        'He wants to be sick.'

(106) Én tanár   vagyok.   Mi tanárok vagyunk.
        I   teacher am   we teachers are

        Te tanár   vagy.   Ti tanárok vagytok.
        you teacher are   you teachers are

        János tanár.   János és   Péter tanárok.
        John teacher   John and Peter teachers

(107) a. János és   Péter tanárok.
        John and Peter teachers
        'John and Peter are teachers.'

    b. János és   Péter tanárok voltak.   János és   Péter tanárok lennének.
        John and Peter teachers were   John and Peter teachers be-COND-3PL

        János és   Péter tanárok lesznek.   János és   Péter legyenek   tanárok!
        John and Peter teachers will.be   John and Peter be-IMPER-3PL teachers

What these examples demonstrate is that adjectival predicates like *beteg* 'sick', and nominal predicates like *tanár* 'teacher' are accompanied by the copula in every tense – whether finite or non-finite – every mood and every person, except for present indicative 3rd person singular and plural. The copula is spelled out when at least one of the morphosyntactic projections in the predicate has a phonologically salient [+suffix] head, which needs a stem to attach to. The present tense marker, the indicative mood marker, and the 3rd person singular subject agreement marker are phonologically null, hence they need no carrier. The present indicative 3rd person plural subject agreement marker is phonologically real; however, its function is also expressed by the plural marker added to the predicative noun or adjective. That is, the copula appears to be an expletive which is present if and only if its presence is required by a morphophonological constraint. In sentences like (105a) and (107a), in which the copula has no role to play, there is no reason to assume one; the predicate phrase must be of the category AdjP/NP. This claim is supported by the fact that in these sentences the predicative adjective or noun, representing the lexical head of the predicate, cannot be extracted, e.g. it cannot undergo contrastive topicalization – unlike an adjective or noun accompanying the copula:

(108) a. * [$_{TopP}$ /**Beteg** [$_{FP}$ JÁNOS]]
         sick   John
         'It is John who is sick.'

       compare:

     b.   [$_{TopP}$ /**Beteg** [$_{FP}$ JÁNOS **volt**]]
         sick   John   was
         'It was John who was sick.'

Notice that the construction represented by (108a), consisting of a contrastive topic and a focus, is not ungrammatical in itself – provided the topic position is filled by a phrase:

(109)   [$_{TopP}$ /**A legsúlyosabb beteg** [$_{FP}$ JÁNOS]]
         the gravest   patient   John
         'It is John who is the gravest patient.'

In sentences in which the copula is spelled out, the focus constituent in Spec,FP must be followed by the copula, whereas the adjectival/nominal verb modifier can stand anywhere in the VP (110a,b). In the case of a nominal/adjectival predicate, the constituent that must be adjacent to the focus is the noun or adjective (110c), so the logical conclusion is that the focus is followed by a noun phrase or adjective phrase:

(110) a.   [$_{FP}$ JÁNOS **volt beteg** a   honvágytól]
         John   was sick   the homesickness-from
         'John was sick with homesickness.'

     b.   [$_{FP}$ JÁNOS **volt** a honvágytól **beteg**]

     c.   [$_{FP}$ JÁNOS **beteg** a   honvágytól]
         John   sick   the homesickness-from
         'John is sick with homesickness.'

     d. * [$_{FP}$ JÁNOS a honvágytól **beteg**]

These examples suggest that, when the copula is not spelled out, it is not merely phonologically null but is absent altogether. Unfortunately, other aspects of the verbless construction, e.g. that in (110c), are not at all clear; for example: does the structure without the copula have a TenseP projection? If it does not, what licenses the nominative case of the subject? If there is a TenseP, does the adjective merge with the phonologically null tense suffix, or does it skip TenseP? As for

(110a), the copula is likely to be inserted as the head of a VP, taking an NP or AdjP complement. Then the NP or AdjP is presumably moved to the specifier of an AspP, to check the [+stative] feature of the Asp head, and the copula is raised to Asp. Crucially, the syntactic relation of a predicative adjective or noun and an expletive does not differ from a verb modifier–lexical verb relation in any respect. Compare the position of a standard verb modifier and a verb, and that of a nominal predicate and a copula in various sentence types:

(111) a. János [$_{AspP}$ **betegre**   **tanulta** magát]
John   sick-TRANSLATIVE learned himself
'John learned himself sick.'

b. János [$_{AspP}$ **beteg volt**]
John   sick   was
'John was sick.'

(112) a. [$_{FP}$ JÁNOS [$_{AspP}$ **tanulta** magát **betegre**]]
'It was John who learned himself sick.'

b. [$_{FP}$ JÁNOS [$_{AspP}$ **volt beteg**]]
'It was John who was sick.'

(113) a. János **betegre**   szokta **tanulni** magát.
John sick-TRANSLATIVE used   to.learn himself
'John used to learn himself sick.'

b. János **beteg** szokott **lenni**.
John sick   used   to.be
'John used to be sick.'

(114) a. Csak **betegre**   nem szabad [$_{CP}$ hogy **tanuld**   magad]!
only sick-TRANSLATIVE not must   that you.learn yourself
'Only you mustn't learn yourself sick!'

b. Csak **beteg** nem szabad [$_{CP}$ hogy **légy**]!
only sick   not must   that you.be
'Only you mustn't be sick!'

According to the evidence of (111)–(114) the distribution of the nominal predicate and the copula is identical with that of the verb modifier and the verb, which follows if nominal and adjectival predicates are included in the class of verb modifiers. A consequence of this tentative solution is that nominal/adjectival predicates end up in Spec,AspP, where they check the [+stative] feature of Asp. The expletive is raised to Asp, and – unless it moves on to a higher functional head – the nominal/adjectival predicate cliticizes to it.

3.8   Summary

This chapter has discussed the structure of the minimal predicate, which consists of a VP extended by morphosyntactic projections, and an AspP. The VP is a V-initial phrase displaying free argument order. It is subject to a referentiality constraint: it can only host referential arguments. Non-referential complements must join the preverbal, predicative section of the sentence via operator movement.

The subject is also internal to the VP.[22] It does not have to be raised into Spec,AgrSP visibly; it only leaves the VP if it is topicalized, or if it undergoes operator movement. The tests which prove the VP-external position of the subject in English prove the VP-external status of the topic in Hungarian. Thus, in Hungarian VP-deletion is a transformation which deletes the V and its non-topicalized complements, and spells out the topic – whether it be represented by the subject or the object. In idiomatic sentences with a non-idiomatic variable the idiom is confined to the VP, and the non-idiomatic variable is in topic position. Further evidence of the lack of a VP-external subject position is provided by the lack of any superiority effect in *wh*-movement. The question of whether the VP is hierarchical, with the subject asymmetrically c-commanding the object VP-internally, is harder to answer. The evidence is controversial: subject–object symmetries in disjoint reference and Weak Crossover, as well as the total freedom of postverbal word order argue for a flat VP. Anaphora and disjoint reference between two lexical noun phrases, on the other hand, provide evidence of a hierarchy of arguments. This hierarchy is other than a subject > object > oblique complement hierarchy; according to the evidence of psych verbs and causative verbs, it is based on thematic prominence.

The VP is extended by a set of morphosyntactic heads including modality, tense, mood, object agreement, and subject agreement. The object agreement marker is of

---

[22] The question in what sense the EPP can be maintained in Hungarian is addressed in É. Kiss (to appear), where the EPP is split into a predication requirement and a requirement on argument ordering, namely:

(i)   *EPP1*
       A sentence expressing predication must contain a topic.
(ii)   *EPP2*
       Of the arguments of a predicate, one must be marked as a subject.

EPP2 has the consequence that each verb taking at least one argument will have a nominative complement – without implying that the given complement is associated with an invariant position. The solution of Alexiadou and Anagnostopoulou (1998), i.e., the checking of the EPP-feature of AgrS via V-to-AgrS movement, is also applicable to Hungarian.

particular interest: it is an invariant suffix appearing on finite verbs taking a definite object. The facts that transitive infinitives take no object agreement marker, and in infinitival constructions with a transitive matrix verb the carrier of AgrO and the source of accusative case are different suggest that AgrO may not be the locus of accusative assignment.

Most verbs have a lexically selected complement represented by a bare head: a so-called verb modifier, which has crucial role in determining the aspect of the VP. It has contradictory, clitic-like syntactic properties: it can move like a phrase, even at long distances – but when immediately preceding the verb, it seems to form a complex head with it. In the proposed analysis it undergoes phrasal movement to Spec,AspP, and then it merges with the V raised to Asp.

4

Focussing

The morphosyntactically extended VP can merge with logical operators expressing exhaustive identification, negation, and quantification. Although these elements appear at the head of the predicate, they act as propositional operators. They can be preceded at most by other (wider scope) propositional operators, and topicalized constituents, which are referring expressions, and hence are outside the scope of all operators, whatever their surface position relative to them.

4.1 The focus function

As was demonstrated in Chapter 3, the predicate phrase of a neutral sentence begins with a 'VM V' string; so a noun phrase preceding a VM + V complex is a predicate-phrase-external topic. A constituent followed by a 'V(...)VM' string, on the other hand, is still internal to the predicate phrase; it represents the semantically and phonologically most emphatic element of the predicate; it functions as a focus:

(1) a. [TopP Pétert [Predicate [Focus JÁNOS] mutatta   be   Marinak]]
         Peter-ACC   John   introduced VM Mary-to
         'As for Peter it was John who introduced him to Mary.'

    b.   [TopP János [Predicate [Focus PÉTERT] mutatta be Marinak]]
         'As for John, it was Peter that he introduced to Mary.'

    c.   [TopP Pétert [Predicate [Focus MARINAK] mutatta be János]]
         'As for Peter, it was to Mary that John introduced him.'

The phonological prominence of the focus (which is marked in the Hungarian text by small capitals throughout this book) arises not only from its primary stress but also from the fact that it obligatorily deletes the stress of the verb following it, and forms a single phonological word with it. (Usually the postverbal constituents of the VP are also unstressed, representing presupposed information.) Semantically, the focus is more than merely non-presupposed information; it expresses exhaustive identification from among a set of alternatives. Consider (1a); this sentence is used in a situation or context in which it can be potentially true of a set of persons, including John, that they introduced Peter to Mary. Example (1a) expresses that of this set it is John and no-one else for whom it holds that he introduced Peter to Mary. That is, an operator performing exhaustive identification is at work in this sentence: it operates on a set of alternative individuals for whom the VP can potentially hold, exhaustively identifying the subset for which the VP holds, and excluding the complementary subset. The focus constituent (or identificational focus according to É. Kiss 1998b) represents the value of this invisible operator.

In (1b) the operator performing exhaustive identification operates on a set of persons of whom it can be potentially true that John introduced them to Mary, and it identifies Peter as the one for whom this holds, excluding everyone else. In (1c) the operation of exhaustive identification is performed on a set of individuals of whom it can be true that John introduced Peter to them, and identifies Mary as the subset of this set for whom this holds, excluding the others. Generalizing our observations:

(2)   *The function of focus*
       The focus represents a proper subset of the set of contextually or situationally
       given referents for which the predicate phrase can potentially hold; it is identified
       as the exhaustive subset of this set for which the predicate phrase holds.[1]

Exhaustive identification is a function of the immediately preverbal focus constituent, and of that constituent only, which can be demonstrated by showing that the exhaustiveness associated with the preverbal focus is absent in other sentence positions. Various tests have been proposed to point out exhaustive identification, and they only give a positive result in the case of the preverbal constituent. A test of Szabolcsi (1981a) is based on a pair of sentences which differ only in that the constituent to be tested for its [+focus] feature consists of two coordinate DPs in the first sentence, one of which is dropped in the second; for example:

(3) a.   János PÉTERT   ÉS   ZOLTÁNT   mutatta   be   Marinak.
         John Peter-ACC and Zoltan-ACC introduced VM Mary-to
         'As for John, it was Peter and Zoltan that he introduced to Mary.'

    b.   János PÉTERT   mutatta   be   Marinak.
         John Peter-ACC introduced VM Mary-to
         'As for John, it was Peter that he introduced to Mary.'

(4) a.   János bemutatta Marinak Pétert   és   Zoltánt.
         John introduced Mary-to Peter-ACC and Zoltan-ACC
         'John introduced Peter and Zoltan to Mary.'

---

[1] The proposed interpretation of the focus function adopts features of the semantic focus definitions of Kenesei (1986), Szabolcsi (1994b), Jacobs (1986), von Stechow and Uhmann (1986), Krifka (1992), and others.

b.   János bemutatta Marinak Pétert.
John introduced Mary-to Peter-ACC
'John introduced Peter to Mary.'

If the (b) sentence is a logical consequence of the (a) sentence, as is the case in
(4) – i.e., if John introducing Peter and Zoltan to Mary implies that John introduced Peter to Mary – then the constituents tested (*Pétert és Zoltánt*; *Pétert*) do
not express exhaustive identification. If the (b) sentence does not follow from the
(a) sentence, on the contrary, it contradicts the (a) sentence, then the constituents
in question are foci expressing exhaustive identification. This latter state of affairs
is the case in (3): if it was Peter and Zoltan whom John introduced to Mary, then
it is not true that it was Peter whom John introduced to Mary. Examples (4a,b), on
the other hand, contain no identificational focus.

Consider also the dialogue in (5). Example (5a) can be continued by (5b) only
because its *Pétert* element expresses exhaustive identification.[2]

(5) a.   János PÉTERT   mutatta   be Marinak.
John Peter-ACC introduced VM Mary-to
'As for John, it was Peter that he introduced to Mary.'

b.   Nem, Zoltánt   is   bemutatta neki.
no   Zoltan-ACC also introduced to.her
'No, he also introduced Zoltan to her.'

Since this dialogue describes a situation in which John did introduce Peter to
Mary, the negation of John introducing Peter to Mary can be interpreted only as
the negation of exhaustivity. If in such a dialogue negation applies to a postverbal
emphatic constituent, as in (6), the dialogue is nonsensical:

(6) a.   János bemutatta Marinak Pétert.
John introduced Mary-to Peter-ACC
'John introduced Peter to Mary.'

b.   * Nem, Zoltánt   is   bemutatta neki.
no   Zoltan-ACC also introduced to.her
'No, he also introduced Zoltan to her.'

Focus is often said to express a contrast. Indeed, often a contrast can be inferred
between the two subsets of the relevant set delineated: the subset of which the
predicate is true, and the complementary subset, of which the predicate is not true.
For example, if in the case of (1a) the relevant persons who could have introduced
Peter to Mary are John and his brother, then the exhaustive identification of John
as the person who introduced Peter to Mary implies a contrast between John and

---

[2] This test of exhaustive identification was proposed by Donka Farkas (personal
communication).

his brother in this respect ('It was John and not his brother who introduced Peter to Mary'). The identificational focus, however, only implies a contrast when the relevant set on which the operation of exhaustive identification is performed is a closed set. If it is an open set, as in (7) below, the complementary subset, for which the predicate does not hold, cannot be reconstructed, and hence no contrast arises.

(7) a.   A Magyar   rapszódiákat   LISZT FERENC írta.
          the Hungarian rhapsodies-ACC Ferenc Liszt   wrote
          'As for the Hungarian rhapsodies, it was Ferenc Liszt who wrote them.'

    b.   Liszt Ferenc 1886-BAN halt meg.
          Ferenc Liszt 1886-in   died VM
          'As for Ferenc Liszt, it was in 1886 that he died.'

The relevant set on which exhaustive identification is performed is an open set of composers in (7a), and an open set of years in (7b); hence, it is not clear which composers the identification of Liszt excludes as the potential authors of the Hungarian rhapsodies, or which years the identification of 1886 excludes as the time of Liszt's death.

The identification of a subset and the exclusion of the complementary subset is an operation interpretable primarily on a set of individuals. Nevertheless, as Szabolcsi (1981c, 1983a) argued, non-individual-denoting expressions (e.g. predicative NPs, AdvPs, AdjPs) can also be focussed, because – by opposing them with their alternatives – focussing individuates them, creating the impression that they denote distinct properties; compare:

(8) a.   János OROSZ LÁNYT   vett feleségül.
          John Russian girl-ACC took as.wife
          'As for John, it was a Russian girl that he married.'

    b.   Péter OKOS LÁNYT   akart   feleségül venni, nem SZÉPET.
          Peter smart girl-ACC wanted as.wife   to.take not beautiful-ACC
          'As for Peter, it was a smart girl that he wanted to marry, not a beautiful one.'

    c.   János FOKOZATOSAN értette   meg a   problémát.
          John gradually   understood VM the problem-ACC
          'As for John, it was gradually that he understood the problem.'

In (8a) the focussing of the predicative expression *orosz lányt* 'Russian girl' suggests that exhaustive identification is performed on a set of properties including 'girl of Russian nationality' and its alternatives, among them 'girl of Hungarian nationality', etc. Whereas nationalities represent a natural class, in the case of (8b) it is not immediately clear what the relevant alternatives to the property *okos lány* are, but the elliptical sentence added to the clause helps: the alternative excluded is the property *szép lány* 'beautiful girl'. In the case of (8c), exhaustive identification is performed on manners. *Fokozatosan* 'gradually' has an inherent opposite, *egyszerre* 'at once', so the identification of *fokozatosan* as the manner in which the action denoted by the VP is performed means the exclusion of *egyszerre*.

The set of individuals or individuated entities on which exhaustive identification is performed is sometimes a set of sets. Consider (9), which contains a noun phrase extended into a numeral phrase in focus position:

(9)   Az osztálykiránduláson TIZENÖT TANULÓ vett részt.
       the class-excursion-on fifteen   student took part
       'It was fifteen students who took part in the class excursion.'

If the numeral is stressed, the relevant alternatives on which the identificational operator operates are subsets of various cardinality of some set of students, i.e., in the case of a class of 30 students, a set of 1 student, a set of 2 students, . . . a set of 29 students, and a set of 30 students. Having identified a set of 15 students as the set for which the predicate holds, the sentence excludes the possibility of 14, or 16 students taking part in the excursion. At the same time, however, it does not also exclude the possibility of any number of adults taking part in it, as well. The sets of adults are not among the entities taken into consideration in (9). This point can also be illustrated by the following example:

(10)   JÁNOS vezet Mercedest.
        John   drives Mercedes-ACC
        'It is John who drives a Mercedes.'

In a situation in which (10) is likely to be uttered, it does not mean that János is the only person on Earth who drives a Mercedes; it means that he is the only one of the relevant persons (those under consideration) at the moment.

Whereas the focus constituent expressing exhaustive identification can be represented by a bare nominal or a numeral phrase, it cannot be represented by a universal quantifier, or an existential quantifier of the *vala-* 'some' type. Consider:

(11) a. * János MINDENKIT   mutatott   be Marinak.
         John everyone-ACC introduced VM Mary-to
         'It was everybody that John introduced to Mary.'

     b. * János MINDKÉT FIÚT   mutatta   be Marinak.
          John both   boy-ACC introduced VM Mary-to
          'It was both boys that John introduced to Mary.'

     c. * János PÉTERT   is mutatta   be Marinak.
          John Peter-ACC too introduced VM Mary-to
          'It was Peter, too, that John introduced to Mary.'

(12)   * János VALAKIT   mutatott   be Marinak.
         John somebody-ACC introduced VM Mary-to
         'It was somebody that John introduced to Mary.'

As illustrated by these examples, both universal quantifiers (among them phrases containing the additive particle *is* 'also') and existential quantifiers of the *valaki* 'somebody' type are barred from focus position. Intuitively, universal quantifiers are unsuitable for the focus role because their function is incompatible with exhaustive identification. Whereas the focus exhaustively identifies a proper subset of some relevant set, excluding the complementary subset, the universal quantifier identifies every element of the relevant set as such for which the content of the VP holds. This is also true of *is* 'also' and *még...is* 'even' phrases, given that a phrase like *Pétert is* is interpreted as 'every relevant person plus Peter'. As is clear from (11b), in the case of a universally quantified expression the relevant set to be taken into consideration is always determined by the restrictor of the universal quantifier, i.e., *mindkét fiú* 'both boys' or *minden fiú* 'every boy' cannot be interpreted as the proper subset of some superset also including *mindkét lány* 'both girls' or *minden felnőtt* 'every adult'. In the focus theory of Szabolcsi (1994b, 1997a), universal quantifiers are excluded from focus position because it can only harbor group-denoting quantifiers.

Existential quantifiers are unsuitable for the focus role because – even if they can be interpreted to identify a subset of some relevant set as such for which the content of the VP holds – the identification they perform is by no means exhaustive. If John introduced somebody to Mary, it does not follow that the given person was the only one that John introduced to Mary.

The identifying operator whose value the focus constituent represents enters into a scope relation with other operators. It takes scope over the operators it c-commands, and it is in the scope of the operators c-commanding it; compare:

(13) a.   MARIT   hívta   meg minden fiú.
           Mary-ACC invited VM every   boy
           'It was Mary that every boy invited.'

     b.   Minden fiú MARIT hívta meg.
           'For every boy, it was Mary that he invited.'

(14) a.   János PÉTERT   nem mutatta   be   Marinak.
           John Peter-ACC not introduced VM Mary-to
           'It was Peter that John did not introduce to Mary.'

     b.   János nem PÉTERT mutatta be Marinak.
           'It was not Peter that John introduced to Mary.'

As is clear from the paraphrases, in (13a) exhaustive identification has scope over universal quantification, whereas in (13b) universal quantification has scope over exhaustive identification. In the latter case exhaustive identification is distributed over the variables bound by the universal quantifier, i.e., the sentence expresses that every boy has a set of persons eligible for invitation associated with him and, for every boy, Mary represents the only member of this set whom he in fact invited. In (14a) negation is in the scope of exhaustive identification, whereas in (14b) exhaustive identification is in the scope of negation.

4.2   The syntax of focus

4.2.1   Deriving the focus–verb adjacency

The reversal of the unmarked 'VM V' order in the 'focus V VM' string (illustrated in (15) below), i.e., the required adjacency of the focus and the verb represents the most conspicuous constraint on the apparently flexible word order of the Hungarian sentence, which has intrigued linguists since the middle of the 19th century.[3]

(15) a.   János **el   ment**.
          John away went
          'John went away.'

     b.   * JÁNOS **el ment**.

     c.   JÁNOS **ment el**.
          'It was John who went away.'

The most obvious way of accounting for this constraint would be to assume that the focus and the verb modifier are in complementary distribution in preverbal position, i.e., that they compete for the same position, which, however, can only harbor a single constituent. Although this approach accounts for the adjacency of the focus and the verb, it raises other unsolvable problems (see Farkas 1986). If the preverbal position is a landing site both for the focus and for the aspectualizer, it cannot be associated with an invariant interpretation. Furthermore, when the sentence contains both an inherently focus-marked constituent and a verb modifier, the preverbal slot will be occupied by the focus, with the verb modifier staying behind the verb – which can only be ensured by an ad hoc ordering constraint. The 'complementary distribution' approach is also undermined by facts of coordination. Namely, in the case of a 'VM V XP' string it is the 'VM V' section that can be subject to coordination (16); in the case of a 'focus V XP' string, on the other hand, it is the 'V XP' section (17), which suggests that the two strings are structured differently ([[VM V] XP] versus [focus [V XP]]).

(16) a.   János össze   szedte a   széttépett levelet,   és   össze   rakta a   darabjait.
          John together picked the torn-up   letter-ACC and together pieced its parts-ACC
          'John collected the torn-up letter and pieced its parts together.'

   →   * János [össze [[szedte a széttépett levelet] és [rakta a darabjait]]]

      compare:

     b.   János [[[össze   szedte] és [össze   rakta]] a   széttépett levelet]
          John   together picked and together pieced the torn-up   letter
          'John collected and pieced together the torn-up letter.'

---

[3] For references of historical interest, see É. Kiss (1987a: 90).

(17)   János [A MARI LEVELÉT [[tépte szét tegnap   este] és [rakta össze
        John the Mary's letter-ACC tore up yesterday night and pieced together
        ma reggel]]]
        this morning
        'As for John, it was Mary's letter that he tore up last night and pieced together
        this morning.'

Deletion provides similar information about the constituency of the 'VM V XP'
versus 'focus V XP' strings: the V XP string is a possible target of deletion only
in the latter case:

(18) a. * János nem sokáig tanulta a verset,   de meg   [tanulta a verset]
          John not long learned the poem-ACC but PERFECTIVE learned the poem-ACC
          'John hasn't been learning the poem long, but he has (learned it).'

    b.   Nem JÁNOS tudja a   verset, hanem PÉTER [tudja a verset].
         not John knows the poem but Peter knows the poem
         'It is not John that knows the poem but Peter.'

Bródy's analysis of focus (1990a, 1990b, 1995) can derive the focus–verb adjacency without involving these problems. Bródy generates an additional functional
projection (FP) for the focus above the projection dominating the VM + V complex. He places the focus constituent into Spec,FP, and assumes V movement
across the VM into the F head.

Let us tentatively adopt Bródy's idea, and let us assume that the AspP projection
of the verb is optionally extended into an FP, which is the projection of the abstract
operator performing exhaustive identification. The focus constituent, representing
the value of this operator, appears in Spec,FP. F attracts the verb, which moves from
Asp to F across the verb modifier in Spec,AspP, yielding the following structure:

(19)

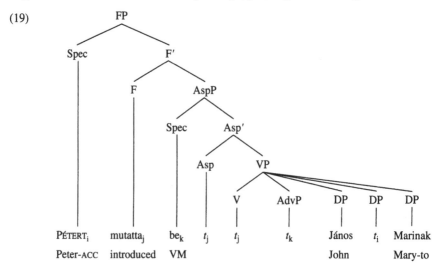

(The derivation of (1b) involves one more step: the topicalization of the nominative DP.) A non-trivial question that this approach raises is how to 'excorporate' the verb from the verb modifier cliticized to it – recall (79)–(80) in Chapter 3 – or how to block the incorporation of the verb modifier into the verb if and only if the verb is raised into F.[4] A further problem is that the proposed derivation predicts that the verb modifier always surfaces in the immediately postverbal position. In fact, the verb modifier can stand anywhere behind the verb; compare the following with (19):

(20) a.   PÉTERT   mutatta   János **be**   Marinak.
       Peter-ACC introduced John   VM Mary-to

   b.(?) PÉTERT mutatta János Marinak **be**.

In order to eliminate these problems, let us assume that the FP projection is not an extension of AspP, but an alternative to it. That is, a VP must be extended either into an AspP or into an FP. This proposal combines the advantages of the complementary distribution approach with the merits of Bródy's theory without raising the problems that they involve. Since a construction containing a VM incorporated into V is not subject to further derivation, the necessity of excorporation does not arise. What is more, since in a focus phrase the VM is in its base-generated position in the VP, its order relative to the other verb complements is predicted to be free. The elimination of AspP from the focus projection is also supported semantically. As was demonstrated in Section 3.6.2., the aspectual operator is neutralized in focus constructions; an FP is either vague or ambiguous aspectually.

The elimination of AspP from the focus projection also makes V movement superfluous to a large extent. The only fact providing some empirical support for the assumption of V movement is the word order of sentences containing both a focus and an adverbial of manner or degree. Adverbials of manner and degree are typically left-adjoined to AspP in a focusless sentence (although they can also stand in the VP). In the presence of a focus, on the other hand, they surface postverbally; compare:

(21) a.   [$_{TopP}$ János [$_{AspP}$ *nagyon* [$_{AspP}$ el   szomorodott]]]
       John   very   VM saddened
       'John became very sad.'

   b. * JÁNOS *nagyon* szomorodott el.
   c.   JÁNOS szomorodott el *nagyon*.
   d.   JÁNOS szomorodott *nagyon* el.

---

[4] Although Bródy (1990a) generates no AspP projection, his approach faces the same excorporation problem: the prefixed verb is generated as a complex head under a node labeled as V+.

(22) a.   [TopP János [AspP *gyorsan* [AspP meg értette   a   feladatot]]]
          John   quickly   VM understood the task
          'John understood the task quickly.'

    b. * Csak JÁNOS *gyorsan* értette meg a feladatot.
    c. Csak JÁNOS értette meg *gyorsan* a feladatot.
    d. Csak JÁNOS értette meg a feladatot *gyorsan*.

The sentences in (21c,d) and (22c,d) would clearly argue for a V-to-F movement only if the adverb of manner or degree immediately followed the V; in fact, however, it can stand anywhere postverbally. I conclude that in the proposed framework the assumption of V-to-F movement is unnecessary. The word order variants in (21b) and (22b), with the adverb intervening between the focus and the V, may be ruled out by a constraint requiring the adjacency of the focus and the V. Some additional motivation for such a constraint is presented in Section 6.2.

4.2.2   The FP projection

In view of the above considerations, we assign to a Hungarian sentence containing a focus the following structure:

(23)

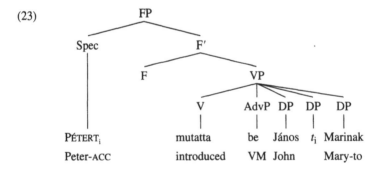

Movement into Spec,FP is an instance of operator movement; the focus phrase binds a variable trace in argument position. This claim is supported by the fact that a focus can license a parasitic gap; for example:

(24)   János [FP HÁROM LEVELET$_i$ dobott ki t_i [PP anélkül,   hogy elolvasott volna t_p]]
       John   three   letter-ACC threw out   without.it that read   had
       'It was three letters that John threw out without reading.'

The empty object in the embedded clause cannot be a pro, because a 3rd person pro counts as a definite object, and would trigger the objective conjugation. The verb *elolvasott*, however, which is obligatorily transitive, does not have the -(*j*)*a* definite object marker; hence, the empty object it agrees with must be bound by the indefinite matrix focus.

The scope of focus – more precisely the scope of exhaustive identification – is the domain c-commanded by the constituent in Spec,FP. Long focus movement is also possible, in which case the focus constituent raised into the matrix Spec,FP, naturally, has matrix scope; for example:

(25) a.　Nem szeretném,　　hogy CSAK MARIVAL　barátkozz.
　　　　　not　like-COND-1SG that　only　Mary-with friends.make-2SG
　　　　　'I wouldn't like that you make friends only with Mary.'

　　　b.　CSAK MARIVAL nem szeretném, hogy barátkozz.
　　　　　'It is only Mary that I wouldn't like you to make friends with.'

In (25a) exhaustive interpretation is in the scope of matrix negation, whereas in (25b) it has scope over it.

Since focus movement is substitution into Spec,FP, the extension of focus can be neither smaller nor bigger than a major sentence constituent. Claims that the focus can be both smaller and larger than an XP are based on a different notion of focus; compare:

(26) a.　JAPÁN　autót　vettél,　　vagy NÉMETET?
　　　　　Japanese car-ACC bought-you or　German-ACC
　　　　　'Is it a Japanese car, or a German one, that you have bought?'

　　　b.　Egy TOYOTÁT　vettem.
　　　　　a　Toyota-ACC bought-I
　　　　　'It is a Toyota that I have bought.'

Since in (26) only the adjectival modifier of the noun phrase is stressed, some linguists claim that the focus extends only over the adjective; the rest of the noun phrase has been pied-piped to Spec,FP.[5] If one interprets the term 'focus' as 'non-presupposed information', then this might be true. In the terminology adopted in this book, however, the focus is the value of exhaustive identification performed on a set of relevant individuals. In the case of (26a) the individuals – one of which the focus of the *yes–no* question identifies – are not nationalities but cars (otherwise the answer given to the question in (26b) would not be adequate). In other words, the entity representing the value of exhaustive identification is the referent of the whole noun phrase.

If the value of exhaustive identification is always the referent of the whole constituent in Spec,FP, then it is not immediately clear why the following sentences are interpreted differently; after all, they share the same focus, and they are also identical in other respects.

(27) a.　Péternek　HÁROM lányt　　kellett elszállásolnia.
　　　　　Peter-DAT three　girl-ACC needed put.up-INF-3SG
　　　　　'Peter had to put up THREE girls.'

---

[5]　See Kenesei (1998).

   b.   Péternek három LÁNYT kellett elszállásolnia.
        'Peter had to put up three GIRLS.'

   c.   Péternek HÁROM LÁNYT kellett elszállásolnia.
        'Peter had to put up THREE GIRLS.'

In fact, each of the three sentences means that, of a set of relevant sets, it was a set of three girls that Peter had to put up. What the sentences differ in is how the set of relevant sets is construed. In the case of (27a) the relevant sets from among which the set of three girls has been identified are sets of girls of different cardinality (e.g. a set of one girl, a set of two girls, a set of six girls, etc.). In the case of (27b), the alternatives are three-member sets of individuals (e.g. a set of three men and a set of three children, in addition to the set of three girls). In the case of (27c) the context does not give any clue to the identification of the alternative sets. The stress pattern of focus affects the construal of the set of relevant alternatives in as much as the destressing of a subconstituent of focus such as *három* 'three' or *lányt* 'girl' indicates that the given subconstituent denotes a presupposed property, more precisely a property shared by all the alternatives.

   Focus movement involves an ill-understood constraint: only head-final constituents can be focussed; namely:

(28)   *The Head-finality Constraint*
       A phrase in Spec,FP must be head-final.[6]

Owing to the Head-finality Constraint, focussed noun phrases tolerate DP and PP modifiers only in an adjectivalized, premodifying version (see Section 7.4.):

(29) a.   * Számomra [DP A   TALÁLKOZÁS PÉTERREL] volt a   legemlékezetesebb.
           for.me   the meeting   Peter-with was the most.memorable
           'For me, it was the meeting with Peter that was the most memorable.'

     b.   Számomra [DP A   PÉTERREL VALÓ TALÁLKOZÁS] volt a   legemlékezetesebb.
          for.me   the Peter-with being meeting   was the most.memorable
          'For me, it was the meeting with Peter that was the most memorable.'

The Head-finality Constraint causes clausal postmodifiers either to be extraposed or to be left-adjoined to the projection containing them:

(30) a.   * Csak [DP AZOK A   VEZETŐK, AKIK MÉG SOHA NEM OKOZTAK BALESETET],
           only   those the drivers   who still never not caused   accident-ACC
           kapnak díjkedvezményt.
           get   discount-ACC
           'It is only the drivers who have never caused any accident that get a discount.'

---

[6] It is not clear what the explanation of the constraint is. Kenesei (1994: 330), and Vogel and Kenesei (1987) derive the prohibition against headless and post-head clauses in Spec,FP from a prosodic constraint: the focus and the verb following it must form a phonological phrase, which cannot subsume a clause.

b. Csak [DP AZOK A VEZETŐK t_i] kapnak díjkedvezményt [CP AKIK MÉG SOHA
    NEM OKOZTAK BALESETET]$_i$

c. Csak [DP AKIK MÉG SOHA NEM OKOZTAK BALESETET, AZOK A VEZETŐK] kapnak
    díjkedvezményt.

(31) a. * [DP (AZ), HOGY KÖD VOLT], nehezítette   meg a   vezetést.
           it   that fog was   made.difficult VM the driving-ACC
           'It was the fact that there was fog that made driving difficult.'

b. [DP AZ t_i] nehezítette meg a vezetést [CP HOGY KÖD VOLT]$_i$

c. [DP HOGY KÖD VOLT, AZ] nehezítette meg a vezetést.

A question that has gained particular significance in current generative theory
is what motivates focus movement. In the Minimalist framework, in which movement is triggered by the need to check morphological features, identificational
focus moves to Spec,FP to check the [+focus] feature of the F head (see Bródy
1995). Since the VP can contain more than one [+focus]-marked constituent,
but projects at most a single FP,[7] it has to be ensured that at least one, and at
most one, of the [+focus] constituents of the clause moves to Spec,FP visibly.
Bródy (1995) achieves this by a Focus Criterion, a generalized version of the
wh-Criterion:

(32) a. At S-structure and LF the spec of a [+F] XP must contain a [+f] phrase.
     b. At LF all [+f] phrases must be in the spec of a [+F] XP.

In the Government and Binding framework focus movement is motivated by the
need for exhaustive identification to assume scope. This approach is particularly
appealing in the case of Hungarian because in Hungarian scope-bearing elements
c-command their scope from their surface positions. Hence, the word order of the
major sentence constituents can be derived from the scope principle, requiring that
operators c-command their scope, without any stipulations.

4.3   Inherent foci

In the Minimalist framework, a constituent can move to Spec,FP to check
the [+focus] feature of F if it also has a matching [+focus] feature. Certain types of
constituents – among them interrogative phrases, *csak* 'only' phrases, negative existential quantifiers, and negative adverbs of frequency, degree, and manner – obligatorily move to Spec,FP (unless Spec,FP is occupied by another [+focus]-marked
constituent). This is presumably because they have an inherent [+focus] feature
assigned to (a subconstituent of) them even in the lexicon. The [+focus] feature of

---

[7] In fact, É. Kiss (1995a,b) and (1998a) argues for the possibility of projecting more than
one FP per clause. Owing to verb movement to the highest F head, all foci but the highest
one will surface postverbally.

interrogative phrases and *only* phrases must be due to the fact that the semantic functions they are associated with represent particular types of exhaustive identification. *Wh*-phrases typically request the exhaustive identification of the subset of a relevant set of individuals for which the predicate holds, whereas *only* phrases combine exhaustive identification with evaluation (see Sections 4.4 and 4.5); compare:

(33) a. * János [$_{AspP}$ be   mutatott kit   Marinak]?
        John   VM introduced whom Mary-to
        'Whom did John introduce to Mary?'

     b. János [$_{FP}$ KIT$_i$ [$_{VP}$ mutatott be t_i Marinak]]?

(34) a. * János [$_{AspP}$ be   mutatta   csak Pétert   Marinak]
        John   VM introduced only Peter-ACC Mary-to
        'John introduced only Peter to Mary.'

     b. János [$_{FP}$ CSAK PÉTERT$_i$ [$_{VP}$ mutatta be t_i Marinak]]

In the case of negative existential quantifiers, negative adverbs of degree, and negative adverbs of manner it is less clear what semantic property is responsible for their inherent [+focus] feature; compare:

(35) a. * János *kevés matematikafeladatot* [$_{AspP}$ meg oldott]
        John few   math-problem-ACC   VM solved
        'John solved few math problems.'

     b. János [$_{FP}$ KEVÉS MATEMATIKAFELADATOT$_i$ [$_{VP}$ oldott t_i meg]]

(36) a. * János *alig* [$_{AspP}$ meg értette   a   matematikafeladatot]
        John hardly   VM understood the math-problem
        'John hardly understood the math problem.'

     b. János [$_{FP}$ ALIG [$_{VP}$ értette meg a matematikafeladatot]]

(37) a. * János [$_{AspP}$ meg oldja a   házi   feladatot *ritkán*]
        John   VM solves the home work   seldom
        'John seldom does the homework.'

     b. János [$_{FP}$ RITKÁN [$_{VP}$ oldja meg a házi feladatot]]

(38) a. * János *rosszul* [$_{AspP}$ meg oldotta a   házi   feladatot]
        John badly   VM solved the home work
        'John did the homework wrong.'

     b. János [$_{FP}$ ROSSZUL [$_{VP}$ oldotta meg a házi feladatot]]

The fact that their [+focus] feature is the manifestation of some semantic property becomes clear from the case of *csúnyán* 'uglily'. *Csúnyán* must only be focussed if it means 'in an ugly manner'. If it is used to express the great degree of some ugly deed, it is not focussed (but is adjoined to AspP);[8] compare:

---

[8] See Kiefer (1967).

(39) a. János [FP CSÚNYÁN [VP írta   meg a   leckét]]
         John   uglily   wrote VM the lesson
         'John wrote the lesson in an ugly way.'

         compare:

   b. * János [AspP csúnyán [AspP meg írta a leckét]]

(40) a. János [AspP csúnyán [AspP el   vágta a   kezét]]
         John   uglily   VM cut   his hand
         'John badly cut his hand.'

   b. Jánost [AspP csúnyán [AspP be   csapták]]
       John-ACC   uglily   VM deceived-they
       'John was badly deceived.'

The [+focus] feature can also be assigned freely, to any argument in the VP. If the VP contains two or more [+focus]-marked constituents, then only one of them will move to the Spec,FP; the rest of them remain in the VP. The constituent raised to Spec,FP will have scope over those left in situ; see (41):

(41) a. Csak MARI kapott   CSAK KÉT TÁRGYBÓL   jelest.
         only Mary received only two subject-from A+
         'It was only Mary who got an A+ only in two subjects.'

   b. Csak KÉT TÁRGYBÓL kapott CSAK MARI jelest.
       'It was only two subjects in which only Mary got an A+.'

These sentences are not ambiguous; as is clear from the paraphrases, the relative scope of the two *only*-phrases depends on their surface c-command relation. This provides evidence against the LF-movement of the postverbal [+focus]-marked constituent into Spec,FP predicted by the Focus Criterion of Bródy (1995), quoted under (32). If it were adjoined invisibly to the phrase occupying Spec,FP, then the two would have identical scopes (as is the case in English multiple questions). In fact, the postverbal [+focus]-marked constituent is interpreted scopally in situ. This must be possible because, the Hungarian VP being flat, it c-commands the material in the predicate also from its base position.[9] This approach predicts that in a sentence containing two VP-internal focus-marked constituents in addition to the one in Spec,FP, the VP-internal foci have identical scopes, i.e., they can be interpreted in any scope order, whatever their linear order should be. This is, indeed, what we attest:

---

[9] The idea of FP-iteration raised in footnote 7 is motivated by multiple focus constructions like (41), in which the postverbal focus also occupies a scope position. If the postverbal focus were in situ, then it would undergo movement to Spec,FP in LF and would end up adjoined to the focus constituent in Spec,FP. As a result of this, they would have identical

(42) a. MELYIK FÉLÉVBEN [_{VP} kapott   CSAK HÁROM LÁNY CSAK KÉT
      which   term-in   received only three   girl   only two
      TÁRGYBÓL   jelest]?
      subject-from A+
      'In which term was it only three girls who received an A+ only in two subjects?'
      'In which term was it only in two subjects that only three girls received an A+?'

   b. MELYIK FÉLÉVBEN [_{VP} kapott CSAK KÉT TÁRGYBÓL CSAK HÁROM LÁNY JELEST]?
      'In which term was it only in two subjects that only three girls received an A+?'
      'In which term was it only three girls who received an A+ only in two subjects?'

Example (42) also illustrates that of a *wh*-phrase and an *only*-phrase, the former must be selected for focus movement. This is presumably because a sentence without a *wh*-phrase in Spec,FP cannot be interpreted as a question; compare also:

(43) a. KI   látta CSAK PÉTERT?
      who saw only Peter-ACC
      'Who saw only Peter?'

   b. * CSAK PÉTERT látta KI?

---

scopes and could be interpreted in any scope order. In the theory of É. Kiss (1995a, 1995b, 1998a), FP is an extension of AspP, it can be iterated, and the V is attracted to the highest F, as follows:

(i)

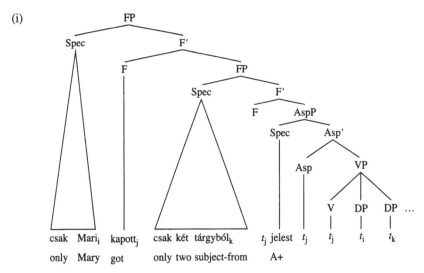

The V undergoes head movement from V into the higher F head passing through Asp and the lower F. Since it must be raised to the higher F, the lower focus constituent will be spelled out in postverbal position. This proposal raises the following problems: first, as Surányi (2000) pointed out, it makes wrong predictions for cases like (42), containing three [+focus]-marked constituents. It predicts a fixed scope order for the postverbal foci, which is contrary to fact. Second, it also wrongly predicts that the second focus immediately follows the verb. In fact, any number of constituents can intervene between them.

Of an inherent focus and a non-inherent focus, the latter must land in Spec,FP (44a), otherwise its [+focus] feature, which is not salient morphologically, will not be interpreted (whereas the inherent [+focus] feature of for example an *only* phrase or a negative adverb cannot become lost).

(44) a.　MINKET hív　fel Péter RITKÁN.
　　　　　us　　　calls up Peter seldom
　　　　　'It is us that Peter calls up seldom.'

　　　b.　RITKÁN hív fel minket Péter.
　　　　　'It is seldom that Peter calls us up.'

Example (44b) is not ungrammatical, but its *minket* constituent cannot be assigned a focus interpretation.

4.4　*Only*-phrases

4.4.1　The syntax of only

Csak 'only'-phrases deserve a more detailed examination. Focussing particles like *only* (similar to additive particles like *also* and *even*) are usually analyzed in the literature as clausal operators generated independently of the focus, and associated with it only in the course of interpretation.[10] This approach is somewhat counter-intuitive for Hungarian native speakers, who share the intuition that *csak* is a modifier of the focus constituent, and has undergone focus movement together with it. This intuition is based partly on the fact that a sentence can contain more than one *csak* phrase – see examples (41)–(42) above.

Word order variation in *csak* sentences also provides some weak support for this view. The particle *csak* usually immediately precedes the focus phrase that it is understood to belong to, qualifying the exhaustive identification expressed by it (in a way to be specified below):

(45) a.　János csak MARINAK mutatta　be　Pétert.
　　　　　John only Mary-to　introduced VM Peter-ACC
　　　　　'It was only to Mary that John introduced Peter.'

　　　b.　János csak PÉTERT　　mutatta　be　Marinak.
　　　　　John only Peter-ACC introduced VM Mary-to
　　　　　'It was only Peter whom John introduced to Mary.'

　　　c.　János csak EGYSZER találkozott Marival.
　　　　　John only once　　met　　　Mary-with
　　　　　'It was only once that John met Mary.'

　　　d.　János csak HÁROM LÁNYT　　tud elszállásolni.
　　　　　John only three　girl-ACC can put.up-INF
　　　　　'It is only three girls that John can put up.'

---

[10] Such an analysis has also been proposed by Szabolcsi (1980) for Hungarian.

Csak can also appear anywhere behind the verb, and still be understood to belong to the focus. The following sentences are merely stylistic variants of those under (45):

(46) a.   János MARINAK mutatta *csak* be Pétert.
'It was only to Mary that John introduced Peter.'

b.   János PÉTERT mutatta be *csak* Marinak.
'It was only Peter whom John introduced to Mary.'

c.   János EGYSZER találkozott Marival *csak.*
'It is only once that John met Mary.'

d.   János HÁROM LÁNYT tud *csak* elszállásolni.
'It is only three girls that John can put up.'

In (46b) a pause between *csak* and *Mary* indicates that *csak* belongs to *Peter*.

This sentence would also be grammatical if *csak* modified *Mary*. (Recall that if the VP contains two [+focus]-marked constituents, one of them will remain in situ.) In fact, there can also be two *csak* particles next to each other (separated by a slight pause), one of which is a stranded *csak* belonging to the focussed constituent; the other one is a *csak* belonging to the phrase that it immediately precedes:

(47) a.   János PÉTERT   mutatta   be   csak csak Marinak.
John Peter-ACC introduced VM only only Mary-to
'As for John, it was only Peter that he introduced only to Mary.'

b.   János PÉTERT mutatta csak be csak Marinak.
'As for John, it was only Peter that he introduced only to Mary.'

If *csak* is inserted into the sentence attached to a VP-internal constituent to be focussed, then the examples in (46) and (47) are instances of *csak*-floating/stranding. *Csak* has no fixed position in the VP because the trace to which it is adjoined can stand anywhere behind the verb.

Csak can also show up in a focusless sentence, left-adjoined to AspP. In such cases exhaustive identification is performed on a set of alternative actions, and the value of exhaustive identification is represented by the action denoted by the given AspP. Since AspP has not undergone any movement, the *csak* modifying it cannot have been stranded. Indeed, a *csak* applying to an AspP cannot stand postverbally; compare:

(48) a.   [$_{AspP}$ *Csak* [$_{AspP}$ rá csapta   János az ujjára   a   kocsiajtót]], más nem
only   on slammed John his finger-on the car-door-ACC else not
történt.
happened
'John only slammed the car door on his finger, nothing else happened.'

b.   * [$_{AspP}$ Rá csapta János *csak* az ujjára a kocsiajtót], más nem történt.

Certain types of non-major categories (e.g. numerals and adverbs of degree) can also be modified by *csak*, which also argues against the propositional operator analysis of *csak*:

(49) a. A *csak* 15 éves   gyanúsítottat letartóztatták.
the only 15 year-old suspect-ACC arrested-they
'The only 15-year-old suspect was arrested.'

   b. A *csak* alig   olvasható szöveget sokan próbálták értelmezni.
the only barely readable text-ACC many tried   to.interpret
'Many tried to interpret the only barely legible text.'

The distribution of *csak* attested follows most straightforwardly if we assume that *csak* can be adjoined to (extended) lexical projections, among them DPs and AspPs. *Csak* has a lexical [+focus] feature, which percolates onto the category that *csak* modifies. If the constituent modified by *csak* is available for focus movement, it will land in Spec,FP. In other cases – e.g. when *csak* is adjoined to an AspP or to a subconstituent of a major constituent – its [+focus] feature will result in a particular interpretation.

4.4.2   The semantics of only

   Csak 'only' phrases are generally believed to express exhaustive identification, i.e., they are associated with the same logical function that plain foci have in Hungarian. Indeed, it is hard to tell what the difference between the meanings of (50a) and (50b) is, if any.

(50) a. János PÉTERT   mutatta   be Marinak.
John Peter-ACC introduced VM Mary-to
'It was Peter whom John introduced to Mary.'

   b. János CSAK PÉTERT   mutatta   be Marinak.
John only Peter-ACC introduced VM Mary-to
'It was only Peter whom John introduced to Mary.'

Both sentences appear to mean that, of a set of relevant individuals, it holds for Peter and for no-one else that John introduced him to Mary. However, there are also contexts in which the focus cannot be accompanied by *csak* – which could not happen if sentences with a *csak*-marked focus and a *csak*-less focus were truly synonymous; compare:

(51) a. János MARIT   szereti a   legjobban.
John Mary-ACC loves the best
'It is Mary whom John loves the best.'

b. * János CSAK MARIT szereti a legjobban.
    'It is only Mary whom John loves the best.'

(52) a. JÁNOS érkezett elsőként.
         John   arrived first
         'It was John who arrived first.'

  b. * CSAK JÁNOS érkezett elsőként.
      'It was only John who arrived first.'

(53) a. Az Európa-bajnokságon   A FRANCIA CSAPAT nyerte az aranyérmet.
         the Europe championship-on the French team   won the gold-medal-ACC
         'At the European championship it was the French team that won the gold medal.'

  b. * Az Európa-bajnokságon CSAK A FRANCIA CSAPAT nyerte az aranyérmet.
      'At the European championship it was only the French team that won the gold
      medal.'

The semantic contribution of *csak* is most transparent in sentences in which the
elements in the domain of exhaustive identification denote quantities or some other
type of gradable elements; for example:

(54) a. Az osztálykirándulásra CSAK HÚSZ GYEREK jött el.
         the class-excursion-on only twenty child   came VM
         'Only twenty children came on the class excursion.'

  b. János CSAK KÖZÉPISKOLÁT végzett.
      John only high-school-ACC completed
      'John completed only high school.'

  c. Az előadás   CSAK KILENCKOR kezdődik.
      the performance only nine-at   begins
      'The performance begins only at nine.'

In the case of these sentences the operator performing exhaustive identification
operates on a set of alternatives that are ordered along a scale. *Csak* expresses that
the referent identified as the value of the identificational operator represents a non-
maximal value on the scale of alternatives. Suppose that (54a) is uttered in a situation involving a class of 30 students. The alternatives of which it can be potentially
true that they came on the excursion include a (sub)set of 30 students, a subset of
29 students, a subset of 28 students, etc. If a focus modified by *csak* indeed represents a non-maximal value on the scale of alternatives, then (55a,b) are possible
sentences in the given situation; (55c), however, is not. This is what we attest:

(55) a. Az osztálykirándulásra CSAK EGY GYEREK jött el.
         the class-excursion-on only one child   came VM
         'Only one child came on the class excursion.'

b.   Az osztálykirándulásra CSAK 29 GYEREK jött el.
     'Only 29 children came on the class excursion.'

c. % Az osztálykirándulásra CSAK 30 GYEREK jött el.
     'Only 30 children came on the class excursion.'

In the case of (54b) the alternatives on which exhaustive identification is performed include different levels of education, among them university, college, high school, and elementary school. Again, *csak* expresses that the alternative identified represents a non-maximal value of this scale. In the case of (54c) the operator of exhaustive identification operates on a set of points of time. These points of time form a scale if they are viewed from a reference point, e.g. the point of time of speaking. *Csak* in (54c) expresses that the time of the beginning of the performance identified is not the earliest possible alternative.

The interpretation of *csak* as an evaluative particle can in fact also be extended to cases in which it applies to noun phrases referring to non-gradable entities; for example:

(56)   A   családból   CSAK JÁNOS ÉS   PÉTER vett   részt az esküvőn.
         the family-from only John   and Peter took part the wedding-in
         'From the family only John and Peter took part in the wedding.'

Suppose that the family in question is a family of four members: János, Péter, Éva, and Mari. Then the subsets of the family that could have taken part in the wedding include the maximal subset {János, Péter, Éva, Mari}, the 3-member subsets {János, Péter, Éva}, {Péter, Éva, Mari}, {János, Éva, Mari}, and {János, Péter, Mari}, the two-member subsets {János, Péter}, {Péter, Éva}, {Éva Mari}, {János, Mari}, {János, Éva}, {Péter, Mari}, and finally the one-member sets {János}, {Péter}, {Éva}, {Mari}. The use of *csak* expresses that the two-member subset identified does not represent the maximal value on the scale of alternatives. That is, *csak* in (56) is the same evaluative particle that we attested in (54a–c). If the alternatives to be evaluated are not inherently graded, then we form subsets of different cardinality from the relevant set of alternatives and arrange the different subsets along a scale. *Csak* expresses that the subset identified represents a non-maximal value on the scale of subsets.

The sentences that do not allow the use of *csak* all include a predicate that can hold only for a single individual. The predicates *John loves x the best*, *x arrived first*, or *x won the gold medal* can only be true of a unique *x*. That is, the maximal value on the scale of sets with which these predicates can be combined is a one-member set. However, *csak* can be used only in case the focus represents a non-maximal value on the scale of alternatives – that is why (51b), (52b), and (53b) are ungrammatical.

4.5   *Wh*-questions

4.5.1   *Simple* wh-*questions*

In Hungarian *wh*-questions the *wh*-phrase must move to Spec,FP – presumably owing to the [+focus] feature of its *wh*-element; compare:

(57) a. [$_{TopP}$ A huzat [$_{FP}$ MELYIK SZOBA ABLAKAIT   törte be]]?
        the draft   which   room's windows-ACC broke in
        'The windows of which room did the draft break?'

   b. [$_{FP}$ MELYIK SZOBA ABLAKAIT törte be a huzat]?
   c. * Melyik szoba ablakait a huzat [$_{AspP}$ be törte]?

The only exception is *miért* 'why'. *Miért* is ambiguous: it can mean 'what for' and 'why'. Its focus movement is not obligatory only under the latter interpretation; compare:

(58) a. [$_{FP}$ MIÉRT   nyúlt   a   baba]?
        what-for reached the baby
        'What did the baby reach for?'

   b. * [$_{FP}$ Miért [$_{FP}$ A BABA nyúlt]]?

      compare:

(59) a. [$_{FP}$ MIÉRT kapott   János díjat]?
        why   received John prize-ACC
        'Why did John receive a prize?'

   b. [$_{FP}$ Miért [$_{FP}$ JÁNOS kapta a díjat]]?
      'Why was it John who received the prize?'

Miért 'why' as a sentence adverbial does not necessarily act as a variable binding operator, requesting the exhaustive identification of a subset of a set of presupposed reasons – that is why its [+focus] feature is not obligatory. When it specifies the reason for the identification expressed by the focus, it is adjoined to the FP. (In view of this fact, we must slightly modify the generalization we arrived at in connection with (42)–(43): for a Hungarian sentence to be interpretable as a *wh*-question, it must have a *wh*-phrase in the checking domain of F.)

The Hungarian pronouns functioning as *wh*-phrases – e.g. *ki* 'who', *mi* 'what' – can also occur in positions other than Spec,FP, where they are associated with functions other than interrogation. They can be relative pronouns, universal quantifiers, and exclamative phrases, among others. The *wh*-pronoun in (60a), located in Spec,CP, acts as a relative phrase, whereas the iterated *wh*-pronoun in (60b), occupying the position of distributive quantifiers, functions as a universal quantifier.

(60) a. [$_{CP}$ **Ki** [$_{FP}$ KORÁN kel]],   aranyat lel.
        who early   gets.up gold-ACC finds
        'He who gets up early finds gold. [The early bird catches the worm.]'

b.   [$_{DistP}$ **Ki-ki** [$_{AspP}$ haza   mehet]]
      who-who   home go-can
      'Everybody can go home.'

This situation led Horvath (1986a) to claim that for a *wh*-pronoun to function as an interrogative operator it must also have the feature [+focus]. Lipták (2000) has a different account of the varying interpretation of *ki* and *mi*. She claims that they are variable pronouns (like their Chinese and German counterparts), and that their *wh*-interpretation results from binding by an interrogative operator, a [+wh] C. Notice that in Hungarian embedded questions the C position is occupied by the equivalent of *that* – hence one and the same subordinator must be assigned either a [+wh] or a [–wh] feature; or, alternatively, the subordinator and the interrogative operator must be assigned to distinct CP and ForceP projections; compare:

(61)   János meg kérdezte, [$_{CP}$ hogy [$_{TopP}$ Pétert [$_{FP}$ ki   mutatta   be   Marinak]]]
       John VM asked   that   Peter-ACC who introduced VM Mary-to
       'John asked who introduced Peter to Mary.'

Yes–no questions (whose word order does not differ from that of declarative sentences) do display a visible *-e* interrogative marker when embedded; however, *-e* appears as a suffix attached to the verb. What is more, it is attached to a verb in situ. The possibility that V-to-C or V-to-F movement has taken place can be excluded; according to the evidence of the straight VM V order, the predicate of the embedded clause is of the category AspP; compare:

(62)   Nem tudom, [$_{CP}$ hogy [$_{TopP}$ Pétert [$_{AspP}$ be mutatta-e   valaki   Marinak]]]
       not know-I   that   Peter-ACC VM introduced-Q someone Mary-to
       'I don't know if someone has introduced Peter to Mary.'

Since most matrix verbs select either a [+wh] or a [–wh] clausal complement, and since they only 'see' the topmost CP projection of their complement, the *-e* interrogative element attached to the verb in (62) must be linked to the complementizer or the force head in some way (presumably via the LF movement of its [+wh] feature to C or force).

4.5.2   Multiple questions

In Hungarian, multiple questions requiring a singular answer and those requiring a pair-list answer have different syntactic structures. Multiple questions triggering a singular answer are rare and highly restricted; nevertheless, they are discussed first because they are the 'true' multiple questions semantically. As is argued below, multiple questions associated with a pair-list answer involve only one *wh*-operator; the rest of *wh*-phrases function as universal quantifiers in them.

In a 'true' double question, one of the *wh*-phrases occupies Spec,FP and the other one remains in situ – given that Spec,FP provides room only for a single

[+focus] constituent; for example:

(63) a. [$_{FP}$ KI vesz el [$_{VP}$ *kit*   a regény végén]]?
   who marries VM whom the novel's end-at
   'Who marries whom at the end of the novel?'

  b. [$_{FP}$ KI verekedett [$_{VP}$ *kivel*]]?
   who fought   who-with
   'Who fought with whom?'

The *wh*-phrase to be raised to Spec,FP can be chosen freely; the Superiority Condition does not favor one *wh*-phrase over the other. Since the subject, too, is internal to the VP, all *wh*-complements are at an equal distance from Spec,FP. The order of *wh*-phrases could also just as well be the reverse in (63a,b):

(64) a. KIT vesz el *ki*   a regény végén?
   whom marries VM who-NOM the novel's end-at
   'Whom does who marry at the end of the novel?'

  b. KIVEL verekedett *ki(csoda)*?
   who-with fought who-NOM
   'With whom fought who?'

(Example (64b) sounds better if the clause-final pronoun is replaced by *kicsoda*, its heavier morphological variant.) Interestingly, this type of double question is only acceptable if the two *wh*-phrases operate on the same domain. The following multiple questions, in which the two *wh*-phrases are unlikely to bind variables in a shared domain, are ungrammatical:

(65) a. *? KI mondott *mit*?
   who said what-ACC
   'Who said what?'

  b. *? KI érkezett *melyik vonattal*?
   who arrived which train-by
   'Who arrived by which train?'

The motivation for this constraint is unclear. If Lipták (2000) is right, and the two pronouns are variables bound by one and the same *wh*-operator in C, then perhaps (65a,b) violate the bijection principle, which prevents an operator from binding two variables. Then (64a,b) are perhaps saved by some kind of anaphoric binding between the two pronouns.

 The type of *wh*-question under discussion does not invite a pair-list answer. Pair-list answers are triggered by a different type of question, which superficially also contains multiple *wh*-phrases. However, only one of them is an interrogative operator in Spec,FP; the others are universal quantifiers sitting in distributive quantifier positions; for example:

(66) a.   [DistP **Ki** [FP MELYIK AJÁNDÉKOT választotta]]?
           who   which   present-ACC chose
           'Who chose which present?'

b.   [DistP **Melyik ajándékot** [FP KI választotta]]?

(67) a.   [DistP **Ki** [FP MELYIK VONATTAL érkezett]]?
           who   which   train-by   arrived
           'Who arrived by which train?'

b.   [DistP **Melyik vonattal** [FP KI érkezett]]?

In these questions only the immediately preverbal *wh*-phrase is located in Spec,FP; and that is also the only one that acts as an interrogative operator. The *wh*-phrase preceding the one in Spec,FP occupies the position of distributive quantifiers (see Chapter 5); and it also functions as a distributive quantifier. In the case of (66a), for example, *ki* 'who' is equivalent to *mindenki* 'everybody': it singles out every member of a relevant set of persons, and links a set of presents to each of them, requesting the exhaustive identification of the present that the given person chose. In the case of (66b), on the other hand, *melyik ajándékot* 'which present-ACC' is interpreted as the universal quantifier 'each present'; and the sentence asks about each element of the set of presents who chose it.

Thus, whereas an English double question is ambiguous – allowing either an answer denoting two individuals or an answer providing a so-called pair-list – in Hungarian the two meanings are expressed by different structures. The answers to the following two questions, for example, could not be exchanged; whereas (68a) must be answered by a single statement involving two individuals, (68b) requires a family of answers.

(68) a.   János KIT   mutatott   be   *kinek*?
           John whom introduced VM who-to
           'Whom did John introduce to whom?'

b.   PÉTERT   mutatta   be   *Marinak*.
      Peter-ACC introduced-he VM Mary-to
      'He introduced Peter to Mary.'

(69) a.   János **kit** KINEK mutatott be?
           'Whom did John introduce to whom?'

b.   Pétert   MARINAK ÉS ÉVÁNAK, Zoltánt   ÉVÁNAK ÉS JÚLIÁNAK,
      Peter-ACC Mary-to and Eve-to, Zoltan-ACC Eve-to and Julie-to,
      Istvánt   pedig   JÚLIÁNAK ÉS MARINAK mutatta   be.
      Stephen-ACC on the other hand Julie-to and Mary-to introduced-he VM
      'He introduced Peter to Mary and Eve, Zoltan to Eve and Julie, and Stephen to Julie and Mary.'

As is also clear from the dialogue in (69), the so-called pair-list answer is not in fact a list of distinct pairs. The members of a set (the variables in the domain of the universal quantifier) are linked to possibly overlapping sets of individuals (those in the domain of the interrogative operator).

It is an interesting question why the content of, for example, (66a) cannot be expressed by means of a regular universal quantifier followed by an interrogative pronoun; i.e., by (70):

(70)   Mindenki MELYIK AJÁNDÉKOT választotta?
        everybody which   present-ACC chose
        'Which present did everybody choose?'

Example (70) is a grammatical question. However, its universal quantifier cannot be understood distributively; it denotes a set as a single entity. Thus, (70) can only be asked in a situation in which the speaker knows that everyone chose one and the same present.[11] The reason why the distributive reading is missing, and why a universal quantifier distributing over an interrogative operator must have the form of an interrogative operator, is unknown. Perhaps the theory of Lipták (2000), in which the *wh*-pronoun is bound by a [+wh] C, will bring us closer to an answer (it might turn out to be a Relativized Minimality effect; perhaps the intervening universal quantifier would block the binding relation between C and the constituent in Spec,FP).

In this type of multiple question the first *wh*-phrase, acting as a universal quantifier, must be [+specific] (or D-linked), i.e., it must apply to a set of individuals present in the context or in the domain of discourse.[12] It is intuitively clear what motivates this constraint (called the Specificity Filter in É. Kiss 1993): the interpretation (i.e., the reference) of the *wh*-pronoun depends on the identity of the individuals in the domain of the universal quantifier. If the universal quantifier is not specific enough in the sense that the individuals in its domain cannot be identified, then the *wh*-phrase cannot be interpreted. The (b) sentences of the following sentence pairs are ungrammatical, or marginal, because they violate the specificity filter, i.e., the specificity requirement on the universal quantifier:

---

[11] Whereas *mindenki* 'everybody' in (70) does not distribute, it has wide scope with respect to exhaustive identification. The sentence in which the universal quantifier has narrow scope with respect to the identificational focus reads as follows:

(i)   Melyik ajándékot   választotta mindenki?
       which present-ACC chose   everybody
       'Which is the present which everybody chose?'

[12] This specificity requirement is also known from other languages; compare Pesetsky (1987), Comorovski (1996), É. Kiss (1993).

(71) a. **Ki** MIT   mondott?
who what-ACC said
'Who said what?'

  b. ? **Mit**   KI   mondott?
what-ACC who said
'What did who say?'

(72) a. **Ki**   HOGYAN viselkedett?
who how   behaved
'Who behaved how?'

  b. ?* **Hogyan** KI   viselkedett?
how   who behaved
'How did who behave?'

(73) a. **Ki**   MIÉRT hazudott?
who why   lied
'Who lied why?'

  b. * **Miért** KI   hazudott?
why   who lied
'Why did who lie?'

At first sight, the marginal (b) sentences seem to violate the Superiority Condition. However, the following acceptable sentences display the same distributions of grammatical functions; the initial constituents in them have merely been replaced by their specific (partitive) counterparts, which presuppose the presence of a set of relevant entities in the domain of discourse:

(74) a. **Melyik mondatot**   KI   mondta?
which   sentence-ACC who said
'Who said which sentence?'

  b. **Melyik módon** KI   oldotta meg a   feladatot?
which   way-in who solved VM the problem
'Who solved the problem in which way?'

  c. **Mely okból**   KI   hazudott?
which reason-for who lied
'Who lied for which reason?'

The Superiority Condition is also undermined by examples in which the object–subject order is grammatical, and the subject–object order is marginal – because the subject is represented by a non-specific *wh*-phrase; for example:

(75) a. **Kire**   HÁNY   SZAVAZAT jutott?
who-on how-many votes   fell
'How many votes fell on whom?'

  b. * **Hány szavazat** KIRE jutott?
'Whom did how many votes fall on?'

(76) a.   Mit   ki   a   fene mondott?
           what-ACC who the hell said
           'Who the hell said what?'

  b. * Ki a fene mit mondott?
       'What did who the hell say?'[13]

Hungarian embedded questions also have empirically and theoretically interesting properties – e.g. they allow partial *wh*-movement. These properties are discussed in some detail in Chapter 10.

4.6   Summary

This chapter has examined the syntax and semantics of the preverbal focus constituent of the Hungarian sentence. It has demonstrated that the focus serves to exhaustively identify the subset of a set of relevant individuals for which the predicate holds, while excluding the complementary subset. The focus constituent must be adjacent to the finite verb – with no verb modifier intervening between them – which is derived by generating the FP projection harboring the focus constituent immediately above the morphosyntactically extended VP – as an alternative to AspP. The movement of the focus constituent to Spec,FP is motivated in current theory by the need of the head of FP to have its [+focus] feature checked. Certain types of constituents – e.g. interrogative pronouns, *csak*-phrases, negative existential quantifiers, negative adverbs of frequency, negative adverbs of degree, and negative adverbs of manner – are moved to Spec,FP obligatorily; this is attributed to their inherent [+focus] feature.

Csak 'only' has been argued to be generated adjoined to a verb complement, lending its inherent [+focus] feature to it. *Csak* functions as an evaluating particle used in the case of exhaustive identification performed on a partially ordered set of gradable entities. It serves to express that the entity identified by the focus constituent represents a non-maximal value on the scale of alternatives.

The surface position of the *wh*-phrase is also in Spec,FP (although the possibility has been raised that it is bound from C). In Hungarian, multiple questions requesting the identification of two individuals, and multiple questions requesting a pair-list answer have different structures. The former are subject to a constraint requiring a shared domain for the two *wh*-phrases, whereas the latter are subject to a specificity filter, but the Superiority Condition is applicable to neither of them.

---

[13] This type of example is quoted from den Dikken and Giannakidou (2000).

5

Quantification

5.1 Distributive quantifiers at the head of the predicate

A characteristic property of Hungarian, shared by few other languages, is that it has a designated structural position for distributive quantifiers at the head of the predicate, before the focus (1a,b) or before the verb modifier (2a,b);[1] for example:

(1) a.   [**Mindenki** [FP JÁNOST hívta meg]]
         everybody   John-ACC invited VM
         'Everybody invited John. [For everybody, it was John whom he invited.]'

    b.   [**Mindenkit** [FP JÁNOS   hívott meg]]
         everybody-ACC John-NOM invited VM
         'Everybody was invited by John. [For everybody, it was John who invited him.]'

(2) a.   [TopP Jánost   [**mindenki** [AspP meg hívta]]]
         John-ACC everybody-NOM VM invited
         'John, everybody invited.'

    b.   [TopP János   [**mindenkit** [AspP meg hívott]]]
         John-NOM everybody-ACC VM invited
         'John invited everybody.'

The universal quantifiers in (1)–(2) are clearly inside the predicate phrase. This is indicated, among other things, by their stress. Whereas the stress of the topic is usually reduced, these quantifiers bear obligatory stress; they bear the first obligatory stress of the sentence, which marks the first major constituent of the predicate phrase. Furthermore, if these quantifiers were in topic position, their order relative to the other topic constituent would be free, which is not true; compare:

(3) a.   * [TopP *Mindenki* [TopP Jánost [AspP meg hívta]]]
         everybody   John-ACC VM invited

---

[1] For earlier descriptions of the quantifier position in the Hungarian sentence, see É. Kiss (1987a, 1991a). The interaction of quantifier position and relative scope was first observed by Hunyadi (1986). A Q-position similar to that attested in Hungarian has been pointed out in KiLega (Kinyalolo 1990), Palestinian Arabic (Khalaily 1995), and Chinese (Bartos 2000b).

b. * [$_{TopP}$ *Mindenkit* [$_{TopP}$ János [$_{AspP}$ meg hívott]]]
      everybody-ACC John-NOM VM invited

The boundary between the topic and the predicate is the rightmost possible position for sentence adverbials. Universal quantifiers cannot precede sentence adverbials, which is evidence of their predicate-internal position:

(4) a. * [$_{TopP}$ János   [**mindenki**   szerencsére [$_{AspP}$ meg hívta]]]
          John-ACC everybody-NOM luckily   VM invited
          'John, luckily, everybody invited.'

    b. * [$_{TopP}$ János [**mindenkit**   szerencsére [$_{AspP}$ meg hívott]]]
          John everybody-ACC luckily   VM invited
          'John, luckily, invited everybody.'

At the same time, a predicate-initial quantifier is clearly not in focus position either. Whereas a constituent in Spec,FP is followed by a bare V, with the verb modifier in postverbal position (5), a quantifier is followed by a VM V string (6).

(5) a. [$_{FP}$ Csak ÉVA hívta   meg Jánost]
          only Eve invited VM John-ACC
          'It was only Eve who invited John.'

    b. [$_{FP}$ KEVÉS KOLLÉGA hívta   meg Jánost]
          few   colleague invited VM John-ACC
          'There were few colleagues who invited John.'

(6)   [**Minden kolléga** [$_{AspP}$ meg hívta   Jánost]]
          every   colleague   VM invited John-ACC
          'Every colleague invited John.'

As is clear from the comparison of (5b) and (6), the predicate-initial quantifier position is not available for every type of quantifier. Thus, negative existential quantifiers (the so-called counting quantifiers of Szabolcsi 1997a) – involving for example *kevés* 'few', *legfeljebb n* 'at most n', *pontosan n* 'exactly n' – are ungrammatical in quantifier position; they must be preposed into Spec,FP (recall that in Section 4.2.3 they were claimed to have an inherent [+focus] feature). Existential quantifiers of the type *valaki* 'somebody', *valami* 'something', *néhány fiú* 'some boys' can appear neither in focus position, nor in quantifier position; they are either topics, as in (7a) and (8a), or are VP-internal bound variables, as in (7b) and (8b).

(7) a. [$_{TopP}$ *Valaki*   szerencsére [$_{AspP}$ meg hívta   Jánost]]
          somebody luckily   VM invited John-ACC
          'Somebody luckily invited John.'

    b. [Minden diákot [$_{AspP}$ meg hívott *valaki*]]
          every   student-ACC VM invited somebody-NOM
          'Every student was invited by somebody.'

(8) a. [$_{TopP}$ *Néhány család* szerencsére [$_{AspP}$ meg hívta   Jánost]]
          some   families luckily   VM invited John-ACC
          'Some families luckily invited John.'

b.　[Minden diákot [$_{AspP}$ meg hívott *néhány család*]]
　　every　　student-ACC VM invited some　　families
　　'Every student was invited by some families.'

Positive existential quantifiers involving *sok* 'many', *számos* 'several', *több mint n* 'more than n', *legalább n* 'at least n', on the other hand, can appear either in focus position or in quantifier position:[2]

(9) a.　[$_{Top}$ Jánost　　[**sok**　**család** [$_{AspP}$ meg hívta]]]
　　　　John-ACC　many family　　　VM invited
　　　　'John, many families invited.'

　　b.　[$_{Topp}$ Jánost [$_{FP}$ SOK CSALÁD hívta　meg]]
　　　　'As for John, it was many families who invited him.'

(10) a.　[$_{Topp}$ Jánost　　[**számos család** [$_{AspP}$ meg hívta]]]
　　　　John-ACC　several family　　　VM invited
　　　　'John, several families invited.'

　　b.　[$_{Topp}$ Jánost [$_{FP}$ SZÁMOS CSALÁD hívta meg]]
　　　　'As for John, it was several families who invited him.'

(11) a.　[$_{Topp}$ Jánost　　[**több, mint hat család** [$_{AspP}$ meg hívta]]]
　　　　John-ACC　more than six family　　　VM invited
　　　　'John, more than six families invited.'

　　b.　[$_{Topp}$ Jánost [$_{FP}$ TÖBB, MINT HAT CSALÁD hívta meg]]
　　　　'As for John, it was more than six families that invited him.'

(12) a.　[$_{Topp}$ Jánost　　[**legalább hat család** [$_{AspP}$ meg hívta]]]
　　　　John-ACC　at.least　six family　　　VM invited
　　　　'John, at least six families invited.'

　　b.　[$_{Topp}$ Jánost [$_{FP}$ LEGALÁBB HAT CSALÁD hívta meg]]
　　　　'As for John, it was at least six families that invited him.'

The set of quantifiers that can only occur in quantifier position from among the preverbal operator slots include universal quantifiers such as *mindenki* 'everybody', *minden fiú* 'every boy', *valamennyi fiú* 'every boy', *mindegyik fiú* 'each boy', *bármelyik fiú* 'any boy', *az összes fiú* 'all the boys', *mindkét fiú* 'both boys';

---

[2] Some (or perhaps all) of these positive existential quantifiers can marginally also be topicalized, in which case they are associated with a referential, partitive interpretation, i.e., they are understood to refer to specific members of a group of individuals present in the domain of discourse; for example:

(i)　Sok　diákot　　/számos diákot　　/legalább hat diákot　　valószínűleg
　　many student-ACC /several student-ACC /at least six student-ACC probably
　　el　　kell　utasítanunk.
　　VM needs refuse-1PL
　　'Many students/several students/at least six students, we will probably need to refuse.'

compare:

(13) a.   [$_{TopP}$ Jánost   szerencsére [**mindegyik család** [$_{AspP}$ meg hívta]]]
           John-ACC luckily   each   family   VM invited
           'John, luckily each family invited.'

    b. * [$_{TopP}$ Jánost [$_{FP}$ MINDEGYIK CSALÁD hívta meg]]

    c. * [$_{TopP}$ *Mindegyik család* [$_{TopP}$ Jánost [$_{AspP}$ meg hívta]]]

Also, for phrases modified by the additive particles *is* 'also', and *még...is* 'even', the predicate-initial position is the only available operator slot for them (14). It is not surprising that universal quantifiers and *is* 'also' phrases group together; after all, *also x* means 'every relevant individual plus x'. (*Még* 'even' in *még x is* adds an evaluative element to *is* 'also'; it expresses that *x* is an unexpected addition to the set of relevant individuals.)

(14) a.   [$_{TopP}$ Éva szerencsére [**még Jánost   is** [$_{AspP}$ meg hívta]]]
           Eve luckily   even John-ACC also   VM invited
           'Eve luckily invited even John.'

    b. * [$_{TopP}$ Éva szerencsére [$_{FP}$ (MÉG) JÁNOST IS hívta meg]]

    c. * [$_{TopP}$ *(Még) Jánost is* [$_{TopP}$ Éva szerencsére [$_{AspP}$ meg hívta]]]

A noun phrase extended by a bare cardinal number behaves like an indefinite: it can be topicalized, focussed, or stand in postverbal position. However, it can also be turned into a quantifier to be moved to predicate phrase initial position – if it is supplied with the particle *is*; compare:

(15) a.   [$_{TopP}$ Jánost   [**három család is** [$_{AspP}$ meg hívta]]]
           John-ACC three   family also   VM invited
           'John was invited by three families.'

    b. * [$_{TopP}$ Jánost [$_{FP}$ HÁROM CSALÁD IS hívta meg]]

    c. * [$_{TopP}$ *Három család is* [$_{TopP}$ Jánost [$_{AspP}$ meg hívta]]]

Szabolcsi (1997a) calls this type of *is* scalar, expressing the idea that the given number is evaluated as many, but its lexical meaning is, in fact, negligible. This type of *is* evidently functions as a grammatical formative, causing the numeral phrase it modifies to land in quantifier position. (Of course, the context can also force a regular, additive interpretation on it.) In other words, *is* must be the spelling-out of the grammatical feature that is responsible for movement to the prefocus operator position. As the facts in (16), observed by Szabolcsi (1997a), illustrate, this feature must be lexically assigned at least in some cases. Namely, whereas a quantifier involving the analytical expression *több, mint n* 'more than n' can land in the prefocus quantifier position, that involving its synthetic equivalent *n-nél több* 'more than n' has to be moved to Spec,FP (although judgments are somewhat fuzzy):

(16) a.   [$_{TopP}$ Jánost   [**több, mint három család** [$_{AspP}$ meg hívta]]]
           John-ACC more than three   family   VM invited
           'John, more than three families invited.'

b.   [TopP Jánost [FP HÁROMNÁL   TÖBB CSALÁD hívta   meg]]
      John-ACC three-ADESSIVE more family   invited VM
      'John, more than three families invited.'

The property that universal quantifiers, *is* phrases, numeral phrases supplied with *is*, and, optionally, phrases involving *sok* 'many', *számos* 'several', etc. share has been identified by Szabolcsi (1994b, 1997a) as the feature of distributivity. A quantifier raised to the initial position of the predicate phrase acts as a distributor, i.e., the content of the rest of the predicate is distributed over every element in its domain. Szabolcsi (1997a) demonstrates the distributivity associated with quantifiers in the predicate-initial operator position by using examples that force a distributive reading despite the fact that it contradicts our knowledge about the world:

(17) a.   [**Minden/valamennyi/mindegyik fiú** [AspP fel emelte a   zongorát]]
           every   /all   /each   boy   up lifted the piano
           'Every boy/all boys/each boy lifted up the piano.'

     b.   [**János is** [AspP fel emelte a   zongorát]]
           John   also   up lifted the piano
           'Also John lifted up the piano.'

These sentences do not allow a reading in which the lifting of the piano was performed by the boys or by some relevant persons plus John collectively. Consider another of Szabolcsi's examples, involving a non-distributive predicate:

(18)   [**Mindhárom birtok** [AspP körül veszi   a   kastélyt]]
        all-three   estate   VM surrounds the manor
        'All the three estates surround the manor.'

Since surrounding is a collective act that cannot distribute over the three members of the subject set, the event of surrounding must be distributed over them. That is, the sentence must be understood in such a way that each of the three estates surrounds the house separately, i.e., they form concentric circles around the house, no matter how unlikely this situation may be.

In the case of universals and *is* phrases, distributivity may be an inherent feature of the quantifier; however, in the case of *számos* 'several' and *sok* 'many', it is a function of the predicate-initial position. The following pairs of sentences differ only in the quantifier versus focus position of their subject. As the English paraphrases make clear, the distributive reading is obligatory only if the subject is in quantifier position.

(19) a.   [**Sok/számos fiú** [AspP fel emelte a   zongorát]]
           many/several boy   up lifted the piano
           'Many/several boys (each) lifted up the piano.'

     b.   [FP SOK/SZÁMOS FIÚ emelte fel a zongorát]
           'It was many/several boys who lifted up the piano.'

A similar semantic difference is attested between a numeral phrase supplied with *is*, occupying quantifier position, and a plain numeral phrase moved to focus or topic position: the former is obligatorily distributive, whereas the latter also allows a collective reading.

(20) a. [**Két fiú** **is** [$_{AspP}$ fel emelte a   zongorát]]
         two boys also   up lifted the piano
         'Two boys (each) lifted up the piano.'

   b. [$_{FP}$ KÉT FIÚ emelte fel a zongorát]
       'It was two boys who lifted up the piano.'

Here is a further example, involving a *több mint* n 'more than *n*' phrase, which can also occur either in quantifier position or in focus position, and which assumes an obligatorily distributive reading only in the former case.

(21) a. [Minden alkalommal [**több, mint hat fiú** [$_{AspP}$ fel emelte a   zongorát]]]
         every   time   more than six boy   up lifted   the piano
         'Every time more than six boys (each) lifted up the piano.'

   b. [Minden alkalommal [$_{FP}$ TÖBB, MINT HAT FIÚ emelte fel a   zongorát]]
       every   time   more than six boy lifted up the piano
       'Every time it was more than six boys that lifted up the piano.'

In sum, the prefocus position of the predicate phrase is reserved for distributive quantifiers. This is the only operator position available for universals and *is* phrases; this is presumably because they are inherently distributive. In the case of phrases involving a positive existential quantifier such as *sok* or *számos*, on the other hand, obligatory distributivity is a function of the given position, which is not the only structural position available for them.

5.2   The DistP projection

Let us assume that distributive quantifiers occupy the specifier slot of a DistP projection.[3] DistP dominates FP or, in the absence of an FP, AspP. Let us assume that it is a projection of a Dist head, which attracts a [+distributive] constituent into Spec,DistP. Universally quantified noun phrases, and noun phrases modified by (*még*). . .*is* are inherently [+distributive]; that is, distributivity is obviously an intrinsic property of the universal determiner *mind-*, and of *is*. *Sok/számos/ legalább* n/*több, mint* n phrases can be assigned the feature [+distributive] optionally; or perhaps they represent two items in the lexicon: they stand both for a [+distributive] quantifier and for an indefinite numeral.

The DistP projection differs syntactically from the AspP and FP projections in that it can have more than one specifier. (It is also conceivable that the whole DistP projection is iterated – but under the latter assumption multiple negative

---

[3] The term DistP has been adopted from Beghelli and Stowell (1997) and Szabolcsi (1997a).

universal quantifiers, licensed by a single negative head, are harder to account for; see Section 6.5.); compare:

(22) a. János [$_{DistP}$ **mindig** [$_{DistP}$ **mindenhová** [$_{DistP}$ **mindkét fiát**   [$_{AspP}$ magával
         John   always   everywhere   all-two   son-3SG-ACC with.him
         viszi]]]]
         takes
         'John always takes both of his sons with him everywhere.'

   b. János [$_{DistP}$ **minden diákjának** [$_{DistP}$ **három dolgozattémát is** [$_{AspP}$ fel
       John   every   student-3SG-DAT three   essay-topic-ACC even   VM
       ajánlott]]]
       offered
       'John offered to each of his students three essay topics.'

In the framework of the Government and Binding theory, the possibility of several distributive quantifiers in a clause follows from the adjunction analysis of Quantifier-Raising, adjunction being an iterable operation. In view of the results of Szabolcsi (1997a), Beghelli and Stowell (1997), and others, however, the Quantifier-Raising transformation of May (1985), applying to quantifiers indiscriminately, is not tenable any more – although it could be reformulated as distributor-raising. In the Minimalist framework, quantifier movement is substitution into Spec,DistP, triggered by the need of the Dist head to have its [+distributive] feature checked.

Movement to Spec,DistP creates scope; hence, sentences containing two quantifiers, derived by two applications of quantifier movement, are disambiguated. Thus, the following sentences have only one reading each; the quantifier which c-commands and precedes the other also has scope over it.

(23) a. [$_{TopP}$ János [$_{DistP}$ **minden diákjának** [$_{DistP}$ **három dolgozattémát is** [$_{AspP}$ fel
         John   every   student-3SG-DAT three   essay-topic   even   VM
         ajánlott]]]]
         offered
         'John offered to each of his students three essay topics.'

   b. [$_{TopP}$ János [$_{DistP}$ **három dolgozattémát is** [$_{DistP}$ **minden diákjának** [$_{AspP}$ fel
       John   three essay-topic even   every   student-3SG-DAT VM
       ajánlott]]]]
       offered
       'John offered three essay topics to each of his students.'

A [+distributive] quantifier can be raised into the specifier of the DistP of a matrix clause, as well, in which case it assumes scope over the matrix VP and matrix focus:

(24) a. A professzor$_j$ [$_{DistP}$ **mindkét diákot**$_i$ [$_{FP}$ MÁMA$_k$ szeretném, [$_{CP}$ ha
         the professor   all.two student-ACC today like-COND-1SG if
         levizsgáztatná t_j t_i t_k]]]
         examined
         'As for the professor, it is today that I would like him to examine both students.'

b.   A professzor$_j$ [$_{DistP}$ **mindenkit**$_i$ [$_{AspP}$ át$_k$ kellene,   [$_{CP}$ hogy
      the professor   everybody-ACC through need-COND-3SG that
      engedjen t_j t_i t_k]]]
      let
      'It would be necessary that the professor let everybody pass.'

Since quantifier raising takes place in visible syntax in Hungarian, a quantifier in Spec,DistP is expected to license a parasitic gap:[4]

(25) a.   A professzor [$_{DistP}$ **tíz diákot**   **is**$_i$ [$_{AspP}$ át   engedett t_i, [$_{PP}$ anélkül,
      the professor   ten student-ACC also   through let   without.it
      [$_{CP}$ hogy alaposan   kikérdezett volna t_p]]]]
          that thoroughly asked   had
      'The professor let ten students pass without examining [them] thoroughly.'

b.   János [$_{DistP}$ **minden ételmaradékot**$_i$ [$_{AspP}$ ki dobott t_i, [$_{PP}$ anélkül, [$_{CP}$ hogy
      John   every leftover-ACC   out threw   without.it that
      megkóstolt volna t_p]]]]
      tasted   had
      'John threw out all leftovers without tasting [them].'

By way of summary, observe the tree diagram of the structure assigned to (23a):

(26)

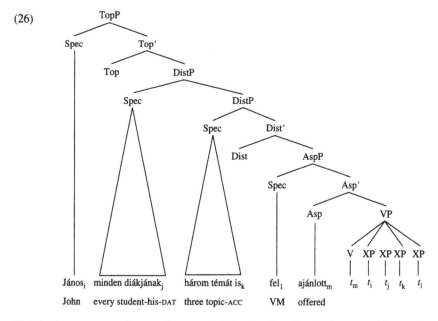

This is the structure of a predicate containing both a distributive quantifier and a focus:

---

[4] For a detailed discussion of the Hungarian parasitic gap construction, see Section 10.6.

(27)

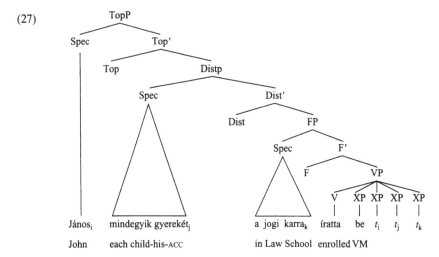

| János$_i$ | mindegyik gyerekét$_j$ | a jogi karra$_k$ | íratta | be | t_i | t_j | t_k |
| John | each child-his-ACC | in Law School | enrolled | VM | | | |

On the basis of their structures, the stress patterns of these sentences can also be predicted. In Hungarian, the Nuclear Stress Rule puts phrasal stress on the left edge of phrases.[5] The topic of the sentence – i.e., the constituent in Spec,Top – constitutes an independent intonation phrase, which is usually subject to stress reduction.[6] In the intonation phrase represented by the predicate (i.e., in the complement of Top), each maximal projection is assigned phrasal stress. Since phrasal stress falls on the left edge, in (26) the VM and the two quantifiers will be stressed, whereas in (27) the quantifier and the focus will be stressed. As follows from the Nuclear Stress Rule, the higher a projection, the heavier its stress will be. The stress assigned to the initial V of a VP immediately dominated by an FP is obligatorily deleted – perhaps because a post-focus V necessarily carries presupposed information.

5.3   The scope principle

5.3.1   Preverbal quantifiers

In the generative framework, operators are assumed to be subject to the following constraint:

(28)   *The scope principle*
An operator c-commands its scope.

English and other languages often contradict this principle on the surface; various mechanisms have, therefore, been proposed to map the structures attested

---

[5] On the Nuclear Stress Rule in Hungarian, see É. Kiss (1988), and Varga (1999).
[6] See Hunyadi (1997, 1999), who outlines a Hungarian metrical phonology (based on phonetic evidence recorded in the form of sonograms). Incidentally, in his system, scope is primarily expressed by stress; an operator has scope over the elements in the phonological phrase of which it is the head.

on structures in which the scope of operators corresponds to their c-command domain. In the Government and Binding framework operators were assumed to satisfy the scope principle in LF, after invisible quantifier raising. More recently it has been claimed that operators satisfy the scope principle at an early stage of the derivation, but subsequent transformations may superficially cover the correspondence between their scope and c-command domain. From the point of view of the scope principle, Hungarian is the 'best-behaving' language of those described in the generative framework: it observes the scope principle trivially, in visible syntax, at surface structure.

In the preverbal operator field of the predicate the scope principle is trivially satisfied: every operator has scope over the constituent it c-commands and precedes. That is, sentences are fully disambiguated; scope relations can be identified both on the basis of c-command and on the basis of surface order. This fact has already been illustrated in the case of a pair of quantifiers: in (23a,b) the reversal of the order of quantifiers results in a reversal of their relative scope.

If one of the theoretically possible scope orders of two quantifiers yields a reading that is pragmatically impossible, the linear order corresponding to the pragmatically impossible order will be unacceptable; for example:

(29) a. **Mindenki minden almát**   meg evett.
         everybody every   apple-ACC up   ate
         'Everybody ate up every apple.'

   b. * **Minden almát mindenki** meg evett.

   c. **Minden almát**   **mindenki** meg vizsgált.
         every   apple-ACC everybody VM examined
         'Everybody examined every apple.'

The wide scope of *minden almát* 'every apple' in (29b) means that every one of a relevant set of apples was eaten up by every one of a set of persons – which is impossible, given that an apple can only be eaten up once. Example (29a), on the other hand, is grammatical because every person in the domain of *mindenki* 'everybody' can have a different set of apples at his or her disposal, which he or she might as well eat up. If we replace the verb *megeszik* 'eat up' with *megvizsgál* 'examine', as in (29c), the uniqueness restriction is lifted, and the order 'universally quantified object – universally quantified subject' becomes acceptable.

Consider also the scope relation of a distributive quantifier in Spec,DistP and a negative existential quantifier (a so-called counting quantifier in the terminology of Szabolcsi 1997a) in Spec,FP:

(30)   [$_{DistP}$ **Mindkét süteményt** [$_{FP}$ KEVÉS GYEREK kóstolta meg]][7]
         all-two cake-ACC   few   child   tasted   VM
         'For both cakes, it was few children that tasted them.'

---

[7] Szabolcsi (1994b, 1997a) claims that *kevés gyerek* 'few children' and similar counting quantifiers are in Spec,AspP (which she calls Spec,PredOp), instead of Spec,FP. Her claim

As is clear from the English paraphrase, the focussed quantifier is unambiguously in the scope of the universal quantifier c-commanding it.

5.3.2   Postverbal unstressed quantifiers

The question arises of what happens if the intended scope relation between a universal quantifier and a focussed quantifier is just the opposite of that illustrated in (30). How could a counting quantifier have scope over a universal when both a counting quantifier marked as [+focus] and a universal quantifier marked as [+distributive] have designated landing sites in the preverbal operator field, and the landing site of the latter c-commands the landing site of the former? The answer is that the narrow scope universal must remain in postverbal position; for example:

(31)   [$_{FP}$ KEVÉS GYEREK$_i$ [$_{VP}$ kóstolta meg t_i **mindkét süteményt**]]
          few   child   tasted   VM all.two cake
          'It was few children who tasted both cakes.'

The question of whether the postverbal universal quantifier is in its base-generated position, or occupies a postverbal operator slot, and whether it takes scope in situ, or is subject to LF movement, has initiated much discussion. É. Kiss (1987a, 1991a) discarded the possibility of the quantifier sitting in a postverbal operator position because the quantifier has no fixed position in the VP, and its word order and scope relative to other postverbal operators is also free; compare:

(32) a.   TAVALY olvasott el   **minden diák   két könyvet is**   a   szintaxis-vizsgára.
           last.year read   VM every   student two book   also the syntax-exam-for
           'It was last year that every student read two books for the syntax exam.'

---

is based on two considerations. First, a sentence like

(i)   KEVÉS FIÚ ette meg az ebédet.
       few   boy ate up   the lunch
       '(It was) few boys who ate the lunch.'

does not exclude the possibility that any number of girls also ate the lunch, i.e., the quantifier does not seem to be associated with the exhaustivity characteristic of focussed constituents. As I argued in Chapter 4, however, in such a case the alternatives on which exhaustive identification is performed are various subsets of the set of boys present in the domain of discourse. That is, what are excluded in the case of (i) are sets of boys of a cardinality other than 'few' – e.g. a set of many boys; a set of all boys, etc. Girls are not among the relevant individuals considered.

Szabolcsi claims that there is another test for deciding whether a constituent occupies Spec,FP or Spec,PredOp: in negated focussed sentences the negative particle is followed by the focus, whereas in negated sentences containing a predicate operator/aspectualizer, the negative particle is followed by the verb. This test also shows *kevés fiút* to be in Spec,FP; compare:

(ii)   Nem kevés fiú   ette meg az ebédet.
        not   few   boy ate up   the lunch
        'It wasn't few boys who ate the lunch.'

(iii)   ?? Nem ette meg kevés fiú az ebédet.

   b. TAVALY olvasott el **két könyvet is minden diák** a szintaxis-vizsgára.
   c. TAVALY olvasott el **minden diák** a szintaxis-vizsgára **két könyvet is.**
   d. TAVALY olvasott el a szintaxis-vizsgára **két könyvet is minden diák.**

According to the evidence of these examples, if a sentence contains two narrow scope quantifiers, then they can appear anywhere behind the verb, which is typical of VP-internal arguments in Hungarian. Operators have fixed positions in the Hungarian sentence. Furthermore, the relative order of the quantifiers does not affect their scope interpretation; each of these sentences is ambiguous (although the scope order that corresponds to the linear order of the quantifiers is slightly preferred in every case). É. Kiss (1987a, 1991a) concludes on the basis of these facts that postverbal quantifiers are in their base-generated positions, and they take scope in situ. The Hungarian VP being flat, they mutually c-command each other, which means that they have identical scopes, i.e., they can be interpreted in any scope order. At the same time, they are in the scope of all preverbal operators.[8]

---

[8] Szabolcsi (1997a) observed that in the postverbal domain a counting quantifier sometimes cannot have wide scope over a universal quantifier preceding it. Observe her example:

   (i) TEGNAP   harapott meg **minden kutya** KEVÉS FIÚT.
        yesterday bit   VM every   dog   few   boy
        'It was yesterday that every dog bit few boys.'

        compare:

   (ii) TEGNAP harapott meg KEVÉS FIÚT **minden kutya.**
        'It was yesterday that few boys were bitten by every dog.'
        'It was yesterday that every dog bit few boys.'

Whereas (ii) is scopally ambiguous, as expected, in the case of (i) it is difficult, or impossible, to obtain the reading in which it holds for few boys that each of them was bitten by every dog. Szabolcsi (1997a) derives this fact from a Hungarian sentence structure that has two sets of operator positions: a set above AgrP, preceding the finite verb, and a set below AgrP, following the finite verb. The relevant section of the lower set of operator positions looks as follows:

   (iii)   CaseP*

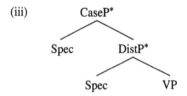

A postverbal universal quantifier occupies Spec,DistP. A postverbal counting quantifier preceding it is in a Spec,CaseP, where it takes scope over the constituent in Spec,DistP. Otherwise it is reconstructed into the VP for interpretation and has narrow scope with respect to the universal quantifier. A counting quantifier following a postverbal universal is in the VP. A constituent in Spec,DistP cannot be reconstructed into the VP, hence it always takes scope over a counting quantifier following it.

   The facts, however, are not quite as clear as would appear from the examples in (i) and (ii). First, we do not get the same effect with every type of distributive quantifiers; e.g. if

A postverbal universal quantifier is also predicted to be scopally ambiguous with respect to a postverbal counting quantifier. The prediction is borne out:

(33)   TAVALY bukott meg **minden tárgyból**   KEVÉS DIÁKUNK.
        last.year failed VM every subject-from few   student-our
        'It was last year that few of our students failed in every subject.'
        'It was last year that in every subject few of our students failed.'

The in situ analysis of postverbal quantifiers raises the question of whether postverbal universal quantifiers also have a [+distributive] feature to check. Beghelli and Stowell (1997) claim that in sentences containing a universal in the scope of negation, the VP-internal narrow-scope universal quantifier is non-distributive; it is simply a variable bound by the wide-scope operator. However, we can construct examples in which a postverbal universal quantifier in the scope of focus distributes over another postverbal quantifier; for example:

(34)   KEVÉS GYEREK adott **mindkét süteményből mindegyik felnőttnek**.
        few   child   gave all.two cake-from   every   adult-to
        'It was few children who gave some from both cakes to every adult.'

What is more, the predicate is also always distributed over a postverbal narrow-scope universal quantifier:

we replace *minden kutya* 'every dog' with *minden kutyánk* 'every dog of ours', inverse scope is not impossible; compare:

(iv)   TEGNAP   harapott meg **minden kutyánk** KEVÉS FIÚT.
        yesterday bit   VM every   dog-1PL few   boy
        'It was yesterday that every dog of ours bit few boys.'
        'It was yesterday that few boys were bitten by every dog of ours.'

(v)   TEGNAP   harapott meg **mindkét kutya** KEVÉS FIÚT.
        yesterday bit   VM all-two dog   few   boy
        'It was yesterday that both dogs bit few boys.'
        'It was yesterday that few boys were bitten by both dogs.'

The relevant difference between *minden kutya* 'every dog', on the one hand, and *minden kutyánk* 'every dog of ours' and *mindkét kutya* 'both dogs', on the other hand, is that the latter quantifiers denote D(iscourse)-linked, or specific, sets. The sentence in (33) evokes a classroom situation involving a specific set of students and a specific set of subjects. The relevant generalization is as follows:

(vi)   *The inverse scope constraint*
        Inverse scope between two quantifiers in situ is impossible if the quantifier that is first in linear order is not D(iscourse)-linked.

(A different generalization also requires the second, wide-scope quantifier to be D-linked/specific; the specificity of the wide scope operator is a condition of grammaticality or interpretability in all sentences involving two operators – whether their order is straight or reverse; compare É. Kiss 1993.) I conclude that the scope difference between (i) and (ii) is not structurally based. The inverse scope reading of (i) is blocked because it would violate the semantically or perceptually motivated constraint in (vi).

(35)   RITKÁN emelte fel **minden fiú** a   zongorát.
      rarely lifted up every   boy the piano
      'Rarely did every boy lift up the piano.'

Lifting the piano is also a separate act for the boys in the case of (35). In view of
this, a universal quantifier always has a [+distributive] feature, whether preverbal
or postverbal. So we have to conclude that the [+distributive] feature of quantified
phrases is interpretable, hence need not be checked.

    If – in a Greed-type framework (see Chomsky 1995: Chapter 3) – we hypothesize
something like a Distributive Criterion, requiring that a [+distributive] feature
always be checked in Spec,DistP, then we can maintain that the scope principle
is observed in overt syntax in Hungarian only at the cost of assuming a recursion
of operator projections, as in É. Kiss (1995a, 1995b, 1998a). In that proposal an
operator surfaces postverbally if a higher F(ocus) head attracts the V across it into
a higher F position; for example:

(36)

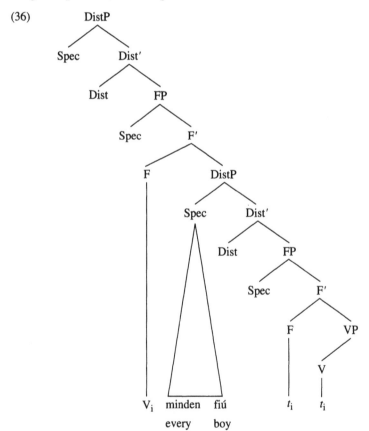

In this framework postverbal inverse scope can be derived by remnant movement
into a specifier position within the postverbal domain.

5.3.3   Postverbal stressed quantifiers

Whereas the facts of Hungarian surveyed so far support, or at least do not contradict, the claim that the scope principle is observed at S-structure/ spell-out, there is a genuine, systematic exception to this generalization. Namely, a [+distributive] quantifier need not be preposed into Spec,DistP to assume scope over FP; a postverbal stressed quantifier can also take scope over FP from inside the VP; for example:

(37)   KEVÉS GYEREK evett ′mindkét süteményből.
        few   child   ate   both   cake-from
        'For both cakes, few children ate from them.'

The universal quantifier in (37) unambiguously takes scope over the counting quantifier in Spec,FP, i.e., (37) is equivalent to (38), in which the universal quantifier occupies Spec,DistP:

(38)   [$_{DistP}$ **Mindkét süteményből** [$_{FP}$ KEVÉS GYEREK evett]]

On the other hand, (38) is different in meaning from (39), in which the same postverbal universal quantifier is unstressed, and has narrow scope:

(39)   KEVÉS GYEREK evett **mindkét süteményből**.
        few   child   ate   both   cake-from
        'Few children ate from both cakes.'

The postverbal stressed universal quantifier can also co-occur with a preverbal universal quantifier occupying Spec,DistP:

(40)   [$_{DistP}$ **Mindenkinek** [$_{FP}$ KÉTSZER kellett vizsgáznia ′**több   tárgyból is**]]
        everybody-DAT   twice   needed to.take.exam several subject-from
        'Everybody had to sit for an exam twice in several subjects.'

The universal quantifier *több tárgyból is* 'from several subjects' has wide scope with respect to *kétszer* 'twice'. Its scope relation to *mindenkinek* 'everybody', on the other hand, is ambiguous; either of them can take scope over the other. That is, (40) has two readings, which are equivalent to (41a) and (41b):

(41) a.   [$_{DistP}$ **Mindenkinek** [$_{DistP}$ **több tárgyból is** [$_{FP}$ KÉTSZER kellett vizsgáznia]]]
           'Everybody had to sit for an exam in several subjects twice.'

    b.   [$_{DistP}$ **Több tárgyból is** [$_{DistP}$ **mindenkinek** [$_{FP}$ KÉTSZER kellett vizsgáznia]]]
           'In several subjects, everybody had to sit for an exam twice.'

Both readings of (40) are different from that of (42), in which the same postverbal universal quantifier is unstressed, and has narrow scope with respect to both the preverbal quantifier and the focus:

(42)   [$_{DistP}$ **Mindenkinek** [$_{FP}$ KÉTSZER kellett vizsgáznia **több tárgyból is**]]
        'For everybody, it was on two occasions that he had to sit for an exam in several subjects.'

The position of the postverbal stressed quantifier is not fixed within the VP; compare:

(43) a. JÁNOS vizsgáztatott 'mindenkit szintaxisból.
John examined   everybody from-syntax
'For everybody, it was John who examined him in syntax.'

   b. JÁNOS vizsgáztatott szintaxisból 'mindenkit.

The number of postverbal stressed quantifiers is not limited to one, and both their word order and their scope order is free. Thus, the following word order variants are all equally grammatical and equally ambiguous:

(44) a. János el   vitte vacsorázni 'mindkét barátnőjét   'többször is.
John VM took to.dine.out both   girl-friend-his-ACC several.times
'John took both of his girl friends to dinner several times.'
'On several occasions, John took both of his girl friends to dinner.'

   b. János el vitte 'mindkét barátnőjét 'többször is vacsorázni.
   c. János el vitte 'többször is 'mindkét barátnőjét vacsorázni.
   d. János el vitte 'mindkét barátnőjét vacsorázni 'többször is.
   e. János el vitte 'többször is vacsorázni 'mindkét barátnőjét.
   f. János el vitte vacsorázni 'többször is 'mindkét barátnőjét.

Whereas the descriptive facts are clear, they are hard to account for in a systematic way. They provide no evidence for a postverbal hierarchy of operator positions. If the operators were right-adjoined to the VP or FP, as in (45a), then their scope order would be the opposite of their linear order. If they were occupying specifier positions of functional projections below FP, which happen to surface postverbally because the V has been preposed across them into a higher functional head, as in (45b), then their scope order would be identical with their linear order.

(45) a.

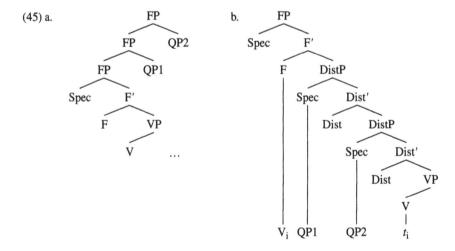

In an early attempt to account for the prosody and interpretation of postverbal stressed quantifiers, É. Kiss (1987a, 1991a) suggested that they occupy the regular prefocus quantifier position at S-structure. The postposing of the quantifier is a Phonetic Form (PF) phenomenon, the result of a stylistic rule (ordered after stress assignment – that is why the postverbal quantifier bears the primary stress assigned to constituents in Spec,DistP). That is, (46a) is derived from (46b):

(46) a.   [$_{AspP}$ Le vizsgázott 'mindenki]
           VM passed   everybody
           'Everybody passed.'

     b.   [$_{DistP}$ **Mindenki** [$_{AspP}$ le vizsgázott]]

Since the quantifier postposing rule yielding (46a) takes place on the PF branch of the derivation, it does not affect scope interpretation.

The proposed rule is not unprecedented: PF extraposition of this type is applied quite extensively also in Chomsky (1999). The rule also has independent motivation in Hungarian. Sentence adverbials, which are generated outside the predicate phrase and are ungrammatical in the operator domain of the predicate, can also occur – somewhat markedly – inside the VP; compare:

(47)   ? A professzor mindenkit   át   engedett **szerencsére** szintaxisból.
          the professor everybody-ACC through let   luckily   syntax-from
          'The professor luckily let everybody pass in syntax.'

The stylistic rule assumed could be formulated as follows:

(48)   *Stylistic Postposing*
        In the phonological component constituents preceding the main assertion can be postposed into the VP.

(Although the notion of 'main assertion' is a semantic–pragmatic notion, it can also be interpreted in phonological terms: it is the rightmost obligatorily stressed element of the predicate phrase: the prefixed verb or, in the presence of a focus, the focussed element.)

The possibility that a postverbal wide-scope quantifier is in argument position, and will be preposed into Spec,DistP at LF (logical form) after spell-out, must be discarded because then there is no way to predict the difference between an unstressed postverbal quantifier having narrow scope with respect to the focus and a stressed postverbal quantifier, taking scope from Spec,DistP.

In an alternative approach, Hunyadi (1997a, 1997b) attempts to derive scope from the surface order and the stress relations of operators. He claims that the stress-bearing head of an intonational phrase has wide scope over the rest of the operators in the same intonational phrase. If a postverbal unstressed operator is in the intonational phrase of the focus, then it is predicted to have narrow scope with respect to the focus. A postverbal stressed operator, on the other hand, starts a new intonational phrase, hence it is not subordinated to the previous operators; their relative scope is determined by a hierarchy of operators stipulated, in which sentence operators outrank universal quantifiers and universal quantifiers outrank the focus. The relative scope of operators of equal ranking is free – hence a stressed postverbal universal quantifier is predicted to have scope over the focus and to be scopally ambiguous with respect to another stressed universal quantifier. Hunyadi's theory has an intuitive appeal and appears to cover a large number of facts across languages, but in its present form it leaves many questions unanswered (e.g. how syntactic structure interacts with prosody in determining scope or what the source of the hierarchy of operators is).

Bródy and Szabolcsi (2000) propose an analysis of postverbal quantifiers in the framework of Bródy's Mirror theory (2000). They assume, following Hallman (1998), that each of AgrS, T, AgrO, and v come with their own 'scope series' [operator projections] in overt syntax. Hence, postverbal quantifiers also occupy Spec,DistP and Spec,FP positions. When we attest inverted scope in the postverbal field – e.g. Q2 has scope over a preceding Q1 – then Q2 is in a higher scope series than Q1. This is possible because in the Mirror theory of Bródy (2000) a specifier can not only precede a head but can also follow it. It follows the head if the head is a morphological head – i.e., a suffix – and precedes it otherwise. Thus, the V Q1 Q2 order arises with Q2 having scope over Q1 if Q2 is a specifier of a morphological Dist head, and Q1 is embedded in the complement of Dist. Preverbal quantifiers occur in a fixed order because there is only one Top*–Dist*–F series above AgrS. In this framework, the stress of a postverbal quantifier obviously indicates that the quantifier belongs to a higher scope series. The coverage of this theory roughly corresponds to that of the 'Stylistic Postposing' approach – but it accounts for the same set of data with a considerably more complex syntactic machinery.

5.3.4   Quantifiers in topic position

Universal quantifiers (as well as counting quantifiers) can also be topicalized – if they are pronounced with a contrastive, rising intonation (marked by the symbol /). A predicate-external quantifier pronounced with a rising intonation always appears to have narrow scope with respect to some operator in the preverbal operator field of the predicate phrase – in apparent violation of the scope principle; for example:

(49) a.   [$_{TopP}$ /Minden könyvet [$_{FP}$ csak KETTEN olvastak el   a   vizsgára]]
           every   book-ACC   only two   read   VM the exam-for
           'All the books were read only by two persons for the exam.'

b. [_{TopP} /*Egynél   több könyvet* [_{FP} KEVESEN olvastak el   a   vizsgára]]
    one-ADESSIVE more book-ACC few   read   VM the exam-for
    'More than one book was read by few persons for the exam.'

c. [_{TopP} /*Kevés hallgatónak* [_{NegP} nem tartok órát]]
    few   student-DAT   not hold-I class-ACC
    'For few students, I do not hold a class.'

These sentences are generally believed to be scopally equivalent to the following sentences, containing a VP-internal unstressed narrow scope quantifier:

(50) a. [_{FP} Csak KETTEN olvastak el *minden könyvet* a vizsgára]
    'Only two persons read all the books for the exam.'

b. [_{FP} KEVESEN olvastak el *egynél több könyvet* a vizsgára]
    'Only few persons read more than one book for the exam.'

c. [_{NegP} Nem tartok órát *kevés hallgatónak*]
    'I do not hold a class for few students.'

The sentences in (49) are problematic not only because their initial quantifiers do not appear to c-command their scope – in violation of the scope principle – but also because they do not seem to observe the restriction that requires topics to be [+referential] and [+specific].

As was argued in Section 2.7, the contrastive topicalization of a quantified noun phrase does not in fact violate any of these restrictions. The contrasting of a non-individual-denoting expression is a means of individuating it, i.e., presenting it as the name of a distinct property. Quantifiers individuated by contrast function as the names of cardinality properties of sets. In (49a) the property 'maximal set of books' is implicitly contrasted with the property 'non-maximal set of books'. As the name of a property, the expression *minden könyvet* 'every book' is a legitimate target of topicalization. In Spec,TopP it functions as the logical subject of predication; it is predicated of it that only two persons read a representative of it. (About the alternative property 'non-maximal set of books', an alternative statement is implied: not only two persons read a representative of it.) In (49b) the property *egynél több könyvet* 'set of books of at least two members' is predicated about; it is predicated about it that few persons read a representative of it for the exam. In (49c) the property 'set of students of few members' is set into an implicit contrast with the property 'set of students of many members'; it is stated about it that the speaker does not hold a class for a representative of it.

In each of these sentences the quantifier functions as the name of a property and, as such, it is outside the scope of all operators; in some sense it has maximally wide scope. It nevertheless gives the impression of a narrow scope quantifier because whatever is predicated about a property is evaluated with respect to concrete representatives of the property, which can be referentially different. This referential variability is superficially similar to that attested in the case of narrow scope quantifiers.

5.3.5   *Noun phrase internal quantifiers*

An area where the scope principle is not observed in the visible syntax of various languages is noun phrase internal quantification. The inverse scope attested in English noun phrases like that in (51) has had a significant role in the emergence of the theory assuming invisible quantifier movement at LF:

(51)   Every entrance to several large downtown stores was smashed in the riot.

In Hungarian, where the scope principle is observed at S-structure, a quantifier in the complement of a noun is not expected to have wider scope than the quantified head. Indeed, the Hungarian equivalent of (51) is ungrammatical (although the structure itself, with the quantifiers removed, is acceptable):

(52) a.   * [Minden bejárat több   nagy boltba] megrongálódott a zavargások alatt.
        every   entrance several large store-to was.damaged   the riots   during
        'Every entrance to several large stores was damaged during the riots.'

    compare:

   b.   [A bejárat a   boltba] megrongálódott a   zavargások alatt.
       the entrance the store-to was.damaged   the riots   during
       'The entrance to the store was damaged during the riots.'

The intended scope order of the two quantifiers in (52a) can be expressed by placing the wider scope quantifier into the position of the genitive specifier, where it c-commands the whole noun phrase:

(53)   Több   nagy bolt   minden bejárata megrongálódott.
      several large store's every   entrance was.damaged
      'Every entrance of several large stores was damaged.'

A noun phrase internal operator can take sentential scope presumably because the operator feature percolates up to the maximal noun phrase projection. The operator feature of a prehead specifier or modifier can percolate up across several cycles, causing the matrix noun phrase to land in the specifier of a functional projection with a matching feature, from where it c-commands the predicate. Observe how deeply the *wh*-pronoun is embedded in the focus-moved noun phrases of the following sentences:

(54) a.   [$_{FP}$ [*MELYIK* ZENESZERZŐ HARMADIK SZIMFÓNIÁJÁNAK 2. TÉTELÉBEN]
          which   composer's   third   symphony's   2. movement-in
          található   ez a motívum]?
          can.be.found this motif
          'In the 2nd movement of which composer's third symphony can this motif be
          found?'

   b.   [$_{FP}$ [JÁNOS *KINEK*   ÍROTT LEVELÉT] fogta el   a   rendőrség]?
        John's who-DAT written letter-ACC seized VM the police
        'John's letter written to whom did the police seize?'

(If we adopt Kayne's antisymmetry of syntax approach, we can ensure clausal
domain for the *wh*-operator in (54a,b) even without assuming feature percolation.
Kayne (1994) analyzes specifiers as adjoined phrases, and he defines c-command
in such a way that the specifier of the specifier of a phrase does asymmetrically
c-command the given phrase.)

The question arises as to what happens if a noun phrase has two quantifiers to
take sentential scope. In the case of (53) the quantifier of the head and the quantifier
of the genitive specifier have matching features: the universal quantifier is intrin-
sically [+distributive], and the quantifier *több* 'more' also has a [+distributive]
reading, so the two features obviously merge, causing the noun phrase to move
to Spec,DistP. The interesting question is how a noun phrase with contradictory
quantifiers behaves. Consider:

(55) a. *? [$_{FP}$ MINDEN CSALÁDTAG   KEVÉS FÉNYKÉPE sikerült   jól]
         every   family.member's few   photos   succeeded well
         'Few photos of all family members succeeded well.'

   b. * [$_{DistP}$ **Minden családtag kevés fényképe** [$_{AspP}$ jól sikerült.]]

(56) a. *? [$_{FP}$ KEVÉS CSALÁDTAG   MINDEN FÉNYKÉPE veszett el]
         few   family.member's every   photo   lost   VM
         'All the photos of few family members got lost.'

   b. * [$_{DistP}$ **Kevés családtag minden fényképe** [$_{AspP}$ el veszett]]

As these examples indicate, if the operator feature percolating up from the quantifier of the head and the operator feature percolating up from the quantifier
of the genitive specifier are distinct – hence cannot merge – the sentence is
ungrammatical. This is because the operator whose feature cannot percolate up to
the noun phrase cannot take sentential scope in violation of the scope principle.
In the Minimalist framework, the ungrammaticality of these sentences must be
due to the fact that one of the contradictory features of the noun phrase cannot be
checked by overt movement. The grammatical way of resolving such conflicts is
to extract the genitive specifier (in fact, a dative-marked noun phrase) into the VP
domain and to move it independently into the functional position with a matching

feature. Here it can also take sentential scope in observance of the scope principle. (For information on the mechanism of possessor extraction, see Chapter 7.)
For example:

(57) a. [$_{DistP}$ **Minden családtagnak**$_i$ [$_{FP}$ [t_i KEVÉS FÉNYKÉPE] sikerült   jól]]
         every family.member-DAT few   photo   succeeded well
         'Of every family member, few photos succeeded well.'

   b. [$_{FP}$ KEVÉS CSALÁDTAGNAK$_i$ [$_{VP}$ veszett el [t_i minden fényképe]]]
       few   family.member-DAT lost   VM every   photo
       'Of few family members did all the photos get lost.'

If the noun phrase internal quantifier that is intended to have wide scope cannot be
formulated as a genitive specifier – e.g. because the head is a pronoun, which cannot
take a genitive specifier – then it can assume the status of an independent quantifier
via extraposition. This is what happens in the (b) example of the following minimal
pair, where the extraposed quantifier phrase is subsequently moved into Spec,DistP.
(The syntactic category of *keves-en* 'few-SUFFIX' is not quite clear; I assume tentatively that it is a NumP consisting of an indefinite numeral and a pro.)

(58) a. * [$_{FP}$ [KEVESEN MINDEN KÖRZETBŐL] szavaztak a   javaslatra]
           few   every   district-from voted   the proposal-for
           'Few persons from every district voted for the proposal.'

   b. [$_{DistP}$ **Minden körzetből**$_i$ [$_{FP}$ [KEVESEN t_i] szavaztak a javaslatra]]
       'From every district, few persons voted for the proposal.'

5.4   Quantifiers or adverbial modifiers?

It was argued in Section 4.2.3. that adverbs expressing a negative frequency, a negative degree, or a negative manner have an inherent [+focus] feature,
which they must check in Spec,FP; for example:

(59) a. [$_{TopP}$ János [$_{FP}$ RITKÁN [$_{VP}$ jár be az órákra]]]
         John   seldom   goes in the classes-to
         'John seldom goes to classes.'

   b. [$_{TopP}$ János [$_{FP}$ ALIG [$_{VP}$ értette   meg az anyagot]]]
       John   barely   understood VM the material
       'John barely understood the material.'

   c. [$_{TopP}$ János [$_{FP}$ LASSAN [$_{VP}$ fogta   fel a   magyarázatot]]]
       John   slowly   understood VM the explanation
       'John slowly understood the explanation.'

The question arises of how the positive counterparts of these adverbs are to be
analyzed. Adverbs of frequency are functionally quantifiers quantifying over actions or events; so it is expected that those expressing a 'universal' frequency such
as *mindig* 'always' or *állandóan* 'constantly' share the distribution of universal

quantifiers, whereas those expressing a non-universal positive frequency such as *sokszor* 'many times' or *gyakran* 'often' share the distribution of positive existential quantifiers. This is exactly what we attest. Universal adverbs of frequency occupy Spec,DistP in the unmarked case:

(60) a. [$_{DistP}$ **Mindig** [$_{DistP}$ **minden diák** [$_{FP}$ A   SZINTAXISÓRÁRÓL késik el]]]
         always   every   student the syntax-class-from is.late VM
         'Always, for every student, it is the syntax class that he is late for.'

   b. [$_{DistP}$ **Mindenki** [$_{DistP}$ **mindig** [$_{FP}$ A SZINTAXISÓRÁRÓL késik el]]]

(61) a. [$_{DistP}$ **Állandóan** [$_{DistP}$ **minden kollégám** [$_{FP}$ AZ INTERNETET böngészi]]]
         constantly   every   colleague-1SG the Internet-ACC browses
         'Every colleague of mine constantly browses the Internet.'

   b. [$_{DistP}$ **Minden kollégám** [$_{DistP}$ **állandóan** [$_{FP}$ AZ INTERNETET böngészi]]]

If we attribute a [+distributive] feature to adverbs of frequency with a [+universal] meaning component, we correctly predict that they cannot stand either in Spec,FP, or in Spec,TopP, or be adjoined to TopP (like sentence adverbials):

(62) a. * [$_{TopP}$ János [$_{FP}$ MINDIG késik el]]
         John   always late.is VM
         'John is always late.'

   b. * [$_{TopP}$ János [$_{FP}$ ÁLLANDÓAN böngészi az internetet]]
         John   constantly browses the Internet

(63) a. * [$_{TopP}$ *Mindig* [$_{TopP}$ János [$_{AspP}$ el késik az óráról]]]
   b. * [$_{TopP}$ *Állandóan* [$_{TopP}$ János [$_{FP}$ AZ INTERNETET böngészi]]]

Like other [+distributive] quantifiers, universal adverbs of frequency can also appear in the VP – either unstressed, having narrow scope with respect to the focus, or stressed, taking wide scope over the focus.

(64) a. [$_{FP}$ KETTEN [$_{VP}$ késnek el *'mindig/állandóan* a   szintaxisóráról]]
         two   are.late VM always/constantly the syntax.class-from
         'It is always/constantly two persons who are late for the syntax class.'

   b. [$_{FP}$ KETTEN [$_{VP}$ késnek el *mindig/állandóan* a szintaxisóráról]]
         'It is two persons who are always/constantly late for the syntax class.'

Adverbs expressing a positive (but non-universal) frequency can move either to Spec,DistP (65a), or to Spec,FP (65b), or they can stand in the VP, unstressed, taking narrow scope (65c), or stressed, taking wide scope (65d). That is, they can occupy the same positions as positive existential quantifiers – presumably because they are also optionally marked as [+distributive].

(65) a. Péter [$_{DistP}$ **sokszor/gyakran** [$_{AspP}$ el felejti megírni a leckéjét]]
         Peter   many.times/often   VM forgets to.write his homework
         'Peter many times/often forgets to write his homework.'

b. Péter [FP SOKSZOR/GYAKRAN felejti el megírni a leckéjét]
    'It is many times/often that Peter forgets to write his homework.'

c. [FP PÉTER felejti el *sokszor/gyakran* megírni a leckéjét]
    'It is Peter who many times/often forgets to write his homework.'

d. Péter [AspP el felejti 'sokszor/gyakran megírni a leckéjét]
    'Peter many times/often forgets to write his homework.'

When they express the frequency of the whole event, they stand outside the predicate phrase, adjoined to TopP – similar to other sentence adverbials:

(66)   [TopP Gyakran [TopP a   tanárok nem tudják minden diákjuk
        often   the teachers not know every student-POSS-3PL
        nevét]]
        name-POSS-ACC
        'Teachers often don't know the name of every student of theirs.'

For adverbs of degree, and adverbs of manner, the position left-adjacent to the AspP projection seems to be the only possibility in the preverbal field (67a). They cannot stand either in Spec, DistP or adjoined to DistP (67b), nor can they occupy Spec,FP (67c) or be adjoined to FP (67d).

(67) a. [DistP Mindenki [*tökéletesen/gyorsan* [AspP meg értette   a
          everybody perfectly/quickly   VM understood the
          relativitáselméletet]]]
          relativity-theory
          'Everybody understood perfectly/quickly the theory of relativity.'

    b. * [DistP **Tökéletesen/gyorsan** [DistP mindenki [AspP meg értette a
          relativitáselméletet]]]

    c. * [DistP Mindenki [FP TÖKÉLETESEN/GYORSAN értette meg a relativitáselméletet]]

    d. * [DistP Mindenki [FP *tökéletesen/gyorsan* [FP A RELATIVITÁSELMÉLETET értette
          meg]]]

In the presence of a focus, the adverb of degree or manner occupies a VP-internal position, as in (68a,b):

(68) a. [DistP Mindenki [FP csak a   relativitáselméletet [VP értette
          everybody   only the relativity-theory-ACC   understood
          tökéletesen /gyorsan meg]]]
          perfectly /quickly VM
          'For everybody, it was only relativity theory that he understood perfectly/quickly.'

    b. [FP Csak a   relativitáselméletet [VP értette   meg János *tökéletesen /gyorsan*
          only the relativity-theory-ACC understood VM John perfectly /quickly
          tegnap]]
          yesterday
          'It was only relativity theory that John understood perfectly/quickly yesterday.'

If we generate the adverb in an AspP-adjoined position, there is no straightforward way of deriving the structure in (68b). The simplest way of deriving (68a,b) is to generate the adverb in the VP and optionally to adjoin it to AspP in the course of the derivation.

Some adverbs of manner can also function as sentence adverbials. In that case they are external to the predicate phrase, being adjoined either to the TopP projection or to the Top head (see also Section 2.6):

(69) a. [*Okosan* [$_{TopP}$ János [$_{DistP}$ a   jegyzeteit is   magával vitte]]]
          smartly   John   his notes-ACC also with.him took
          'Smartly, John also took his notes with him.'

    b.   [János [$_{Top}$ *okosan* [$_{DistP}$ a jegyzeteit is magával vitte]]]
          'Smartly, John also took his notes with him.'

The VP-internal position of the adverbs of manner and degree in (68a,b) suggests that these types of adverbs should be generated in the VP and should be preposed into a pre-AspP position transformationally. Their preposing can be adjunction, or substitution into the specifier of a MannerP or DegreeP projection, depending on our theoretical assumptions.

5.5   Summary

In the Hungarian sentence, universal quantifiers and phrases modified by *is* 'also', *még... is* 'even' have a designated position at the head of the predicate phrase: they occupy the specifier of a functional projection called DistP. Spec,DistP is also available for positive existential quantifiers. A quantifier moved to Spec,DistP is associated with a distributive interpretation: the predicate holds separately for every element in the domain of the quantifier. The quantifier in Spec,DistP has scope over the domain it c-commands. In fact, every preverbal operator position is a scope position; the scope principle, requiring that operators c-command their scope, is satisfied at S-structure/spell-out in the Hungarian sentence. Since the functional projection harboring distributive quantifiers is above the focus projection, a distributive quantifier can only have narrow scope with respect to the focus if it is left in argument position. (Alternatively, a postverbal narrow-scope quantifier can be analyzed to occupy a Spec,DistP in a lower series of operator positions.) A stressed postverbal distributive quantifier has scope over FP; its VP-internal position may be the result of stylistic postposing from Spec,DistP. (Alternative ways of assigning wide scope to it were also quoted from the literature.) A noun phrase internal quantifier assumes sentential scope by feature percolation, or by being extracted into the VP domain, and undergoing operator movement into scope position on its own. Adverbs of frequency also share the syntactic behavior of quantifiers.

6

Negation

6.1   Two NegP projections[1]

In the Hungarian sentence, negation is performed by the negative particle *nem*. It can appear before the verb, or before the focus, or before the universal quantifier, i.e., we can negate the action or state expressed by VP (1a,b), or the exhaustive identification expressed by FP (1c), or the universality of the quantification expressed by DistP (1d).

(1) a.   János *nem* táncolt a   feleségével.
        John not danced his wife-with
        'John didn't dance with his wife.'

   b.   János A FELESÉGÉVEL *nem* táncolt.
        'It was his wife that John didn't dance with.'

   c.   János *nem* A FELESÉGÉVEL táncolt.
        'It was not his wife that John danced with.'

   d.   *Nem* **mindenki** A   FELESÉGÉVEL táncolt.
        not everybody his wife-with   danced
        'Not everybody danced WITH HIS WIFE.'

The different layers of the predicate can also be negated simultaneously, although triple negation is not easy to interpret.

(2) a.   János *nem* A   FELESÉGÉVEL *nem* táncolt.
        John not his wife-with   not danced
        'It wasn't his wife that John didn't dance with.'

   b.   *Nem* **mindenki** A   FELESÉGÉVEL *nem* táncolt.
        not everybody his wife-with   not danced
        'It is not true for everybody that it was his wife that he didn't dance with.'

   c.   *Nem* **mindenki** *nem* A FELESÉGÉVEL táncolt.
        'It wasn't true for everybody that it wasn't his wife that he danced with.'

---

[1] The first theory of Hungarian negation involving two NegP projections was put forth in Olsvay (2000a, 2000b). Some of the issues discussed here were first raised by Piñon (1992). Hungarian negation is discussed in detail in Puskás (1998, 2000).

d.   *Nem* **mindenki** *nem* FELESÉGÉVEL *nem* táncolt.
     'It wasn't true for everybody that it wasn't his wife that he didn't dance with.'

The negative particle preceding VP negates the action or state expressed by the predicate, which is a function associated with a NegP projection in Universal Grammar. Therefore, we place it in the head position of a NegP dominating VP. This negative particle must be adjacent to the finite verb; no verb modifier can intervene between them. The adjacency of the negative particle and the verb must have the same reason as the adjacency of the focus and the verb. That is, if the adjacency of the focus and the verb is derived by verb movement from the head of AspP into F (compare Bródy 1990a, 1990b, 1995), then the adjacency of the negative particle and the V must also be derived by V movement from Asp to Neg, as follows:

(3)   János [$_{NegP}$ *nem* hívta$_i$ [$_{AspP}$ fel t_i a   feleségét]]
       John   not called   up   his wife
       'John didn't call up his wife.'

This solution would, however, raise at least two problems. First, whereas the instances of head movement in the literature involve the left-adjunction of the moved head to the target, V-to-Neg movement is adjunction to the right. The problem cannot be eliminated by claiming that the negative particle is sitting in Spec,NegP and that the verb is moved into the empty Neg head – because in the case where NegP is dominated by FP, the V must move on into F, and it takes the negative particle along; that is:

(4)   János [$_{FP}$ A   FELESÉGÉT [$_{F'}$ [nem hívta$_i$]$_j$ [$_{NegP}$ t_j [$_{AspP}$ fel t_i [$_{VP}$ t_i]]]]]]
       John   his wife-ACC   not called   up
       'It was his wife that John didn't call up.'

The second problem with the V movement approach is that the focus-negating particle is not adjacent to the V. If it also represents the head of a NegP, it is hard to explain why one of the Neg heads attracts the verb, and the other does not. If focus negation could be proved to represent constituent negation then, naturally, this argument would be invalid; however, both semantic and syntactic considerations – to be reviewed below – indicate that focus negation, too, is predicate negation involving a NegP. It therefore seems less problematic to assume that the VP-negating particle and the V are adjacent because no AspP is projected. That is, NegP is not an extension of AspP, but is an alternative to it – as represented in (5):

(5)

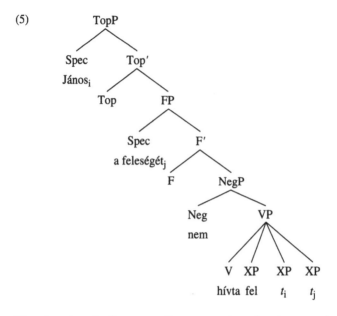

Negation does in fact neutralize aspect, i.e., the absence of AspP in a negative sentence is a semantically motivated assumption; compare:

(6) a.   A vonat (már) [_AspP_ át [_Asp′_ ment a hídon,   amikor a baleset történt]]
           the train (already) across went the bridge-on when the accident happened
           'The train had (already) gone across the bridge when the accident happened.'

   b.   A vonat (épp) [_AspP_ [_Asp′_ ment át   a hídon,   amikor a baleset
           the train (just)   went across the bridge-on when the accident
           történt]]
           happened
           'The train was (just) going across the bridge when the accident happened.'

   c.   A vonat (még) nem ment át   a hídon,   amikor a baleset történt.
           the train (yet) not went across the bridge-on when the accident happened
           'The train did not go across the bridge (yet) when the accident happened.'

Whereas the main clause of (6a) is clearly perfective, and that of (6b) is clearly progressive, the negated equivalent in (6c) is vague aspectually: it can be used both in a situation in which the crossing of the bridge by the train has not taken place at all and in a situation in which it has started but has not been completed yet. Example (6b), with the progressive aspect clearly preserved, could only be negated in a circumscribed way; for example:

(7)   Nem igaz, hogy a vonat épp ment át   a hídon...
        not true that the train just went across the bridge-on
        'It is not true that the train was just going across the bridge...'

The assumption that the prefocus negative particle is not adjoined to the focussed constituent but is the head of a NegP is based on various types of evidence. First, the unstressed verb following the focussed constituent does not necessarily represent presupposed information. That is, (8a) can be continued also with (8b) (see Szabolcsi 1980, 1981a), in which case negation is understood to extend over the whole FP projection:

(8) a.   János nem A   FELESÉGÉT hívta fel.
        John not his wife-ACC   called up
        'John didn't call up HIS WIFE.'

    b.   Inkább A LÁNYÁNAK   küldött táviratot.
        rather his daughter-DAT sent   telegram-ACC
        'He rather sent a telegram TO HIS DAUGHTER.'

The following argument was put forth by Olsvay (2000b). Let us assume tentatively that the negative particle + focus sequence, such as that in (8a), forms a constituent. So as to rule out (9a), i.e., to ensure that the negated constituent always lands in focus position, we must also assume that the negative particle has an inherent [+focus] feature, which spreads over the whole negated phrase. In sentences containing two [+focus] constituents, e.g. two *wh*-phrases or *only* phrases, one of them always stays behind the verb. This should also be the case if one of the [+focus] constituents is a negated phrase. A postverbal negated constituent, however, is ungrammatical, or very marginal in double focus constructions; see (9b–d). This is inexplicable, unless we have wrongly assumed that the negative particle + focus sequence forms a negated constituent.

(9) a.   * János fel hívta *nem a   feleségét.*
        John up called not his wife-ACC
        'John called up other than his wife.'

    b. *? KI   hívta fel NEM A FELESÉGÉT?
        who called up not his wife
        'Who didn't called up HIS WIFE?'

    c. * JÁNOS nem hívta fel NEM A   FELESÉGÉT.
        John   not called up not his wife
        'It was John who didn't call up other than his wife.'

    d. ?* Nem JÁNOS hívta fel NEM A FELESÉGÉT.
        not   John   called up not his wife
        'It wasn't John who called up other than his wife.'

The clearest evidence for the negative head status of the focus-negating particle is that it shares crucial properties of the VP-negating particle, analyzed as the head of NegP. First, it licenses the same type of negative pronominal elements beginning with the morpheme *se-*; compare:

(10) a.   *Senki   nem* [vp hívta fel a   feleségét]
          nobody not   called up his wife
          'Nobody called up his wife.'

   b.   *Senki   nem* [FP A FELESÉGÉT hívta fel]
        nobody not   his wife-ACC called up
        'Nobody called up HIS WIFE.'

When immediately preceded by a *se*-pronoun, both the focus-negating *nem* and
the VP-negating *nem* can apparently alternate with a *sem* particle (discussed in
detail in Section 6.3):

(11) a.   *Senki   sem* [vp hívta fel a   feleségét]
          nobody not   called up his wife
          'Nobody called up his wife.'

   b.   *Senki   sem* [FP A FELESÉGÉT hívta fel]
        nobody not   his wife-ACC called up
        'Nobody called up HIS WIFE.'

The negative particle negating a prefocus universal quantifier, e.g. that in (1d) or
in (12a) below, on the other hand, does not license a negative pronoun, and does
not alternate with *sem*:

(12) a.   Nem **mindenki** A FELESÉGÉT hívta fel.
          not everybody his wife-ACC called up
          'Not everybody called up HIS WIFE.'

   b. * *Soha nem* **mindenki** A FELESÉGÉT hívta fel.
        never not everybody his wife-ACC called up
        'Never did everybody call up his wife.'

   c. * *Soha sem* **mindenki** A FELESÉGÉT hívta fel.

These facts suggest that the negation of the universal quantifier is of a different
kind than the negation of VP and FP. Whereas the negative particle negating the FP,
as well as that negating the VP, sits in the head positions of NegP projections, the
negative particle negating *mindenki* 'everybody' represents constituent negation,
with *nem* adjoined to the quantified noun phrase.

The negative particle can in fact also precede an AspP if the *nem* 'not' phrase
is coordinated with a *hanem* 'but also' phrase:

(13)   János nem [AspP 'fel hívta a   fiúkat], hanem [AspP 'meg látogatta őket]
       John not   up called the boys   but   VM visited them
       'John did not call the boys up, but visited them.'

The *nem . . . hanem* pair can presumably take AspP complements because they
are coordinators combining two predicate phrases rather than being operators
extending a VP.

That the *nem* element of the *nem... hanem* pair is not the head of a NegP is also clear from its prosody. Whereas a regular *nem* forms a single phonological word with the constituent following it, bearing the word-initial stress, the *nem* coordinated with *hanem* is unstressed; for example:

(14)   Nem 'JÁNOS hívta fel a   fiúkat, hanem 'PÉTER látogatta meg őket.
        not John   called up the boys   but   Peter visited VM them
        'What happened was not JOHN calling up the boys but PETER visiting them.'

The prosodic behavior of the *Neg* head is similar to that of the focus: not only is it stressed, but it also deletes the stress of the constituent following it. If we mean by 'main assertion' the part of the content of a sentence that cannot be presupposed, then in a VP the main assertion is represented by the V, in an FP it is represented by the focus, whereas in a NegP dominating FP it is represented by the negative particle. After all, if the focus is in the scope of negation, even the content of focus becomes presupposed. The stress pattern of the assertive part of the Hungarian sentence is determined by the following principle:

(15)   *The stressing of the predicative section of the Hungarian sentence*
        The assertive elements following the constituent representing the main assertion
        (that which cannot be presupposed) are unstressed.[2]

(A distributive quantifier in Spec,DistP can convey presupposed information, hence it is not analyzed as the carrier of main assertion. Consequently, it is not predicted to delete the stress of the constituent following it.)

The assumption that a negated universal quantifier represents a constituent is in fact not sufficient to account for its peculiar word order behavior. Consider first the word order of a non-negated universal quantifier (16a), then that of a negated universal quantifier in a focusless sentence (16b–c), and finally the word order of a negated universal quantifier in the presence of a focus (16d):

(16) a.   [DistP **Mindenki** [AspP fel hívta a   feleségét]]
                  everybody   up called his wife
           'Everybody called up his wife.'

     b.   [FP Nem **mindenki** hívta fel a   feleségét]
                not everybody called up his wife

     c. * [DistP Nem **mindenki** [AspP fel hívta a feleségét]]

     d.   [DistP Nem **mindenki** [FP A FELESÉGÉT hívta fel]]
           'For not everybody was it his wife that he called up.'

A non-negated universal quantifier occupies Spec,DistP (16a), and so does a negated universal quantifier in the presence of a focus as well (16d); the negated

---

[2] The claim that the function of focus is to express the main assertion in the sentence has been adopted from Herburger (1997).

universal quantifier of a focusless sentence, on the other hand, appears to land in Spec,FP (16b). We can derive these facts if we assume that *nem mindenki* is inserted into its base-generated position in the VP associated with both the [+focus] feature of negative existential quantifiers and the [+distributive] feature of universal quantifiers; moreover – for reasons of economy – it checks by overt movement the feature which it can check first, in a closer projection. In (16b) the Spec,FP position is open for *nem mindenki*, so it moves there to check its [+focus] feature overtly.[3] In (16d), on the other hand, Spec,FP is occupied; only the more distant Spec,DistP is available; so *nem mindenki* checks its [+distributive] feature overtly.

6.2   The locus of negative pronouns licensed by *nem*

As was illustrated under (10) and (11), a negative particle functioning as the head of a NegP can license negative pronouns and proadverbs beginning with the *se-* morpheme. Although these *se*-phrases are identified as negative elements by native speakers, they always require the presence of a negative particle, and the co-occurrence of one or more *se*-phrases and the negative particle does not yield multiple negation semantically. This type of spreading of the [+negative] feature over indefinite pronominals is often referred to in the literature as negative concord (compare, for example, Puskás 2000).

The distribution of *se*-phrases is similar to that of distributive quantifiers (e.g. positive universals and *is* 'also' phrases) – apart from the fact that in the sentence types in which they occur the presence of the negative particle blocks the projection of an AspP and the preposing of the verb modifier into a preverbal position. Thus in a focusless sentence, the *se*-phrase either immediately precedes the negated VP, or stands postverbally, bearing a heavy stress:

(17) a.   János *'semmit 'nem* hallott a   függöny mögül.
       John nothing not   heard the curtain   behind
       'John didn't hear anything from behind the curtain.'

---

[3]   In the case of a focussed negated universal quantifier, the negative particle can marginally also license a *se*-pronoun, and in the presence of a *se*-pronoun it can also alternate with *sem*; for example:

(i)   ? Soha nem/sem MINDENKI hívja fel a   feleségét.
       never not   everybody calls up his wife
       'Never does everybody call up his wife.'

This construction may be marginally possible because the linear position of the negative particle adjoined to the universal quantifier is non-distinct from that of a focus-negating *nem*; hence, it can be marginally reanalyzed as such.

b. János *'nem* hallott *'semmit* a   függöny mögül.
    John not   heard   nothing the curtain behind
    'John didn't hear anything from behind the curtain.'

c. János *'nem* hallott a   függöny mögül *'semmit.*
    John not   heard the curtain behind nothing
    'John didn't hear anything from behind the curtain.'

The preverbal *se*-phrase in (17a) seems to occupy the same Spec,DistP position that a positive universal quantifier would occupy (18a). The postverbal *se*-phrases in (17b,c), on the other hand, seem to correspond to a positive universal quantifier subjected to the rule of Stylistic Postposing, proposed under (48) in Section 5.3.3. This rule allows constituents preceding the main assertion to be postposed behind the verb, carrying along the stress assigned to them in their preverbal operator position (18b,c):

(18) a. János [$_{DistP}$ **'mindent** [$_{VP}$ hallott a   függöny mögül]]
         John   everything   heard the curtain behind
         'John heard everything from behind the curtain.'

     b. János hallott **'mindent** a függöny mögül.
     c. János hallott a függöny mögül **'mindent.**

As in the case of positive distributive phrases and other types of operators, as well, the position of the *se*-phrase is independent of its grammatical function. Thus a subject *se*-phrase has the same word order possibilities as an object *se*-phrase:

(19) a. *'Senki 'nem* jött be a   szobába.
         nobody not   came in the room-into
         'Nobody came into the room.'

     b. *'Nem* jött be a   szobába *'senki.*
         not   came in the room-into nobody
         'Nobody came into the room.'

     c. *'Nem* jött be *'senki* a szobába.

Since the DistP projection at the head of the predicate phrase can have more than one specifier, it provides space for any number of positive distributive quantifiers, some or all of which can subsequently also undergo Stylistic Postposing into postverbal positions. *Se*-phrases have the same word order possibilities:

(20) a. Mari *soha senkinek   nem* beszélt a   terveiről.
         Mary never nobody-DAT not spoke   her plans-about
         'Mary never spoke about her plans to anybody.'

     b. Mari *soha nem* beszélt a terveiről *senkinek.*
     c. Mari *senkinek nem* beszélt *soha* a terveiről.

    d.   Mari *nem* beszélt a terveiről *soha senkinek.*

    e.   Mari *nem* beszélt *soha* a terveiről *senkinek.*

In the presence of a focus, a *se*-phrase can only be licensed by a negative particle above the focus; compare:

(21) a.   *Senki   nem* [FP JÁNOST [VP hívta   meg]]
          nobody not   John-ACC   invited VM
          'Nobody invited JOHN.'

    b.   * *Senki* [FP JÁNOST [NegP *nem* [VP hívta meg]]]

The possibility of Stylistic Postposing is, naturally, also open for prefocus *se*-phrases (similar to prefocus positive universal quantifiers):

(22) a.   *'Senki   nem* VONATTAL érkezett.
          nobody not train-with arrived
          'Nobody arrived BY TRAIN.'

    b.   *Nem* VONATTAL érkezett *'senki.*

The Spec,DistP position of a negated sentence cannot contain a positive distributive quantifier (23a,b) unless a focus intervenes between Spec,DistP and the negative particle, as in (23c):

(23) a.   * **Mindenki** *nem* JÁNOST   hívta   meg.
          everybody not John-ACC invited VM
          'For everybody, it wasn't John that he invited.'

    b.   * **Mindenki** *nem* hívta meg Jánost.
          'Everybody didn't invite John.'

    c.   **Mindenki** (csak) JÁNOST   *nem* hívta   meg.
          everybody only John-ACC not invited VM
          'For everybody, it was only John that he didn't invite.'

A VP-negating *nem* separated from Spec,DistP by a focus can only license a VP-internal unstressed *se*-phrase (24a). The construction in (24a) is parallel to that in (24b), which contains a positive distributive quantifier in the scope of focus, left in situ, receiving no stress.

(24) a.   Csak JÁNOST   *nem* hívta   meg *senki.*
          only John-ACC not invited VM nobody
          'It was only John whom nobody invited.'

    compare:

    b.   Csak JÁNOST   hívta   meg mindenki.
          only John-ACC invited VM everybody
          'It was only John whom everybody invited.'

A structure like (24a) could also contain a positive distributive quantifier in its Spec,DistP, in addition to its VP-internal *se*-phrase:

(25)   **Mindig** csak JÁNOST   *nem* hívja   meg *senki*.
        always only John-ACC not   invites VM nobody
        'It is always only John whom nobody invites.'

It is a matter of discussion whether the negative pronouns accompanying the negative particle in the negative concord constructions of various languages represent indefinites with no quantificational force of their own, bound by a negative operator (compare Ladusaw 1992, 1994); whether they are negative operators themselves forced to move to Spec,NegP by the Neg Criterion so as to check the [+neg] feature of the Neg head (compare Haegeman and Zanuttini 1991, Haegeman 1995, Zanuttini 1997, Puskás 2000); or whether they are negative polarity universal quantifiers subject to Q-Raising (see Giannakidou 2000). The facts of Hungarian reviewed above seem to support a combination of the latter two theories. Hungarian *se*-phrases appear in the canonical positions of distributive quantifiers, primarily in Spec,DistP – provided that DistP is in the local environment of a negative particle. To be able to predict the possible structural positions and the prosody of *se*-phrases, we make the following assumptions:

i.   A *se*-phrase has the features [+negative, +distributive].
ii.   The functional heads Neg and Dist, instantiating these features, can fuse, projecting a joint DistNegP.

Then it follows that a *se*-phrase will immediately precede the negative particle, landing in the specifier of the joint DistNegP, checking the [+dist, +neg] features of the head, and will have scope over DistNeg'. It also follows that the specifier of a DistNegP cannot be filled with a positive distributive quantifier. A *se*-phrase in Spec,DistNegP is, naturally, subject to Stylistic Postposing. If an intervening focus blocks the fusion of NegP with DistP, then the *se*-phrases generated in the VP will have no scope position to move to. Hence, it will stay in situ unstressed, and will take scope only over the VP. In this case the [+negative] feature of the *se*-phrase is checked against that of the negative particle covertly.

Under these assumptions, the preverbal *se*-phrases in (17a), (19a), (20a,b,c), (21a), and (22a) all occupy Spec,DistNegP. In (17b,c), (19b,c), (20b,c,d,e), and (22b) the [+distributive, +negative] quantifiers surfacing postverbally have undergone Stylistic Postposing, as well, i.e., they have been moved back to postverbal position, preserving both the stress and the scope assigned to them in Spec,DistNegP. In (24a) the *nem* preceded by a focus cannot fuse with a non-adjacent Dist head, hence it provides no preverbal landing site for the *se*-phrase. Therefore, the *se*-phrase it licenses remains in situ, unstressed, having narrow scope with respect to

the focus. A Spec,DistP not adjacent to, and not fused with, *nem* is available for a
positive distributive quantifier, as is illustrated in (25).

These are the structures assigned, for example, to (21a) and (24a):

(26)

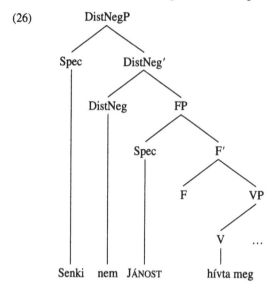

(27)   [FP Csak JÁNOST [NegP nem [VP hívta meg senki]]]

6.3   The status of *sem*

In a negative environment, the *is* 'also' particle adjoined to various types
of distributive phrases is replaced by *sem* 'neither'.

(28) a.   El   jött   Péter *is*.
           VM came Peter also
           'Peter, too, came.'

     b.   El   jött   két diák *is*.
           VM came two student
           'Two students (even) came.'

(29) a.   *Nem* jött   el   Péter *sem*.
           not   came VM Peter neither
           'Peter didn't come, either.'

     b.   *Nem* jött   el   egy diák   *sem*.
           not   came VM one student even
           'No student [not even one student] came.'

In (28a) *is* functions as an additive particle, the equivalent of 'also'; in (28b), on
the other hand, it is a scalar particle expressing that the given number is considered

many. Accordingly, *sem* in (29a) functions as an anti-additive particle, whereas in (29b) it is the negative counterpart of the scalar particle, expressing that the given number is few. (So, while *is* is typically added to numbers higher than one, *sem* is typically combined with *egy* 'one'.)

Interestingly, when no Stylistic Postposing is performed, the negative particle *nem* expected to follow the *sem* phrase is not spelled out:

(30) a.   Péter *sem*   jött el.
          Peter neither came VM
          'Peter didn't come, either.'

   b.   Egy diák   *sem*   jött el.
        one student neither came VM
        'No student came.'

Just as the particle *is* can accompany certain types of universal quantifiers (e.g. *bárki (is), akárki (is)* 'anybody') as well, *sem* can also be freely combined with *se*-quantifiers – e.g. *senki (sem)* 'nobody'. In sentences containing a *se*-phrase supplied with *sem* we find the same distribution of *sem* and *nem* as was attested in (29)–(30): *nem* is only spelled out if the *se*-phrase + *sem* complex stands postverbally.

(31) a.   Mari *semmit*   *sem* mondott.
          Mary nothing-ACC not said
          'Mary said nothing.'

   b.   Mari *nem* mondott *semmit sem.*

(32) a.   Mari *soha senkinek*   *sem* beszélt a   terveiről.
          Mary never nobody-DAT not spoke her plans-about
          'Mary never spoke to anybody about her plans.'

   b.   Mari *nem* beszélt *soha senkinek sem* a   terveiről.
        Mary not spoke   never nobody-DAT her plans-about
        'Mary didn't ever speak about her plans to anybody.'

(33) a.   Mari *senkinek*   *semmit*   *sem* ígért.
          Mary nobody-DAT nothing-ACC not promised
          'Mary didn't promise anybody anything.'

   b.   Mari *nem* ígért   *senkinek*   *semmit sem.*
        Mary not promised nobody-DAT nothing-ACC
        'Mary didn't promise anything to anybody.'

In the (a) sentences of (31)–(33) *sem* seems in a certain sense to stand for *nem*. Relying on this intuition, traditional Hungarian grammars analyze this type of *sem* as an allomorph of *nem*. In fact, however, the situation is more complex. First, the prosody of *sem* is surprisingly different from that of *nem*: whereas *nem* is stressed and forms a phonological word with the subsequent verb, *sem* is unstressed and forms a phonological word with the preceding noun phrase. That *sem* is not simply an allomorph of *nem* is shown particularly clearly by the (b) versions of (31)–(33), involving Stylistic Postposing, in which *nem* remains in preverbal position, whereas *sem* moves together with the postposed *se*-elements. In these examples *sem* is understood to be simply the negative equivalent of the distributive particle *is*.

I propose the following account of these facts. Let us assume that the particle *sem* (and presumably *is*, as well) is an optional spelling-out of the head of DistP, which, when present, is obligatorily cliticized to the constituent in Spec,DistP. When Dist and Neg fuse, sharing a single projection, the joint DistNeg head cannot be doubly realized: either *nem* or *sem* must be dropped. When *sem* is retained, it will be cliticized to the constituent in Spec,DistP. If the filler of Spec,DistP, with *sem* cliticized to it, undergoes Stylistic Postposing, the empty DistNeg head is left without a local identifier, hence it must be spelled out by *nem*.

The assumption that *sem* is the head of DistP is confirmed by the fact that in sentences with more than one negative quantifier, only the rightmost one can be followed by *sem*:

(34) a.   * János *soha sem sehová sem* autóval megy.
       John never   nowhere   car-with goes
       'John never goes by car anywhere.'

   b.   János *soha sehová sem* autóval megy.

A numeral phrase is interpreted as a negative quantifier only with the scalar *sem* adjoined to it (obviously because it has neither a negative morpheme, nor a distributive morpheme in itself). In a series of [+negative,+distributive] phrases, the numeral phrase can only be the rightmost one, since elsewhere it would not be adjacent to *sem*:

(35) a.   * János *egy szót* senkinek *sem* szólt.
       John a   word nobody-DAT said
       'John didn't say a word to anybody.'

   b.   * János *egy szót sem* senkinek *sem* szólt.
   c.   János senkinek egy szót *sem* szólt.

If *sem* is the head of a DistP with multiple specifiers, then it will follow that it can only appear after the last one of a series of negative quantifiers.

6.4   The universal and existential readings of negative pronouns

Se-phrases sometimes appear to function as the negative equivalents of universal quantifiers; other times they seem to act as the negative equivalents of existential quantifiers; compare:

(36) a. *Senki   sem/nem* érkezett.
      nobody not   arrived
      'Nobody arrived. [There wasn't anybody who arrived.]'

    b. *Nem* érkezett *senki (sem).*
      'Nobody arrived. [There wasn't anybody who arrived.]'

(37) a. *Senki   sem/nem* érkezett meg.
      nobody not   arrived VM
      'Nobody arrived. [It is true for every person in question that he did not arrive.]'

    b. *Nem* érkezett meg *senki (sem).*
      'Nobody arrived. [It is true for every person in question that he did not arrive.]'

(38) a. János *semmit   sem/nem* mondott.
      John nothing-ACC not   said
      'John said nothing.'

    b. János *nem* mondott *semmit (sem).*
      'John didn't say anything.'

(39) a. János *semmit sem/nem* mondott el.
      John nothing not   said   VM
      'John didn't disclose anything. [It is true for everything that John didn't disclose it.]'

    b. János nem mondott el *semmit (sem).*
      'John didn't disclose anything. [It is true for everything that John didn't disclose it.]'

Whereas the *se*-phrases in (36)–(39) have either only the existential or only the universal interpretation, certain *se*-phrases are ambiguous; for example:

(40) a. János *senkivel   sem/nem* találkozott.
      John nobody-with not   met
      'John didn't meet with anybody.'

    b. János *nem* találkozott *senkivel (sem).*

The fact that the (a) and (b) sentences in (36)–(40) have identical interpretations suggests that the existential or universal reading is not a function of the position of the *se*-phrase relative to the negative particle or to the verb; rather it depends on what type of predicate the sentence has. The predicates of (36) and (38) (*érkezik* 'arrive (imperfective)' and *mond* 'say') require their argument represented by the *se*-phrase to be [–specific], whereas those of (37) and (39) (*meg érkezik* 'arrive (perfective)', and *el mond* 'tell, disclose') require it to be [+specific]. The verb *találkozik* 'meet' in (40) allows its theme to be either [–specific] or [+specific]. These selectional restrictions can be demonstrated by independent evidence. Observe that the relevant arguments of the verbs of (36) and (38) cannot be represented by any type of specific (strong) noun phrase, whereas the relevant arguments 'of the verbs of (37) and (39) cannot be represented by any type of non-specific (weak) noun phrase.[4]

(41) a. Érkezett *a   vendég/*mindenki/valaki.
         arrived the guest/ everybody/somebody
         'There arrived *the guest/*everybody/somebody.'

     b. Mondtam *az érdekes   dolgot/*minden érdekes   dolgot/érdekes
         said-I   the interesting thing/ every   interesting thing/interesting
         dolgokat.
         things
         'I said *the interesting thing/*every interesting thing/interesting things.'

(42) a. Meg érkeztek *vendégek/a   vendégek.
         VM arrived   guests   /the guests
         '*Guests/the guests arrived.'

     b. El   mondtam ??érdekes   dolgokat /minden érdekes   dolgot.
         VM said-I   interesting things /every   interesting thing
         'I said (disclosed) ??interesting things/every interesting thing.'

The specificity feature of the noun phrase representing the theme of *találkozik* 'meet' is not constrained by the predicate:

(43)   Találkoztam fiúkkal /a   fiúval   /mindenkivel.
         met-I   boys-with/the boy-with/everybody-with
         'I met with boys/with the boy/with everybody.'

These facts lead to the conclusion that the interpretation of a *se*-phrase is determined by the specificity feature associated with the argument of the given predicate that it represents. A [–specific] *se*-phrase is understood as an existential quantifier, whereas a [+specific] *se*-phrase is interpreted as a universal quantifier. A *se*-phrase is ambiguous if it represents a [+/–specific] argument.[5]

This conclusion appears, at first sight, to be contradicted by the fact that a prefocus *se*-phrase is always understood as a universal quantifier, no matter whether it represents an argument required to be [+specific] or [–specific]; compare:

---

[4] The verbs claimed here to require a non-specific theme, e.g. *érkezik* 'arrive', *mond* 'say' are not 'indefiniteness-effect' verbs in English; compare:

(i)   *John* arrived.
(ii)   John said *his lesson*.

In Hungarian, only the prefixed, perfective counterparts of these verbs can take a specific theme; the non-prefixed verbs in question are like the English *there is...* construction; they accept nothing but a non-specific argument.

[5] For further discussion of this topic, see Sections 2.5 and 7.2.

(44) a. Senki   sem/nem TEGNAP   érkezett.
         nobody not   yesterday arrived
         'For nobody was it yesterday when he arrived.'

  b. Senki   sem/nem TEGNAP   érkezett meg.
      nobody not   yesterday arrived VM
      'For nobody was it yesterday when he arrived.'

Recall, however, that in Section 2.5 we argued that if a predicate is subsumed by a focus phrase, then the specificity restrictions associated with its arguments are neutralized. At the same time, a specificity restriction of a different kind, called the Specificity Filter in É. Kiss (1993), is activated (see also Section 4.5.2):

(45)   *The Specificity Filter*
       If Op_i is an operator which has scope over Op_j and binds a variable in the scope of Op_j, then Op_i must be specific.

A *se*-phrase is a quantifier having scope over the focus, and binding a variable in the scope of the focus – hence it is subject to the Specificity Filter, which forces a specific universal reading on it.

Since the canonical position of the different types of *se*-phrases is invariably the specifier of a DistP fused with NegP, it seems surprising at first sight that *se*-phrases have a variable interpretation: they can be understood either existentially or universally. After all, in non-negative sentences, Spec,DistP typically harbors universal quantifiers of the *minden* 'every' type, which are generally believed to be inherently [+specific], and to be barred from contexts allowing only a [–specific] indefinite (compare **Minden fiú érkezett* 'Every boy arrived'). In fact, however, Spec,DistP can also be filled with a *sok . . .* 'many . . .' phrase, as well as with numeral phrases modified by *is* such as *két fiú is* 'two boys (even)', which are existential quantifiers, and can represent non-specific arguments; compare *Két fiú is érkezett* 'Two boys arrived'.

Spec,DistP is also the canonical landing site of pronouns involving the morphemes *bár* and *akár* 'any', which, although traditionally categorized as universals, can also be interpreted either existentially or universally in non-veridical contexts. Their interpretation, too, depends on whether the argument they represent is selected by the verb as [–specific] or as [+specific]; compare:

(46) a. [$_{TopP}$ Mari [$_{DistP}$ akármit/bármit [$_{AspP}$ el   mondhat a   szüleinek]]]
           Mary   anything   VM can.tell her parents-DAT
         'Mary can tell her parents anything.'

  b. Mari akármit/bármit mond, senki   nem hisz   neki.
      Mary anything   says nobody not believes her
      'Whatever Mary says, nobody believes her.'

What is more, even certain types of universals involving the morpheme *mind* 'every' can function as [–specific] existentials in Spec,DistP; compare:

(47) a. Minden   történt   már   a mi házunkban: betörés, rablás, gyilkosság.
         everything happened already in our house: burglary, robbery, murder
         'There has already been everything in our house: burglary, robbery, murder.'

  b. Mindenféle ember érkezett.
      every-kind man arrived
      'There arrived all kinds of men.'

That is, the feature that the head of DistP instantiates and that the potential fillers of Spec,DistP share is not the feature [+universal] but the feature [+distributive]. According to the evidence of sentences like (48) *se*-phrases also possess this feature:

(48) *Senki   sem* emelte fel a   zongorát.
      nobody not lifted up the piano
      'Nobody lifted the piano.'

Example (48) does not mean that nobody participated in a collective lifting event; it rather expresses that nobody performed a separate lifting act.

In sum: the existential versus universal reading of a *se*-pronoun correlates primarily with the specificity feature of the argument it represents. The position of the pronoun plays only an indirect role in its interpretation: a *se*-pronoun with scope over the focus is always universal because the Specificity Filter forces a [+specific] feature on it, no matter what verb it belongs to.[6]

---

[6] Puskás (2000) argues on the basis of tests proposed by Zanuttini (1997) that *se*-phrases always function as universal quantifiers. Thus, both existentially and universally interpreted *se*-phrases can be modified by *almost/absolutely*, which is a property of universal quantifiers not shared by existentials; compare:

(i)   * Majdnem valaki   érkezett.
        almost   somebody arrived
        'Almost somebody arrived.'

(ii) Majdnem mindenki meg érkezett.
      almost   everybody VM arrived
      'Almost everybody arrived.'

(iii) Majdnem senki   nem érkezett (meg).
      almost   nobody not arrived   VM
      'Almost nobody arrived.'

(iv) Nem érkezett (meg) majdnem senki.
      not arrived VM   almost   nobody
      'Almost nobody arrived.'

Puskás's second argument for the universal quantifier status of *se*-phrases involves donkey anaphora. Whereas existential quantifiers can establish anaphoric links from a

6.5   Long distance negative polarity

The claim that *se*-phrases are not indefinites bound by negation but are distributive quantifiers with a negative feature is also supported by the fact that they are only licensed by a clause-mate NegP. If they were indefinites in the scope of negation, we would also expect them to be licit in a clause subordinated to a negated sentence – as is the case with English negative polarity items. In fact, indefinite pronouns in the scope of matrix negation cannot have a *se*-morpheme; they have the form of indefinite pronouns occurring in other types of non-veridical contexts (e.g. in conditional, interrogative, optative, etc. sentences): they are represented by pronominal elements containing a *vala-* 'some-', a *bár-* 'any-', or an *akár-* 'any-' morpheme (see also Tóth 1999). Non-veridical *vala-* 'some-' pronouns are obligatorily supplied with the distributive *is* particle. *Is* can be attached to *bár-* and *akár-* pronouns, as well; compare:

(49) a.   Nem ígérték,   hogy az ügyemben *bármit/akármit/valamit is* tesznek.
           not promised-they that my case-in   anything-ACC   do-they
           'They didn't promise that they would do anything in my case.'

    b.   Kétlem, hogy *bárki/akárki/valaki is* [$_{AspP}$ meg érkezne   ma délután]
           doubt-I that anybody   VM would.arrive   this afternoon
           'I doubt that anybody would arrive this afternoon.'

    c.   Nem hiszem, hogy *bárki/valaki is* [$_{FP}$ JÁNOST   támogatná]
           not believe-I that anybody   John-ACC would.support
           'I don't believe that, for anybody, it is John that he would support.'

---

non-c-commanding position, *se*-phrases, like universal quantifiers, cannot bind a pronoun which they do not c-command; compare:

   (v)   Azok a   lányok, akik valamilyen lovat$_i$ vettek, azt   mondták, hogy pro$_i$ rúg.
          those the girls   who some   horse bought it-ACC said   that pro kicks
          'The girls who bought some horse said that it kicked.'

   (vi)   * Azok a   lányok, akik minden lovat$_i$ meg vettek, azt   mondták, hogy pro$_i$
          those the girls   who every   horse VM bought it-ACC said   that pro
          rúg.
          kicks
          'The girls who bought every horse said that it kicked.'

   (vii) * Azok a   lányok, akik nem vettek egy lovat sem$_i$, azt   mondták, hogy pro$_i$
          those the girls   who not bought one horse neither it-ACC said   that pro
          rúg.
          kicks
          'The girls who bought no horse said that it kicked.'

These tests would, however, have a compelling force only if the roles of the features [+/–universal], [+/–specific], and [+/–negative] in licensing *almost/absolutely* and donkey anaphora were tested and explained separately.

To all appearances, the *bármit (is)/valamit is* elements of the embedded clauses occupy Spec,DistP. (Their position is above AspP, as is clear from (49b), and also above FP, as is clear from (49c).) The particle *is*, spelling out the Dist head to be cliticized to the filler of Spec,DistP, provides morphological evidence of their Spec,Dist position. Like other types of distributive quantifiers, they are also subject to Stylistic Postposing:

(50)   Nem hiszem, hogy JÁNOST   támogatná   ′bárki/valaki is.
        not   believe-I that John-ACC would.support anybody
        'I don't believe that, for anybody, it is John that he would support.'

The fact that the non-veridical pronouns in question must also raise to Spec,DistP suggests that they are also [+distributive] quantifiers rather than bound indefinites, and they are related to the licensing matrix negation by being in its scope, rather than by being bound by it.[7]

6.6   The negative existential verb

The constraint in (15) requires that the V be adjacent to the VP-negating particle, and form a phonological word with it. If the verb involved is the indicative present tense 3rd person verb of existence, the Neg +V sequence merges into a single word not only prosodically, but also morphologically: Neg + EXIST-IND-PRES-3 is replaced by the morphologically non-compositional *nincs*; compare:

(51)   én nem vagyok otthon   mi nem vagyunk otthon
        I   not   am   at.home   we not   are   at.home

        te   nem vagy otthon   ti   nem vagytok otthon
        you not   are   at.home   you not   are   at.home

        ő nincs otthon   **ők nincsenek** otthon
        he isn't at.home   they aren't   at.home

The *nem* incorporated into the verb of existence behaves syntactically exactly as a non-incorporated *nem* does; i.e., it blocks the AspP projection (the verb modifier must stay in its postverbal, base-generated position):

(52) a.   János [AspP **itt** van]
          John   here is
          'John is here.'

      b.   János [NegVP nincs **itt**]
           John   isn't here

---

[7] For a different view, see Tóth (1999) who claims – following Giannakidou and Quer (1995) – that *valaki is* type pronouns are bound non-selectively by the closest non-veridical operator.

The FP-negating *nem*, which is not adjacent to the verb, naturally does not fuse morphologically with the verb of existence:

(53)   Nem [FP JÁNOS van itt]
        not   John   is   here
        'It isn't John who is here.'

Nincs licenses non-specific *se*-pronouns:

(54)   Semmi nincs a   hűtőszekrényben.
        nothing isn't the refrigerator-in
        'There isn't anything in the refrigerator.'

In such cases the Neg + EXIST-IND-PRES-3 complex also fuses with the head of Dist. When Dist is spelled out by *sem*, the joint DistNegV head is realized as *sincs* (55a), unless *sem* is cliticized to a *se*-pronoun undergoing Stylistic Postposing; compare:

(55) a.   Senki   *sincs* otthon.
           nobody isn't   at.home
           'Nobody is at home.'

     b.   *Nincs* otthon senki *sem*.

6.7   Summary

This chapter has argued that in the Hungarian sentence either the VP level, or the FP level, or both can be negated. Both the VP-negating particle and the FP-negating particle project a NegP. The negative particle negating the universal quantifier, on the other hand, represents constituent negation.

Hungarian displays negative concord: the Neg heads can license negative *se*-pronouns. The canonical location of *se*-phrases is the specifier of the projection of a Dist head fused with Neg. A *se*-pronoun in Spec,DistNegP can also undergo Stylistic Postposing, an operation moving it into postverbal position together with the stress and scope assigned to it in Spec,DistP. A *se*-quantifier in the scope of focus remains in its base-generated VP-internal position unstressed.

Se-pronouns are interpreted universally or existentially depending on whether they are assigned the feature [+specific] or [–specific]. The specificity feature of a *se*-pronoun is primarily determined by the verb selecting it. For example, the theme of an indefiniteness-effect verb is [–specific], hence existential. The syntactic position of a *se*-pronoun affects its interpretation through the Specificity Filter: a *se*-phrase preceding the focus, and binding a variable in the domain of focus, is necessarily specific, hence universal.

Sem, the negative counterpart of the distributive/additive/scalar *is* particle, has been argued to represent the head of a negative DistP, cliticized to the quantifier in Spec,DistP. The head of a joint DistNegP projection can be spelled out either as *sem* or as *nem* – unless *sem* is cliticized to a phrase removed via Stylistic Postposing, leaving *nem* as the only option.

Indefinite pronouns in the scope of the negative particle of a superordinate sentence are of the type *bármi/akármi/valami is*. They also land in the Spec,DistP position of their clause, which is evidence of their quantifier status.

7

The noun phrase

The inner structures of the various types of verb complements resemble the inner structure of the extended verb phrase in their outlines: they consist of a lexical phrase embedded in morphosyntactic projections and operator projections. The noun phrase, too, will be analyzed as a complex containing a lexical kernel (the NP proper) subsumed by operator projections extending it into an indefinite numeral phrase (NumP) and/or a definite determiner phrase (DP). The full range of morphosyntactic projections that play a role in the noun phrase will become evident in the analysis of the possessive construction.[1]

7.1   The basic syntactic layers of the noun phrase

The minimal noun projection appearing in the Hungarian sentence is a bare singular case-marked noun; for example:

(1) a.   János **könyvet**   olvas.
John book-ACC reads
'John is book-reading.'

b.   János **moziba**   ment.
John cinema-to went
'John went to (the) cinema.'

---

[1] The first syntactic theory of the Hungarian noun phrase was put forth by Szabolcsi (1981b, 1983b, 1992a, 1992b, 1994a, Szabolcsi and Laczkó 1992). Noticing that the Hungarian noun phrase contains too many specifiers to fit into the single slot provided by X-bar theory, she identified the article as the head of a functional projection. Her observations and her proposal contributed to the emergence of the idea of noun phrase internal functional projections in generative grammar.

The Hungarian noun phrase aroused renewed interest in the Minimalist framework of the late 1990s, particularly because of its interesting pattern of agreement and anti-agreement in the possessive construction, and because of the role that the definiteness feature of the noun phrase plays in verb–object agreement; compare Bartos (1997, 1999a, 2000a), den Dikken (1999a), and É. Kiss (1998d, 2000a).

In the unmarked case such nouns function as verb modifiers. In Section 3.6 verb modifiers were shown to display both phrase-like and head-like properties: they move into Spec,AspP like a phrase, and merge with the V in Asp like a head, which suggests that they are both minimal and maximal, i.e., they are phrases containing merely a head. They can also undergo operator movement into Spec,FP and Spec,DistP, and can even be topicalized if contrasted (see Section 2.7), which is clear evidence of their phrasal status. Consequently, bare nouns will be analyzed as noun phrases (NPs proper). An NP is a lexical projection consisting of an N, and in case N is an argument-taking head, also of a noun phrase or postpositional phrase complement – a possibility to be investigated in Section 7.4. The NP can also be modified by adjectival phrases and, when used in a sentence, it is embedded in a Case phrase (KP). That is:

(2)

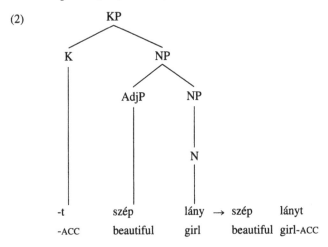

The morphophonological linearization of the noun phrase is represented on the right-hand side of the arrow. Bartos (1999a) assumes that the structure in (2) is a three-dimensional tree whose K element is marked as a head in syntax and as a suffix in morphology. Since a syntactic head precedes its complement, whereas a morphological suffix is right-adjoined to its lexical stem, the tree must be linearized differently in syntax and in morphophonology.

Hungarian noun phrases can be supplied with either a (suffixal) plural marker or a numeral – but not both. The plural marker is assumed to appear in the head position of a numeral phrase (NumP) projection dominating NP (3a), whereas the numeral is assumed to appear in Spec,NumP (3b). In case Spec,NumP is filled, an economy principle (akin to the Doubly-filled Comp Filter) blocks the spelling-out of the [+plural] feature of the Num head.[2]

---

[2] The principle at work may be the principle 'Economize functional heads' proposed by Dimitrova-Vulchanova (1998).

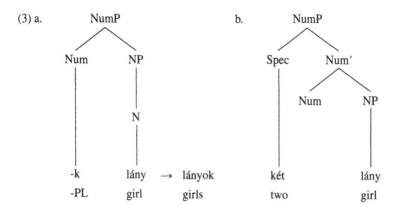

(3) a.   NumP   b.   NumP

| Num | NP |
| lány → lányok |

ját...

The numerals appearing in Spec,NumP include cardinal numbers (among them *egy* 'one', which, when unstressed, is interpreted as an indefinite article), as well as *néhány* 'some', *számos* 'several', *sok* 'many', *minden* 'every', *hány* 'how many', etc. 1st and 2nd person pronouns also count as NumPs; see footnote 11 of Chapter 3.

A NP or a NumP can be further extended by a quantifier ending in *-ik* (e.g. *mindegyik* 'each', *bármelyik* 'any', *valamelyik* 'a certain', *semelyik* 'no', *melyik* 'which') into a quantifier phrase (QP) (4), and/or by a demonstrative of the *e/eme/ezen* 'this', *ama/azon* 'that' type into a demonstrative phrase (DemP) (5a,b).

(4)

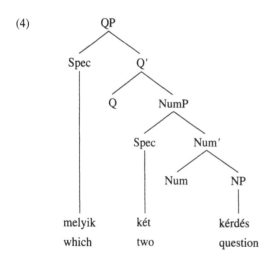

(5) a.   [_DemP_ e [_NumP_ két [_NP_ kérdés]]]
             this   two   question
          'these two questions'

   b.   ? [_DemP_ ezen [_QP_ bármelyik [_NP_ kérdés]]]
             this   any   question
          'any of these questions'

Noun phrases extended by an -*ik* quantifier or an *e/eme/ezen* type demonstrative act as definite noun phrases (in ways to be specified below); i.e., -*ik* quantifiers and demonstratives also seem to play the role of a definite determiner. The default definite determiner, the definite article *a/az*, is only spelled out – presumably in the head position of a DP projection – if the noun phrase has no quantifier determiner or demonstrative determiner – as in (6a) – or if the quantifier or the demonstrative determiner it has is not the highest element in the noun phrase but is buried, for example, under a non-finite restrictive relative clause adjoined to QP or DemP (7a,b).

(6) a.   [DP a [NumP két [NP fiú]]]
         the   two   boy

  b.   * [DP a [QP mindegyik [NP fiú]]]   c.   * [DP az [DemP ezen [NP fiú]]]
        the   each   boy   the   this   boy

      but:

(7) a.   [DP a [QP Marinak   bemutatott [QP mindegyik fiú]]]
        the   Mary-DAT introduced   each   boy
      'each boy introduced to Mary'

  b.   [DP a [DemP tőled   kapott [DemP eme levél]]]
        the   you-from received   this letter
      'this letter received from you'

To capture the fact that QPs and DemPs behave like DPs, we can assume that they always project a DP, and the quantifier or the demonstrative must be raised from Spec,QP/Spec,DemP into Spec,DP – presumably to check the [+definite] feature of the D head. Once Spec,DP is filled by movement, the D head cannot be spelled out (owing to the economy principle also active in the NumP). In (7b) the movement from Spec,QP to Spec,DP is blocked by the intervening participial clause.[3] Third person personal pronouns and proper names are also DPs; they may involve movement from N to D.

---

[3] Noticing that the definite article in e.g. (7a,b) does not change the referential properties of the noun phrase, Szabolcsi (1983b, 1992a, 1994a) concludes that the definite article is not a determiner. She claims it to be a complementizer-like element, a subordinator, whose function is to turn a nominal expression into the argument of a predicate. At the same time, it also carries the feature [+definite] or [−definite]. The definite subordinator is spelled out as *a/az*, whereas the indefinite one is phonetically null (the so-called indefinite article, *egy* 'an/one', being in fact a numeral). The article projects a DP. A noun phrase appearing in a sentence is syntactically always a DP; however, phonologically the DP projection can be vacuous. It is not only the indefinite article that is phonologically empty; the definite article is also deleted if it is immediately followed by a determiner (whether a contentful determiner or another definite article belonging, for example, to a genitive specifier).

7.2   Evidence for the different noun phrase projections

The categorial distinction between predicative noun phrases (NPs), indefinite noun phrases (NumPs), and definite noun phrases (DPs) is supported by semantic, morphosyntactic, syntactic, and lexical evidence. These noun phrase types have different semantic functions: NPs denote properties, NumPs denote individuals identified by a property, whereas DPs denote individuals identified (more or less) uniquely. Definite and indefinite noun phrases also behave differently on the morphosyntactic level: only DP objects trigger the presence of a visible object agreement marker on the V (see Section 3.5.2).

NPs, NumPs, and DPs also have different distributions across sentence positions. Although NPs, i.e., bare singulars, can represent any argument of a predicate, including its subject, they are barred both from postverbal argument positions and from the topic position. They can only occur in the operator slots: Spec,AspP, Spec, FP, and Spec,DistP (compare Section 3.2). Non-specific NumPs (for example, bare plurals) are only barred from the topic position (compare Section 2.5).[4] (Generic plurals and mass terms have a definite article in Hungarian; hence, they can be topicalized and predicated about.)

As was discussed in Section 2.5, predicates may subcategorize for the category of their noun phrase complement. Thus, predicates with the meaning component '(come to) exist/appear' – e.g. *van* 'is', *születik* 'is born', *keletkezik* 'arise', *alakul* 'is formed' – or with the meaning component 'cause to (come to) exist/appear' – e.g. *készít* 'prepare', *rajzol* 'draw', *főz* 'cook', *kap* 'receive' – require their theme to be a mere NP or a non-specific NumP. These predicates assert the existence, or coming into being, of their theme; that is why their theme cannot be expressed by a noun phrase carrying an existential presupposition – as happens in (8d) and (9b).[5]

(8) a.　Született egy gyerek.
　　　was.born a　child
　　　'A child was born.'

　b.　Született sok　gyerek.
　　　was.born many child
　　　'Many children were born.'

　c.　Születtek gyerekek.
　　　were.born children
　　　'Children were born.'

　d.　* Született a gyerek/mindegyik gyerek/eme gyerek.
　　　was.born a child　/each　　　child　/this child
　　　'The child/each child/this child was born.'

---

[4]　This observation is due to Alberti (1997b).
[5]　For details, see Szabolcsi (1986) and É. Kiss (1995c).

(9) a.   Kaptunk egy díjat /sok   díjat /díjakat.
          we.got   a   prize/many prize/prizes
          'We got a prize/many prizes/prizes.'

   b.   * Kaptuk a   díjat /mindegyik díjat /ezen díjat.[6]
         we.got the prize/each   prize/this prize
         'We got the prize/each prize/this prize.'

Minden 'every' phrases functioning as objects trigger the subjective conjugation of the V, i.e., they must be NumPs; still verbs requiring a non-specific theme do not accept them as their theme:

(10) a.   * Született minden gyerek.   b.   * Kaptunk minden díjat.
           was.born every   child   we.got   every   prize-ACC
           'Every child was born.'   'We got every prize.'

The reason for the ungrammaticality of (10a,b) must be that *minden* is an inherently specific numeral (after all, it always refers to a set already present in the universe of discourse).

   There are also predicates requiring that their arguments be represented by a DP or a specific NumP. Such are predicates expressing a state; compare:

(11) a.   * Szeretnek lányok operákat.
           love   girls operas-ACC
           '(Some) girls love (some) operas.'

---

[6] Example (9b) can also be grammatical – provided the verb is focussed, in which case the main assertion is other than the assertion of the theme's coming into being:

   (i)   KAPTUK a díjat,   nem KÁRTYÁN NYERTÜK.
          got-we the prize-ACC not cards-at won-we-it
          'We GOT the prize, we did not WIN it at CARDS.'

   The indefiniteness effect is, in general, neutralized if the sentence contains a focus; for example:

   (ii)   TAVALY kaptuk a   díjat.
          last.year got-we the prize-ACC
          'We got the prize LAST YEAR.'

   It also saves the sentences if the verb is supplied with a perfectivizing suffix – presumably because in that case the main assertion is the completion of the event of the theme's coming into being:

   (iii) Meg született a   gyerek.
          PERF was.born the child
          'The child has been born.'

   (iv)   Meg kaptuk az üzenetet.
          PERF got-we the message-ACC
          'We have got the message.'

b.   A lányok szeretik az operákat.
     the girls   love   the operas
     'Girls love operas.'

In view of these facts it seems expedient to distinguish categorially different noun phrase types; after all, NPs, NumPs, and DPs not only have different referring functions but also figure in various morphological, morphosyntactic, and syntactic operations and constraints.

7.3   The possessive construction

7.3.1   The facts

In the Hungarian possessive construction, the possessive relation is marked primarily on the possessed noun: it bears a suffix indicating its possessedness, and it may also bear an agreement marker, matching the person and number of the possessor. The possessor can bear a dative suffix, or can be caseless. The presence versus absence of dative case on the possessor, and the presence versus absence of agreement on the possessed noun, interact with the syntactic structure of the possessive construction in an intricate way. Here are the essential facts to be accounted for:

The dative-marked possessor either occupies the initial position in the extended projection of the possessed noun (12a), or it is external to it, sitting among the complements of the matrix verb, on a par with the projection of the possessed noun (12b). (The latter pattern is referred to as the cleft possessive construction.)

(12) a.   Jánosnak a   könyv-e
          John-DAT the book-POSS
          'John's book'

     b.   Jánosnak ellopták   a   könyvét.
          John-DAT stole-they the book-POSS-ACC
          'John's book was stolen.'

The caseless possessor cannot leave the projection of the possessed noun:

(13) a.   János könyv-e
          John book-POSS
          'John's book'

     b. * János ellopták   a   könyvét.
          John stole-they the book-POSS-ACC
          'They stole John's book.'

Whereas the dative-marked possessor precedes the definite article of the possessed noun, the caseless possessor usually blocks the spelling-out of the article of the possession (14a). The article is spelled out in two cases. Its presence is obligatory when the caseless possessor is represented by a personal pronoun (14b), and it is optional when it is represented by a personal name (14c). A caseless possessor always follows the article of the possession.

(14) a.   Magyarország fővárosa
           Hungary   capital-POSS
           'Hungary's capital'

     b.   az ő könyve
           the he book-POSS
           'his book'

     c.   (a) János könyve
           (the) John book-POSS
           '(the) John's book'

Most speakers reject a pronominal possessor in pattern (12a) as a dative-marked possessor internal to the projection of the possessed noun:

(15)   ?* Csak (én)nekem a   könyvem   veszett el.
          only I-DAT   the book-POSS-1SG lost   VM
          'Only my book got lost.'

As for the morphosyntax of possession, the possessed noun bears a possessive suffix and often also an additional agreement suffix corresponding to the person and number of the possessor. The possessive suffix and the agreement suffix are fused in many cases. However, in the case of a plural possessed noun they are clearly distinct; they are separated by the plural marker. (The plural marker of possessed nouns (-*i*) happens to be different from the regular -*k* plural marker.) That is:

(16)   az én diák -ja -i -m   a mi diák -ja -i -nk
        the I student-POSS-PL-1SG   the we student-POSS-PL-1PL
        'my students'   'our students'

        a te diák -ja -i -d   a ti diák -ja -i -tok
        the you student-POSS-PL-2SG   the you student-POSS-PL-2PL
        'your students'   'your students'

        az ő diák -ja -i -0   az ő diák -ja -i -k
        the he student-POSS-PL-3SG   the he student-POSS-PL-3PL
        'his students'   'their students'

Notice that the 3rd person plural personal pronoun (*ők* 'they') loses its -*k* plural marker when used as a caseless possessor, which some of the (anti)agreement theories to be discussed below attribute great significance to. The principal target of these theories is the phenomenon that the agreement marker of the possession is missing if the possessor is represented by a lexical noun phrase. Since the 3rd person singular agreement marker is phonologically empty, the absence of agreement becomes evident only in the case of a plural lexical possessor, which would trigger the -*k* agreement marker:

(17) a.   a   fiú   könyv-e   -i   b.   a   fiúk   könyv-e   -i
          the boy book -POSS-PL   the boys book -POSS-PL
          'the boy's books'   'the boys' books'

Agreement between the lexical possessor and the possessed noun is optional in the cleft pattern:

(18)   A   fiúknak   elvesztek a   könyv-e   -i   -(k).
         the boys-DAT got.lost   the book -POSS -PL-3PL
         'The boys' books got lost.'

In the Minimalist approach of Bartos (1999a) the possessedness marker and the agreement marker surrounding the plural suffix on the possessed noun are analyzed as the heads of the functional projections PossP and AgrP, respectively. Relying on the Mirror Principle of Baker (1985), according to which morphological derivation is the mirror image of syntactic derivation, Bartos argues that PossP immediately dominates NP, and AgrP immediately dominates NumP. Consider the relevant section of the extended noun phrase projection:

(19)

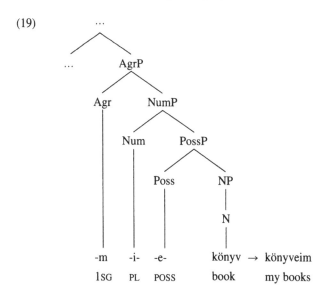

The structure in (19), again, should be conceived as three dimensional. Agr, Num, and Poss surface on the right-hand side of the N because each of them is marked as suffixal, which means that it must right-adjoin to the lexical head of its complement.

7.3.2   Relating the caseless and the dative possessor

A crucial question that a description of the Hungarian possessive construction must answer is how to relate the three possible realizations of the possessor: the caseless possessor, the -nak/nek-marked possessor internal to the extended projection of the possessed noun, and the cleft -nak/nek-marked possessor. As Szabolcsi (1992a) first argued, the three possessor types are realizations of the same unspecified theta role, assigned to the possessor by the possessed noun. The possessed noun, consisting of a noun and a possessedness suffix, is an argument-taking head, denoting a referent that bears an unspecified relation to an individual (the possessor). If the noun combined with the possessedness suffix is a theta-role assigner in itself, e.g. it is a deverbal noun denoting an action, then the possessor will have the specific theta role determined by the noun. In such cases the possessedness suffix only plays a role in licensing the case of the possessor.[7] The fact that the three types of possessors share the same theta role suggests that they originate in the same position.

The 'standard' theory of the Hungarian possessive construction, elaborated by Szabolcsi (see Szabolcsi 1981b, 1983b, 1992a, 1992b, 1994a, Szabolcsi and Laczkó 1992, etc.), is based on the insight that the relation between the possessor and the possession is both functionally and formally similar to the relation between the subject and the predicate. The possessor bears the same agreement relation to the possessed noun that the subject bears to the verb, and it is assigned the same nominative case by nominal inflection that the subject is assigned by verbal inflection. The role of Tense is played by the Poss(essedness) element in the nominal domain. Every noun phrase is associated with an inflection complex containing a [+/−Poss] element, and, like [+Tense], [+Poss] is accompanied by agreement.

In this theory, the primary realization of the possessor is the apparently caseless variant. If we interpret Szabolcsi's theory on structure (19) (which is an updated version of her original proposal), then the possessor is generated in Spec,PossP, where it also receives its theta role. It bears a phonologically null

---

[7] On the theta role of the possessor, see Szabolcsi (1992a, 1994a, etc.) and Alberti (1995).

nominative case, which is assigned/checked by Poss. Then the possessor moves on to Spec,AgrP, the surface position of nominative possessors. The nominative possessor in Spec,AgrP is predicted to follow the definite article and to precede every other determiner and numeral – correctly, as is demonstrated in (20a,b):

(20) a. a te minden szavad   b. János ezen szavai
         the you every word-POSS-2SG   John this word-POSS-PL
         'your every word'   'these words of John'

Szabolcsi assumes a phonological rule deleting the definite article followed by another determiner. D-deletion takes places whatever the structural relation between the two adjacent determiners is, and whichever type the second determiner represents. Hence, when the nominative possessor has a determiner of its own, it will delete the definite article of the possessed noun (21a). The definite article of the possessed noun may in fact also be missing when the possessor has no visible determiner of its own; e.g. it is absent in front of a determinerless geographical name (21b). It can also be missing in front of a possessor represented by a personal name; thus, (21c) is perhaps even more common than the variant with an article. Szabolcsi claims that geographical names and, optionally, personal names too have a zero determiner, which is, however, visible for the determiner of the possessed noun, and deletes it.

(21) a. 0 [ezen fiú] könyve
            this boy book-POSS
         'this boy's book'

     b. 0 [0 Budapest] hídjai
            Budapest bridge-POSS-PL
         'the bridges of Budapest'

     c. 0 [0 János] ezen szavai
            John this word-POSS-PL
         'these words of John'

A nominative possessor in Spec,AgrP can move on into Spec,DP, where it assumes a *-nak/nek* operator marker (22). (Szabolcsi claims that this *-nak/nek* is other than the dative case suffix. The suffix *-nak/nek* also serves un-case-like purposes in Hungarian, such as marking modifiers in left dislocation, e.g. *Boldog-nak boldog vagyok* 'Happy I am'.)

(22)

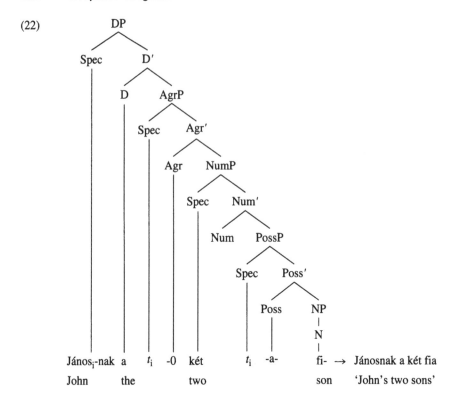

János$_i$-nak a t_i -0   két t_i -a-   fi- →   Jánosnak a két fia

John   the   two   son   'John's two sons'

The -*nak/nek*-marked possessor in Spec,DP is correctly predicted to precede both the article and the quantifiers/numerals of the possessed noun, without causing the deletion of the matrix D.

If D plays the same role in the nominal domain as C plays in the sentence, then Spec,DP must also be a functional equivalent of Spec,CP, serving as an (intermediate) landing site for operators. The operator position status of Spec,DP is said to be confirmed also by the observation that possessors with an inherent operator feature, e.g. *wh*-phrases and quantifiers, are somewhat marked when left in Spec,AgrP, bearing a null nominative case. A *wh*-phrase in Spec,AgrP sounds particularly archaic; Szabolcsi even marks it as ungrammatical; compare:

(23) a. ? Ki   könyve   van az asztalon?
      who book-POSS is   the table-on
      'Whose book is on the table?'

   b.   Kinek   a   könyve   van az asztalon?
       who-DAT the book-POSS is   the table-on
       'Whose book is on the table?'

(24) a.(?) Mindenki   könyve   az asztalon van.
         everybody book-POSS the table-on is
         'Everybody's book is on the table.'

   b. Mindenkinek a   könyve   az asztalon van.
         everybody-DAT the book-POSS the table-on is
         'Everybody's book is on the table.'

The facts in (23)–(24), however, do not clearly support the claim that Spec,DP filled with the -nak/nek-marked possessor is an operator position. The whole of the subject of (23) occupies Spec,F(ocus)P – the location of wh-phrases – and the whole of the subject of (24) occupies Spec,DistP – the location of universal quantifiers – i.e., the operator feature of the possessor percolates up to the matrix noun phrase in both cases, and causes it to move into a position where the given operator feature can be checked. The mild (or, for some speakers, significant) acceptability difference between the (a) and (b) sentences in (23) and (24) suggests merely that the operator feature of the possessor can percolate up to the matrix noun phrase more easily from Spec,DP than from Spec,AgrP. Contrary to what Szabolcsi's theory predicts, it is not necessary for a possessor to have an operator feature to be able to land in Spec,DP and to assume a -nak/nek operator marker. Any possessor of any noun phrase can occupy Spec,DP (unless it is a personal pronoun; compare (15)).

Spec,DP – like Spec,CP – serves as an escape hatch: a possessor raised into Spec,DP and supplied with -nak/nek can be extracted into the domain of the matrix verb. In the following pair of examples the possessor is generated in Spec,PossP, where it has its nominative case checked, and – after passing through Spec,AgrP – it moves on to Spec,DP. Then it is extracted into the matrix VP (25a), where it may undergo topicalization (25b).

(25) a.   Elveszett [$_{DP}$ t_i' a [t_i pénze   ]   Jánosnak$_i$]
         got.lost   the money-POSS John-DAT
         'John's money got lost.'

   b.   Jánosnak$_i$ elveszett [$_{DP}$ t_i' a [t_i pénze] t_i'']

Szabolcsi's basic claim – that the three types of possessors derive from the same underlying structure – has been generally accepted. At the same time, some of her specific proposals have been challenged. For example, her analysis of the -nak/nek suffix as an operator marker is not supported by independent evidence. It is not plausible that a language that has no operator markers on the sentence level should have one on the noun phrase level and, what is more, this operator marker should be identical with the dative case ending.

Demonstratives of the ez/az type represent a further problem for this theory. Ez/az stands in a pre-article position in the noun phrase, and it agrees in number with the head noun, also sharing its case – an accusative in (26a). One of the open questions is the position of *ez/az*. The only pre -article position in Szabolcsi's theory is Spec,DP, which, however, is taken by the *-nak/nek* possessor; see, for example, (26b). Furthermore, an *ez/az* occupying Spec,DP should bear the *-nak/nek* operator marker assigned (or checked) in Spec,DP instead of sharing the case of the matrix NP.

(26) a. ezeket   a könyveket
          these-ACC the books-ACC
          'these books-ACC'

    b. a fiúnak   ezt   a könyvét
        the boy-DAT this-ACC the book-POSS-ACC
        'this book-ACC of the boy'

The use of *ez/az* in possessive constructions is also restricted in unexplained ways. A possessed noun can only have an *ez/az*-type demonstrative if the possessor bears the *-nak/nek* ending; compare (26b) and (27a). A possessor, too, can only be associated with *ez/az* if it is a possessor marked by *-nak/nek* (27b,c).

(27) a. * ezt   a fiú könyvét
          this-ACC the boy book-POSS-ACC
          'this book of the boy'

    b. * ez a fiú könyvét
        this the boy book-POSS-ACC
        'this boy's book'

    c. ennek   a fiúnak   a könyvét
        this-DAT the boy-DAT the book-POSS-ACC
        'the book of this boy'

An adequate analysis of the possessive construction should also account for the facts illustrated in (26b) and (27).

Seeking to eliminate the problems listed above, den Dikken (1999a) proposes the following account of the nominative–dative alternation. The primary variant is the *-nak/nek*-marked possessor, whose suffix is the regular dative case ending, employed for the encoding of the possessor theta role in many languages. Possession is claimed to be expressed universally by means of a predication structure, in which the possessor is predicated of the possessum, as follows:

(28)   [$_{SC}$ POSSESSUM [$_{PP}$ P$_{dat}$POSSESSOR]]

The possessor receives its theta role in the dative PP. The dative P has two allomorphs. It can be overt, in which case it is spelled out as *-nak/nek*. It can also be null, in which case it must meet a licensing condition, as a consequence of which the PP will undergo Predicate Inversion (see den Dikken 1995: Chapter 3).

(English Dative Shift is claimed to be the output of the same Predicate Inversion rule.) Predicate Inversion yields a construction of the following type (disregarding agreement for the time being):

(29)   [$_{DP}$ a [$_{FP}$ [$_{PP}$ P$_e$ János]$_i$ F [$_{SC}$ kalap t_i]]]
        the   John   hat

(FP, whose specifier position the caseless possessor occupies, means 'functional projection', which can presumably be identified with the PossP projection of structure (19).) If the dative P is realized as an overt -*nak/nek* suffix, then the -*nak/nek*-marked possessor is preposed from the predicate position of the small clause directly into Spec,DP.

   The dative-marked possessor is also the primary variant in the approach of É. Kiss (2000a). It is generated as a post-head complement of the possessed noun – contrary to den Dikken (1999a), and similar to Szabolcsi (1992a, etc.). As for the caseless variant, it is argued that certain types of arguments can not only be realized as post-head complements but can also appear as specifiers or modifiers. When realized as complements, they are licensed by a case or a preposition merged with them. As specifiers or modifiers, they need different categorial features – e.g. the modifiers of nouns are typically of the category AdjP. Certain types of adjuncts display a similar categorial alternation in post-head and prehead position. Thus, in the (b) examples in (30)–(33) the prenominal arguments and adjuncts either lack their K or P, or have it buried under an AdjP:

(30) a.   a student [$_{PP}$ of chemistry] [$_{PP}$ with long hair] →
     b.   a [long-haired] [chemistry] student

(31) a.   egy papírvágó   kés [$_{KP}$ ébenfából] →
           a   paper.cutting knife ebony-from
           'a paper knife of ebony'

     b.   egy [ébenfa] papírvágó   kés
           an ebony   paper.cutting knife
           'an ebony paper knife'

(32) a.   tüntetés [$_{PP}$ a megszállás ellen] →
           demonstration the occupation against
           'demonstration against the occupation'

     b.   [$_{AdjP}$ [$_{PP}$ a megszállás ellen] -i]   tüntetés
                     the occupation against-ADJ demonstration
           'demonstration against the occupation'

(33) a.   harc [$_{KP}$ a   függetlenségért] →
           fight   the independence-for
           'fight for independence'

b.   [$_{AdjP}$ [$_{KP}$ a   függetlenségért] való] harc
      the independence-for being fight
  'fight for independence'

The dative possessor–caseless possessor alternation is claimed to be of the same kind. That is, the possessor argument can be licensed either as a complement or as a specifier – i.e., it can be generated either in the complement position, or as the specifier of the N + Poss complex. It will need a Case (a Dative) only in the former case. Dative case serves to denote the unspecified theta role that the complement of a possessed noun bears to its head.

Let us assume that the possessor, which uniquely identifies the possessum, has a [+determiner] feature. The possessum is of the category DP, whose [+determiner] head attracts the possessor into its checking domain. A caseless lexical possessor, generated in Spec,PossP, is moved into Spec,DP in order to check the [+determiner] feature of D. If Spec,DP is filled, D will remain phonologically empty owing to economy requirements (compare Dimitrova-Vulchanova 1998); for example:

(34)

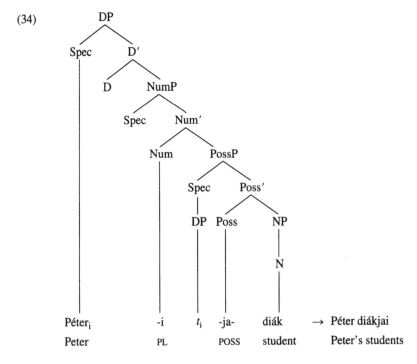

AgrP is believed to play no role in the derivation, since lexical possessors – unlike pronominal possessors – do not bear an agreement marker. Thus, (35a,b) represent a minimal pair: the 3rd person pronoun has a phonologically null agreement suffix, whereas the lexical noun phrase does not have any:

(35) a. az ő diák -ja -i -0
    the he student-POSS-PL-0
    'his students'

   b. a Péter diák -ja -i
    the Peter student-POSS-PL
    'Peter's students'

The presence of the phonologically null agreement suffix in (35a) is supported by the fact that the construction is part of a paradigm of overt agreement suffixes; compare:

(36) az én diák -ja -i -m   a mi diák -ja -i -nk
    the I student-POSS-PL-1SG   the we student-POSS-PL-1PL
    'my students'   'our students'

    a te diák -ja -i -d   a ti diák -ja -i -tok
    the you student-POSS-PL-2SG   the you student-POSS-PL-2PL
    'your students'   'your students'

    az ő diák -ja -i -0   az ő diák -ja -i -k
    the he student-POSS-PL-3SG   the he student-POSS-PL-3PL
    'his students'   'their students'

The claim that the possession of a singular lexical possessor, e.g. that in (35b), does not bear a zero agreement suffix is supported by two pieces of evidence. First, the 3rd person plural agreement marker is the phonologically salient -$(u)k$ – see (36) – and it is also absent in the case of a plural lexical possessor. Compare the following minimal pair:

(37) a. az ő diák -ja -i -k
    the he student-POSS-PL-3PL
    'their students'

   b. a fiúk diák -ja -i
    the boys student-POSS-PL
    'the boys' students'

Bartos (1999a) also found a second argument for the different morphological make-up of pronominal and lexical possessors. In coordinated possessive constructions the shared possession of a lexical possessor and a 1st or 2nd person pronominal possessor can undergo Right Node Raising, whereas the shared possession of a 3rd person pronoun and a 1st or 2nd person pronoun cannot do so:

(38) a. ?a Péter és a te diákjaid
    the Peter and the you student-POSS-PL-2SG
    'Peter's and your students'

b. * az ő és a te diákjaid
the he and the you student-POSS-PL-2SG
'his and your students'

In (38a) Right Node Raising is possible because, although the two possessed nouns to be represented by the same element are not identical (*diák-ja-i* versus *diák-ja-i-d*), at least one subsumes the other. In (38b), on the other hand, the two possessed nouns cannot be identified because they contain conflicting agreement morphemes (*diák-ja-i-0* versus *diák-ja-i-d*).

If lexical possessors have no agreement suffix, then presumably they do not pass through an AgrP projection; in fact, they do not even activate an AgrP. AgrP is only projected if the possessor has a person feature that needs checking, i.e., if it is a personal pronoun. The pronominal possessor moves from Spec,PossP to Spec,AgrP, as follows:

(39) $[_{DP} [_{D'} a [_{AgrP} te_i [_{Agr'} -d [_{NumP} -i- [_{PossP} t_i [_{Poss'} -ja- [_{NP} diák]]]]]]]]$

The pronominal possessor in Spec,AgrP apparently has its [+determiner] feature checked by merging into D.[8] Although first it lands in the specifier position of AgrP, it consists of a mere head (a D); this is why it is able to proceed into the checking domain of the matrix D. The possibility of a head category in non-head position merging into a head immediately preceding it has been demonstrated by Dobrovie-Sorin (1993) in connection with Romance clitics. The operation of head merge assumed by her is reanalysis-like in that it does not change the linear order of the adjacent heads involved. That is, (39) is mapped on (40):

(40) $[_{DP} [_{D'} a + te_i [_{AgrP} t_i [_{Agr'} -d [_{NumP} -i- [_{PossP} t_i [_{Poss'} -ja- [_{NP} diák]]]]]]]]$
        → a te diákjaid
        the your students

For those who allow the article of the possessed noun to be spelled out also in front of a possessor represented by a personal name, personal names can also undergo feature checking via head merge; after all, they are also mere heads (Ns raised to D position). That is:

(41) $[_{DP} [_{D'} a + Péter_i [_{NumP} -i- [_{PossP} t_i [_{Poss'} -ja- [_{NP} diák]]]]]] →$ a Péter diákjai
                                                        the Peter's students

Apparently, the dative-marked possessor also has a [+determiner] feature to check because it also has to be preposed into the checking domain of D. The specifiers of functional projections extending the noun phrase are not open to KPs

---

[8] The possibility of feature checking via head merge has been argued for by Alexiadou and Anagnostopoulou (1998).

and PPs (unlike the specifiers of clause-level functional projections). Therefore, the dative-marked possessor cannot land in Spec,DP; it can check its [+determiner] feature only in a DP-adjoined position. A constituent adjoined to DP does not block the spelling-out of the determiner:

(42)   [$_{DP}$Péternek$_i$ [$_{DP}$ a [$_{NumP}$ -i [$_{PossP}$ -ja- [$_{NP}$ diák t_i]]]]] → Péternek a   diákjai
                                                                      Peter-DAT the students
                                                                      'Peter's students'

Under these assumptions, the ungrammaticality of (15), containing a dative-marked pronominal possessor, can also be accounted for. If the pronominal possessor is realized as a dative-marked complement, it can move on from post-nominal position only to a DP-adjoined position, the specifiers of the intervening functional projections not being available to a KP. That is, it cannot pass through Spec,AgrP to have its [+person] feature checked. A possessor can only land in Spec,AgrP if it is caseless. A caseless possessor moved to Spec,AgrP and then merged with D, on the other hand, is not a possible target of adjunction to DP.

The distribution of *ez/az*, the case-marked demonstrative – problematic for the theory of Szabolcsi (1992a, 1992b, etc.) – also becomes more predictable under these assumptions. Consider again the relevant examples. To make it more transparent whether the demonstrative modifies – and shares the case of – the possessor or the possession, the possession will be in the accusative.

The demonstrative modifier of the possessed noun cannot co-occur with a lexical possessor consisting of a D/Num + NP sequence:

(43) a. * a   kisfiú ezt   a   barátját
           the boy   this-ACC the friend-POSS-ACC
           'this friend of the boy-ACC'

     b. * ezt   a   kisfiú barátját
           this-ACC the boy   friend-POSS-ACC
           'this friend-ACC of the boy'

         compare:

     c.   a   kisfiúnak ezt   a   barátját
           the boy-DAT this-ACC the friend-POSS-ACC
           'this friend-ACC of the boy'

A caseless possessor constituted by a personal name, on the other hand, can marginally follow a demonstrative, similarly to a possessor constituted by a personal pronoun:

(44) a. ? ezt   a   Mari barátját
           this-ACC the Mary friend-POSS-ACC
           'this friend-ACC of Mary's'

b. ezt   a te barátodat
this-ACC the you friend-POSS-2SG-ACC
'this friend-ACC of yours'

If we assume, following Kenesei (1992) and Bartos (1999a), that the *az/ez* demonstrative is generated in Spec,DP, then the only unexpected property of *az/ez* is that it requires the presence of a definite article in D, i.e., it is an exception to the principle 'Economize functional heads'. It follows that (43a,b) are ungrammatical – as their Spec,DP is doubly filled. In (43c), and (44a,b), on the other hand, Spec,DP is open for *ez*: in (43c) the possessor is adjoined to DP, whereas in (44a,b) it is merged with D.

Recall the other demonstrative-related constraint to be accounted for: the possessor can have a demonstrative modifier of its own only if it is in the dative; compare:

(45) a. * ez a lány barátját
        this the girl friend-POSS-ACC
        'this girl's friend-ACC'

    b. ennek a lánynak a barátját
        this-DAT the girl-DAT the friend-POSS-ACC
        'this girl's friend-ACC'

Bartos (2001) argues on the basis of independent considerations that *ez/az* must always be case-marked. This constraint explains why (45a) is ungrammatical: the possessor which *ez* modifies, and whose case it should share, is caseless. (Notice that an independently used *ez* cannot function as a caseless possessor either: **ez szín-e* 'the colour of this'.)

7.3.3   Agreement and anti-agreement in the possessive construction

The fact that only a pronominal possessor agrees with the possessed noun, and that a lexical possessor does not, is seen by Szabolcsi (1992a) and den Dikken (1999a) as a phenomenon analogous to the anti-agreement effect attested in the Welsh sentence. In fact, the Hungarian data include an additional complication. Whereas a lexical possessor referring to a plurality of possessors does bear a plural suffix, a 3rd person plural pronominal possessor lacks the plural marker expected: it is non-distinct from a singular 3rd person pronoun. Consider the relevant data again:

(46) a. az ő diák -ja -i -0   a professzor diák -ja -i
         the he student-POSS-PL-0   the professor student-POSS-PL
         'his students'   'the professor's students'

b. az ő diák -ja -i -k   a professzoro-k diák -ja -i
    the he student-POSS-PL-3PL   the professor -PL student-POSS-PL
    'their students'   'the professors' students'

Den Dikken (1999a) applies Rouveret's account of Welsh anti-agreement (Rouveret 1991) to Hungarian. Recall that in den Dikken's theory of the Hungarian possessive construction the caseless possessor is preposed into Spec,PossP. Den Dikken assumes that it does not move on from there to Spec,AgrP. The pronominal possessor is capable, nevertheless, of establishing an agreement relation with the Agr head via head movement. A crucial element of this explanation is the assumption that pronominal noun phrases project a NumP – unlike lexical noun phrases, which project a DP. The abstract Num head is claimed to require licensing via movement to a higher head. A Num embedded in a DP is licensed by raising to D. This is what happens in the case of lexical possessors in the possessive construction. The head of a pronominal possessor, on the other hand, has no D head to be raised to, hence it raises to Agr. That is:

(47) $[_{DP}$ az $[_{AgrP}$Agr + Num$_n$ $[_{PossP}$ $[_{NumP}$ t_n $[_{NP}$ pro/ő$]]$ $[_{Poss'}$ Poss ... diák ...$]]]]$

Den Dikken does not split a possessedness morpheme off the agreement morpheme (given that they are fused in many cases), i.e., he places the -ja suffix under the Agr head, and analyzes the -juk 3rd person plural suffix as Agr merged with Num. The fact that a 3rd person plural pronominal possessor lacks the usual -k plural marker is seen as prima facie evidence of Num-to-Agr movement: it is the -k missing on the pronoun that appears in Agr.

In case Spec,PossP is occupied by a lexical possessor, Agr is realized as a default 3rd person singular -ja – whether the possessor is in the singular or in the plural. Whereas a caseless lexical possessor does not reach Spec,AgrP in the projection, a dative-marked possessor skips it, moving directly to Spec,DP. Agr is realized as the default -ja in this case, too.

Despite its apparent success, some of the premises on which den Dikken's theory is built seem problematic. First, as was argued above, in Hungarian NumPs and DPs trigger different agreement paradigms on the V (DPs trigger the objective conjugation, including a definite object agreement marker; NumPs, on the other hand, trigger the subjective conjugation); hence, DPs and NumPs can easily be told apart. First and 2nd person pronominal objects trigger the indefinite conjugation, so they are indeed NumPs; 3rd person pronouns, however, clearly act like DPs: they require the objective conjugation. Bartos (1999a) also has a morphological argument against den Dikken's theory: he claims that the -juk ending on the possessed noun cannot be the combination of the -ja- suffix and the -k plural suffix, which would yield -jak. In fact, it is the regular phonological realization of the -ja-possession marker plus the -uk 3rd person plural agreement marker sequence.

The explanation of anti-agreement advocated by Bartos (1999a) and Szabolcsi (1992a, etc.), adopted from traditional descriptive literature, is nonetheless problematic. It is an explanation based on economy, stating that the plurality of the possessor can be marked only once: either on the head or on the possessor – but not on both. What it fails to explain is why plurality is marked on the possessor when the possessor is lexical, and why it is marked on the possessed noun when the possessor is pronominal – and not the other way round, for example. Furthermore, such redundancies are accepted in the language in other cases – e.g. a plural subject, whether pronominal or lexical, takes a verb with a 3rd person plural agreement marker.

Den Dikken (1999a) also provides an explanation of the optional agreement attested between a cleft lexical possessor and the possessed noun (compare (18) above). Consider the facts again:

(48) a.　A fiúknak　ellopták　a　labdá-já　-t.
　　　　the boys-DAT stole-they the ball　-POSS-ACC
　　　　'The boys' ball was stolen.'

　　 b.　A fiúknak　ellopták　a　labdá-j　**-uk** -at.
　　　　the boys-DAT stole-they the ball　-POSS-3PL-ACC
　　　　'The boys' ball was stolen.'

(49) a. * Nekik　ellopták　a　labdá-já　-t.
　　　　they-DAT stole-they the ball　-POSS-ACC
　　　　'Their ball was stolen.'

　　 b.　Nekik　ellopták　a　labdá-j　**-uk** -at.
　　　　they-DAT stole-they the ball　-POSS-3PL-ACC
　　　　'Their ball was stolen.'

In den Dikken's theory a -nak/nek-marked lexical possessor moves from its original small clause position directly to Spec,DP, without passing through Spec,Agr. If this is, indeed, the case then it is expected not to participate in agreement. This is what we attest in (48a). Only a pronominal possessor triggers agreement with the possessed noun; hence, the noun phrase with the agreeing possessum in (48b) must contain a null pronominal possessor. Den Dikken concludes that in (48b) the dative lexical noun phrase extracted into the VP domain is coindexed with a null resumptive pronoun, instead of a trace.

7.3.4　The non-specific possessive construction

As was argued in Section 7.3.2, the possession, uniquely identified by the possessor, projects a DP. The [+determiner] feature of the D head attracts the possessor, which must be raised to the domain of D – whether it is expressed by a caseless or dative-marked noun phrase. The caseless possessor lands in Spec,DP, whereas the dative-marked possessor is adjoined to DP. Indeed, an object constituted by a possessive construction containing a caseless or a dative-marked possessor always triggers the objective verb conjugation. (As was argued in Section 3.5.2, a definite object requires the presence of a -*(j)a/-j(a)/i* object agreement marker on the V. The agreement marker triggered by an indefinite object is phonologically empty.) Observe (50). (Since it is crucial that the possessor be internal to the object noun phrase, the object is preposed into Spec,FP, which takes a single constituent.)

(50)   Csak [$_{DP}$ egy diáknak [$_{DP}$ [$_{NumP}$ két [$_{PossP}$ dolgozatát]]]] talált-a /
        only   one student's   two   papers-ACC   found-DEF/
        * talált-0   jutalomra méltónak a   zsűri.
        * found-INDEF of.prize   worthy   the jury
        'The jury found only one student's two papers worthy of a prize.'

In the possessive construction in (50) both the possessum and the possessor are indefinite; still, the noun phrase is of the category DP, triggering the objective conjugation.

   Section 7.2 enumerated several verbs – those with the meaning component '(cause to) (come to) exist' – which require that their theme argument be represented by a non-specific NumP or an NP. Does that mean that these verbs do not allow their theme to be expressed by a possessive construction? Let us check:

(51) a.   Született Marinak   egy gyereke.
           was.born Mary-DAT a   child
           'A child was born to Mary.'

     b. * Csak Marinak   egy gyereke született.
           only Mary-DAT a   child   was.born
           'Only a child to Mary was born.'

     c.   Csak Marinak született egy gyereke.

Születik 'be born' is a verb requiring a non-specific argument. Example (51a) seems to suggest that it also accepts a possessive construction as its subject. However, this possessive construction fails the constituency test in (51b): it cannot be squeezed into the focus slot of the sentence. Evidently the possessor and the possessum are independent constituents in (51a) and (51c) alike. That is, if an argument is required to be represented by a non-specific noun phrase, its possessor, if any, must be external to it. It is clear why. The non-specific noun phrase cannot project a DP to harbor a possessor. A caseless possessor cannot survive in a position other than Spec,DP. A dative-marked possessor, on the other hand, is also viable on its own – it is not ruled out by the Case Filter. Therefore, it must be extraposed.

A dative-marked possessor – similar to the non-possessor complement of a nominal head – cannot remain in a post-head complement position. It must undergo obligatory extraposition, presumably because its case-marking would interfere with the case-marking of the matrix noun phrase. That is, a constraint of the following type must be at work in Hungarian:

(52)　　*The Case Constraint*
　　a.　　The case suffix must cliticize to the right edge of the noun phrase.
　　b.　　The case suffix cannot cliticize to a K or a P.

A case-marked possessor is subject to extraposition also when it is represented by a phonologically empty pro. Szabolcsi (1994a) based this claim on the following evidence. A possessive construction can be coordinated with a [–poss] noun phrase (53a). In (53b) the same coordinate structure is ungrammatical. The explanation for its ungrammaticality is that the pro possessor has been removed from one of the conjuncts, thus violating the coordinate structure constraint:

(53) a.　　Vizes lett　　a　kalapod　　és　a　sál.
　　　　　　wet　became the hat-POSS-2SG and the shawl
　　　　　　'Your hat and the shawl became wet.'

　　b.　*　Van kalapod　　és　sál.
　　　　　　is　hat-POSS-2SG and shawl
　　　　　　'There is a hat of yours and a shawl.'

With the possessor removed, the possessum in (51a,c) need not project a category higher than NumP. As the examples in (54), containing a plural lexical possessor, indicate, the possessum can optionally also agree with its extracted possessor, i.e., it is allowed to project an AgrP, as well, with a null resumptive pronoun in Spec,AgrP:

(54) a.　　A　fiúknak　　két　kabátja　　van.
　　　　　　the boys-DAT two coat-POSS are
　　　　　　'The boys have two coats.'

　　b.　　A　fiúknak　　két　kabátjuk　　　van.
　　　　　　the boys-DAT two coat-POSS-3PL are
　　　　　　'The boys have two coats.'

The structure assigned to the possessed noun phrase of (54b) is represented in (55) below. Apparently a noun phrase required to be non-specific can merge with any functional head up to Agr. The functional projections obligatorily associated with the feature [+specific] are QP, DemP, and DP.

(55)　　　　$[_{AgrP}$ pro$_i$ $[_{Agr'}$ -uk $[_{NumP}$ két $[_{PossP}$ $t_i[_{Poss'}$ -ja $[_{NP}$ kabát]]]]]]

The pro in Spec,AgrP is the phonologically empty equivalent of the Caseless 3rd person plural pronoun *ők* 'they'. The difference between the pro forced to leave the non-specific noun phrase in (53b), and that allowed to stay in it in (54b)/(55) is that the latter only has person and number, without also having Case, and represents an intermediate chain link, coindexed with a 'hanging topic'.

As Szabolcsi (1992a, 1992b) pointed out, the so-called verbs of possession in Hungarian are none other than the existential *van* 'be' and *nincs* 'not be' taking a subject with a possessor; for example:

(56) a. A fiúknak   van pénze.
         the boys-DAT is   money-POSS
         'The boys have money.'

     b. A fiúknak   van pro pénzük.
         the boys-DAT is   pro money-POSS-3PL
         'The boys have money.'

     c. Nekem nincs pénzem.
         I-DAT isn't money-POSS-1SG
         'I have no money.'

The existential verbs require a non-specific subject (similar to the English *there is*...), hence when their subject has a possessor, it is obligatorily extraposed, and always bears the *-nak/nek* dative suffix. The traditional analysis of the so-called possession verbs as two-place predicates taking a nominative and a dative complement is untenable – in part because it cannot explain why the alleged co-arguments can agree with each other.

7.4   Non-possessor arguments in the noun phrase

7.4.1   *The subject and object of the verbal stem in event noun phrases*

Whereas most nouns are incapable of assigning a theta role in themselves, without merging with a Poss head, deverbal nouns denoting a complex event preserve the theta role assigning capability of their verbal stem. Confirming Grimshaw's results (1990), Laczkó (1985, 1990, 1995a), Szabolcsi (1992b, 1994a), and Szabolcsi and Laczkó (1992) argue that Hungarian deverbal nouns derived by the suffix *-ás/és* under a complex event interpretation are associated essentially with the same theta-grid as their verbal stems. (This does not hold for deverbal nouns derived by *-ás/és* under the result reading.) The argument structure of the verbal stem, nevertheless, is realized in a modified form in the corresponding noun phrase – partly because the extended nominal projection provides only one structural Case, and partly because the Case Constraint prevents the possibility of post-nominal complements and adjuncts.

Whereas in the extended VP there are two structural Cases available for the encoding of arguments – Nominative and Accusative – in the extended NP only a single non-inherent case can be assigned – the Dative (provided the noun head is merged with Poss). Thus, in the case of an event nominal derived from a verb taking a mere subject, the subject is realized as a possessor; for example:

(57) a. Mari énekel.
         Mary sings

     b. Mari(nak az) éneklése
         Mary(DAT the) singing-POSS
         'Mary's singing'

When nominalizing a transitive verb, the object is expressed as the possessor, and the agent subject can optionally appear as an *által* 'by' phrase:

(58) a. Mari el énekli a dalt.
         Mary VM sings the song-ACC

     b. a dal(nak) (Mari által való) eléneklése
         the song(DAT) (Mary by being) singing
         'the singing of the song by Mary'

(*Való* is originally a participial form of the verb *van* 'be', which has been grammaticalized as an adjectivalizer turning the argument or adjunct of an event nominal into a premodifier.[9]) The expression of the subject is not always optional; a non-human agent or experiencer, or a force often cannot be omitted upon nominalization; compare:

(59) a. A betegek méh által való megcsípése veszélyes.
         the sick   bee by   being stinging-POSS dangerous
         'The stinging of the sick by a bee is dangerous.'

     b. A betegek megcsípése veszélyes.
         the sick   stinging-POSS dangerous
         'The stinging of the sick is dangerous.'

(60) a. Hallatszik a szél(nek a) fújása.
         is.heard the wind-DAT the blowing-POSS
         'The blowing of the wind can be heard.'

     b. Hallatszik a fújás.[10]
         is.heard the blowing
         'The blowing can be heard.'

---

[9] For details, see Laczkó (1995b).
[10] The examples and the argumentation have been adopted from Szabolcsi (1994a).

The non-human subject of the verb stem (whether agent, force, or experiencer) cannot be omitted in the course of nominalization because if it is omitted, the missing subject is reconstructed as [+human]. Thus, *a betegek megcsípése* in (59b) can only mean the stinging of sick people by humans. The missing argument in (60b), too, can only be reconstructed as a person instead of the wind.

Szabolcsi and Laczkó (1992) and Szabolcsi (1994a) explain this fact as follows. In the case of an event nominal, the external argument of the verbal stem not expressed lexically must be realized as a PRO. The PRO argument of a noun, just like that of a verb, is either controlled by a matrix argument – as happens, for example, in (61b) – or is interpreted as PRO$_{arb}$.

(61) a.   Bízom a   beteg   gyógyulásában.
          I.trust the patient's recovery.in
          'I trust in the patient's recovery.'

     b.   Bízom a   gyógyulásban.
          I.trust the recovery.in
          'I trust in the recovery.'

The control of the PRO argument of a nominal head is possible only in the presence of an appropriate 'control' predicate such as *elkezd* 'start', *folytat* 'continue', *befejez* 'finish', *abbahagy* 'stop', *megtagad* 'refuse', *un* 'be bored with', etc. None of these predicates happens to be able to control the force PRO of an event nominal. There being no potential controller either in (59b) or in (60b), only a PRO$_{arb}$ reading is possible. PRO$_{arb}$, however, is known to require a [+human] interpretation universally – hence its referent cannot be identified with a bee.

A further question is where the invisible PRO argument is located. In the noun phrase structure proposed by Szabolcsi and Laczkó (1992) and Szabolcsi (1994a) there is no room for a PRO argument, hence they suggest that PRO is realized merely in the lexicon without appearing in syntax. The noun phrase structure proposed in the previous sections of this chapter does in fact provide room for a PRO argument. It is plausible to assume that PRO has an underspecified [+person] feature, hence it triggers the projection of an AgrP, whose specifier it occupies, checking the underspecified [+person] feature of Agr.

7.4.2   Oblique arguments and adjuncts

The lexically case-marked arguments and adjuncts of the nominal head would be expected to follow the head (as also happens in the verb phrase) – if the Case Constraint were not in effect. Since the Case Constraint in (52) blocks this possibility, there are two options left: the argument or adjunct must be realized as a modifier, or it must be extraposed. (These are the options that are also available for the adjuncts of nouns denoting other than complex events.) Extraposition is in fact not completely free; there must be some kind of (ill-understood) compatibility between the extraposed complement and the argument structure of the matrix verb. Extraposition is easier with adjuncts than with arguments; compare:

(62) a. ? [A beszélgetés t_i] nagyon   tetszett   a művésznővel$_i$.
         the interview   very.much pleased.me the artist-with
         'The interview with the artist pleased me very much.'

   b. [A művésznővel való beszélgetés t_i] nagyon   tetszett   a TV-ben$_i$.
      the artist-with   being interview   very.much pleased.me the TV-in
      'The interview with the artist on the TV pleased me very much.'

The regular, fully productive way of legitimizing a lexically case-marked complement is to insert it into an adjectival phrase headed by *való* or *történő*, or by some other contentful participle. This is what happens to the complement of the noun *beszélgetés* 'interview' in (62b), while its adjunct is extraposed. Observe the structure attributed to a noun taking a complement or adjunct formulated as a premodifier. Only one of the two adjacent definite articles is pronounced.[11] It is an open question whether the argument in premodifier position, or the PRO assumed, binds a trace in complement position.

(63)

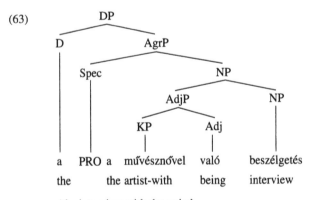

'the interview with the artist'

Arguments and adjuncts of the category PP can also be adjectivalized by being inserted into an AdjP headed by the suffix *-i*, to be cliticized to P:

---

[11] This phonological rule is a limited version of the D-deletion rule proposed by Szabolcsi (1992a, Szabolcsi and Laczkó 1992). This rule is triggered only by two adjacent definite articles.

(64)

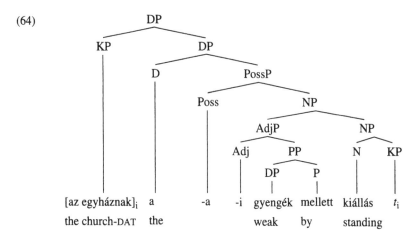

→ az egyháznak a gyengék melletti kiállása
'the church's espousal of the weak'

Certain lexically case-marked arguments can apparently also precede the head noun without being adjectivalized:

(65) a.   a   piacra   menés
        the market-to going
        'the going to market'

     b.   az   ágyban fekvés
        the bed-in lying
        'the lying in bed'

These arguments are heads incorporated into the verb prior to nominalization; i.e., the noun phrases in (65a,b) have been derived by the nominalization of complex N + V units. Whereas a lexically case-marked argument does not lose its case ending, an incorporated object undergoes nominalization without its accusative case ending:

(66) a.   János újságot   olvas.
        John newspaper-ACC reads
        'John is newspaper-reading'

     b.   János újságolvasása
        John newspaper-reading-POSS
        'John's newspaper-reading'

7.5   Summary

Three different noun phrase projections have to be distinguished in Hungarian syntax: the NP, a lexical projection with a predicative function; and its extensions by operators expressing various quantifying-identifying functions, the indefinite NumP and the definite DP. The three noun phrase projections have different distributions across sentence positions and across predicate types, and also figure in various syntactic and morphosyntactic constraints. (For example, the object triggers a definite object agreement on the V if and only if it is represented by a DP.)

The possessive relation is marked primarily on the possessum – by a possessedness suffix – and in cases where the possessor is a pronominal, also by an Agr marker. The possessor can be realized as a dative-marked complement or as a caseless determiner. The Case-assigner of the dative possessor is the possessedness suffix, whereas its theta-role assigner is the possessed noun + possessedness suffix complex. The possession, uniquely identified by the possessor, projects a DP. The caseless possessor moves to Spec,DP, whereas the dative-marked possessor is adjoined to DP in order to check the [+determiner] feature of D. A pronominal possessor checks the [+determiner] feature of D by merging into the article realizing D.

The full possessive construction is always definite. An argument required by the subcategorization properties of its predicate to be non-specific can only be represented by a possessive construction if the possessor is extraposed. The so-called possession sentence of Hungarian contains the verb *van* 'be' and an obligatorily non-specific subject with its dative-marked possessor extraposed.

The argument-taking capabilities of nominal heads are limited. Event nominals derived from verbs can keep only one of their arguments marked with a structural case, which will be realized as a possessor. The subject of a nominalized transitive verb can only be expressed as a *by*-phrase or as a controlled or arbitrary PRO. Arguments in oblique cases and adjuncts can join the nominal head as adjectivalized premodifiers, or under appropriate circumstances they can be extraposed.

8

The postpositional phrase

8.1   Restricting the category of postpositions

In traditional Hungarian grammars postpositions form a large and varied class, including postpositions taking a noun phrase complement with a lexical case (1a), idiomatic participles taking a noun phrase complement with a lexical case (1b), and postpositions taking a caseless noun phrase complement (1c).

(1) a.   Jánossal **együtt**
          John-with together
          'together with John'

    b.   termetére   **nézve**
          on.his.stature looking
          'concerning his stature'

    c.   János **mellett**
          John near
          'near John'

As Marácz (1986a, 1989) noted, the presence versus absence of lexical case on the complement of the postposition correlates with another property: a postposition taking a caseless noun phrase complement – e.g. that in (2c) – may bear an agreement marker corresponding to the person and number of its complement. Postpositions taking a case-marked complement, e.g. those in (2a,b), on the other hand, cannot be combined with an agreement suffix.[1]

(2) a.   veled   együtt
          with.you together
          'together with you'

---

[1] Marácz (1986a, 1989) analyzed the apparently caseless noun phrase complement of postpositions to be in the nominative. He noticed that the lack of lexical case on the complement correlates with the presence of agreement on the postposition, which led him to the conclusion that the complement without a case suffix bears nominative case licensed by inflection.

b. rád   nézve
    on.you looking
    'concerning you'

    but:

c. te   mellett-**ed**
    you near-2SG
    'near you'

The categories illustrated in (1a), (1b), and (1c) differ not only in the presence
or absence of a case suffix on their complement, and in the presence or absence
of an agreement marker on their head. In type (1a) the order of the head and
the complement can be reversed; in type (1b) and (1c), on the other hand, this is
impossible:

(3) a. együtt Jánossal
    b. * nézve termetére
    c. * mellett János

Furthermore, degree adverbs modifying phrases of type (1a) immediately precede
the head of the phrase, whereas those modifying phrases of type (1c) precede
the whole construction. Phrases of type (1b) do not usually tolerate an adverb of
degree, but if they accept one, it is adjoined to the whole construction; compare:

(4) a. Jánossal **teljesen**   együtt
        John-with completely together
        'completely together with John'

    b. * **teljesen** Jánossal együtt

(5) a. * januártól   **egészen** kezdve
        January-from quite   beginning

    b. **egészen** januártól kezdve
        'beginning quite from January'

(6) a. * János **pontosan** mellett
        John   exactly   next.to

    b. **pontosan** János mellett
        'exactly next to John'

The different status of the three types of postpositions becomes particularly clear
if their noun phrase complement is supplied with a demonstrative:

(7) a. azzal   a fiúval   **együtt**
        that-with the boy-with together
        'together with that boy'

b. attól   a   perctől   **kezdve**
    that-from the minute-from beginning
    'since that minute'

c. az **alatt** a fa **alatt**
    that under the tree under
    'under that tree'

Whereas the postposition in (7c), taking a caseless complement, is copied both on the demonstrative and on the head noun, the postpositions in (7a,b), taking a complement with a lexical case, are spelled out only once.[2]

These heterogeneous properties make it highly questionable that the elements illustrated in (1a–c) are representatives of one and the same syntactic category. In fact, the type of postpositions illustrated in (1a) do not differ in any significant respect from adverbs; to all appearances they are adverbs taking an argument. *Együtt* 'together', when occurring without an argument, is analyzed as an adverb in traditional grammars. The fact that it is occasionally complemented with an overt noun phrase should not affect its categorization.[3] The handful of idiomatic participles, on the other hand, do not differ in any significant respect from participles proper. Even though they must follow their complement (compare (3b)), this is a consequence of the fact that their complement occupies verb modifier

[2] This fact was observed and interpreted as evidence of the Kase-like status of postpositions with a caseless complement by Kenesei (1992).

[3] There is a single problem case: *képest* 'compared to'. It is adverb-like in that it cannot bear an agreement marker; it requires a noun phrase complement in the allative case (see (i)–(ii)); and it is not spelled out twice when merging with a noun phrase containing a demonstrative (iii). On the other hand, unlike adverbs of type (1a), it cannot precede its complement (iv), and cannot be separated from it by a modifier (v).

(i)   hozzám képest
       to.me   compared
       'compared to me'

(ii)   Jánoshoz képest
       John-to compared
       'compared to John'

(iii) ahhoz   a   fiúhoz képest
       that-to the boy-to compared
       'compared to that boy'

(iv)   * képest   Jánoshoz
         compared John-to

(v)   * Jánoshoz egészen   képest
         John-to   completely compared

We can predict all these properties if we categorize *képest* as an adverb obligatorily incorporating its complement.

position, as usually happens in the case of idioms. Therefore, in the present analysis the elements illustrated in (1a) are analyzed as adverbs, those illustrated in (1b) are categorized as participles, and the class of postpositions is restricted to the elements illustrated in (1c).

8.2   The formal properties of postpositional phrases

8.2.1   Distribution

If we exclude from the category of postpositions both heads taking a noun phrase with a lexical case, and participles, then we arrive at a syntactically homogeneous class of entities, including: *alá* 'to under', *alatt* 'under', *alól* 'from under', *elé* 'to before', *előtt* 'before', *elől* 'from before', *felé* 'towards', *felől* 'from', *fölé* 'to above', *fölött* 'above', *fölül* 'from above', *köré* 'round', *körül* 'around', *közé* 'between', *között* 'in between', *közül* 'from between', *által* 'by', *ellen* 'against', *ellenére* 'despite', *helyett* 'instead of', *szerint* 'according to', *iránt* 'towards', *miatt* 'because of', *nélkül* 'without', *után* 'after', *végett* 'because of', and *révén* 'by means of'. These postpositions take a caseless noun phrase complement (1c), which they follow (3c), and to which they are adjacent (6a,b). If their complement is pronominal, they bear an agreement marker (2c).

The order and the strict adjacency of the postposition and its complement seem reminiscent of the relation of a noun phrase and its case ending, which constitute a word. The prosody of PPs is also similar to that of KPs: the postposition, like a case ending, is unstressed. At the same time, however, coordinated PPs also allow the ellipsis of either the postposition or the complement, which is impossible in the case of coordinated KPs; compare:

(8) a.   a ház előtt és a ház mögött   → a ház előtt és mögött
          the house before and the house behind   the house before and behind
                                                       'before and behind the house'

  b.   * a háztól   és a házból   → * a háztól   és -ból
          the house-ABLATIVE and the house-ELATIVE   the house-ABLATIVE and ELATIVE
                                                         'from inside and from outside the house'

(9) a.   a ház előtt és a garázs előtt   → a ház és a garázs előtt
          the house before and the garage before   the house and the garage before
                                                        'before the house and the garage'

  b.   * a háznál   és a garázsnál   → * a ház- és a
          the house-ADESSIVE and the garage-ADESSIVE   the house and the
                                                         garázsnál
                                                         garage-ADESSIVE
                                                         'at the house and the garage'

The ellipsis attested in (8a) and (9a) does not, in fact, refute the morphosyntactic wordhood of the noun phrase + P unit. Compounds and even derived words consisting of a stem and a sufficiently heavy suffix may allow word-internal ellipsis under certain conditions; for example:

(10) a. orvosképzés   és -továbbképzés
         doctor-education and continuing-education
         'doctors' training and continuing training'

     b. orvos- és bábaképzés
         doctor and midwife-education
         'doctors' and midwives' training'

     c. feleség- és anyaként
         wife   and mother-ESSIVE
         'as wife and mother'

The crucial difference between a noun phrase + P combination and a noun phrase + K combination seems to be that the wordhood of the latter also extends to the level of morphophonology. Whereas the vowel quality of postpositions is invariable, case endings have developed allomorphs, and participate in vowel harmony.

Following Grimshaw (1991), van Riemsdijk (1998), and, with respect to Hungarian, Payne and Chisarik (2000), let us assume that postpositions, similar to cases, are functional (or semi-lexical) heads extending a noun phrase, relating its referent to the predicate semantically, hence enabling the noun phrase to function as an argument or adjunct. The analysis of the PP as a functional extension of the noun phrase is supported by the fact that the clause-internal position of a PP is determined by the referential properties of its noun phrase complement. For example, just as a bare NP is excluded from a postverbal argument position (see the discussion of the 'referentiality effect' in Section 3.2), an NP dominated by a PP cannot stand there either; it must be preposed into the preverbal section of the sentence:

(11) a. * A gyerekek elbújtak farakás   mögé.
           the children hid   wood-stack behind

     b. Az egyik gyerek FARAKÁS   MÖGÉ bújt (el), a   másik gyerek BOKOR MÖGÉ.
         the one   child wood-stack behind hid (VM) the other child bush behind
         'One of the children hid BEHIND A WOOD-STACK, the other one, BEHIND A BUSH.'

The parallelism between the syntactic position of K and that of P in the extended noun projection is also evident in their parallel behavior when merging with a noun phrase containing a demonstrative. Both a P and a K must be copied on the demonstrative, as well:

(12) a.   ennél   a   háznál
            this-ADESSIVE the house-ADESSIVE
            'at this house'

     b.   e   mellett a   ház   mellett
            this near   the house near
            'near this house'

8.2.2   Agreement and anti-agreement phenomena

If the complement of the postposition is a personal pronoun, then the postposition will bear an agreement marker. Apparently, a pronominal complement has a person feature to check, and therefore the PP must project an AgrP. Observe the full paradigm:

(13)   én mellett-em   mi mellett-ünk
         I   near -1SG   we near   -1PL
         'near me'   'near u͂s'

         te mellett-ed   ti   mellett-etek
         you near -2SG   you near   -2PL
         'near you'   'near you'

         ő mellett-e   ő mellett-ük
         he near -3SG   he near -3PL
         'near him'   'near them'

The inflection appearing on the P is identical with the inflection appearing on the possessed noun in the case of a pronominal possessor. Compare the possessive agreement paradigm, repeated in (14), with the postpositional agreement paradigm in (13). Not only are the suffixes the same, but there is also no plural -*k* suffix on the 3rd person plural pronominal complement/possessor.

(14)   az én nev -em   a   mi nev -ünk
         the I   name-POSS-1SG the we name-POSS-1PL
         'my name'   'our name'

         a te nev -ed   a ti   nev -etek
         the you name-POSS-2SG the you name-POSS-2PL
         'your name'   'your name'

         az ő nev -e   az ő nev -ük
         the he name-POSS-3SG   the he name-POSS-3PL
         'his name'   'their name'

Recall that possessive inflection consists of a possessedness suffix and an agreement marker sometimes fused, sometimes – e.g. in the plural – kept apart; compare:

(15) az én nev -e -i -m 'my names'   a mi nev -e -i -nk
      the I name-POSS-PL-1SG   the we name-POSS-PL-1PL

      a te nev -e -i -d   a ti nev -e -i -tek
      the you name-POSS-PL-2SG   the you name-POSS-PL-2PL

      az ő nev -e -i -0   az ő nev -e -i -k
      the he name-POSS-PL-3SG   the he name-POSS-PL-3PL

The identity of the two inflection paradigms would suggest that the postposition also bears both a possessedness suffix and an agreement marker. However, if the postposition and its complement would, indeed, realize a possessive relation, then the possessedness suffix should also be present on the postposition in the case of a non-pronominal, lexical possessor. In the case of a lexical complement, however, the postposition bears no suffix. Compare a lexical possessor–possession relation with a noun phrase–postposition relation:

(16) a. Péter nev -e   b. Péter mellett
         Peter name-POSS   Peter near
         'Peter's name'   'near Peter'

In fact, as Marácz (1986a) noted, the possessedness marker can also appear on a postposition with a complement other than a personal pronoun – but only if the possessor has been extracted:

(17) a. Kinek   futottál után-**a**?
         who-DAT ran-you after-POSS
         'Whom did you run after?'

     b. A fiúknak   szép   jövő áll   előtt -**ük**.
         the boys-DAT beautiful future stands ahead-POSS-3PL
         'A beautiful future is ahead of the boys.'

As in the case of possessive constructions, agreement between the extracted complement and the postposition is optional. Thus, in addition to (17b), (18) is also possible, in which the postposition bears a possessedness suffix without an agreement marker:

(18) A fiúknak   szép   jövő áll   előtt -**e**.
      the boys-DAT beautiful future stands ahead-POSS
      'A beautiful future is ahead of the boys.'

If we extend the analysis of the possessive construction to PPs, the non-agreeing pattern in (18) is an instance of plain extraction. Example (17b), on the other hand, contains a pro possessor (the trigger of agreement), and a hanging-topic-like lexical possessor generated outside the possessive construction, and coindexed with pro.

Let us attempt to assign to the different types of Hungarian postpositional phrases structures from which their properties discussed in Sections 2.1 and 2.2 follow without any stipulations.

8.3   The structure of the postpositional phrase

A postpositional phrase extending a lexical noun phrase is assigned the following structure:

(19)

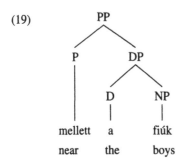

The assumed underlying order has been constructed in observance of the principle that syntactic heads precede their complements. That is, the PP is syntactically a prepositional phrase; P will turn into a postposition only in the morphological component. Traditionally, the noun phrase complement of a postposition is assumed to be preposed into Spec,PP. That approach, however, could not account for the case-suffix-like properties of the Hungarian postposition; for example, it could not explain its behavior in constructions of type (12b), involving a P taking a noun phrase modified by a demonstrative, in which the postposition is copied both on the demonstrative and on the head noun. Therefore, we will rather extend the analysis of case projections (KPs) proposed by Bartos (1999a) to postpositional phrases. We will assume – in the spirit of Minimalism – that the syntactic relation of a P and its noun phrase complement is a non-linearized relation in abstract space. It becomes linearized with the P following the noun phrase as a consequence of the [+suffix] feature of P, which corresponds to the linearization command 'right-adjoin to the lexical head of the projection'. The feature [+suffix] of the postposition also accounts for the invariable surface order and the obligatory adjacency of the noun phrase complement and the postposition. In this framework, both P and K(ase) share the same [+suffix] morphosyntactic feature, and the closer unity of the noun phrase + Kase sequence is of a morphophonological nature.

A P with a pronoun or pro complement bears an agreement suffix. From a Minimalist perspective, if the PP is extended into an AgrP, the [+person] feature of

Agr must be checked against that of a pronoun. (Recall from the discussion of agreement in the noun phrase in Section 7.3.3 that we attribute a [+person] feature only to personal pronouns.[4]) As was pointed out above, the agreement marker of postpositions with a pronominal complement is also merged with a possessedness suffix. This is particularly clear in 3rd person singular, where the agreement suffix is null, and the *-(j)a/(j)e* morpheme appearing on the P is the bare possessedness suffix. (The *-ja/je* appearing on 3rd person singular verbs in the definite conjugation, on the other hand, is the object agreement marker.) The possessedness suffix, capable of assigning/licensing dative case and a theta role, does not appear to play a syntactic or semantic role in this case (the noun phrase receives its theta role from P, and it does not need a case word-internally). Therefore, let us assume that the presence of the possessedness morpheme is merely phonologically motivated: given that the agreement and possessedness morphemes (not separated by a plural suffix) are fused phonologically, the presence of one also brings about the presence of the other. Syntactically, however, Agr and Poss represent a single projection. That is, we assign to a PP containing a pronominal complement, e.g. to *én mellettem* 'near me', the following structure:

(20)

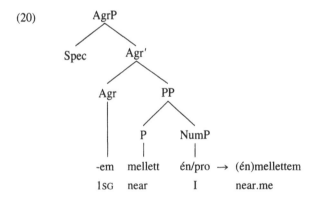

The [+suffix] features of Agr and P result in a complete reversal of the underlying order represented in (20). (That is, in the proposed approach, the pronoun does not move overtly to Spec,AgrP.)

Historically, the postpositions under investigation were all case-marked nouns, expressing relative location, used in genitive constructions (meaning 'at the head

---

[4] For a different analysis of the distribution of agreement across Hungarian PP types, see Ackerman (1987). In his analysis, the agreement marker appearing on the postposition in the case of a pronominal complement is the incorporated pronoun itself. This account can explain the lack of agreement in the case of a lexical complement, but has difficulties, for example, with the cleft PP, whose head always bears inflection, whether its removed complement is lexical or pronominal; see (17)–(18) above.

of . . . , at the bottom of . . .', etc.). They developed their [+suffix] feature after
their locative case-ending had become obsolete. According to the evidence of the
cleft PP construction illustrated in (17)–(18), the [+suffix] feature is still not an
obligatory attribute of them. They can also be marked as [–suffix], in which case
their complement needs case; the PP must, therefore, be extended into a PossP
projection so that Poss can assign dative case to the complement of P; that is:

(21)

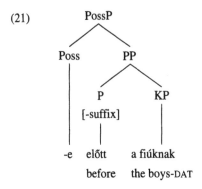

The Case Constraint forces the KP complement to be adjoined to PossP, from
where it can be extracted into the matrix syntactic domain (22a). If the head of the
cleft PP projects an AgrP as well, in addition to PossP, then the complement of P
must be represented by a pro, coindexed with a PP-external dative noun phrase.
This is how the 'agreeing' variant of the cleft PP construction is derived (22b).

(22) a.   A fiúknak$_i$ szép   jövő áll   [$_{PossP}$ t_i [$_{PossP}$ előtt -e t_i]]
           the boys-DAT beautiful future stands   ahead-POSS
           'A beautiful future is ahead of the boys.'

    b.   A fiúknak$_i$ szép   jövő áll   [$_{AgrP}$ pro$_i$ [$_{PossP}$ előtt -ük]]
          the boys-DAT beautiful future stands   ahead-POSS.3PL
          'A beautiful future is ahead of the boys.'

The complement of P is extraposed if either the complement or the remnant PP is
intended to play an operator role in itself. In (17) the complement of P, a *wh*-phrase,
has been focussed; in (22) it has been topicalized. Most often the complement of
P is extracted so that the remnant PP, consisting of a mere head, can function as a
verb modifier; for example:

(23) a.   [$_{AspP}$ [t_i Utána]   futottam a fiúknak$_i$]
                      after-POSS ran-I   the boys-DAT
           'I ran after the boys.'

    b.   [$_{AspP}$ [pro$_i$ Utánuk]   futottam a fiúknak$_i$]
                     after-POSS-3PL ran-I   the boys-DAT
          'I ran after the boys.'

The construction in (21), containing a [–suffix] postposition combined with a Poss morpheme, is acceptable in present-day Hungarian only if the dative-marked complement of P is extraposed:

(24) a. * A fiúknak   előtte   szép   karrier áll.
        the boys-DAT before-POSS beautiful career stands
        'The boys have a beautiful career ahead of them.'

        compare:

     b.   A fiúk előtt szép karrier áll.

The fact that a P can be analyzed as a [–suffix] head only in a context that excludes the possibility of a [+suffix] analysis may follow from economy considerations.

8.4   PPs as verb modifiers

If the referential complement of the postposition has been extracted, the remnant PP can be assigned a [+V(erb)M(odifier)] feature. The assignment of a [+VM] feature to a postposition is very common, but is subject to a constraint; compare (25), (26), and (27). In the case of (25), the (b) version, involving a cleft PP with the P acting as a VM, is even more common and more unmarked than the (a) version. In the case of (26), the (b) version is slightly marked, whereas in the case of (27) it is totally impossible.

(25) a. János a cél   mellé   lőtt.
        John the target beside shot
        'John shot beside the target.'

     b. János mellé   lőtt a célnak.
        John beside-POSS shot the target-DAT[5]

(26) a. János Mari mellett állt.
        John Mary by   stood
        'John stood by Mary.'

     b. János mellette   állt   Marinak.
        John beside-POSS stood Mary-DAT

(27) a. János futott Mari mellől.
        John ran   Mary near-from
        'John ran from Mary.'

     b. * János mellőle   futott Marinak.
        John near-from-POSS ran   Mary-DAT

---

[5] The -e possessedness suffix is only morphosyntactically present; phonologically it is fused with the -é stem vowel.

The PPs in (25)–(27) have different theta roles. That in (25) expresses a goal, that in (26) expresses a location, whereas that in (27) expresses a source. Interestingly the adverbs unambiguously identified as verb modifiers by native speakers – *ki* 'out', *be* 'in', *le* 'down to', *fel* 'up to', *el* 'away', *át* 'across', *rá* 'onto', *ide* 'to here', *oda* 'to there', *össze* 'together', *vissza* 'back', *szerte* 'apart', *szét* 'apart', etc. – also all denote a goal in their primary meaning (even if this fact cannot always be expressed by their English translations). The verb modifier status of adverbs expressing location such as *kint* 'outside', *bent* 'inside', *lent* 'down', *fent* 'up', *itt* 'here', *ott* 'there' is less clear; some grammars include them in the class of verb modifiers, others do not, and native speakers also hesitate as to whether to spell a location adverb + verb sequence as one word (as must be done if the adverb is a verb modifier), or as two words. No source adverb such as *kintről* 'from outside', *lentről* 'from down', *innen* 'from here', *onnan* 'from there' has ever become a verb modifier.

These facts are related to the aspectual operator function of the verb modifier. A verb modifier raised to Spec,AspP, its canonical position, serves primarily to specify the aspect of the action described in the VP, i.e., to express whether the given action is to be looked upon as an action completed, or as an action in progress. Most bare verbs denote a process; for example:

(28)   János futott.
        John ran

If the V is supplemented with a goal complement, the VP also allows a perfective interpretation – because an action with an endpoint can be looked upon as either an action in progress or as an action completed; for example:

(29)   János a   fa   alá   futott.
        John the tree to.under ran
   a.   'John ran/has run (to) under the tree.'
   b.   'John was running (to) under the tree.'

If the complement of the postposition is extraposed, then the remnant PP marked as [+VM] will move to Spec,AspP, and will eventually be incorporated into the V. If a verb incorporates its goal complement, then its interpretation becomes unambiguously perfective. The incorporated postposition in (30a) has the same perfectivizing effect that the regular verbal prefix has in (30b):

(30) a.   János alá   futott a   fának.
          John to.under-POSS ran   the tree-DAT
          'John ran/has run under the tree.'

b. János oda   futott a   fa   alá.
    John to.there ran   the tree under
    'John ran/has run under the tree.'

An incorporated postposition of a location role, on the other hand, turns a VP unambiguously progressive. Compare the following sentences:

(31) a. János fut   a   patak mellett, és légzőgyakorlatokat   végez.
         John runs the stream near   and breathing.exercises-ACC does
         'John runs near the stream and does breathing exercises.'

    b.   János mellette fut a   pataknak, és légzőgyakorlatokat   végez.
         John near-POSS runs the stream-DAT and breathing.exercises-ACC does
         'John is running near the stream and is doing breathing exercises.'

Although the V *fut* 'run' denotes a process, the aspect of the VP of the first clause of (31a) need not be progressive. The two processes in the two clauses need not be simultaneous; they can also be consecutive – because both clauses can refer for example to regular activities. That is, the aspect of the sentence can be general imperfective rather than progressive.[6] The incorporated location adverb in (31b), on the other hand, anchors the process in space and time; hence, the sentence will only allow a progressive interpretation. The same aspectual interpretation can also be achieved by a regular VM expressing location, i.e., the meaning of the first clause of (31b) is identical with that of (32):

(32)   János ott   fut a   patak mellett.
        John there runs the stream near
        'John is running near the stream.'

An adverb or a PP of a source function does not make a good VM because aspectual interpretation – e.g. the progressive or perfective nature of the VP – does not depend on whether or not the starting point of the action is named. Thus, the interpretation of the following sentences is independent of whether or not they contain a source PP; it is determined by the presence or lack of a perfectivizing VM.

(33) a. János futott a   fa   alól.
         John ran   the tree from.under
         'John was running from under the tree.'

    b.   János el   futott a   fa   alól.
         John away ran   the tree from.under
         'John ran/has run from under the tree.'

We can summarize our observations in the form of the following generalization:[7]

(34)   A source constituent cannot assume a [+VM] feature.

---

[6] On the imperfective and progressive aspects in Hungarian, see Kiefer (1994a).
[7] For further details, see É. Kiss (1999a).

8.5   Case-marked pronouns or PPs?

Hungarian personal pronouns supplied with a lexical case surface as pro + case + agreement sequences.[8] If they are set into a contrast, the pro element is replaced by a pronoun; for example:

(35)   én + val/vel = (én)-vel-em 'with me'   mi + val/vel = (mi)-vel-ünk
      I   INSTR   (I) -with-1SG   we   INSTR   (we)-with-1PL

      te + val/vel = (te)-vel-ed   ti + val/vel = (ti)-vel-etek
      you INSTR   (you)-with-2SG   you INSTR   (you)-with-2PL

      ő + val/vel = (ő)-vel-e   ők + val/vel = (ő)-vel-ük
      he INSTR   (he)-with-3SG   he.PL INSTR   (he)-with-3PL

(36)   én + nál/nél = (én)-nál-am 'at me'   mi + nál/nél = (mi)-nál-unk
      I ADESSIVE   (I)-at-1SG   we ADESSIVE   (we)-at-1PL

      te + nál/nél = (te)-nál-ad   ti + nál/nél = (ti)-nál-atok
      ő + nál/nél = (ő)-nál-a   ők + nál/nél = (ő)-nál-uk

For traditional Hungarian grammars these forms are morphological idiosyncrasies. However, having analyzed the syntactic behavior of PPs, we cannot fail to notice that the strings in (35)–(36) have the same structure as postpositional phrases with a pronominal complement. Historically, lexical case endings were, in fact, postpositions – as is demonstrated by the following fragment from *Tihanyi alapítólevél* 'Tihany Deed of Foundation' from 1055, in which the present-day sublative suffix *-ra/re* is represented by the postposition *rea*:

(37)   feheruuaru rea meneh hodu   utu rea
      Fehérvár   onto going military road onto
      'on the military road going to Fehérvár'

Towards the end of the Middle Ages such postpositions became cliticized to the lexical head to which they were adjoined, forming a morphophonological word with it. They became subject to vowel harmony, and started developing allomorphs. Hungarian being a pro-drop language, a postposition attached to a pronominal should nearly always have cliticized to a phonologically empty head, which is obviously impossible. In such cases cliticization did not take place, and the postposition preserved its category. That is, Hungarian has no personal pronouns bearing a lexical case; it has postpositions with a pro or pronoun complement instead.

---

[8] On the structure and derivation of the accusative forms of 1st and 2nd person pronouns (*engem* 'me', *téged* 'you', *minket/bennünket* 'us', *titeket/benneteket* 'you'), see den Dikken (1999b).

Lexical case endings seem to have preserved their P status in another context as well: in PPs having their complement extraposed, functioning as verb modifiers; compare:

(38) a. János [$_{AspP}$ ért-ük   ment a   gyerekekért az óvodába]
John   for-POSS-3PL went the children-for the kindergarten-to
'John went for the children to the kindergarten.'

b. János [$_{AspP}$ nek-i   szaladt egy járókelőnek]
John   into-POSS ran   a   passer.by-into
'John ran into a passer-by.'

c. János [$_{AspP}$ rá   vágott a   kerítésre]^9
John   on-POSS struck the fence-on
'John struck at the fence.'

d. János [$_{AspP}$ bel-e   szólt a   beszélgetésbe]
John   into-POSS spoke the discussion-into
'John spoke in(to) the discussion.'

It is not immediately obvious if the postposition-like element in the Spec,AspP of these sentences is a verb modifier lexically selected by the verb, or if it is indeed a PP with an extraposed complement, assigned a [+VM] feature, and eventually incorporated into the V in syntax. If it has been grammaticalized as a verb modifier, then it is not expected to agree with one of its coarguments – as it does in (38a). (Agreement is a matter internal to PP, taking place in its AgrP projection.) Furthermore, it should not be sensitive to whether the complement of the verb it modifies is lexical or pronominal. In fact, it cannot co-occur with a pronominal complement; compare:

(39) a. János **rá** szólt **Marira**.
John on called Mary-on
'John admonished Mary.'

b. * János **rá /rám**   szólt **rám**.
John on/on-1SG called on-1SG

c. János **rám**   szólt.
John on-1SG called
'John admonished me.'

(40) a. János **hozzá** vágta a   labdát **a   fiúkhoz**.
John at   threw the ball   the boys-at
'John threw the ball at the boys.'

---

^{9} The -*a* possessedness suffix is only morphosyntactically present; phonologically it is fused with the -*á* stem vowel.

b. * János **hozzá/hozzájuk** vágta a   labdát **hozzájuk**.
   John at   /at-3PL   threw the ball   at-3PL

c.   János **hozzájuk** vágta a   labdát.
   John at-3PL   threw the ball
   'John threw the ball at them.'

The facts in (39)–(40) support the PP incorporation analysis: the VM blocks the spelling-out of a pronominal argument obviously because the VM itself represents the very same argument. However, there is also a fact arguing against incorporation. Whereas in the case of regular incorporation the extraposed complement of the postposition bears dative case, in the case under discussion – e.g. in the examples in (38) – the complement is combined with the same morpheme that also appears as the incorporated postposition in VM position (*ért* in (38a), *nek* in (38b), *re* in (38c), *be* in (38d)), i.e., a kind of doubling takes place. To account for these apparently contradictory facts, let us assume that the sentences in (38), (39a,c), and (40a,c) all contain a PP argument complemented by a pro, which is moved to Spec,AspP, where it is incorporated into the V. What is more, these sentences also contain a case-marked adjunct coindexed with the incorporated PP. That is, the goal theta role in the theta grid of, for example, (38a) is expressed by the following pair of coindexed elements, with AgrP representing the argument proper, and KP representing an adjunct:

(41)

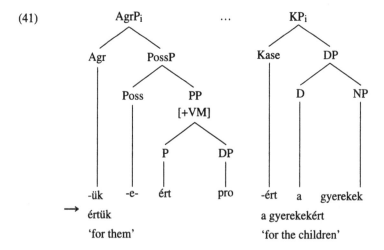

This structure predicts the facts discussed above. The argument and the adjunct instantiate the same theta role by means of the same morpheme – hence the doubling effect. Two identical pronominals cannot enter into an appositive relation – that is why (39b) and (40b) are ungrammatical; the adjunct is only licensed if it conveys lexical information.

There is, nevertheless, a slight problem left: when coindexed with a plural lexical noun phrase, the 3rd person PP does not necessarily bear a plural marker:

(42) a. János **nekik**_i   ment a   járókelőknek_j.
      John into-POSS-3PL went the passers.by-DAT
      'John ran into the passers-by.'

    b. János **neki**_i   ment a   járókelőknek_j.
      John into-POSS went the passers.by-DAT
      'John ran into the passers-by.'

(43) a. ?? János **nekik**_i   vágta a   labdát az üvegtábláknak_j.
      John into-POSS-3PL threw the ball   the window.panes-into
      'John threw the ball against the window-panes.'

    b. János **neki**_i   vágta a   labdát az üvegtábláknak_j.
      John into-POSS threw the ball   the window.panes-into
      'John threw the ball against the window-panes.'

The lack of the plural marker on the P is reminiscent of the lack of the plural marker on the pronominal possessor in constructions of type (44):

(44) a. az **ő** kalapjuk
      the he hat-POSS-3PL
      'their hat'

According to Bartos (1999a) and Szabolcsi (1992a), the pronominal possessor is not in the plural because its plural marker would be redundant, given that the plurality of its referent is expressed by the plural agreement marker. Perhaps the plurality of the 3rd person possessor in (42b) and (43b) need not be marked on the postposition because it would also be redundant, as the plurality of its referent is denoted on the adjunct providing the lexical content of the PP.[10]

8.6   Summary

In the present analysis, the class of postpositions is restricted to a set of elements that are essentially semi-independent case endings. They form the extended projection of a noun phrase, and – owing to their [+suffix] feature – they

---

[10] Ackerman and Webelhuth (1997) account for the facts attested in (39)–(43) in a lexicalist framework. They rely on the assumption that the VM + V combinations in question are lexical expressions, and derive the lack of agreement e.g. in (43a), or the impossibility of spelling out an independent pronoun alongside the agreeing VM, from a morphological blocking principle. According to this principle a lexical representation with a certain information content and synthetic expression tends to block the use of an analytic expression of a lexical representation conveying the same information.

are spelled out right-adjoined to the noun that they extend. The noun + postposition sequence, however, only constitutes a word on the morphosyntactic level; on the morphophonological level the noun and the postposition represent two separate domains for word-internal processes such as vowel harmony.

A postposition taking a personal pronoun complement is inflected, i.e., the PP projects an AgrP. A postposition can also assume a [−suffix] feature, in which case it takes a dative complement assigned case by a possessedness morpheme merging with the PP. The case-marked complement of a [−suffix] P can be extraposed, and the remnant PP can act as a VM. Postpositions expressing a goal are particularly susceptible to the aspectualizer role associated with verb modifiers. Postpositions of a source theta role, on the other hand, never become verb modifiers.

Lexical case endings, which were postpositions until the end of the Middle Ages, have preserved their P status in contexts in which they have no lexical complement to merge into; namely, in the case when their complement is a pro(noun), and in the case when they function as verb modifiers, with their complement extraposed.

9

Non-finite and semi-finite verb phrases

9.1   Introduction

If a VP merges with an infinitival suffix instead of a finite Tense, the resulting infinitival phrase can assume the role of a complement or adjunct in a matrix clause. If the subject of the infinitive is controlled by an argument of the matrix predicate, it is represented by a caseless PRO. If, on the other hand, the matrix predicate has no argument, and therefore cannot provide an adequate controller, the infinitive has a case-marked subject represented by a lexical noun phrase or a pro(noun), and it also bears an agreement marker. Infinitival phrases – whether agreeing or non-agreeing – can merge with the same types of operators that can extend a finite VP into a predicate phrase, and they can also combine with topic phrases into a TopP. Or, alternatively, both types of infinitives can be unified with their matrix V into a complex predicate.

9.2   Subject and object control constructions

9.2.1   *Subject and object control verbs*

A number of Hungarian verbs, among them those listed under (1a,b), are marked in the lexicon as selecting an infinitival phrase with a phonologically empty PRO subject controlled by the matrix subject.

(1) a.   *szeret* 'like', *utál* 'hate', *imád* 'adore', *elkezd* 'begin', *megpróbál* 'try', *elfelejt* 'forget', *fél* 'be afraid', *szégyell* 'be ashamed of', *habozik* 'hesitate', *igyekszik* 'strive', *siet* 'hurry'

   b.   *szeretne* 'would like', *kezd* 'begin', *készül* 'prepare', *próbál* 'try', *bír* 'manage', *kíván* 'desire', *óhajt* 'wish', *mer* 'dare', *szándékozik* 'intend', *tud* 'can'
        (compare L. Kálmán et al. 1986, C. Kálmán et al. 1989)

The verbs listed under (1a) are subject control verbs whose infinitival complement is a distinct clause-like entity – even if it is not introduced by a complementizer;

for example:

(2)   János megpróbál [$_{DistP}$ minden hétvégén [$_{AspP}$ moziba   menni PRO]]
       John tries   every   weekend   to.cinema to.go
       'John tries to go to the cinema every weekend.'

The verbs listed under (1b) either act as subject control verbs, taking an infinitival clause complement (3a), or form a complex predicate with their infinitive, sharing a single set of functional projections with it (3b).

(3) a.   János szeretne [$_{TopP}$ a gyerekeivel [$_{DistP}$ minden hétvégén [$_{AspP}$ moziba
          John would.like   with.his.children   every   weekend   to.cinema
          menni PRO]]]
          to.go
          'John would like to go to the cinema with his children every weekend.'

          compare:

    b.   [$_{TopP}$ János [$_{TopP}$ a gyerekeivel [$_{DistP}$ minden hétvégén [$_{AspP}$ moziba   szeretne$_i$
                 John   with.his.children   every   weekend   to.cinema would.like
          [$_{VP}$ t_i menni]]]]]
                to.go
          'John would like to go to the cinema with his children every weekend.'

Object control verbs are only marginally present in Hungarian grammar; *lát* 'see' and *hall* 'hear' may be their only instances; for example:

(4)   Láttam a   napot$_i$ [PRO$_i$ felkelni]
       I.saw   the sun-ACC   to.rise
       'I saw the sun rise.'

The evidence for the claim that the object of the matrix verb is the noun phrase *a napot* rather than the clause *a napot felkelni* is semantic. Whereas (5) below, in which *a nap* is inside a finite object clause, can also be true if what I saw was the appearance of the reflection of the sunrays, (4) is true only if what I saw was the sun itself.

(5)   Láttam, hogy felkel a   nap.
       I.saw   that rises the sun
       'I saw that the sun was rising.'

It also argues against placing the accusative noun phrase in the embedded clause that it cannot represent the subject of an embedded idiom. Thus, (6a) has no idiomatic meaning:

(6) a.   Láttam a   szöget kibújni   a zsákból.
          I.saw   the nail-ACC to.come.out from.the.bag
          'I saw the nail come out of the bag.'

    b.   Kibújt   a   szög a zsákból.
          out.came the nail from.the.bag
          'The cat is out of the bag.'

On the basis of similar arguments, Tóth (2000a) concludes that the complement of the permissive verbs *hagy* 'let' and *enged* 'allow' is an accusative with infinitive construction rather than an object control construction; compare:

(7)   Hagytam [_{InfP} a   szöget   kibújni   a zsákból]
        I.let   the nail-ACC to.come.out from.the.bag
        'I let the nail come out of the bag.'

9.2.2   The inner structure of the infinitive phrase

The infinitive phrases in the control constructions under (2), (3a), and (4) project the same types of operator phrases that finite VPs do. That is, they are clause-like – apart from the fact that they do not merge with a complementizer. Similar to a finite VP, the infinitival VP can be extended into an AspP, FP, NegP, DistP, and a TopP.

The constraints determining the word order possibilities of finite clauses are also operative in infinitival clauses. Thus, a focusless infinitive phrase cannot contain a postverbal bare NP; it must be preposed into an operator position; compare:

(8) a.   * Mari meg próbált [_{InfP} táncolni magas fiúval]
          Mary VM tried   to.dance tall   boy-with

    b.   Mari meg próbált [_{FP} MAGAS FIÚVAL táncolni]
          'Mary tried to dance WITH A TALL BOY.'

Constituents with a morphological operator feature must also land in the specifier position of a functional head sharing the same feature in infinitival clauses. Thus, a verb modifier of an aspectualizer role will land in Spec,AspP (9a), a [+focus] constituent will land in Spec,FP (9b), a negative quantifier will land in Spec,NegP (9c), a universal quantifier will land in Spec,DistP (9d), whereas a [+referential], [+specific] constituent can land in Spec,TopP (9e).

(9) a.   János megpróbált [_{AspP} fel készülni a   vizsgára]
          John tried   up to.prepare the exam-for
          'John tried to prepare for the exam.'

    b.   János megpróbált [_{FP} A JEGYZETEIBŐL [_{VP} készülni fel a   vizsgára]]
          John tried   his notes-from   to.prepare up the exam-for
          'John tried to prepare for the exam FROM HIS NOTES.'

    c.   János megpróbált [_{NegP} *semmire*   nem [_{VP} gondolni]]
          John tried   nothing-on not   to.think
          'John tried not to think of anything.'

    d.   János megpróbált [_{DistP} **mindkét vizsgára** [_{AspP} fel készülni]]
          John tried   both   exam-for   up to.prepare
          'John tried to prepare for both exams.'

e.   János megpróbált [$_{TopP}$ a   jegyzeteiből [$_{DistP}$ **mindkét vizsgára** [$_{AspP}$ fel
     John   tried   his notes-from   both   exam-for   up
     készülni]]]
     to.prepare
     'John tried to prepare from his notes for both exams.'

The [+focus], [+distributive quantifier], and [+referential], [+specific] complements of the infinitive can also be raised into the corresponding specifier positions
of the matrix sentence, assuming matrix scope; for example:

(10) a.   [$_{TopP}$ János [$_{FP}$ A   JEGYZETEIBŐL$_i$ [$_{VP}$ próbált meg [$_{AspP}$ fel készülni   a
          John   his notes-from   tried   VM   up to.prepare the
          vizsgára t_i]]]]
          exam-for
          'It was from his notes that John tried to prepare for the exam.'

    b.   [$_{TopP}$ János [$_{DistP}$ **mindkét vizsgára**$_i$ [$_{AspP}$ meg [$_{VP}$ próbált [$_{AspP}$ fel
          John   both   exam-for   VM   tried   up
          készülni t_i]]]]]
          to.prepare
          'For both exams John tried to prepare.'

    c.   [$_{TopP}$ A   szintaxisvizsgára$_i$ [$_{AspP}$ meg [$_{VP}$ próbált János [$_{FP}$ A   JEGYZETEIBŐL
          the syntax.exam-for   VM   tried   John   his notes-from
          [$_{VP}$ készülni   fel t_i]]]]]
          to.prepare up
          'For the syntax exam, John tried to prepare FROM HIS NOTES.'

Even though the operator projections extending the verb phrase are identical
whether the V combines with a tense morpheme or with the non-finite -ni suffix, there is an ill-understood difference between the FPs and NegPs of finite and
non-finite sentences: in the infinitival clause the V does not have to be adjacent to
the focus or to the negative particle; the verb modifier can intervene between them.
For many speakers, the F V VM or Neg V VM orders are in fact more marked than
the F VM V and Neg VM V orders; compare:

(11) a.   ? Nem tudtam KIT   **hívni   meg**.
          not   knew-I whom to.invite VM
          'I did not know whom to invite.'

    b.   Nem tudtam KIT **meg hívni**.

(12) a.   Szeretnék CSAK KÉT TÁRGYBÓL **írni   dolgozatot**.
          I.would.like only two subject-from to.write paper-ACC
          'I would like to write a paper ONLY IN TWO SUBJECTS.'

    b.   Szeretnék CSAK KÉT TÁRGYBÓL **dolgozatot írni**.

(13) a. ? Szeretnék   nem **bukni meg**.
　　　　I.would.like not   to.fail VM
　　　　'I would like not to fail.'

　　b.　Szeretnék nem **meg bukni**.

An adverb of manner, canonically adjoined to AspP, can also intervene between the focus/negative particle and the VM + V unit, which indicates that the category with which the focus merges in such examples is an AspP; compare:

(14)　　Miért szeretnél　[$_{FP}$ CSAK SZINTAXISBÓL [$_{AspP}$ gyorsan [$_{AspP}$ le
　　　　why   you.would.like only from.syntax　　　 quickly　　 VM
　　　　vizsgázni?]]]
　　　　to.pass.an.exam
　　　　'Why would you like to quickly pass an exam only in syntax?'

The fact that the focus (and the negative particle) must merge with a VP in a finite clause, whereas it can merge either with a VP or with an AspP in a non-finite clause is not easy to explain. The situation appears to be less problematic if the -*ni* infinitival suffix is not looked upon as the spelling-out of the [–Tense] head of TenseP, but is analyzed as a nominalizing suffix taking a [–Tense] (or tenseless) VP/AspP. Then the infinitival phrase of the (a) examples in (11)–(13) has the structure [$_{InfP}$ -ni [$_{VP}$ . . .]], where that in the (b) examples, as well as that in (14) has the structure [$_{InfP}$ [$_{AspP}$. . .[$_{VP}$. . .]]]. The focus and the negative particle will take an InfP complement no matter whether it immediately dominates an AspP or only a VP.

9.2.3　Long distance object agreement?

　　　　Despite its clausal nature, the infinitive phrase is transparent for object agreement: a transitive matrix verb agrees with the object of its infinitive; compare:

(15) a.　Megpróbálo**k** ritkábban　　veszíteni el　**dolgokat**.
　　　　try-INDEF.1SG more.seldom to.lose　VM things-ACC
　　　　'I try to lose things more seldom.'

　　b.　Megpróbálo**m** ritkábban　　veszíteni el　**az esernyőmet**.
　　　　try-DEF-1SG　more.seldom to.lose　VM my umbrella-ACC
　　　　'I try to lose my umbrella more seldom.'

　　c.　Megpróbál**lak** nem el　veszíteni **benneteket** a　tömegben.
　　　　try-2$_{OBJ}$-1SG$_{SUBJ}$ not　VM to.lose　you-PL-ACC the crowd-in
　　　　'I try not to lose you in the crowd.'

What we witness in (15a–c) is merely long distance verb–object agreement, without any long distance accusative assignment, as well (as pointed out by Bartos 1999a).

The infinitive is perfectly capable of accusative case assignment – as is clear from (16), whose matrix verb is intransitive:

(16)   Sietek   felvenni a telefont.
        hurry-INDEF.1SG to.pick.up the phone-ACC
        'I hurry to pick up the phone.'

In (16) the verb does not agree with the object – obviously because the intransitive matrix verb cannot project an AgrO Phrase. In fact, intransitive matrix verbs can also apparently agree with a 2nd person object at least in the past tense; compare:

(17)   Siettelek   meglátogatni benneteket.
        hurried-2_{OBJ}-$1SG_{SUBJ}$ to.visit   you-PL-ACC

As was discussed in Section 3.5.2, the *-lak/lek* suffix is an idiosyncratic element in the morphological system of Hungarian; it is used in the case of a 1st person singular subject and a 2nd person object. According to den Dikken (1999b), its *-l-* element is a 2nd person object clitic cliticized to the regular *-k* 1st person singular subject agreement marker, i.e., (17) is an instance of long distance clitic movement.

Returning to (15a–c), the infinitive phrase projects no object agreement phrase; the transitive verb selecting the infinitive phrase, on the other hand, does project one. The primary candidate for agreement with the matrix verb is the object of the infinitive. If it is definite, as in (15b), the matrix verb bears a definite object agreement suffix. If it is indefinite, as in (15a), the matrix verb bears a null indefinite object agreement marker. If it is a 2nd person indefinite object, and the matrix verb is in the 1st person singular, long distance clitic movement takes place.

If the infinitive is intransitive, the object agreement marker on the transitive matrix verb agrees with the infinitive phrase, which counts as an indefinite object; for example:

(18)   Megpróbálok énekelni.
        try-INDEF.1SG to.sing
        'I try to sing.'

That the object of the infinitive should take precedence over the infinitive phrase subsuming it in triggering agreement on the matrix verb is an unexpected situation, which represents a violation of the A-over-A principle. The problem can perhaps be avoided if the [+definite] feature of the object of the infinitive is allowed somehow to percolate up to InfP, turning it into [+definite].

It might also appear to be unmotivated at first sight that whereas a finite object clause acts as a definite object, an infinitival clause is indefinite; compare:

(19) a. Utálom   (azt),   ha énekelsz.
         hate-DEF-1SG (it-ACC) if you.sing
         'I hate if you sing.'

   b. Utálok   énekelni.
       hate-INDEF.1SG to.sing
       'I hate to sing.'

The relevant difference between the two constructions lies in the fact that the finite clause is associated with a (pro-dropped) pronominal head, i.e., it is embedded under a DP node; the infinitive, on the other hand, is not.

9.3   Infinitival complex predicates

9.3.1   The licensing of verbal complex formation

Whereas the subject control verbs listed under (1a) treat the infinitive phrase as one of their arguments, assigning a theta role to it, other verbs of temporal or modal meaning combine with the infinitival head and assign theta roles together with it to a set of shared arguments. Some verbs appear to be totally incapable of independent theta-role assignment, hence they always combine with an infinitival head. The verbs listed under (1b), on the other hand, can apparently either assign a theta role to an infinitival clause, or can combine with an infinitival head and assign theta roles together with it. Following Kenesei (2000), let us call the former set of verbs – including *fog* 'will', *szokott* 'used to', and *talál* 'happens to' – auxiliaries. The verbs listed under (1b), i.e., those which can be used either as subject control verbs or as auxiliaries, will be called semi-auxiliaries.

A complex predicate can contain at most one auxiliary (which is always finite), one or more semi-auxiliaries, and a theta-role-assigning lexical verb (which is always infinitival). If the complex predicate consists of three or more verbal elements, interesting word order possibilities arise, which have inspired a large amount of literature, including a monograph by Koopman and Szabolcsi (2000) (see also Bródy 2000, É. Kiss 1999b, Alberti 1999, Bartos 1999b, Olsvay 1999, Szendrői 1999).

9.3.2   The straight verbal complex

If the sentence containing the infinitival complex predicate involves no focussing or negation, then the surface order of the elements of the verbal complex corresponds to their underlying order: the highest, finite verb (to be referred to as V1) stands first, and the lowest, lexical verb (to be referred to as V4) stands last;

for example:

(20)   A fogoly haza fog akarni próbálni szökni.
        the captive home will to.want to.try   to.flee
        'The captive will want to try to flee home.'

As is clear from the example in (20), the verb modifier selected by the lexical V4 appears in the specifier of an AspP dominating V1, i.e., the elements of the V1–V2–V3–V4 verbal complex share one AspP – as expected, given that the verbal complex describes a single action or state. This AspP, however, can also remain 'downstairs', immediately dominating the projection of the lexical verb. Observe what happens if the verbal complex is dominated by an FP or a NegP:

(21) a.   A fogoly HIÁBA fog akarni próbálni **haza** szökni.
           the captive in.vain will to.want to.try   home to.flee
           'In vain will the captive want to try to flee home.'

     b.   ? A fogoly HIÁBA fog **haza** akarni próbálni szökni.
     c.   ?* A fogoly HIÁBA fog akarni **haza** próbálni szökni.

(22) a.   A fogoly nem fog akarni próbálni **haza** szökni.
           the captive not will to.want to.try   home to.flee
           'The captive will not want to try to flee home.'

     b.   ? A fogoly nem fog **haza** akarni próbálni szökni.
     c.   ?* A fogoly nem fog akarni **haza** próbálni szökni.

The possibility of a VM left-adjoined to the lexical verb to which it belongs is excluded if the verbal complex does not project an FP or NegP:

(23)   % A fogoly fog akarni próbálni haza szökni.
          the captive will to.want to.try   home to.flee

Example (23) is ungrammatical as a neutral sentence, with *a fogoly* in topic position (but it is acceptable if *fog* expresses assertion: the denial of a previous denial, in which case it has presumably been raised to F). To all appearances, an auxiliary or a semi-auxiliary cannot stand in the initial position of the predicate phrase. This constraint must be due to the following phonological constraint (recall that in Hungarian both word stress and phrasal stress fall on the left edge).

(24)   *The Auxiliary Constraint*
        An auxiliary cannot bear phrasal stress.

(Naturally, the constraint also applies to semi-auxiliary verbs when they are used as auxiliaries.) Let us assume that it is optional whether the AspP extending a lexical verb in a verbal complex immediately dominates the projection of the lexical verb, or dominates the whole of the verbal complex; i.e., let us assume that both of the following options are available:

(25) a.   b.

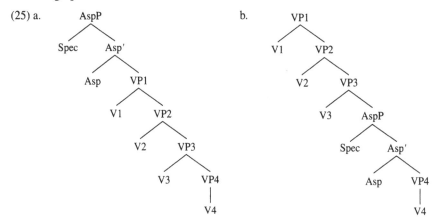

(For those who also accept the pattern illustrated in (21b) and (22b), the verb modifier/aspectualizer of the lexical verb can also merge with the infinitival complex, consisting of V2 + V3 + V4, excluding the finite verb.) Pattern (25a) is acceptable in all contexts. Example (25b), on the other hand, is ruled out by the Auxiliary Constraint in sentences involving no focus or negation.

The question arises how the violation of the Auxiliary Constraint can be avoided if the lexical verb in the verbal complex selects no verb modifier. Then V4 does not project an AspP; however, the verbal complex as a whole does project one, whose specifier will be occupied by the lexical infinitive itself. The infinitive phrase can be analyzed as a verb modifier if it consists of a mere head, i.e., if its complements have been extraposed; for example:

(26)   Mari [$_{AspP}$ énekelni$_i$ fog akarni   tanulni t_i]
         Mary   to.sing   will to.want to.learn
         'Mary will want to learn to sing.'

The verbal elements that share a single AspP projection – e.g. the V1–V2–V3–V4 complex in (25a) – must be interpreted to denote a single event. If the AspP projection dominates the lowest infinitive, as in (25b), then the single event interpretation is not enforced; compare:

(27) a.   A   fogoly **újra** haza fog akarni   próbálni szökni.
            the captive again home will to.want to.try   to.flee
            'The captive will again want to try to flee home.'

     b. ?? A fogoly haza fog akarni **újra** próbálni szökni.

     c.   A   fogoly HIÁBA fog **újra** akarni   próbálni haza szökni.
            the captive in.vain will again to.want to.try   home to.flee
            'In vain will again the captive want to try to flee home.'

   d.   A fogoly HIÁBA fog akarni **újra** próbálni haza szökni.
        'In vain will the captive want again to try to flee home.'

   e.   A fogoly HIÁBA fog akarni próbálni **újra** haza szökni.
        'In vain will the captive want to try again to flee home.'

Whereas in (27a,b) the repetition expressed by *újra* 'again' can apply only to the complex event of wanting to try to flee home, in (27c–e) it applies either to wanting, or to trying, or to fleeing home, depending on its position.

The verbal elements of the straight order complex predicate form only a loose unit syntactically. They need not be adjacent; they can be separated not only by a VM but by adjuncts, as well:

(28) a.   A fogoly haza fog **Karácsonykor** akarni próbálni szökni.
        the captive home will Christmas-at   to.want to.try   to.flee
        'The captive will want to try to flee home at Christmas.'

    b. ?? A fogoly haza fog akarni **Karácsonykor** próbálni szökni.

    c. A fogoly haza fog akarni próbálni **Karácsonykor** szökni.

Complex predicate formation presumably means in syntactic terms that the stacked VPs are interpreted as a single extended verb projection (à la Grimshaw 1991, van Riemsdijk 1998). Apparently, an adjunct adjoined to an intermediate VP level does not block this process.

An intervening lexical verb, on the other hand, does prevent complex predicate formation:

(29)   * A fogoly haza fog **félni**   próbálni szökni.
        the captive home will to.fear to.try   to.flee
        'The captive will be afraid to try to flee home.'

Whereas the semi-auxiliary *próbálni* 'to try' can form a verbal complex with *szökni* 'to escape', the lexical *félni* 'be afraid' cannot join them; it can only be the head of another extended verb projection, together with *fog*. This higher verbal complex is not available for the elements of the lower verbal complex, among them the VM *haza* 'home'. *Haza* must move to the Spec,AspP of the lower verbal complex, whereas the Spec,AspP position of the higher verbal complex must be filled with *félni* 'be afraid', there being no other available candidate; that is:

(30)   A fogoly [félni fog [haza próbálni szökni]]
        the captive to.fear will home to.try   to.flee
        'The captive will be afraid to try to flee home.'

9.3.3   The inverse verbal complex

When the verbal complex is preceded by a focus or a negative particle triggering V movement, the non-finite elements of the verbal complex can also appear in an inverse order:

(31)   A fogoly HIÁBA fog haza szökni próbálni akarni.   (V1 VM V4 V3 V2)
         the captive in.vain will home to.flee to.try   to.want
         'In vain will the captive want to try to flee home.'

In addition to the V1 VM V4 V3 V2 order, illustrated in (31), the V1 V2 VM V4 V3 order is also possible, i.e., the inverse order can be restricted only to the bottom part of the verbal complex:

(32)   A fogoly HIÁBA fog akarni haza szökni próbálni.   (V1 V2 VM V4 V3)

The elements in the inverse order section of the verbal complex must be strictly adjacent; the straight and the inverse order section, however, can be separated by non-verbal elements; for example:

(33) a.   A fogoly nem fog **most** haza szökni próbálni akarni.
            the captive not   will now home to.flee to.try   to.want
            'The captive will not want to try to flee home now.'

     b.   * A fogoly nem fog haza szökni **most** próbálni akarni.
     c.   * A fogoly nem fog haza szökni próbálni **most** akarni.

The complement–head order, typical of word internal domains, as well as the strict adjacency of the infinitival elements, have led Bródy (2000) and É. Kiss (1999b) to the conclusion that the infinitival elements have undergone cyclic incorporation – in fact, compounding – resulting in a complex word.[1] Bartos (1999b) derives the inverted order of the verbal elements from the assumption that (semi-)auxiliaries may optionally assume a [+suffix] feature, which causes them to be realized in morphology on the right-hand side of their lexical complement. The [+suffix] feature of *próbálni* 'to try' licenses the order in (32), and the [+suffix] features of *próbálni* and *akarni* 'to want' license the order in (31).

The initial structure that (31) and (32) are derived from is a V1 V2 V3 VM + V4 structure, with VM incorporated into V4 (34a). Then, as a next step, the VM + V4 unit is incorporated into V3 (34b). Eventually V3 (with V4 incorporated into it) is incorporated into V2 (34c).

(34) a.   A fogoly nem fog akarni próbálni [haza szökni]
     b.   A fogoly nem fog akarni [[hazaszökni]$_i$ próbálni] t_i
     c.   A fogoly nem fog [[hazaszökni próbálni]$_i$ akarni] t_i

---

[1] Koopman and Szabolcsi (2000) deny this conclusion; they analyze both the straight order construction and the inverse order construction as (remnant) phrasal movement.

It is not quite clear why the complex V2 cannot be incorporated into the finite V1, i.e., why (35) is ungrammatical:

(35)   * A fogoly [[hazaszökni próbálni akarni]ᵢ fog] t_i

In any case, the ungrammaticality of (35) cannot be an accident, because in German we find the same distribution of grammaticality over the different orders: whereas the V1 V2 V4 V3 and the V1 V4 V3 V2 orders are grammatical, the V4 V3 V2 V1 order is impossible; compare:

(36) a.   ...dass er hätte können herein kommen wollen   (V1 V2 VM V4 V3)
           that   he had can   in   to.come to.want
           'that he could have wanted to come in'

     b.   ...dass er hätte herein kommen wollen können   (V1 VM V4 V3 V2)
     c.   * ...dass er herein kommen wollen können hätte   (*VM V4 V3 V2 V1)

It must be the Tense on V1 that blocks incorporation into V1. This hypothesis is supported by the fact that in infinitival constructions involving no finite V, e.g. that in (37) below, roll-up, i.e., cyclic left-adjunction and incorporation, can proceed all the way in the verbal complex.

(37)   [[[Haza szökni] próbálni] akarni] hiábavaló dolog.
         home to.flee to.try   to.want useless   thing
         'Wanting to try to flee home is a useless thing.'

If the verbs except the lowest one are indeed suffixal in this type of roll-up structure, as claimed by Bartos (1999b), then the verb that represents the root for the Tense suffix apparently cannot assume a [+suffix] feature (or, alternatively, Tense cannot merge with a [+suffix] element).

9.4   Agreeing infinitives with a case-marked subject

9.4.1   Their formal properties

In infinitival complements of impersonal predicates, which provide no controller for a PRO subject, the infinitive can have a case-marked subject represented by a lexical noun phrase, a pronoun, or a pro; for example:

(38) a.   Korábban kellett volna Jánosnak haza men-ni-e.
           earlier   needed COND John-DAT home go-INF-3SG
           'John needed to have gone home earlier.'

     b.   Korábban kellett volna neked/pro haza menned.
           earlier   needed COND you-DAT home go-INF-2SG
           'You needed to have gone home earlier.'

Infinitives with a lexical or pronominal subject bear a subject agreement marker. Observe the full paradigm of infinitival agreement:

(39)   (Nekem) haza kell men-n-em.   (Nekünk) haza kell men-n-ünk.
        I-DAT   home need go-INF-1SG   we-DAT   home need go-INF-1PL

        (Neked) haza kell men-n-ed.   (Nektek) haza kell men-n-etek.
        you-DAT home need go-INF-2SG   you-DAT home need go-INF-2PL

        (Neki) haza kell men-ni-e.   (Nekik) haza kell men-ni-ük.
        he-DAT home need go-INF-3SG   they-DAT home need go-INF-3PL

Apart from the case-marked subject and the agreement marker on the infinitival head, the syntactic properties of the infinitive phrase are identical with those of non-agreeing infinitive phrases. Thus, its VP can project an AspP, FP, NegP, DistP, and/or a TopP. As is expected, the infinitival suffix can merge either with VP or with AspP, i.e., the focus or the negative particle can be left-adjacent either to the verb or to the verb modifier; for example:

(40)   Érdemes   volt [$_{DistP}$ mindkét feladatra [$_{FP}$Marit   fel kérnünk
        worthwhile was   both   job-for   Mary-ACC VM ask-INF-1PL
        /kérnünk   fel]]
        /ask-INF-1PL VM
        'It was worthwhile to ask Mary for both jobs.'

Impersonal modal auxiliaries selecting an agreeing infinitive with a case-marked subject form a verbal complex with it; i.e., the modal and the infinitive share a single set of arguments and project a single set of operator phrases. The auxiliary is subject to the Auxiliary Constraint, i.e., unless it forms a phonological word with a focus or a negative particle, the auxiliary must be preceded by the VM of the infinitive or, in case it has none, by the infinitive itself:

(41) a. Jánosnak mindkét lányt   **fel kell** hívnia.
         John-DAT both   girl-ACC up must call-INF-3SG
         'John must call up both girls.'

     b. Jánosnak **telefonálnia**   **kell**.
         John-DAT telephone-INF-3SG must
         'John must make a phone call.'

Because of the lack or scarcity of matrix arguments in this type of construction, the matrix topic and focus positions are often occupied by arguments of the infinitive even if the matrix predicate and the infinitive do not share an aspectual projection. This is not an indication of clause union; topic and focus movement can also cross a finite clause boundary; compare:

(42) a. [TopP Jánosnaki sikerült [AspP elérnie   ti a   vonatot]]
         John-DAT succeeded   catch-INF-3SG the train-ACC
         'John succeeded in catching the train.'

    b.   Jánosnak [FP CSAK A KÉSŐI VONATOTi sikerült[AspP elérnie ti]]
         John-DAT   only the late train-ACC succeeded catch-INF-3SG
         'As for John, it was only the late train that he managed to catch.'

9.4.2   The distribution of the agreeing infinitive and the dative subject

It is not easy to disentangle the contexts in which an agreeing infinitive with a case-marked subject is licensed. Two types of complications blur the picture. On the one hand, the dative-marked noun phrase interpretable as the subject of the infinitive may occasionally represent the experiencer argument of the matrix predicate, controlling or binding a phonologically empty subject inside the infinitive phrase. On the other hand, the agreement marker of the infinitive may occasionally be missing in contexts that otherwise allow agreement. It remains to be clarified whether the missing agreement marker is merely phonologically null or is also syntactically absent in such cases.

In a monograph devoted to Hungarian inflected infinitives, Tóth (2000a) lists the following types of contexts in which inflected infinitives with a case-marked subject occur:

I   Monadic predicates, among them:

(i)   epistemic modals: *kell* 'must'

(43)   Ég   a villany, Kovácséknak   már   otthon kell lenniük.
        shines the light   Kovács-PL-DAT already at.home must be-INF-3PL
        'The light is on, the Kovácses must be at home already.'

(ii)   non-directed deontic modals: *kell* 'need', *szabad* 'may'

(44)   Rég nem esett, nem szabadna a   földnek vizesnek lennie.
        long not rained not should   the soil-DAT wet-DAT be-INF-3SG
        'It hasn't rained for long, it shouldn't be the case that the soil be wet.'

(iii)   nominal predicates: *gonoszság* 'viciousness', *szemtelenség*
        'impertinence', *illetlenség* 'impoliteness'

(45)   Szemtelenség Jánosnak ilyet   feltételeznie.
        impertinence John-DAT such-ACC surmise-INF-3SG
        'It was impertinence for John to surmise such a thing.'

II   Dyadic predicates taking an experiencer in addition to the infinitive phrase:[2]

(i)   evaluative predicates: *fontos* 'important', *kellemes* 'pleasant', *kellemetlen* 'unpleasant', *lehetetlen* 'impossible', *nehéz* 'hard', *könnyű* 'easy'

(46)   Fontos   volna   Jánosnak megtudnia   az igazat.
        important would.be John-DAT learn-INF-3SG the truth-ACC
        'It would be important for John to learn the truth.'

(ii)   subject-oriented deontic modals: *kell* 'need', *lehet* 'may', *illik* 'be becoming', *sikerül* 'succeed', *muszáj* 'must', *szabad* 'may'

(47)   Jánosnak nem szabad haza mennie.
        John-DAT not must   home go-INF-3SG
        'John must not go home.'

(iii)   nominal predicates with an ablative: *gonoszság* 'viciousness', *szemtelenség* 'impertinence', *illetlenség* 'impoliteness', *szép dolog* 'a nice thing', *ügyes dolog* 'a skillful thing'

(48) a. Jánostól nem volt szép dolog cserben hagyni   minket.
        John-ABL not was nice thing in.lurch leave-INF us
        'It wasn't a nice thing of John to leave us in the lurch.'

    b. Butaság volt Jánostól   olyan korán haza menni.
        stupidity was John-ABL so   early home go-INF
        'It was stupidity of John to go home so early.'

III   Permissive verbs taking a dative permissee: *hagy* 'let', *enged* 'allow', *segít* 'help'

(49) a. Hagytam Jánosnak levágni a   hajamat.
        I.let   John-DAT cut-INF my hair
        'I let John cut my hair.'

    b. Engedtem levágnia   a   hajamat.
        I.let   cut-INF-3SG my hair
        'I let him cut my hair.'

---

[2] Tóth (2000a) analyzes the copula taking a relative clause, e.g. that in (i) below, as a monadic predicate.

(i)   Nincs Marinak   mit   fölvennie.
        isn't Mary-DAT what-ACC wear-INF-3SG
        'There is nothing for Mary to wear.'

In fact, it behaves more like an optionally dyadic predicate, with the dative interpretable as either the subject of the infinitive, or both the subject of the infinitive and the beneficiary of the matrix verb.

    c.   Segítettem felvinniük   a   szekrényt a   padlásra.³
       I.helped   take-INF-3PL the cupboard the loft-to
       'I helped them to take the cupboard to the loft.'

The lexical noun phrase or pronoun interpreted as the subject of the agreeing infinitive bears the dative case. When the matrix predicate is monadic, as those in (43)–(45), the dative-marked lexical noun phrase is clearly an argument of the infinitival verb.

(50) a.   Jánosnak már   otthon kell lennie.
         John-DAT already home must be-INF-3SG
         'John must already be at home.'

     b.   Nem szükséges a   padlónak felmosva lennie.
         not necessary the floor-DAT scrubbed be-INF-3SG
         'It is not necessary for the floor to be scrubbed.'

     c.   Szemtelenség Jánosnak ilyet   kérdeznie.
         impertinence John-DAT such-ACC ask-INF-3SG
         'It is impertinence for John to ask such a thing.'

Note that in this case the presence of the agreement marker on the infinitive is obligatory:

(51) a. * Jánosnak már   otthon kell lenni.
         John-DAT already home must be-INF
         'John must already be at home.'

     b. *? Nem szükséges a   padlónak felmosva lenni.
         not necessary the floor-DAT scrubbed be-INF
         'It is not necessary for the floor to be scrubbed.'

     c. * Szemtelenség Jánosnak ilyet   kérdezni.
         impertinence John-DAT such-ACC ask-INF
         'It is impertinence for John to ask such a thing.'

---

³ Tóth (2000a) adopts – or rather adapts – Borer's theory of anaphoric Agr (Borer 1989). She argues that what licenses an agreeing infinitive with a case-marked subject is the lack of agreement between the controller of its subject and the matrix verb. The agreement in the infinitive phrase is anaphoric on the matrix agreement, and control is established through this anaphoric relation if both the controller is coindexed with the matrix agreement, and the controllee is coindexed with the embedded agreement. When there is no controller, or the designated controller is a matrix dative argument not coindexed with agreement, the infinitive needs a lexical subject of its own, which is assigned dative case by the embedded Agr. For a rich array of further facts and arguments, see Tóth (2000a). The present description of inflected infinitives adopts only some of her solutions because it also intends to account for the obligatoriness or optionality of the presence of agreement on the infinitive, as well as the occasional anti-agreement, to which Tóth does not attribute any significance.

When the matrix predicate selecting the agreeing infinitive is a dyadic predicate allowing a dative experiencer, as those in (46)–(47), the dative-marked noun phrase seems to be interpretable either as the subject of the infinitive, or as simultaneously both the subject of the infinitive and the experiencer of the matrix predicate. In such cases the agreement on the infinitive is optional; for example:

(52) a.   Jánosnak fontos   megjelenni(e)   az ünnepélyen.
          John-DAT important appear-INF(3SG) the ceremony-at
          'It is important for John to appear at the ceremony.

     b.   Jánosnak muszáj otthon tartózkodni(a).
          John-DAT must   home   stay-INF(3SG)
          'It is necessary for John to stay at home.'

When the matrix predicate is a noun phrase taking an ablative complement, the ablative functions semantically both as a matrix argument and as the subject of the infinitive. Agreement on the infinitive is impossible:

(53)   Szemtelenség volt tőled   nem köszönni /?* köszönnöd.
       impertinence was you-ABL not greet-INF /   greet-INF-2SG
       'It was an impertinence of you not to say hello.'

The claim that – at least on the level of semantics – the dative/ablative noun phrase functions simultaneously both as the experiencer of the matrix predicate and the subject of the infinitive is supported by the fact that the matrix experiencer and the infinitival subject cannot both be spelled out:

(54) a.   * Jánosnak kellemetlen Péternek ilyet   kérnie.
          John-DAT unpleasant Peter-DAT such-ACC ask-INF-3SG
          'It was unpleasant for John for Peter to ask such a thing.'

     b.   * Jánosnak$_i$ kellemetlen neki$_i$/$_j$ ilyet   kérnie.
          John-DAT unpleasant he-DAT such-ACC ask-INF-3SG
          'It is unpleasant for John for him to ask for such a thing.'

Tóth (2000a) demonstrates that when the permissive verbs *hagy*, *enged*, and *segít* occur with a dative permissee and an infinitive, the dative is a complement of the matrix verb; it is always inside the matrix clause. When the permissee is the subject of an embedded idiom, i.e., when it is clearly part of the embedded phrase, it cannot appear in the dative. (The alternative accusative permissee, on the other hand, is part of the embedded clause; see (7) above.)

(55)   * Engedtem a szögnek kibújni   a   zsákból.
       I.allowed the nail-DAT to.get.out the sack-from
       'I allowed the cat to get out of the bag.'

In permissive constructions with a lexical dative permissee the infinitive cannot bear an agreement marker; compare:

(56) a. Az inasoknak   nem hagytam levágni(*uk) a hajamat.
         the apprentices-DAT not let-I   cut-INF(*3PL) my hair
         'I didn't let the apprentices cut my hair.'

   b. Segítettem a gyerekeknek megírni(*uk)   a leckét.
       I.helped   the children-DAT write-INF(*3PL) the lesson
       'I helped the children write the lesson.'

Note that the agreement marker cannot even be spelled out in the presence of a pronominal permissee:

(57) Nem hagytam nekik   levágni(*uk) a hajamat.
      not let-I   they-DAT cut-INF(*3PL) my hair
      'I didn't let them cut my hair.'

Summarizing our observations: the presence or absence of the agreement marker on the infinitive correlates with whether or not the lexical subject belongs to the infinitive. Where it is thematically part of the infinitive phrase, agreement is obligatory. Where it can belong either to the matrix predicate or to the infinitive, agreement is optional. Where the dative is clearly an argument of the matrix clause, agreement is impossible. Let us attempt to account for these facts.

Let us assume that in sentences with a monadic matrix predicate, whose sole argument is the infinitive phrase, the dative (or its trace) is also syntactically part of the infinitive phrase. Then the sentences in (50a–c) have the following type of structure:

(58) a. Jánosnak$_i$ már   otthon kell [t_i lennie]
         John-DAT already home must   be-INF-3SG
         'John must already be at home.'

   b. Nem szükséges [a padlónak felmosva lennie]
       not necessary the floor-DAT scrubbed be-INF-3SG
       'It is not necessary for the floor to be scrubbed.'

Let us assume, furthermore, that in the case of a potentially dyadic matrix predicate with an optional dative experiencer, the dative may be the experiencer subcategorized by the matrix predicate, controlling a PRO subject in the infinitive phrase which has no agreement marker. (For a similar proposal, see Dalmi 1995: Section 7.4.) The ablative argument of a nominal predicate also controls a PRO subject in an uninflected infinitive phrase.

(59) a. Jánosnak$_i$/neki$_i$ muszáj [PRO$_i$ otthon tartózkodni]
         John-DAT/he-DAT must   home stay
         'It is necessary for John to stay at home.'

   b. Jánosnak$_i$ kellemetlen [PRO$_i$ ilyet   kérni]
       John-DAT unpleasant   such-ACC ask-INF
       'It is unpleasant for John to ask for such a thing.'

c. Szemtelenség Jánostól_i [PRO_i ilyet   kérni]⁴
    impertinence John-ABL   such-ACC ask-INF
    'It is impertinence of John to ask for such a thing.'

If these predicates are used monadically, then the dative-marked lexical subject is
generated inside the infinitive, and the infinitive agrees with it:

(60) a. Jánosnak_i/neki_i   muszáj [t_i otthon tartózkodnia]
         John-DAT/he-DAT must   home stay-INF-3SG
         'John must stay at home.'

    b. Jánosnak_i kellemetlen [t_i ilyet   kérnie]
        John-DAT unpleasant   such-ACC ask-INF-3SG
        'It is unpleasant for John to ask for such a thing.'

    c. Szemtelenség [a fiúknak   ilyet   kérniük]
        impertinence   the boys-DAT such-ACC ask-INF-3PL
        'It is impertinence for the boys to ask for such a thing.'

Permissive verbs, whose dative argument – whether lexical or pronominal – is
always outside their infinitival complement, take an infinitive with a controlled
PRO subject:

(61) a. Az inasoknak_i   nem hagytam [PRO_i levágni a   hajamat]
         the apprentices-DAT not   let-I   cut-INF my hair
         'I didn't let the apprentices cut my hair.'

    b. Segítettem a gyerekeknek_i [PRO_i megírni a   leckét]
        I.helped   the children-DAT   write-INF the lesson
        'I helped the children write the lesson.'

    c. Segítettem nekik_i [PRO_i megírni   a   leckét]
        I. helped   they-DAT   write-INF the lesson

When in the case of a monadic (or monadically used) matrix predicate the agreeing
infinitive has no visible subject, as in (62), its subject is a dative pro internal to the
infinitival phrase. As Tóth (2000a) points out, a dative pronoun can be dropped
because its features are recoverable from agreement.

---

⁴ Tóth (2000a) claims that the subject of the infinitive in these cases is a case-marked pro.
She assumes that the predicative adjective always agrees in case with the subject; hence,
the dative case of the adjective in (i) is evidence of a dative-marked pro subject:

(i) Jánosnak kellemetlen [pro rámenősnek lenni]
     John-DAT unpleasant   pushy-DAT be-INF
     'It is unpleasant for John to be pushy.'

However, Tóth's premise is false; the predicative adjective in an infinitival phrase can
always bear dative case – even when its subject is in the accusative:

(ii) Engedtem [Jánost   rámenősnek lenni]
      I.allowed John-ACC pushy-DAT be-INF
      'I allowed John to be pushy.'

(62)   Fontos [pro idejében haza   érkezned]
        important in.time home arrive-INF-2SG
        'It is important for you to arrive at home in time.'

In the case of dyadic predicates allowing a controlled PRO in the infinitive phrase, a missing controller results in an arbitrary PRO reading:

(63) a.   Kellemetlen [PRO ilyet   kérni]
           unpleasant   such-ACC ask
           'It is unpleasant to ask for such a thing.'

    b.   Nem hagyom [PRO levágni a   hajamat]
           not let-I   cut-INF my hair
           'I don't allow my hair to be cut.'

Obligatorily monadic predicates (i.e., epistemics and non-directed deontic modals), which do not license a caseless subject in their infinitival complement, do not allow a PRO$_{arb}$, either. Thus, the modal in the following example cannot have a non-directed deontic reading:

(64)   Június vége van, Magyarországon már   aratni   kell.
        June's end is   in.Hungary   already harvest-INF must
        'It is the end of June, they must already harvest in Hungary.'

There remains one pattern to account for: permissive verbs can have an agreeing infinitival complement when the permissee is not spelled out phonologically; compare:

(65) a.   Hagytam levágniuk   a   hajamat.
           I.let   cut-INF-3PL my hair
           'I let them cut my hair.'

    b.   Segítek megírnod   a   leckét.
           I.help   write-INF-2SG the lesson
           'I help you write the lesson.'

Apparently these constructions involve an infinitival phrase with a pro subject. If the subject is lexical or pronominal, it is obligatorily interpreted as the permissee argument of the matrix verb controlling a PRO. It seems idiosyncratic that a construction should allow a pro but should rule out a pronoun or a lexical noun phrase in its subject position.

9.4.3   The source of the dative case

The next question to answer is, naturally, what the mechanism of checking or assigning the dative case of the subject of the infinitive is in infinitival phrases complementing a monadic(ally used) predicate. Tóth (2000a) stipulates that the dative case of the subject of an infinitive is a structural case assigned/checked in Spec,AgrP. Whereas [+Tense, +Agr] inflection checks nominative case, [−Tense, +Agr] inflection checks dative case.

There is in fact a way of eliminating the stipulative element from this proposal. There is indication that agreement in the infinitive domain is parallel in relevant respects to that in the nominal domain. The agreement morphemes appearing on the infinitive are identical with the inflection morphemes appearing on the possessed noun, which were analyzed in Section 7.3 as consisting of a -(j)a/(j)e suffix expressing 'being possessed', and an agreement marker. The two morphemes are fused in many cases, but in the plural the intervening -i- plural suffix makes their morphosyntactic independence evident:

(66)　　a pro birtok-a-i-m 'my estates'　　　a pro birtok-a-i-nk
　　　　the estate-POSS-PL-1SG　　　　　　the estate-POSS-PL-1PL

　　　　a pro birtok-a-i-d　　　　　　　　　a pro birtok-a-i-tok
　　　　the estate-POSS-PL-2SG　　　　　　the estate-POSS-PL-2PL

　　　　a pro birtok-a-i-0　　　　　　　　　a pro birtok-a-i-k
　　　　the estate-POSS-PL-3SG　　　　　　the estate-POSS-PL-3PL

The paradigm arising from the fusion of the suffix meaning 'being possessed' and the agreement marker in the case of a singular possessed noun is identical with the agreement paradigm appearing on the infinitival head:

(67)　　a birtok-om 'my estate'　　　rajzol-n-om 'draw-INF-1SG'
　　　　a birtok-od　　　　　　　　　rajzol-n-od
　　　　a birtok-a　　　　　　　　　 rajzol-ni-a
　　　　a birtok-unk　　　　　　　　rajzol-n-unk
　　　　a birtok-otok　　　　　　　　rajzol-n-otok
　　　　a birtok-uk　　　　　　　　　rajzol-ni-uk

(The -i vowel of the infinitival suffix is dropped in front of a suffix consisting of a vowel + consonant sequence.) If the two paradigms are, indeed, identical, then the suffix of the infinitive must also represent the fused sequence of an -a/e morpheme and an agreement marker. The -a morpheme, however, was argued in Section 7.3 to be a theta-role assigner/licenser and a dative case assigner. Although we referred to the -(j)a/(j)e morpheme in Section 7.3 as the morpheme of possessedness, in fact, as has been made clear by Szabolcsi (1983b, 1994a) and Alberti (1995), it expresses 'being related to x in a way determined by the lexical head' rather than 'being possessed by x'. In a possessive construction the relation between the so-called possessor and the so-called possessed noun can also be a whole–part relation (*János lába* 'John's leg'), a genealogical relation (*János nagyapja* 'John's grandfather'), a local relation (*János iskolája* 'John's school'), etc., depending on what type of relations the given noun participates in in a lexical network.[5] If the lexical head with which the -(j)a/(j)e suffix combines is a theta-role assigning event nominal, the suffix merely licenses the theta role assigned by the lexical head (e.g. *János* in *János kiabálása* 'John's shouting' will receive an agent role, that in *János megverése* 'John's beating' will receive a theme role). In any case, a lexical head supplied with the -*a* suffix bears a (specific or non-specific) relation to an individual; hence, it has the given individual as its argument, and acts as its case-assigner/case-checker. Just as a noun merged with the -(j)a/(j)e suffix assigns dative case to its argument, an infinitive merged with -*a/e* assigns dative case to its subject. Whereas the possessor of a noun can also be realized as a caseless determiner in Spec,DP, the infinitive projects no DP; hence, this possibility is not open.

If the structure of an infinitive phrase with a case-marked subject is parallel in relevant respects to the structure of a possessive construction, then we expect to attest the same anti-agreement phenomenon we attested in the case of a lexical possessor in Section 7.3.3. Recall that we claimed that AgrP is only projected in a possessive construction if the possessor is a pronominal with a [+person] feature. The optional presence of Agr on the head in the case of an extracted lexical possessor was interpreted to indicate that the noun phrase external lexical possessor can form a chain not only with a noun phrase internal trace, but, alternatively, also with a noun phrase internal pro. (Either pro is a resumptive pronominal spelling out the trace of extraction, or the lexical possessor is a hanging topic or adjunct base-generated outside the possessive construction, coindexed with pro). Anti-agreement does occur with a lexical dative subject, as well, although it is slightly substandard:

(68) a. ? A fiúknak   nem kell még haza mennie.
         the boys-DAT not need yet home go-INF-3SG
         'The boys don't need to go home yet.'

         compare:

     b.   A fiúknak   nem kell még haza menniük.
         the boys-DAT not need yet home go-INF-3PL

The greater acceptability of (68b) might mean that an infinitive supplied with -*a/e* can project agreement not only in the presence of a pronominal subject with a [+person] feature, but in the case of a lexical subject, as well – e.g. because the -*a/e* suffix and the agreement marker, never separated by a plural suffix, are fused in a joint Inflection Phrase. It can also be the case that the lexical subject associated with an agreeing infinitive is always a hanging topic coindexed with a pro subject inside the infinitive phrase. This latter view is supported by the fact that a dative lexical subject + infinitive sequence fails the constituency tests: it cannot be a

---

[5] On the notion of lexical network, see L. Kálmán (1990).

focus in Spec,FP, and it cannot be a distributive phrase surrounded by *még ... is* 'even'; compare:

(69) a. * [CSAK AZ EBÉDNEK KÉSZ LENNIE]   kellene.
          only   the lunch-DAT ready be-INF-3SG need-COND
          'Only the lunch should be ready.'

    b. * [Még Jánosnak úsznia is]   sikerült.[6]
          even John-DAT swim-INF-3SG succeeded
          'It was possible even for John to swim.'

9.5   Adverbial participle phrases

An (extended) VP can be merged with a *-va/ve* or *-ván/vén* adverbial suffix, assuming an AdvP status. As such, it can either function as a VP-adjunct expressing the manner and/or time of the action denoted by the finite verb, or it can function as a predicate, expressing the state of the subject or object of the finite verb. Adverbial participle phrases of adjunct and predicate role also differ in their derivation; they are therefore discussed separately.[7]

9.5.1   *Adjunct adverbial participle phrases*

Adjunct adverbial participle phrases can be derived by the suffix *-ván/vén*, and by the suffix *-va/ve*. The participles *-ván/vén* are used to describe an event anterior to the main event of the clause. The following sentence can only mean that John's smoking was anterior to his sitting on the bench:

(70)   Cigarettázván, János ült a padon.
        smoking   John sat on-the-bench
        'Having smoked, John was sitting on the bench.'

Although it has no complementizer, the *-ván/vén* participle phrase has clausal properties. It occupies peripheral position with respect to the matrix clause, and, crucially, it can have a nominative lexical subject; compare:

---

[6] Notice that *sikerül* 'succeed' is not a semi-auxiliary verb in standard Hungarian; hence, (69b) does not violate the Auxiliary Constraint, requiring that the matrix verb and the infinitive form a complex predicate.

[7] For comprehensive analyses of Hungarian adverbial participle phrases, see Komlósy (1992, 1994), Laczkó (1995a), and Tóth (2000b). Various aspects of them are also discussed in Alberti (1997a, 1998).The present classification of adverbial participle phrases essentially follows that of Laczkó (1995a) without adopting his terminology. What I call adjunct adverbial participle phrases are called adverbial participle phrases of manner by him, and what I call predicative adverbial participle phrases are called adverbial predicate phrases of state by him.

(71)   A   kapu becsukódván, Aladdin egy barlangban találta magát.
      the gate closing,   Aladdin a   cave-in   found himself
      'The gate having closed, Aladdin found himself in a cave.'

Since -*va/ve* participles can have no case-marked subject, the licenser of nominative case in -*ván/vén* phrases must be the -*n* morpheme, presumably the realization of Tense.[8]

Interestingly, the subject of the -*ván/vén* participle cannot be a personal pronoun, which seems to indicate that the participle phrase cannot project an AgrP; compare:

(72)   * Én nem lévén otthon/ *ti   nem lévén otthon, a postás   nem tudott
      I   not being at.home/you-PL not being at.home the postman not could
      bejutni.
      get.in
      'I/you not being at home, the postman could not get in.'

When the subject of the -*ván/vén* phrase is phonologically empty, it is understood to be coreferent with the matrix subject; compare:

(73) a.   pro$_i$/*$_j$ Belépvén a   patikába, Mari$_i$ észre   vette Jánost$_j$.
          entering the drugstore Mary in.sight took John-ACC
          'Having entered the drugstore, Mary noticed John.'

    b.   pro$_i$/*$_j$ Belépvén a   patikába, JÁNOST$_j$ vettem észre pro$_i$.
          entering the drugstore JOHN-ACC took-I in.sight
          'Having entered the drugstore, it was John that I noticed.'

    c. ?? pro$_i$ Rálépve/vén a   sínekre, Jánost$_i$ elütötte a   vonat.
          stepping   the rails-on John-ACC hit   the train
          'Stepping/having stepped on the rails, the train hit John.'

Given that the -*ván/vén* phrase does not project an AgrP, its pro subject can only be licensed by being coindexed with the matrix subject, sharing its person and number. Or perhaps the subject of the -*ván/vén* phrase is a case-marked PRO, assigned nominative by the -*n* Tense morpheme.

The -*va/ve* participle phrase does not express an independent event; it functions as an adverbial of manner (or time). It has no Tense of its own, and cannot have a case-marked subject. Its PRO subject is obligatorily controlled by the matrix subject:

(74) a.   János$_i$ mosolyogva$_{i/*j}$ megszólította Marit$_j$.
          John smiling   approached Mary-ACC
          'Smiling, John approached Mary.'

---

[8] Tóth (2000b) analyzes the -*n* element of the -*ván/vén* complex as a complementizer, capable of nominative assignment.

b. Marit$_j$ mosolyogva$_{i/*j}$ megszólította János$_i$.
Mary-ACC smiling   approached   John
'Mary, John approached smiling.'

The extended verb phrase in the -*va/ve* and -*ván/vén* phrases has a regular structure: it is a VP possibly extended into an AspP, FP, NegP, DistP, and TopP; for
example:

(75) a. János [$_{TopP}$ kalapját [$_{AspP}$ le véve fejéről]]   belépett a   patikába.
John   his.hat-ACC   off taking his.head-from entered the drugstore
'Taking his hat off his head, John entered the drugstore.'

b. János [$_{DistP}$ mindkét kesztyűjét [$_{AspP}$ le húzva]] belépett a   patikába.
John   both   his.glove-ACC off pulling   entered the drugstore
'Pulling off both of his gloves, John entered the drugstore.'

Similar to infinitival constructions, the participial suffix can merge either with VP
or with AspP, i.e., the focus and negative particle can precede either the verb or
the verb modifier; for example:

(76) a. János [$_{NegP}$ nem **véve le** kalapját] be lépett   a   patikába.
John   not taking off his.hat in stepped the drugstore-to
'Not taking off his hat, John entered the drugstore.'

b. János [$_{NegP}$ nem **le véve** kalapját] be lépett a patikába.

Participle phrases in -*va/ve* occupy the canonical positions of adverbials of manner
in the matrix sentence: they are either left-adjoined to AspP – as in (76a,b) – or
they are focussed – as in (77). Since the focus must be head-final, in the latter case
not only the verb modifier must precede the participial V, but also its post-head
arguments must be preposed, undergoing a kind of phrase-internal topicalization:

(77)   János [$_{FP}$ [KALAPJÁT [NEM LE VÉVE]] [$_{VP}$ lépett   be   a   patikába]]
John   his.hat-ACC not off taking   entered VM the drugstore
'Not taking off his hat did John enter the drugstore.'

9.5.2   Predicative adverbial participle phrases

Predicative adverbial participle phrases are also derived by the -*va/ve*
suffix. Whereas any VP + -*va/ve* combination (with -*va/ve* cliticized to the V) can
function as an adjunct, only a subset of the VP + -*va/ve* combinations can function
as predicates: those whose subject is a theme undergoing a change of state. The
verbs involved include unaccusatives, such as:

(78) a. A csirke   meg van sül-ve.
the chicken VM is   fry(INTR)-ed
'The chicken is fried.'

b. A csirkét   csak ropogósra sülve   szeretem.
the chicken-ACC only crispy   fry(INTR)-ed like-I
'I like chicken only fried crispy.'

Transitive verbs figure in predicative adverbial participle phrases detransitivized, with their subject argument suppressed, and with their object promoted to subject role. This change in argument structure is not accompanied by a change in verb morphology; it is therefore a matter of debate whether it can be regarded as passivization and, if it can, what mechanism of passivization is at work (see Komlósy 1994, Laczkó 1995a, Alberti 1998, Tóth 2000b); compare:

(79) a. A csirke ki   van sütve.
the chicken VM is   fry(TR)-ed
'The chicken is fried.'

b. A csirkét   csak (?a feleségem által) ropogósra süt-ve   szeretem.
the chicken-ACC only (my wife   by) crispy   fry(TR)-ed like-I
'I like chicken only fried crispy by my wife.'

Komlósy (1994) suggests that we attribute to transitive verbs both an 'active stem' and a 'passive stem' in the lexicon. The passive and active stems are homophonous, but they are associated with different theta grids. The passive stem is selected by a handful of suffixes: the predicative *-va/ve*, as well as *-ható/hető* '-ible/able' (e.g. *ehető* 'edible'), *-atlan/etlen/tatlan/tetlen* 'un-/in- . . . -ed' (e.g. *íratlan* 'unwritten', *fűtetlen* 'unheated'), and the *-t/tt* suffix of past participles to be discussed below. That is, according to Komlósy, the passivization of the non-finite verb of (79a,b) takes place in the lexicon. According to Laczkó (1995a), the suppression of the external argument in predicative adverbial participle phrases takes place in syntax, and is triggered by the predicative *-va/ve* suffix. Tóth (2000b) eliminates the external argument by adjoining the participial suffix to a VP-shell below the external argument. The latter two views, naturally, presuppose a hierarchical VP.

The subject of the predicative participle phrase is represented by a PRO (except for the case when the participle and the matrix verb form a complex predicate, to be discussed below). Depending on the matrix verb, the controller of PRO is the matrix subject (80), or the matrix object (81), or either the subject or the object (82) – but never an oblique argument.

(80) a. János$_i$ [PRO$_{i/*j}$ meghajolva] megszólította Marit$_j$.
John   bowing   approached   Mary-ACC
'Bowing, John approached Mary.'

b. Marit$_j$ [PRO$_{i/*j}$ meghajolva] megszólította János$_i$.
'Mary, John approached bowing.'

(81) a. János$_i$ [PRO$_j$ az autóban ülve] hagyta Marit$_j$.
John   in.the.car sitting left   Mary-ACC
'John left Mary sitting in the car.'

b. János$_i$ [PRO$_j$ az autóban ülve] találta Marit$_j$.
John   the car-in   sitting found Mary-ACC
'John found Mary sitting in the car.'

(82)   Az orvos$_i$ [PRO$_{i/j}$ levetkőzve] vizsgálja a   betegeket$_j$.[9]
the doctor   undressed   examines the patients
'The doctor examines the patients undressed.'

As for the inner structure of the predicative adverbial participle phrase, it is a VP extended into an AspP and possibly into further operator projections. In (83) it is of the category FP, and in (84) it is of the category NegP. For some reason, this type of participle phrase is only felicitous if it is head-final. This also means that the VM must always precede the verb, whether or not the participle phrase also contains a focus or a negative particle; compare:

(83) a.   A   tojást [$_{FP}$ CSAK AZ EGYIK OLDALÁN [$_{AspP}$ meg sütve]] tálalták   fel.
the egg-ACC only   the one   side-on   VM fried   served-they VM
'They served the egg fried on only one side.'

b. * A tojást [$_{FP}$ CSAK AZ EGYIK OLDALÁN [$_{VP}$ sütve meg]] tálalták fel.

(84) a.   Az adóbevallást [$_{NegP}$ nem [$_{AspP}$ alá   írva]] nem fogadják   el.
the tax-return-ACC   not   under signed not   accept-they VM
'They do not accept the tax return not signed.'

b. * Az adóbevallást [$_{NegP}$ nem [$_{VP}$ írva alá]] nem fogadják el.

When the predicative adverbial participle phrase accompanies a finite copula, the copula and the participial head form a complex predicate, sharing all operator projections, including AspP; compare:

(85)   [$_{TopP}$ A   kérdőív [$_{AspP}$ ki van$_i$ [$_{VP}$ t_i töltve]]]
the form   in is   filled
'The form is filled in.'

As an auxiliary, the copula is subject to the Auxiliary Constraint: it cannot stand at the head of the predicate phrase because it cannot bear phrasal stress. Therefore, unless it forms a phonological word with a preceding focus or negative particle, it must be preceded by a constituent in Spec,AspP. The VM of its participial complement must be raised there – as in (86b,c); or, if it has no VM, the participle itself must be raised; compare:

(86) a. * [$_{TopP}$ A   kerítés [$_{VP}$ van [be   festve]]]
the fence   is   VM painted
'The fence is painted.'

---

[9] The verb *levetkőzik* 'undress self' does have an affected theme, as required; it is represented by the reflexive suffix on the verb.

b. [$_{TopP}$ A kerítés [$_{AspP}$ be$_i$ van [t_i festve]]]

c. [$_{TopP}$ A kerítés [$_{AspP}$ frissen$_i$ van [t_i festve]]]
the fence   freshly is   painted
'The fence is freshly painted.'

d. [$_{TopP}$ A kerítés [$_{AspP}$ festve$_i$ van t_i]]
the fence   painted is
'The fence is painted.'

Naturally, if the copula is in an unstressed position following a focus or a negative particle, then the VM will surface in front of the participle it belongs to:

(87) a. [$_{FP}$ A   KERÍTÉS van [be   festve]]
the fence   is   VM painted
'It is the fence that is painted.'

b. A kerítés [$_{NegP}$ nincs [be   festve]]
the fence   isn't   VM painted
'The fence isn't painted.'

The copula + adverbial participle phrase complex functions as a kind of passive construction – see Alberti (1998) (regular passive verb morphology is extinct in present-day Hungarian). The imperfective and the perfective variants of the copula result in aspectually different interpretations, corresponding to the English passive constructions derived by the auxiliary *be* and *get*, respectively:

(88) a. A   kapu be   van festve.
the gate VM is   painted
'The gate is/has been painted.'

b. A   kapu be   lett   festve.[10]
the gate VM became painted
'The gate has got painted.'

Example (88a) expresses a state resulting from a completed action; (88b), on the other hand, expresses a completed action resulting in a state.

    The distribution of this construction is markedly different from that of the English passive. On the one hand, it is narrower; it can only be used if its subject is an affected theme undergoing a change of state; compare:

(89) a. * Mari meg van látva.
Mary VM is   seen
'Mary has been seen.'

---

[10] The perfective copula *lesz* also has an imperfective meaning: it can be interpreted as the future tense equivalent of the imperfective *van*.

b. Mari meg van hatva.
    MaryVM is   moved (emotionally)
    'Mary has been moved.'

At the same time, the distribution of this passive-like construction is also wider than that of the English-type passive: intransitive verbs with an affected theme can also be 'passivized' in this way. (They allow only the imperfective copula.) For example:

(90) a. A virág el   van hervadva.
         the flower VM is   wilted
         'The flower is wilted.'

   b. A ruha ki   volt fakulva.
       the dress VM was faded
       'The dress was faded.'

Alberti (1997a, 1998) claims that passivization can be interpreted as agent suppression, or patient preferring, or both. Hungarian opts for interpreting passivization as patient preferring, which also licenses passivization in the case of unaccusative verbs with an affected subject. Choosing this type of 'passive' instead of the active verb form – i.e., choosing (91a) instead of (91b) – has primarily aspectual consequences; compare:

(91) a. A ruha ki   volt fakulva.
         the dress VM was faded
         'The dress was faded.'

   b. A ruha ki   fakult/ Ki fakult a   ruha.
       the dress VM faded/ VM faded the dress
       'The dress faded.'

In (91b) we predicate a (past) event, and we have the option of predicating it of the subject, or of an invisible pronominal element referring to the given spatiotemporal location. In (91a), on the other hand, we predicate a (past) state of the subject (resulting from a completed event). 'Preferring the patient' in the case of (91a) means that the affectedness of the patient is focussed on.

9.6   Adjectival participle phrases

If a VP is merged with an -ó/ő or -t/tt suffix (to be cliticized to the V), it assumes an AdjP-like status, and can be used attributively in the sentence. Its PRO subject is coreferent with the noun phrase modified by the participle phrase.

The *-ó/ő* suffix can be added to any type of verb, whether it is agentive, unaccusative, or transitive; compare:

(92) a.   az éneklő primadonna
          the singing prima donna

     b.   az elhangzó dal
          the sounding song

     c.   a dalt   eléneklő primadonna
          the song-ACC singing prima donna
          'the prima donna singing the song'

The *-t/tt* suffix, on the other hand, is merged in standard Hungarian only with verbs whose surface subject is a theme. It combines, on the one hand, with unaccusatives (93a) and, on the other hand, with the passive stem of transitive verbs (93b), but it cannot combine with agentive verbs (93c). (Therefore, the possibility of merging with the *-t/tt* participial suffix is a test of unaccusativity.)

(93) a.   az elhangzott dal
          the sounded   song

     b.   az elzongorázott darab
          the performed   piece

     c. * a   zongorázott fiú
          the performed   boy

Since the *-ó/ő* suffix can be combined with all stems, unaccusative verbs, which also allow the *-t/tt* suffix, can be extended into both types of adjectival participle phrases. In their case, as Laczkó (1995a) points out, the two suffixes have come to be associated with different interpretations; compare:

(94) a.   az elhangzó dal
          the sounding song
          'the song sounding [being performed]'

     b.   az elhangzott dal
          the sounded   song
          'the song having sounded [having been performed]'

In the case of unaccusatives, the *-ó/ő* participle expresses simultaneity, and the *-t/tt* participle expresses anteriority.

The adjectival participle suffix is merged with an AspP, which can also be further extended by logical operators and topics (95). As has been well known at least since Emonds (1978), an attributive phrase must be head-final. This means that not only must the VM always precede the participial head, but the arguments and adjuncts must also undergo phrase-internal topicalization.

(95)   [_TopP a   határidőig [_NegP nem [_AspP be   nyújtott]]] pályázatok
        the deadline-by   not   VM submitted applications
        'the applications not submitted by the deadline'[11]

9.7   Summary

This chapter has argued that infinitival and participial phrases have the
inner structure of an extended VP: they project an AspP, and possibly an FP, NegP,
DistP, and TopP, as well. The movement possibilities of their constituents are
determined by the same constraints that are also operative in finite verb projections.
Non-finite and finite verb projections differ in one respect: the non-finite verb
projection merging with the focus or the negative particle need not be a VP; it can
also be an AspP, containing a preverbal verb modifier.

Since the subject of an uninflected non-finite verb phrase has no case as-
signer/checker, it is represented by a PRO. Inflected infinitives, as well as *-ván/vén*
adverbial participles merged with a Tense head, on the other hand, take a case-
marked lexical subject. The subject of the inflected infinitive is assigned dative case
by the *-a/e* suffix of the infinitive (also present on the possessor in possessive constructions), whereas the subject of the *-ván/vén* participle is assigned nominative by
the *-n* Tense suffix. The inflected infinitive also participates in person agreement.

The infinitival or participial suffix with which the VP/AspP is merged deter-
mines the function that the non-finite VP projection can have in a matrix clause.
The infinitive phrase functions as a complement of the matrix verb, the adverbial
participle phrase functions as an adjunct (an adverbial of manner or time, or a
predicate), whereas the adjectival participle phrase functions as an attribute.

Infinitives (whether inflected or uninflected) and predicative adverbial participles can also form a complex predicate with an auxiliary or semi-auxiliary finite
verb, in which case they share a single functional domain.

---

[11] In negated non-finite verb phrases the verb modifier can, in fact, also precede the negative
particle. In this case the participial suffix is merged with a VP instead of an AspP, and
the verb modifier undergoes left-adjunction to NegP – similar to the other complements
and adjuncts of the head in the obligatorily head-final participial phrase:

(i)   a   határidőig **be** nem nyújtott   pályázatok
       the deadline-by in   not   submitted applications
       'the applications not submitted by the deadline'

10

The subordinate clause

10.1   Introduction

The internal structure of subordinate clauses is essentially identical with the structure of matrix clauses. They differ from matrix clauses only to the extent that, on the one hand, they contain a complementizer, and, on the other hand, they are often associated with a pronoun, which serves to pick up the case assigned to the clause by the matrix predicate, and/or to represent the clause in a matrix operator position that is not available for clausal constituents; for example:

(1) a. János **azt**   **is**   meg ígérte,   [**hogy segíteni fog**]
        John that-ACC also VM promised   that to.help will
        'John also promised that he would help.'

   b.   János CSAK ARRÓL beszélt, [AMIT TAPASZTALT]
        John only about.it spoke   what he.experienced
        'John spoke only about what he experienced.'

In (1a) *azt* (*is*), an accusative pronoun in Spec,DistP, expresses that the *hogy*-clause, or *that*-clause, has the grammatical function of an object, and the logical function of a distributive phrase. In (1b) (*csak*) *arról*, an oblique pronoun in Spec,FP, expresses that the relative clause functions as the oblique argument of the matrix predicate, and it represents the value of the matrix focus operator.[1]

10.2   *That*-clauses

10.2.1   The structure of clausal arguments

In Hungarian, the unmarked subordinating operator is *hogy* 'that', occupying the head position of a CP projection. The CP is associated with a pronoun,

---

[1] For a detailed analysis of subordination in Hungarian, see Kenesei's monograph published both in Hungarian and in English (Kenesei 1992, 1994).

which picks up the case assigned to the argument by the matrix predicate; for example:

(2) a.   *Az,* [*hogy Éva szereti Gergőt*], *nyilvánvaló.*
         it   that Eve loves Gergő   obvious
         'That Eve loves Gergő is obvious.'

   b.   *Azt*   hiszem, [*hogy Éva szereti Gergőt*]
        that-ACC think-I   that Eve loves Gergő
        'I think that Eve loves Gergő.'

   c.   Hallottál *róla,*   [*hogy Éva szereti Gergőt*]?
        heard-you about.it that Eve loves Gergő
        'Have you heard about it that Eve loves Gergő?'

The pronoun also serves to represent the subordinate clause in the matrix operator positions that cannot take a clausal constituent. Thus, in (2b) the pronoun is in Spec,AspP, expressing the aspectualizer function of the subordinate clause. Observe also (3a–d), in which the clausal object functions as the focus of the matrix clause. Both (3a), in which Spec,FP is taken by the pronoun + clause complex, and (3b), in which Spec,FP is taken by the subordinate clause alone, are ungrammatical. Spec,FP must be occupied by the pronoun, and the clause must be extraposed – either to the right, or to the left of the predicate phrase. (I use the term 'extraposition' merely as a metaphor, expressing the non-adjacency of the pronoun and the clause.) The constraint prohibiting a clause in Spec,FP may be syntactic: focus constituents must be head-final for some reason. According to Kenesei (1992), and Vogel and Kenesei (1987), on the other hand, the restriction against clausal foci is phonological: the focus constituent must constitute a single phonological phrase with the verb following it.

(3) a.   * János [$_{Spec,FP}$ CSAK [AZT,   [HOGY NYÍLIK AZ AJTÓ]]] vette   észre.
          John   only that-ACC that opens the door   noticed VM
          'John only noticed that the door was opening.'

   b.   * János [$_{Spec,FP}$ CSAK [HOGY NYÍLIK AZ AJTÓ]] vette észre.

   c.   János [$_{Spec,FP}$ CSAK AZT] vette észre, [HOGY NYÍLIK AZ AJTÓ]

   d.   ? János, [HOGY NYÍLIK AZ AJTÓ], [$_{Spec,FP}$ CSAK AZT] vette észre.

The pronoun coindexed with the *that*-clause is the regular pronoun referring to an inanimate singular 3rd person referent or antecedent. This pronoun has the form of a 3rd person singular personal pronoun in VP-internal position, and the form of a demonstrative in the preverbal operator position. Pronouns are subject to pro-drop up to recoverability in the VP, which means that VP-internal subject pronouns are always missing; object pronouns are dropped in the singular; and oblique pronouns are dropped, but their case endings are spelled out, supplied with an agreement morpheme (see Section 8.5) Pro-drop is also possible in topic position: a pronoun in Spec,TopP is only spelled out if it is set into a contrast.

Observe the pronominal head of a subject clause (4) and an oblique argument clause (5), representing the clause in topic position (a), distributive quantifier position (b), focus position (c), and VP-internal argument position (d).

(4) a.　　[$_{TopP}$ *Az*/pro nyilvánvaló volt, [*hogy Éva szereti Gergőt*]]
　　　　　　　it　　obvious　was　that Eve loves　Gergő
　　　　　　'It was obvious that Eve loved Gergő.'

　　b.　　[$_{DistP}$ **Az is** nyilvánvaló volt, [**hogy Éva szereti Gergőt**]]
　　　　　'It, too, was obvious that Eve loved Gergő.'

　　c.　　[$_{FP}$ CSAK AZ volt nyilvánvaló, [HOGY ÉVA SZERETI GERGŐT]]
　　　　　'Only that was obvious that Eve loved Gergő.'

　　d.　　[$_{AspP}$ Nyilvánvaló volt pro, [*hogy Éva szereti Gergőt*]]
　　　　　'It was obvious that Eve loved Gergő.'

(5) a.　　[$_{TopP}$ *Abban* bíztak,　[*hogy hamarosan megérkezik a　segítség*]]
　　　　　　　in.that trusted-they that　soon　　　arrives　　the help
　　　　　　'They counted on it that help would soon arrive.'

　　b.　　[$_{DistP}$ **Abban is** bíztak, [**hogy hamarosan megérkezik a segítség**]]
　　　　　'They counted on that, too, that help would soon arrive.'

　　c.　　[$_{FP}$ CSAK ABBAN bíztak, [HOGY HAMAROSAN MEGÉRKEZIK A SEGÍTSÉG]]
　　　　　'Only that did they count on that help would soon arrive.'

　　d.　　[$_{VP}$ Bíztak *benne$_i$*, [hogy hamarosan megérkezik a segítség]]^2
　　　　　'They counted on it that help would soon arrive.'

Perhaps the most common type of subordinate clauses is represented by the clausal object of verbs of saying, and verbs expressing mental activities; for example:

(6) a.　　*Azt*　　gondoltam/hittem,　[*hogy János késni　fog*]
　　　　　that-ACC thought-I /believed-I　that John be.late will
　　　　　'I thought/believed that John would be late.'

　　b.　　János *azt*　akarta/szerette volna,　[*hogy induljunk　el　idejében*]
　　　　　John that-ACC wanted/have.liked.would　that leave-SUBJ-1PL VM in.time
　　　　　'John wanted/would have liked that we leave in time.'

It is not immediately obvious whether the pronoun coindexed with the object clause occupies Spec,AspP or Spec,FP. Whether or not the pronoun + clause complex functions as a focus can be tested by the focus test proposed in

---

^{2} *Benne* 'in-POSS.3SG' is an instance of a PP with the pro complement of P dropped. The version without pro-drop would be *ő-benn-e* 'he-about.POSS-3SG'; see Section 8.5.

Section 4.1, namely:

(7) a. János *azt*   mondta, [[*hogy késni fog*], és [*hogy ne várjuk*]]
John that-ACC said   that be.late will-he and that not wait-SUBJ-1PL
'John said that he would be late and that we shouldn't wait for him.'

b. János *azt*   mondta, [*hogy késni fog*]
John that-ACC said   that be.late will-he
'John said that he would be late.'

Example (7b) is a logical consequence of (7a), i.e., (7a) and (7b) can be simultaneously true, which means that the pronoun + clause complexes do not express
exhaustive identification; hence, they are not foci. Consequently, the pronoun coindexed with the extraposed clause must be sitting in Spec,AspP. In examples like
(7b), the pronoun indeed clearly functions as an aspectualizer: by supplying the
process verb with an object, it turns it into terminative–resultative, in other words,
it turns it into an accomplishment verb.

If these predicates are modified by *úgy* 'so', they take a clausal complement
without a visible pronoun associate. *Úgy*, which serves semantically to express a
reservation concerning the truth of the subordinate proposition, appears to be an
alternative of the demonstrative pronoun associated with the subordinate clause.
Compare:

(8) a. *Azt*   gondolom/hiszem, [*hogy igazad van*]
that-ACC think-I   /believe-I that right   are-you
'I think you are right.'

b. *Úgy* gondolom/hiszem, [*hogy igazad van*]
so   think-I   /believe-I that right   are-you
'I think you are right.'

With certain predicates, *úgy* seems to be the only alternative:

(9) a. *Úgy/*az* tűnik, [*hogy már   találkoztunk valahol*]
so / it seems that already met-we   somewhere
'It seems that we have already met somewhere.'

b. *Úgy/??az*   döntöttem /határoztam, [*hogy elfogadom az ajánlatot*]
so / that-ACC concluded-I/decided-I   that accept-I   the offer
'I concluded/decided that I would accept the offer.'

In fact, the subordinate clause must also have an invisible pro coindexed with it in
these sentences. This is indicated by the objective conjugation of the matrix verb,
which is only used in the presence of a definite object. Apparently, the adverb *úgy*
functions as the verb modifier instead of *azt* in these sentences; that is why it must

land preverbally, in Spec,AspP. The pronoun associated with the clause must stay postverbally, where it undergoes pro-drop. It is unclear though why it cannot be, for instance, topicalized; compare:

(10)   * *Azt   úgy* tudom, [*hogy János orvosi   egyetemre jelentkezett*]
       it-ACC so   know-I that   John   medical school-to   applied
       'I know it so that John applied to medical school.'

The noun phrase associated with the clausal complement can also be lexical, denoting a proposition – e.g. *a hír* 'the news', *az állítás* 'the claim'. A lexical noun phrase associated with a *that*-clause is also accompanied by a demonstrative pronoun. Its function is to facilitate interpretation, by indicating that the noun phrase still has a clausal constituent to come (usually at the end of the matrix sentence); for example:

(11) a.   [$_{TopP}$ *Azt a   hírt*   PÉTERTŐL hallottam, [*hogy Jánost   kinevezik*
       that the news-ACC Peter-from heard-I   that   John-ACCappoint-they
       tanszékvezetővé]]
       head.of.department
       'I heard the news that John would be appointed head of the department from Peter.'

    b.   [$_{DistP}$ **Azt a hírt is** Pétertől hallottam, [**hogy Jánost kinevezik tanszékvezetővé**]]
       'I heard also the news that John would be appointed head of the department from Peter.'

    c.   [$_{FP}$ AZT A HÍRT hallottam Pétertől, [HOGY JÁNOST KINEVEZIK TANSZÉKVEZETŐVÉ]]
       'It was the news that John would be appointed head of the department that I heard from Peter.'

    d.   [$_{FP}$ Tegnap [$_{VP}$ hallottam (azt) *a   hírt* Pétertől, [*hogy János   kinevezik*
       yesterday   heard-I   that the news Peter-from   that   John-ACC appoint-they
       tanszékvezetővé]]]
       head.of.department
       'Yesterday, I heard from Peter the news that John would be appointed head of the department.'

The relation between the pronoun and the embedded clause coindexed with it has been a matter of discussion in the literature. According to Kenesei (1992, 1994), the pronoun and the clause form an expletive–associate chain, and they are related by coindexing. In a recent variant of the expletive–associate analysis, proposed by Lipták (1998), the pronoun is generated in the specifier of the embedded CP projection. Argument clauses are claimed by her to have a C head which has all the categorial, case, and phi-features that a corresponding nominal argument would have, and the demonstrative is argued to share/check these features via spec–head agreement. This is the structure she would assign to the clausal object of (1a):

(12)

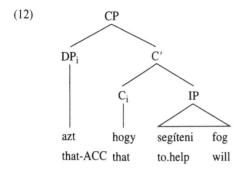

azt	hogy	segíteni	fog
that-ACC	that	to.help	will

According to É. Kiss (1987a, 1990, 1991c), on the other hand, the pronoun and the clause associated with it constitute a complex noun phrase, with the clause subject to extraposition. In this framework pronouns associated with bare *that*-clauses, pronouns associated with *that*-clauses having a lexical head, as well as pronouns associated with headless relatives are analyzed in parallel ways. Compare the structure attributed to a *that*-clause associated with a bare pronoun, and that attributed to a *that*-clause associated with a lexical noun phrase:

(13) a.   b.

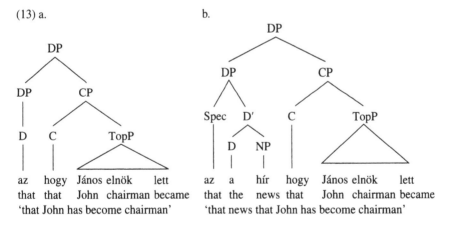

Further merits and disadvantages of the structures in question will become evident in the analysis of complex sentences involving long operator movement, which is presented in Section 10.5.

Clausal complements of structure (13a,b) can complement not only a verb, or a predicative adjective – as in (4a–d) – but also a noun, or an adverb. Here is a clause complementing an adverb. The resulting adverbial phrase functions as a sentence adverbial modifying the matrix clause.

(14)   [AdvP *Azon*   túl [CP *hogy anyagi kárt   okoztak*]],   a
        that-SUPERESS beyond that financial loss-ACC caused-they our
        hírnevünket   is   tönkretették
        reputation-ACC also damaged-they
        'In addition to the fact that they caused a financial loss, they also damaged our
        reputation.'

In our analysis (resembling that of Stowell 1981), a clause accompanying a noun
phrase denoting a proposition such as *a hír* 'the news' is not a complement of the
given noun; it bears an appositive relation to the noun phrase. Nouns that allow
a real clausal complement are derived from verbs and adjectives taking a clausal
complement. Nouns derived from such verbs can only take a complement if they
are supplied with a possessedness suffix, capable of assigning dative case to the
pronoun associated with the clause (see Section 7.3.2); for example:

(15) a.   [DP *Annak*   valószínűség-e, [CP *hogy János elkésik*]], nagyon kicsi.
           that-DAT probability-POSS   that John is.late   very   small
           'The probability of it that John would be late is very small.'

     b.   Én nem hiszek [DP *annak*ᵢ   lehetőségében,   [*hogy Jánost   felveszik*
           I   not believe   that-DAT possibility-POSS-in that John-ACC admit-they
           az orvosi   egyetemre]]
           the medical school-to
           'I don't believe in the possibility of it that John would be admitted to medical
           school.'

10.2.2   The position of the subordinate clause in the matrix sentence

In the examples quoted above the complement clause is rarely adjacent
to the pronoun or lexical noun phrase coindexed with it; it is usually extraposed.
(At least in a metaphorical sense. In the framework proposed by Lipták (1998), the
separation of the complement clause from the pronoun is primarily a consequence
of pronoun extraction.) It is time to examine what constraints are involved in
determining its surface position.

    An embedded clause cannot occupy an internal position in a lexical projection;
for example, the clausal complement of a noun cannot be internal to the noun phrase,
or the clausal complement of an adverb cannot be internal to the adverbial phrase:

(16) a.   * Kicsinek tűnt [DP [DP *annak*, [CP *hogy Jánost   felveszik   az orvosi*
           little   seemed   that-DAT   that John-ACC admit-they the medical
           egyetemre]], a   valószínűsége] számunkra.
           school-to   the probability-POSS us-to
           'The probability of John being admitted to medical school seemed little to us.'

     b.   * [AdvP [DP *Azon,*   [*hogy anyagi   kárt   okoztak*]],   túl]   a
           that-SUPERESS that financial loss-ACC caused-they beyond our
           hírnevünket   is   tönkretették.
           reputation-ACC also damaged-they
           'In addition to causing a financial loss, they also damaged our reputation.'

Whereas (16b) can be remedied by extraposing the embedded clause to the right edge of the phrase containing it, in the case of (16a) this is not enough:

(17) a. ?? Kicsinek tűnt [DP [DP *annak*   a   valószínűsége] [CP *hogy Jánost*
little   seemed   that-DAT the probability   that   John-ACC
felveszik   az orvosi   egyetemre]] számunkra.
admit-they the medical school-to   to.us

b.   [AdvP [AdvP *Azon*   túl] [CP *hogy anyagi   kárt   okoztak*]]   a
that-SUPERESS beyond that   financial loss-ACC caused-they our
hírnevünket   is   tönkretették.
reputation-ACC also damaged-they

The trouble with (17a) must be that the subordinate clause extraposed to the right edge of the noun phrase is still internal to the VP. Whereas a subordinate clause center-embedded in a VP is still comprehensible as opposed to a subordinate clause center-embedded in a noun phrase or an adverbial phrase, it is, nevertheless, marginal – so the following generalization emerges:

(18)   That-*clause Constraint*
A *that*-clause cannot be internal to a lexical projection.

(It remains to be examined to what extent (18) can be extended to languages other than Hungarian; (18) is not expected to hold in languages in which argument clauses are not associated with a nominal element.)

In order to satisfy (18), the subordinate clause on the right periphery of the noun phrase in (17a) must be extraposed once more, this time to the right edge of the VP:

(19)   Kicsinek tűnt [DP *annak*   a   valószínűsége]   számunkra, [CP *hogy Jánost*
little   seemed that-DAT the probability-POSS to.us   that   John-ACC
felveszik   az orvosi   egyetemre]
admit-they to medical school

The *that*-clause Constraint in (18) does not rule out a constituent with a right peripheral subordinate clause sitting in the specifier of a functional projection – still a complex noun phrase in Spec,FP is ungrammatical; the requirement that the focus constituent be head-final forces extraposition:

(20) a. * [Spec,FP [DP CSAK ANNAK A   VALÓSZÍNŰSÉGE [CP HOGY JÁNOST
only   that-DAT the probability   that   John-ACC
FELVESZIK AZ ORVOSI EGYETEMRE]]] tűnt   kicsinek számunkra.
admit-they the medical school-to   seemed little   to.us
'It was only the probability of John being admitted to medical school that seemed little to us.'

b.   [Spec,FP [DP CSAK ANNAK A VALÓSZÍNŰSÉGE]] tűnt kicsinek a számunkra
[CP HOGY JÁNOST FELVESZIK AZ ORVOSI EGYETEMRE]

A clausal constituent modified by the distributive particle *is* 'also' or *még...is* 'even' is also ungrammatical, or marginal, in Spec,DistP – presumably because the particle *is* is unable to cliticize to the right edge of a clause:

(21) a. *? [_{Spec,DistP} [_{DP} **Annak a valószínűsége,** [_{CP} **hogy János   felveszik az**
            that-DAT the probability-POSS   that John-ACC admit-they the
        orvosi egyetemre]], is] kicsi.
        medical school-to   also small
        'Also the probability of John being admitted to medical school is small.'

    b. *? [_{Spec,DistP} [_{DP} **Annak a valószínűsége] is,** [_{CP} **hogy Jánost felveszik az orvosi
        egyetemre]],** kicsi.

    c.   [_{Spec,DistP} [_{DP} **Annak a valószínűsége] is]** kicsi, [_{CP} hogy Jánost felveszik az
        orvosi egyetemre]

A constituent with a peripheral embedded clause moved to Spec,TopP, on the other hand, does not violate any constraint. Nevertheless, the extraposition of the embedded clause is also an option in such cases. Marginally, also extraposition to the left is possible, particularly from Spec,TopP position.

(22) a.   [_{Spec,TopP} [_{DP} *Annak* a valószínűsége, [_{CP} *hogy Jánost felveszik az orvosi
        egyetemre*]]], kicsinek tűnt számunkra.
        'The probability of it that John would be admitted to medical school seemed little
        to us.'

    b.   [_{Spec,TopP} [_{DP} *Annak* a valószínűsége]] kicsinek tűnt számunkra, [_{CP} *hogy Jánost
        felveszik az orvosi egyetemre*]

    c.   [_{CP} *Hogy Jánost felveszik az orvosi egyetemre*], [_{Spec,TopP} [_{DP} *annak* a
        valószínűsége]] kicsinek tűnt számunkra.
        'That John would be admitted to medical school, its probability seemed little
        to us.'

If a clause extraposed from the specifier of a functional projection is adjoined to the given projection, it follows that in the case of multiple extraposition, the higher its source, the more external the extraposed clause will be. Indeed, this is what we attest:

(23) a.   CSAK ABBÓL_i   gondolom pro_j [*hogy János beteg*]_j [HOGY NEM JELENT MEG
        only that-from think-I   that John sick   that not showed up
        AZ ÓRÁN]_i
        at class
        'Only from that do I think that John is sick that he did not show up at class.'

    b. * CSAK ABBÓL_i   gondolom pro_j [HOGY NEM JELENT MEG AZ ÓRÁN]_i
        only that-from think-I   that not showed up   at class
        [*hogy János beteg*]_j
        that John sick
        'Only from that do I think that he did not show up at class that John is sick.'

10.2.3   *Interrogative* that-*clauses*

Embedded questions are also subordinated to the matrix predicate by the complementizer *hogy*. In Hungarian *wh*-questions the interrogative phrase occupies Spec,FP, hence it will follow *hogy*, and possibly even topic constituents can intervene between them; for example:

(24)   János azt   kérdezte, [$_{CP}$ hogy [$_{Top}$ Péter [$_{FP}$ melyik egyetemre   készül]]]
        John that-ACC asked   that   Peter   which university-to applies
        'John asked to which university Peter would apply.'

Non-embedded *yes–no* questions are marked by a special rise and fall in the intonation of the last two syllables of the sentence, or by a particle *-e* cliticized to the right-hand side of the verb. In embedded questions only the latter option is available; for example:

(25)   János meg kérdezte, [$_{CP}$ hogy [$_{TopP}$ Péter [$_{FP}$ orvosi   egyetemre
        John VM asked   that   Peter   medical school-to
        [$_{VP}$ jelentkezett-e]]]]
             applied-Q
        'John asked if Peter has applied to medical school.'

As in other languages, such embedded questions occur only in the context of matrix verbs selecting a question, among them *kérdez* 'ask', *tud* 'know', *megmond* 'tell', *kíváncsi* 'be curious', etc.; compare:

(26) a. János azt   kérdezte tőlünk a   színház után, hogy hogyan tetszett az
         John that-ACC asked   of.us   the theater after that how   pleased the
         előadás.
         performance
         'John asked of us after the theater how the performance pleased us.'

    b. * János azt   mondta, hogy hogyan tetszett az előadás.
         John that-ACC said   that how   pleased the performance
         'John said that how the performance pleased us.'

That is, there is a link between the matrix verb and the interrogative phrase in the Spec,FP of the embedded clause, or the interrogative particle cliticized to the embedded verb – despite the intervening maximal projections. The link is presumably established through the CP projection of the embedded question; perhaps *hogy* is marked as [+/–wh]; or perhaps it has an invisible interrogative operator adjoined to it.[3]

In the sentence type illustrated in (24), (25), and (26a), containing an interrogative clause associated with a personal or demonstrative pronoun, interrogation

---

[3] See Lipták (2000).

is a matter internal to the subordinate clause; the interrogative operator has scope only over the embedded proposition. If the subordinate question is associated with a matrix interrogative pronoun instead of the demonstrative or personal pronoun, on the other hand, interrogation has matrix scope. As Horvath (1995, 1997, 1998) has shown, in such cases the subordinate question bears the same kind of relation to the interrogative pronoun that other types of subordinate clauses bear to the demonstrative or personal pronoun coindexed with them;[4] for instance:

(27) a. János mit   ígért,   (hogy) hányra   érkezik?
         John what-ACC promised that   by.what.time arrives
         'By what time did John promise that he would arrive?'

     b. Mire   számítasz, (hogy) mekkora fizetésemelést kapsz?
         what-on count-you   that   how.big pay.raise-ACC get-you
         'How big a pay raise do you count on getting?'

The interrogative clause can be multiply embedded, in which case each superordinate clause contains an interrogative pronoun associated with the next lower question:

(28) Mit$_i$ mondott Éva, [hogy mit$_j$ hallott, [hogy mit$_k$ ígért
      what-ACC said   Eve that what-ACC heard-she that   what-ACC promised
      János, [hogy hányra   érkezik]$_k$]$_j$]$_i$?
      John   that by.when arrives
      'By what time did Eve say that she heard that John promised that he would arrive?'

This construction is not permitted with verbs selecting a [+wh] complement; compare:

(29) a. * János mit kérdezett, hányra   érkeznek a   vendégek?
         John what asked   by.when arrive   the guests
         'By what time did John ask that the guests would arrive?'

     b. * Mire   vagytok kíváncsiak, kiket   hívtam   meg?
         what-of are-you curious   who-PL-ACC invited-I VM
         'Whom do you wonder that I invited?'

This fact is interpreted by Horvath (1995, 1997, 1998) to indicate that the *wh*-operator of the embedded sentence has matrix scope, i.e., in a sense, the matrix *wh*-phrase serves as a scope marker for the embedded question. At the same time, as Horvath argues, the two *wh*-phrases do not form a chain (they differ in case

---

[4] For the first analysis of this Hungarian construction, referred to as 'partial *wh*-movement' in recent literature, see Marácz (1988).

and theta role). The locality relation between the two *wh*-phrases is also different from the locality relation between two chain links. Namely, although the lower *wh*-phrase cannot be embedded in a complex NP, it can be embedded in an adjunct:

(30)   * Mit   mondott Éva, mit   hallotta [_DP_ a hírt   [hogy János
         what-ACC said   Eve what-ACC heard-she the news-ACC that John
         hányra érkezik?]]
         by.when arrives
         'By what time did Eve say that she heard the news that John would arrive?'

       but:

(31)   Miért voltál   dühös, mert   mire   akartak   rávenni?
       why   were-you angry because what-into wanted-they to.reason
       'Why were you angry? What did they want to persuade you to do?'

This 'subjacency paradox' cannot be accounted for if the matrix *wh*-phrase and the embedded *wh*-phrase are assumed to form a chain, but is easily explained if the embedded question is analyzed as the associate of the *wh*-pronoun, as proposed by Horvath (1995). Namely, the *wh*-pronoun can only be associated with a [+wh] clause; however, in (30) its potential associate is a [−wh] complex noun phrase; that is why it is ruled out. Example (31) is grammatical because nothing is extracted from the adjunct clause (if it is moved in LF, it is moved as a whole).

Horvath (1995) claims that the *wh*-phrase and the *wh*-clause are in the same relation that holds between an expletive and its associate, e.g. in a *there is* construction. Namely, the principle of full interpretation requires that at LF the whole *wh*-clause be left-adjoined to the *wh*-expletive, as represented in (32b):

(32) a.   *wh*-expl ...[_CPi_ *wh*-phrase_j_...e_j_...]...]...

     b.   LF: [[[_CP_ *wh*-phrase_j_...e_j_...]_i_ *wh*-expl]...e_i_...]...

The *wh*-feature of the interrogative operator of the embedded clause is transferred to the CP node, as a result of which CP assumes an operator feature, whereas the interrogative phrase in Spec,FP/CP ceases to be an operator – that is why it can only complement a verb selecting a non-*wh*-proposition (compare Horvath 1995). The identification of the matrix *wh*-phrase with the embedded question results in assigning to the clausal interrogative operator the scope corresponding to the c-command domain of the matrix *wh*-pronoun. In the case of multiple embedding, the association of the matrix *wh*-pronoun with the embedded *wh*-question takes place from bottom up, in every cycle. The lack of an interrogative pronoun in an intermediate cycle results in ungrammaticality:

(33)   * Mit   mondott Éva, hogy hallott(a),   hogy mit   ígért   János,
        what-ACC said   Eve that   heard(DEF)-she that   what-ACC promised John
        hogy hányra   érkezik?
        that   by.when arrives-he

10.2.4 Adjunct that-clauses

That-clauses can also accompany verbs that do not select a complement other than an agent. In such cases the *that*-clause need not be associated with a pronoun – obviously because the matrix verb has no case to assign; compare:

(34)   János csengetett/szólt   /mutogatott, hogy menjünk   be.
        John rang   /called.out /signalled   that go-SUBJ-1PL in
        'John rang/called out/signalled that we should go in.'

The *that*-clause associated with the intransitive verbs in (34) is not a complement of the verb; it does not express the theme of the action; it is an adjunct loosely related to the verb, specifying the meaning, or the purpose of the action denoted by the verb.[5]

A group of matrix verbs is optionally transitive. When they are used transitively, they take a *that*-clause complement associated with an accusative pronoun (35a, 36a). The pronoun is dropped in postverbal position; nevertheless, its presence can be reconstructed from the objective conjugation of the matrix verb. When used intransitively, these verbs can be accompanied by an adjunct *that*-clause. The adjunct *that*-clause is not associated with a pronoun, hence, the verb is in the subjective conjugation (35b, 36b).

(35) a.   János (**azt**)   telefonálta,   hogy ötkor érkezik.
        John (that-ACC) phone-PAST-DEF-3SG that   five-at arrives
        'John phoned (it) that he would arrive at five.'

    b.   János telefonált,   hogy ötkor érkezik.
        John phone-PAST-INDEF.3SG that   five-at arrives
        'John phoned that he would arrive at five.'

---

[5] *Szól* 'say' can take a non-specific indefinite object in some idiom-like expressions such as *mit szólsz* 'what do you say', *nem szólt semmit* 'he didn't say anything'; however, it is clearly ungrammatical with a specific object; compare:

(i)   * János ezt   szólta.
        John this-ACC said
        'John said this.'

(ii)   * János mindent   szólt.
        John everything-ACC said
        'John said everything.'

(36) a. János (**azt**)   üzente,   hogy ötkor érkezik.
         John that-ACC send.message-PAST-DEF-3SG that five-at arrives
         'John sent the message that he would arrive at five.'

  b. János üzent,   hogy ötkor érkezik.
      John send.message-PAST-INDEF.3SG that five-at arrives
      'John sent a message that he would arrive at five.'

Another group of predicates can optionally take an oblique complement. If their complement is represented by a subordinate clause, the oblique case selected by the matrix predicate is realized on the pronoun belonging to the clause. In this case the pronoun + subordinate clause complex is analyzed as an argument. If the pronoun is missing, the clause functions as an adjunct loosely associated with the predicate; compare:

(37) a. Mari büszke volt (**rá**), hogy a   gyerekei ilyen jó   eredményt értek   el.
         Mary proud   was (on.it) that her children such good result-ACC achieved VM
         'Mary was proud (of it) that her children achieved such a good result.'

  b. Mari dicsekedett/hencegett (**vele**), hogy a   gyerekei milyen jó   eredményt
      Mary bragged/showed.off   (with.it) that her children what   good result
      értek   el.
      achieved VM
      'Mary was bragging/showing off what a good result her children achieved.'

  c. Mari panaszkodott (**róla**),   hogy a   gyerekei milyen rossz eredményt
      Mary complained   (about.it) that her children what   bad   result-ACC
      értek   el.
      achieved VM
      'Mary complained (about it) what a bad result her children achieved.'

  d. Mari kiváncsi volt (**rá**), hogy a   gyerekei milyen eredményt
      Mary curious was (on.it) that her children what   result-ACC
      értek   el.
      achieved VM
      'Mary was curious (of it) what result her children achieved.'

10.3   Relative clauses

Relative clauses are introduced by a relative phrase which simultaneously fills an argument or adjunct slot in the embedded clause and functions as a subordinating operator. The relative phrase is raised to Spec,CP – presumably to have its [+complementizer] feature checked. The relative pronoun is formally a *wh*-pronoun with an optional *a*- prefix, which is an obsolete pronominal element. (It is the remnant of the demonstrative *az*, which functioned originally as the head of the relative, then came to be cliticized to the pronoun, and is interpreted by present-day speakers merely as an optional morpheme distinguishing relative pronouns from interrogative ones.) For example:

(38)   [$_{CP}$ (A)ki [$_{TopP}$ másnak [$_{AspP}$ vermet ás]]], maga   esik bele.
        who   other-DAT   pit-ACC digs   himself falls in.it
        'Who digs a pit for someone else, falls in it himself.'

In fact, the relative phrase could marginally also follow one or more of the topicalized constituents of the relative clause; i.e., *Másnak aki vermet ás...* would also be an acceptable variant of (38). Therefore, Kenesei (1994) does not raise the relative phrase into Spec,CP; he adjoins it to IP (which would correspond to topicalizing it in the present framework). The fact that the post-topic position of a relative phrase is rare and sounds archaic nevertheless suggests that its topicalization is merely a marked alternative of its movement to Spec,CP. As is well known (e.g. from Horvath 1986a), relative phrases and interrogative phrases do not share the same position in the Hungarian sentence. If the subject of the subordinate clause in (38) were an interrogative phrase, the clause would have the following structure:

(39)   [$_{CP}$ [$_{TopP}$ Másnak [$_{FP}$ ki [$_{VP}$ ás   vermet]]]]?[6]
        other-DAT   who digs pit-ACC
        'Who digs a pit for someone else?'

Relative clauses share the behavior of *that*-clauses in various respects. They form a constituent with a pronominal or a lexical phrase at some level of representation, although they often get extraposed from it. Free relatives are associated with a demonstrative pronoun, whose function is to pick up the case assigned by the matrix predicate to the argument represented by the relative clause, and to represent the clause in various internal positions of the matrix sentence that are not available for clausal complements:

(40) a.   [$_{Spec,TopP}$ *Azt/pro, amiről   beszéltünk*], felejtsd   el!
          that-ACC what-about talked-we   forget-IMPER-2SG VM
          'Forget what we talked about!'

     b.   [$_{Spec,DistP}$ **Arról   is**] tudok, [**ami a színfalak mögött történt**]
          that-about also know-I what the scenes   behind happened
          'I also know about what happened behind the scenes.'

---

[6] This difference between the positions of Hungarian relative *wh*-phrases and interrogative *wh*-phrases leads Horvath (1986a) to the conclusion that, universally, a *wh*-phrase can function as an interrogative operator only if it also has a [+focus] feature.

c. [_{Spec,FP} CSAK AZT]   hiszem   el,   [AMIT A   SAJÁT SZEMEMMEL LÁTTAM].
    only   that-ACC believe-I VM   what my own   eye-with   saw-I
    'Only that do I believe what I saw with my own eyes.'

d. Nem hiszek   [*abban, amit mond*]
    not   believe-I that-in what says-he
    'I don't believe in what he says.'

e. Felejtsd el   [*azt/pro, amiről   beszéltünk*]
    forget   VM   that   what-about talked-we
    'Forget what we talked about!'

In (40a) the pronoun + relative clause complex functions as a topicalized object; in (40b) it functions as an oblique distributive phrase; in (40c) it is a focussed object; in (40d) it is a VP-internal oblique complement; and in (40e) it is a VP-internal object. Whereas the VP-internal pronoun associated with a *that*-clause is a personal pronoun, a relative clause is always associated with a demonstrative – whether the pronoun is in preverbal or postverbal position. Pro-drop is possible in the VP or in Spec,TopP if the pronoun can be reconstructed from the conjugation of the V – i.e., if it is a subject or object pronoun (40a,e). The fact that an oblique pronoun associated with a relative clause with no lexical head cannot be omitted indicates that Hungarian has no true free relatives; apparent free relatives have a pro head.

Lexical noun phrases modified by a relative clause also contain a demonstrative element:

(41) a. **az** a könyv, amelyet   olvasok
    that the book   which-ACC read-I
    'that book which I am reading'

b. **annyi** könyv, ahányat   te egy évben el   olvasol
    so.many book   as.many-ACC you one year-in VM read
    'so many books as you read in one year'

c. egy **olyan** könyv, amilyet   olvasok
    a   such book   which-ACC read-I
    'such a book that I am reading'

The function of the demonstrative element is to indicate which layer of the noun phrase the relative clause modifies. The pro-adjective *olyan* indicates that the relative clause is to be adjoined to NP, *annyi* expresses that the relative clause is to be adjoined to NumP, whereas *az* expresses that it is to be adjoined to DP. These are the structures associated with (41a–c):

(42) a.

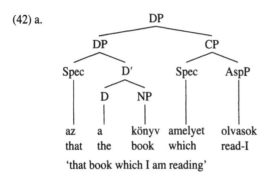

'that book which I am reading'

b.

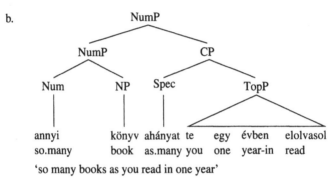

'so many books as you read in one year'

c.

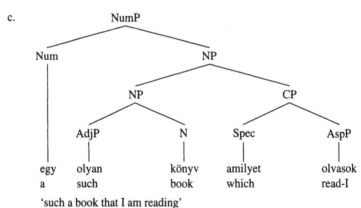

'such a book that I am reading'

The demonstrative in (42a) is sometimes omitted – presumably because the definite determiner can take over its function.

Non-restrictive relative clauses, e.g. relatives adjoined to proper names, differ from restrictive ones in that the noun phrase to which they are adjoined has no demonstrative element; for example:

(43)   *Kodályt,   aki   a   Köröndön lakott,* sokszor   láttam a   környéken
        Kodály-ACC who the Körönd-on lived   many.times saw-I   the neighborhood-in
        sétálni.
        to.walk
        'Kodály, who lived on Körönd square, I often saw walking in the neighborhood.'

A demonstrative element in front of the proper name would mean that the person denoted by the noun phrase + CP complex is one of several persons of the same name:

(44)   Azt a   Kodályt,   aki a   Köröndön lakott, ...
        that the Kodály-ACC who the Körönd-on lived
        'the Kodály who lived on Körönd square'

A relative clause appears to form a closer syntactic and phonological unit with the demonstrative or lexical noun phrase to which it belongs than a *that*-clause; in any case, its extraposition (e.g. from the middle of the VP) is not obligatory. A postmodifying relative clause in Spec,FP, however, is ungrammatical, because it violates the requirement that the focus constituent be head-final; compare:

(45)   * [$_{Spec,FP}$ CSAK AZ, [AKI UTOLSÓNAK LÉPETT   FEL]], kapott nagy tapsot.
        only   that who last   performed VM   got   great applause-ACC
        'Only he who performed last got great applause.'

The construction is better if the relative clause is left-adjoined to the constituent in Spec,FP, allowing it to be head-final (46a), but the unmarked solution is extraposition:

(46) a.   [$_{Spec,FP}$ CSAK [AKI UTOLSÓKÉNT LÉPETT FEL], AZ] kapott nagy tapsot.
    b.   [$_{Spec,FP}$ CSAK AZ] kapott nagy tapsot, [AKI UTOLSÓNAK LÉPETT FEL]
    c.   [AKI UTOLSÓKÉNT LÉPETT FEL], [$_{Spec,FP}$ CSAK AZ] kapott nagy tapsot.

Apart from this case, extraposition is a possible, but non-obligatory option for restrictive relative clauses; compare:

(47) a.   [$_{Spec,TopP}$ Azt a   tornászt,   aki elsőnek szerepel], mindig le   pontozza
        that the gymnast-ACC who first   performs   always down marks
        néhány bíró.
        some   judge
        'The gymnast who performs first is always marked down by some judges.'

    b.   [$_{Spec,TopP}$ Azt a tornászt] mindig lepontozza néhány bíró, [aki elsőnek szerepel]

Non-restrictive clauses are less mobile. Since the modifier–modifiee relation is not marked on the noun phrase to which the non-restrictive relative belongs, extraposition would make it hard to reconstruct the original position of the relative clause. Nevertheless, extraposition from Spec,FP is forced by the requirement that the focus constituent be head-final; compare:

(48) a.   ? [Spec,TopP *Kodállyal*]   sokszor találkoztam a   környéken,   [*aki a*
Kodály-with often   met-I   the neighborhood-in who the
Köröndön lakott].
Körönd-on lived
'With Kodály, who lived on Körönd square, I often met in the neighborhood.'

   b.   [Spec,FP CSAK KODÁLLYAL] találkoztam sokszor, [AKI A   KÖRÖNDÖN LAKOTT].
only Kodály-with met-I   often   who the Körönd-on lived
'Only with Kodály, who lived on Körönd square, did I often meet.'

10.4   Adverbial clauses

Adverbial clauses are mostly relative clauses with an optional head.
The relative pro-adverb introducing them is an adjunct of the embedded predicate, raised to Spec,CP. The head is the demonstrative equivalent of the relative
adverb; for example:

(49) a.   A parlagfű [AdvP **ott   is**] meg jelenik, [**ahol   azelőtt soha nem tapasztalták**].
the ragweed   there too up shows where before never not attested-they
'Ragweed shows up also where it has never been attested.'

   b.   Sokan [AdvP CSAK AKKOR] irtják   a   parlagfüvet, [AMIKOR MÁR
many   only then   extirpate the ragweed   when   already
ELHULLATTA A   MAGJÁT].
shed-it   its seed
'Many extirpate ragweed only when it has already shed its seeds.'

Since the relative adverb introducing the embedded clause expresses the adverbial
function that the clause plays in the matrix sentence, the pro-adverb associated
with the clause as its head is semantically redundant; its role is merely to represent
the clausal complement in positions that are not available for clausal constituents –
as is the case in (49a,b), where it stands in the Spec,DistP, and Spec,FP positions
of the matrix sentence, respectively. In other sentence positions the spelling-out of
the pro-adverb is optional:

(50) a.   [(Ott) [ahol meg bolygatták a   talajt]], meg jelenik a   parlagfű.
there where up broke-they the soil   up shows the ragweed
'Where the soil has been broken up, ragweed appears.'

   b.   [(Akkor) [amikor a   parlagfű már   el   virágzott]], késő irtani.
then   when the ragweed already VM flowered   late to.extirpate
'When ragweed has already flowered, it is late to extirpate it.'

In certain cases, the relative pronoun introducing the adverbial relative cannot in
fact be interpreted as an adjunct of the embedded proposition; for example:

(51) a.   (Azóta) **amióta**   meg érkezett, még nem szólt   egy szót sem.
          since.that since.what VM arrived-he yet not said-he a   word neither
          'Since he arrived he hasn't said a word yet.'

   b.   (Azelőtt) **mielőtt**   a   szomszédunkba költöztek, vidéken   laktak.
        before.that before.what our neighborhood-to moved-they country-in lived-they
        'Before they moved to our neighborhood, they lived in the country.'

   c.   (Azután) **miután**   letette   az utolsó vizsgáját, nem vett   szakkönyvet
        after.that after.what passed-he his last   exam   not took-he technical-book
        a   kezébe.
        his hand-in
        'After he passed his last exam, he did not touch a technical book.'

Although *ami-óta* 'since when', *mi-előtt* 'before what', *mi-után* 'after what' are formally relative pronouns merged with a postposition, they do not denote the time of the event described in the relative clause. *Megérkezik* 'arrive', *költözik* 'move', *letesz* 'pass' express momentary actions, which cannot combine with *since*, *before*, and *after* phrases, expressing duration. Consequently, the apparently relative elements introducing these clauses are not relative pronouns extracted from inside the subordinate proposition, but must be adverbial complementizers generated in C or Spec,CP. (They consist of a pronominal element *mi-* 'what', to which the clause bears an appositive relation, and a postposition expressing the temporal relation that the event described in the clause bears to the matrix predicate.)

Interestingly, there is a parallelism requirement concerning the matrix pronominal element and the complementizer: they must bear the same case or postposition:

(52) a.   **Akkorra, amikorra** elmentek a   vendégek, a   háziak teljesen
          by.then   by.when   left   the guests   the hosts completely
          kimerültek.
          got.exhausted
          'By the time the guests left, the hosts became completely exhausted.'

   b.   **Azért** késett   el, **mert**   lekéste a buszt.
        that-for late.was-he VM what-for missed the bus
        'He was late because he missed the bus.'

(53) a.   * **Akkorra, amikor** elmentek a   vendégek...
          by.then   when   left   the guests

   b.   * **Azelőtt,   amikor** férjhez ment...
        before.that when   married got-she

If these sentences are introduced by a contentive adverbial complementizer indicating the function of the embedded clause in the matrix sentence, then the question is what role the demonstrative pro-adverb optionally associated with them plays.

Obviously, adverbial clauses can be generated in an appositive relation with a matching AdvP or PP for the same reason as adverbial relatives proper can be associated with a head: because occasionally the clause must be represented in a slot of the matrix sentence that is not available for clausal complements. This was the case in (52b), and this is the case in (54):

(54)　　[Spec,FP CSAK AZUTÁN] doktorált　　le, [MIUTÁN SZÜLT
　　　　　　only　after.that took.Ph.D-she VM　after.what bore-she
　　　　HÁROM GYEREKET]
　　　　three　children
　　　　'It was only after bearing three children that she took her Ph.D.'

An adverbial clause introduced by a complementizer that is not of the form (a)mi + Kase/P, i.e., that cannot be identified formally with a relative pronoun, cannot be associated with a demonstrative AdvP or PP, hence it cannot be focussed or used as a distributive phrase; for example:

(55) a.　　Mihelyt le　　ült,　　rá　gyújtott egy cigarettára.
　　　　　　as.soon.as down sat-he VM lit-he　a　cigarette-on
　　　　　　'As soon as he sat down, he lit a cigarette.'

　　　b.　　Minthogy/Mivel　fáradt volt,　le　feküdt.
　　　　　　as　　　　　/because tired　was-he down lay-he
　　　　　　'As he was tired, he went to bed.'

10.5　Long operator movement

10.5.1　The types of operators subject to long movement

It is an old observation of Hungarian grammarians[7] that the material of the subordinate clause and that of the matrix clause can 'intertwine'. More precisely, material from the embedded clause can appear in the preverbal, operator domain of the matrix clause; i.e., certain types of complex sentences form a single domain for operator movement. Every type of operator can undergo long movement, among them the focus:

(56) a.　　[FP KITi　szeretnél　[CP hogy meg hívjunk ti a　　születésnapodra?]]
　　　　　　whom would.like-you that　VM invite-we your birthday-for
　　　　　　'Whom would you like that we invite for your birthday?'

---

[7] See Zolnay (1926), as well as de Groot (1981), É. Kiss (1987a, 1991c), Haader (1998), etc.

b.   [$_{TopP}$ János [$_{FP}$ CSAK MARIT$_i$ nem engedte [$_{CP}$ hogy meg hívjam t_i]]]
     John   only Mary-ACC not allowed   that VM invite-I
     'It was only Mary that John didn't allow that I invite.'

The *wh*-phrase in (56a) and the *only* phrase in (56b) take matrix scope; thus, the
scope of the *only* phrase extends over the matrix negation. The extraction of the
wh-phrase out of (56a) is in fact obligatory, given that the matrix verb selects
a non-interrogative complement. (Another strategy of satisfying the selectional
restriction of the matrix verb would be to move the *wh*-phrase into the Spec,FP
position of the embedded clause, and to associate the clause with a matrix interrogative pronoun; see Section 10.2.3 above.)

Positive and negative distributive quantifiers originating in the embedded sentence can also land in the Spec,DistP and Spec,NegP positions of the matrix clause:

(57) a.   [$_{DistP}$ **Jánost**   **is**$_i$ szeretném [$_{CP}$ ha meg hívnánk t_i]]
          John-ACC too would.like-I if VM invited-we
          'John, too, I would like us to invite.'

     b.   [$_{TopP}$ János [$_{DistNegP}$ *semelyikkollégámat*   *sem*$_i$ engedte [$_{CP}$ hogy
          John   no   colleague.my-ACC not allowed   that
          meghívjam t_i]]]
          invite-I
          'None of my colleagues did John allow me to invite.'

In the case of (57b), long operator movement is in fact unavoidable, because
the negative quantifier generated in the embedded clause is required to move
to Spec,DistNegP – however, the embedded clause does not contain a NegP
projection.

The long movement of an aspectual operator (constituted by a verb modifier)
is licensed only by modal matrix verbs (those that also license it in infinitival
constructions; compare Sections 9.2–9.4). In the case of verb modifier movement
into a matrix Spec,AspP the embedded and the matrix predicates form a single
domain for aspect marking – i.e., they form a kind of complex predicate (58a,b).
Accordingly, the embedded clause cannot contain logical operators, e.g. a focus
or a quantifier, and even a topic intervening between the embedded verb and the
complementizer decreases acceptability (58c,d).

(58) a.   [$_{TopP}$ János [$_{AspP}$ meg$_i$ akarja [$_{CP}$ hogy beszéljük t_i a   problémákat]]]
          John   over wants   that talk-we   the problems
          'John wants us to talk over the problems.'

     b.   [$_{AspP}$ Meg$_i$ kell [$_{CP}$ hogy beszéljük t_i a   problémákat]]
          over needs that talk-we   the problems
          'It is necessary that we talk over the problems.'

c. * [$_{AspP}$ Meg$_i$ kell [$_{CP}$ hogy [$_{FP}$ CSAK A   PROBLÉMÁKAT [beszéljük t_i]]]]
over needs that   only the problems-ACC talk-we
'It is necessary that it be only the problems that we talk over.'

d. ? [$_{AspP}$ Meg$_i$ kell [$_{CP}$ hogy [$_{TopP}$ a   fiúk beszéljék t_i a   problémákat]]]
over needs that   the boys talk   the problems
'It is necessary that the boys talk over the problems.'

Unlike local VM movement into Spec,AspP, VM climbing across a finite clause boundary is not obligatory. Furthermore, the less independent semantic content the climbing verb modifier has, the more marginal the output of long VM movement will be. Den Dikken (1999b: footnote 28) interprets these facts as evidence that a verb modifier undergoing long movement actually lands in the matrix focus position.

The topic of the matrix sentence can also originate in the embedded clause; for example:

(59) a.   [$_{TopP}$ Jánossal$_i$ nem akarom [$_{CP}$ hogy meg beszéljünk bármit is t_i]]
John-with not want-I   that over talk-we   anything
'With John, I don't want us to discuss anything.'

b.   [$_{TopP}$ Marit$_i$ PÉTER ígérte   meg [$_{CP}$ hogy fel hívja t_i]]
Mary-ACC Peter   promised VM   that up calls
'Mary, PETER promised to call up.'

10.5.2 Constraints on long operator movement

Since extraction is universally subject to the Condition on Extraction Domains (CED), adjunct clauses are expected to block the long operator movement of their constituents. Indeed, an adjunct *that*-clause, or an adverbial clause is impermeable for long operator movement:

(60) a. * A kollégáim EGY DIÁK$_i$ figyelmeztettek [$_{CP}$ hogy keresett t_i]
my colleagues a   student warned-me   that sought-me
'My colleagues warned me that a student was looking for me.'

b. * **Mindenki**$_i$ el indulunk [$_{CP}$ mihelyt   megérkezett t$_i$]
everybody off go-we   as.soon.as arrived
'We leave as soon as everybody has arrived.'

Since the subject is in the government domain of the verb in Hungarian, subject clauses are not expected to be affected by the CED. Indeed, they allow extraction:

(61) a.   János$_i$ nyilvánvaló [$_{CP}$ hogy nagyon tehetséges t_i]
John obvious   that very   talented
'It is obvious that John is very talented.'

b.   JÁNOST$_i$ a   legvalószínűbb [$_{CP}$ hogy felveszik   az   egyetemre t_i]
     John-ACC the likeliest   that admit-they the university-to
     'John is the likeliest to be admitted to the university.'

At the same time, it is not the case that all types of argument clauses are potential sources of long extraction. The set of bridge verbs attested in Hungarian is similar to that found in other languages. It includes primarily modal predicates taking a subject or object clause, among them *akar* 'want', *szeretne* 'would like', *kell* 'need', *szabad* 'may', *lehet* 'is possible', *nyilvánvaló* 'is obvious', *valószínű* 'is likely', as well as verbs of saying and verbs denoting mental activities, among them *mond* 'say', *ígér* 'promise', *állít* 'claim', *gondol* 'think', *hisz* 'believe', etc. These predicates do not necessarily introduce an event different from that expressed in the subordinate clause; they serve to report the event described in their subordinate clause, or to evaluate it, or to modify it by a modal operator, etc. The fact that at least on the conceptual level sentences allowing long operator movement involve a complex proposition describing a single event is confirmed by the fact that long operator movement is more acceptable from subjunctive and conditional sentences than from sentences with an independent tense; compare:

(62) a.   János HOLNAP$_i$ akarja [$_{CP}$ hogy induljunk t_i]
          John tomorrow wants   that leave-SUBJ-we
          'It is tomorrow that John wants us to leave.'

     b.   János HOLNAP$_i$ szeretné [$_{CP}$ ha indulnánk t_i]
          John tomorrow would.like   if leave-COND-we
          'It is tomorrow that John would like us to leave.'

     c.   ? János HOLNAP$_i$ mondta [$_{CP}$ hogy indulunk t_i]
          John tomorrow said   that leave-we
          'It is tomorrow that John said we leave.'

In the framework in which argument clauses are embedded under a noun phrase, bearing an appositive relation to a pronoun, extraction from an argument clause is expected to be blocked by the Complex Noun Phrase Constraint (CNPC). Indeed, the pronoun associated with the argument clause, i.e., the head of the complex noun phrase, cannot be spelled out in the case of extraction:

(63) a.   * Azt$_j$ János HOLNAP$_i$ akarja [$_{CP}$ hogy induljunk t_i]$_j$
          that-ACC John tomorrow wants   that leave-we

     b.   * Az$_j$ JÁNOST$_i$ a   legvalószínűbb [$_{CP}$ hogy felveszik   az   egyetemre t_i]$_j$
          that-NOM John-ACC the likeliest   that admit-they the university-to

The blocking effect of the pronoun would follow from the CNPC only under the assumption that a projection containing no phonologically realized material is transparent for subjacency. Then the noun phrase subsuming the argument clause would activate the CNPC only when its nominal head is spelled out phonologically. (Naturally, the transparency of phonologically vacuous projections would have to be confirmed by independent evidence. It should, for instance, be examined if the English *that*-trace effect could be reinterpreted along these lines.)

In the framework proposed by Lipták (1998), the CNPC has no role to play. The complementarity of long extraction from a *that*-clause, and the presence of an expletive pronoun follow from the assumption both that extraction proceeds through Spec,CP, and that the expletive pronoun is located in Spec,CP.

Given that a *wh*-phrase occupies Spec,FP instead of Spec,CP, the Spec,CP of an embedded question is available as an escape hatch, hence an embedded question is not an island; compare:

(64) a. [$_{FP}$ Kit$_i$ nem tudsz [$_{CP}$ t_i hogy mikor vizsgázik t_i?]]
         whom not know-you that when sits.for.exam
         'Whom do you wonder when (he) will sit the exam?'

   b. [$_{DistNegP}$ Senkit   sem$_i$ tudok [$_{CP}$ t_i hogy mikor vizsgázik t_i]]
         nobody-ACCnot know-I   that when sits.for.exam
         'Of nobody do I know when he sits the exam.'

10.5.3 The procedure of long operator movement

In view of the facts considered so far, it seems likely that long operator movement involves the extraction of a constituent from the VP of the embedded clause through Spec,CP into a matrix operator position. The fact that for example a *wh*-phrase can be extracted across a *wh*-phrase occupying the Spec,FP of the lower sentence into the matrix Spec,FP indicates that it does not have to use the lower Spec,FP position as an intermediate landing site. This is also confirmed by the interaction of the constituent undergoing long focus movement with the embedded aspectual operator:

(65) a. Kit$_i$ akarsz [$_{CP}$ t_i hogy [$_{AspP}$ haza menjen t_i]]?
         whom want-you that   home go-SUBJ-3SG
         'Whom do you want to go home?'

      compare:

   b. Ki$_i$ [$_{VP}$ ment haza t_i]?
         who   went home

If *kit* 'whom' had landed temporarily in Spec,FP in the lower cycle, no AspP projection would have been generated, because it cannot be projected in the presence of an FP.

Whereas the raised constituent skips the operator positions in the embedded clause, it must pass through every Spec,CP on the way to its landing site, its extraction must be licensed by bridge verbs, and it must observe the CED and the

CNPC on every cycle, as happens in (66):

(66)   JÁNOSTÓL$_i$ mondták, [$_{CP}$ t_i hogy szeretnék, [$_{CP}$ t_i ha ajánlást
        John-from said-they   that   would.like-they if recommendation-ACC
        hoznék t_i]]
        brought-I
        'It is John that they said that they would like if I brought a recommendation from.'

An intervening non-bridge verb, such as *figyelmeztet* 'warn', taking an adjunct
that-clause, blocks extraction:

(67)   * JÁNOSTÓL$_i$ mondta, [$_{CP}$ **hogy figyelmeztették,** [$_{CP}$ t_i hogy hozzon
        John-from said-he   that   warned-they-him   that   bring-SUBJ-he
        ajánlást t_i]]
        recommendation
        'It is John that he said that he was warned that he should bring a recommendation
        from.'

Notice the effect of an intervening complex noun phrase (i.e., the effect of an
argument clause being embedded in a non-vacuous noun phrase projection):

(68)   * JÁNOSTÓL$_i$ mondták, [$_{CP}$ hogy azt   szeretnék, [$_{CP}$ t_i ha ajánlást
        John-from said-they   that   that-ACC would.like-they if recommendation-ACC
        hoznék t_i]]
        brought-I
        'It is John that they said that they would like if I brought a recommendation from.'

A subject extracted from an object clause assumes accusative case in the course
of the derivation – as in various British English dialects:

(69)   Kit$_i$ javasolsz, [$_{CP}$ t_i hogy [elnök   legyen t_i]]?
        whom suggest-you   that   president become
        'Whom do you suggest should be the president?'

Chomsky (1981: 174) suggests that in such constructions the raised constituent
receives accusative case from the intermediate verb when passing through the
specifier of the lowest CP. It is only a nominative-marked constituent, bearing a
phonologically null case marker, whose case can be superseded by an accusative
assigned by the matrix verb. The case of a raised accusative-marked constituent
obviously remains accusative, and the case of a raised oblique-marked constituent
also remains oblique:

(70)   [$_{FP}$ Kinek$_i$ akarod [$_{CP}$ t_i hogy [a   kitüntetést adjuk t_i?]]]
             whom-DAT want-you   that   the award-ACC give-we
        'Whom do you want that we give the award to?'

The fact that only a nominative case is subject to case-reassignment follows if nominative is, indeed, the lack of case, as in the theory of Bittner and Hale (1996).

Lipták (1998) has reinterpreted this account of case change in the Minimalist framework. She assumes that the C head of a clausal argument with a structural case has a +D/N categorial feature, as well as a case and phi-features. In the unmarked case, the checking of these features is carried out by the expletive pronoun; e.g. the case feature of C is checked by the expletive raising to a matrix AgrP. There is also an alternative option: the features of C can be checked locally, if a constituent with a matching +D/N feature is raised to Spec,CP from the embedded clause. The +D/N constituent raised to Spec,CP will enter into spec–head agreement with C, sharing its case feature – i.e., if a nominative is raised out of an object clause, it will assume the accusative of C. (Constituents with an oblique case are assumed to have a +P or +Adv feature instead of +D/N – that is why the long operator movement of an oblique constituent does not involve a case change.) According to Lipták's theory, an accusative raised out of a subject clause should also assume nominative case in Spec,CP. It does not, which Lipták explains away by claiming that raising out of a subject clause is marginal, in general.

If the constituent undergoing long operator movement is an object, or subject-turned-object, it will trigger definiteness-agreement on the matrix verb. In complex sentences containing an object clause and involving no long operator movement, the matrix verb agrees with the object clause, which counts as definite (71a). If an indefinite object is raised out of the object clause, the matrix verb will be in the subjective conjugation used in the presence of a NumP object (71b) (although for example Bartos (1999a) also accepts the objective conjugation). Lipták's framework can easily account for these facts: in the former case the expletive pronoun generated in the specifier of the object clause; in the latter case the constituent raised from inside the object clause will land in the matrix Spec,AgrOP, carrying there its own definiteness feature.

(71) a.   Hallott**ad**,   hogy azt   szeretné**k**,   hogy
           hear-PAST-DEF-2SG that   that-ACC like-COND-DEF-3PL that
           válasszunk   valakit   elnöknek?
           choose-SUBJ-INDEF.1PL someone-ACC president
           'Have you heard that they would like us to choose somebody president?'

       b.   Kit$_i$ hallott**ál**   [$_{CP}$ t_i hogy szeretnének   [$_{CP}$ t_i hogy
            whom hear-PAST-INDEF.2SG that   like-COND-INDEF.3PL that
            megválasszunk   elnöknek t_i?]]
            choose-SUBJ-INDEF.1PL president
            'Whom have you heard that they would like us to choose president?'

The fact that the definiteness feature of a raised object takes precedence over that of the source clause in movement to Spec,AgrOP is derived by den Dikken (1999a) from economy conditions: the trace/copy of the raised object in Spec,CP is closer to the matrix AgrO than C, which is assumed by him to carry the definiteness feature of CP. It is not clear how den Dikken would ensure that the *hogy* complementizer of an adjunct clause – e.g. that of (35b) – has no [+definite] feature. In the framework advocated here the definiteness of an object clause derives from the fact that it is embedded under a DP headed by a pronoun. The problem for the latter view would be that this DP is closer to AgrO than the object trace in the specifier of the CP embedded under DP – i.e., the question why the matrix verb agrees with the object trace instead of the DP containing it would remain unexplained (unless the constituent triggering agreement is not the object trace in Spec,CP but the raised object itself).

Lipták's approach also solves a further mystery of long operator movement. Whereas the spelling-out of the complementizer of an argument *that*-clause is mostly optional,[8] long movement across Spec,CP makes the spelling-out of the complementizer obligatory:

(72) a.   [$_{FP}$ János$_i$ akarom [$_{CP}$ t_i hogy [$_{AspP}$ meg válasszuk t_i]]]
      John-ACC want-I   that   VM elect-we
      'It is John that I want that we elect.'

   b. * [$_{FP}$ János$_i$ akarom [$_{CP}$ t_i [$_{AspP}$ meg válasszuk t_i]]]
      'It is John I want we elect.'

   compare:

   c.   Azt   akarom, [$_{CP}$ (hogy) JÁNOST   válasszuk meg]
      that-ACC want-I   that John-ACC elect-we VM
      'I want that we elect John.'

The complementizer plays a crucial role in carrying the categorial, case, and phi-features of the clausal argument, and sharing them via spec–head agreement with the constituent raised to Spec,CP – presumably that is why it cannot be deleted.

Den Dikken (1999b) proposes an alternative analysis of the case change attested in (69). He points out that 1st and 2nd person pronouns can also undergo case change, e.g. a *te* 'you' extracted from an object clause becomes *téged* 'you-ACC'. The accusative forms of 1st and 2nd person pronouns, however, are non-compositional (the regular accusative of *te*, for instance, would be *té-t*) – hence they cannot be the output of syntactic morpheme composition. He concludes that the accusative-marked subject is accusative from the start; it is generated as such in Spec,VP. The constituent appearing in the morphosyntactic projections of the embedded verb, bearing nominative case, is a pro. He argues that the 2nd person

---

[8] For certain constraints on *hogy* deletion, see Kenesei (1994: 333–339).

accusative pronoun is represented by a clitic-doubling-like possessive construction, consisting of a clitic and the *te* 'you' pronoun supplied with the 2nd person possessedness inflection. When it is subject to long operator movement, the whole pronominal complex is raised from the embedded Spec,VP to Spec,CP, as follows:

(73)   ...[$_{CP}$ [CL$_{2sg}$ téged]$_i$ [hogy [$_{IP}$ pro [$_{VP}$$t_i$ ...
              you-ACC that

Téged has a focus feature, which needs to be checked in the matrix Spec,FP. The clitic part (an *-l* morpheme), on the other hand, moves to the matrix Spec,AgrOP, and subsequently cliticizes to the *-k* subject agreement suffix, resulting in a *-lak* morpheme complex (compare Section 3.5.2); that is:

(74)   [$_{FP}$ TÉGED$_i$ akarlak [$_{CP}$ t_i hogy pro t_i meglátogasd   Jánost]]
              you-ACC want-I   that   visit-SUBJ-DEF-2SG John-ACC
         'It is you that I want to visit John.'

10.5.4 A base-generated construction

Long topicalization apparently does not need to observe the constraints that long focussing or long distributive quantifier movement are subject to. Thus:

(i)   It can violate the CED:

(75)   János már   dél felé   járt az idő, amikor felébredt.
         John already noon towards went the time when   awoke
         'John, it was already about noon when (he) woke up.'

(ii)   It can violate the CNPC:

(76) a. Jánost   nincs [$_{DP}$ az az ember [$_{DP}$ aki fel   tudná bosszantani]]
         John-ACC isn't   that the man   who VM   could make.angry
         'John, there is no man who could make (him) angry.'

    b.   Jánost   [$_{DP}$ azt   a pletykát t_i] hallottam [$_{CP}$ hogy el   fogják
         John-ACC   that-ACC the gossip-ACC heard-I   that VM will-they
         bocsájtani]$_i$
         fire
         'John, I heard the gossip that they will fire.'

(iii)   The raised subject need not pick up the accusative assigned by the matrix verb, as opposed to what we attested in (69):

(77)   János azt   hiszem, hogy elfogadja a javaslatot.
         John that-ACC think-I that accepts   the proposal
         'John, I think that (he) accepts the proposal.'

(iv)   The matrix verb does not agree with the raised object, or
        subject-turned-object, e.g. in (78) it agrees with the definite object
        clause instead of the indefinite object raised from it:

(78)   Ennyi   vendéget nem gondolom,   hogy le   tudunk ültetni.
        so.many guest-ACC not think-DEF-1SG that VM can-we to.seat
        'So many guests, I don't think that we can seat.'

(v)   The complementizer of the source clause can be omitted:

(79)   Jánossal   azt   hiszem, nem érdemes   vitatkozni.
        John-with that-ACC think-I not worthwhile to.argue
        'With John, I think it is not worthwhile to argue.'

(vi)   The topic constituent can be followed by a coreferent pronoun
        cliticized to it:

(80) a. Jánost,   azt nincs az az ember, aki fel   tudná bosszantani.
        John-ACC him isn't that the man   who angry could make
        'John, there is no man who could make him angry.'

    b. Jánossal, azzal   azt   hiszem, nem érdemes   vitatkozni.
        John-with he-with it-ACC think-I not worthwhile to.argue
        'With John, I think it is not worthwhile to argue with him.'

The matrix topic in (75)–(80), coindexed with an empty complement position
in the subordinate clause, is in all probability base-generated as a hanging topic.
At the same time, a matrix topic belonging lexically to the subordinate clause can
also satisfy the stricter conditions of long operator movement: thus, it can pick up
the accusative assigned by the matrix verb – i.e., long topic movement is also an
option provided by Hungarian grammar; for example:

(81)   Jánost   nem mindenki szeretné,   hogy elnök   legyen.
        John-ACC not everybody would.like that   president become
        'John, not everybody would like to be president.'

In a matrix sentence in which both the topic and the focus bind argument positions
in the subordinate clause, only the focus has passed through Spec,CP; the topic
must have been base-generated in the matrix clause; for example:

(82) a. *János* AZ ELNÖKSÉGRE$_i$ szeretnénk,   ha pályázna t_i.
        John the presidency-to would.like-we if aspired
        'We would like John to aspire TO THE PRESIDENCY.'

    b. *Az elnökségre*   JÁNOST$_i$ szeretnénk,   ha pályázna t_i.
        the presidency-to John-ACC would.like-we if aspired
        'To the presidency, we would like JOHN to aspire.'

In (82a) the oblique complement has been extracted through Spec,CP from the
embedded clause. The subject has been base generated in front of the complex

sentence as a hanging topic – consequently it cannot assume the accusative case licensed/assigned by the matrix verb:

(83)   * *Jánost*   AZ ELNÖKSÉGRE szeretnénk,   ha pályázna.
        John-ACC the presidency-to would.like-we if aspired
        'We would like if John aspired to the presidency.'

In (82b), on the other hand, it is the oblique complement of the embedded verb that is generated in front of the matrix clause as a hanging topic, and the subject passes through Spec,CP, assuming accusative case on the way.

10.6   Parasitic gaps

In the Hungarian sentence, the topic, the distributive quantifiers, and the focus, too, can license a parasitic gap,[9] i.e., each of these elements can simultaneously bind two variables in two different clauses; for example:

(84) a.   *Egy cikket*$_i$ elveszített a   szerkesztő t_i, még mielőtt elolvasott-volna pg_i.
        an   article-ACC lost   the editor   still before he.had.read
        'The editor lost an article still before reading.'

    b.   A szerkesztő **minden cikket**$_i$ elveszített t_i, még mielőtt
        the editor   every   paper-ACC lost   still before
        elolvasott-volna pg_i.
        he.had.read
        'The editor lost every paper still before reading.'

    c.   HÁNY   CIKKET$_i$ dobott ki a   szerkesztő t_i anélkül,   hogy
        how.many paper-ACC threw   out the editor   without.it that
        elolvasott-volna pg_i?
        he.had.read
        'How many papers did the editor throw out without reading?'

    d.   * A   szerkesztő ki   dobott cikkeket$_i$, anélkül,   hogy elolvasott-volna pg_i.
        the editor   out threw papers   without.it that he.had.read
        'The editor threw out papers without reading.'

The embedded clauses in (84) contain a parasitic variable rather than a pro because a pro would count as a definite pronoun, a DP, and would trigger the objective verb conjugation. The embedded verbs of these sentences, however, are in the subjective conjugation, i.e., they agree with an indefinite object.

---

[9] The first analysis of Hungarian parasitic gaps was put forth by É. Kiss (1985–86). Horvath (1990, 1992) pointed out a problem with the theory, and proposed an alternative solution. É. Kiss (2001) is a revised version of É. Kiss (1985–86), with the problem found by Horvath eliminated.

The parasitic gap construction is legitimate if both variables are linked to the antecedent by legitimate chains, which happen to merge at some point. The requirement that each of the variables be linked to the operator by a series of legitimate chain links does not necessarily mean case identity between the antecedent and the two variables. Compare the following examples. In (85a,b) the lack of case identity between the antecedent and one of the variables leads to ungrammaticality; however, (86), displaying apparently the same case-mismatch, is grammatical.

(85) a. * **Több tanulmányra is**$_i$ hivatkoztál t_i, anélkül, hogy elolvastál-volna pg_i.
several study-to   also referred-you without.it that you.had.read
'You referred to several studies without reading.'

  b. * MILYEN CIKK$_i$ jelent   meg t_i, anélkül, hogy elolvastál-volna pg_i?
what   article appeared VM   without.it that you.had.read
'What article appeared without you reading?'

(86)   MILYEN TANULMÁNYT$_i$ akartál,   anélkül, hogy elolvastál-volna pg_i,
what   study-ACC   wanted-you without.it that you.had.read
hogy megjelenjen t_i?
that appear-SUBJ-3SG
'What study did you want to appear without reading?'

The problem with (85a,b) is that the parasitic gap cannot be linked to the operator binding the real gap by a legitimate chain. In both sentences, the parasitic gap is in the accusative, whereas in (85a) the antecedent is in an oblique case, and in (85b) it is in the nominative. In (86) the antecedent (as well as the parasitic gap) is in the accusative, whereas the real gap is in the nominative. Nevertheless, the nominative variable is linked to the antecedent by a legitimate chain: the nominative is superseded by an accusative assigned to the Spec,CP of the clause in which the nominative argument was generated. Consider also the example in (87):

(87)   * MELYIK CIKKET$_i$ dobta   ki a szerkesztő t_i, mielőtt
which paper-ACC threw-DEF-3SG out the editor   before
elolvasott-volna pg_i?
read-PAST-INDEF.3SG
'Which paper did the editor throw out before reading?'

Example (87) is ungrammatical because the chain linking the parasitic gap to the operator is illegitimate: the parasitic variable has the feature [−definite] (as is indicated by the subjective conjugation of the verb), whereas the operator is [+definite]. The fact that the parasitic gap must share all the grammatical features of the operator binding the real gap is theoretically important because it provides evidence that the parasitic gap construction constitutes a forking chain. No other construction can ensure a match of features between the antecedent and the parasitic gap. In Chomsky (1986), for example, the parasitic gap is bound by a null operator, which is linked to the operator binding the real gap through strong binding. A binding relation, however, does not require that the binder and the bound element share all grammatical features (e.g. in the sentence *A man shot himself* the binder is [–definite], and the bound element is [+definite]).

Hungarian parasitic gap constructions have the locality properties known from other languages: the parasitic branch of the forking chain is located in an adjunct, i.e., the highest parasitic variable is separated from the nearest licensing variable by an extra barrier. Observe the structure of the parasitic gap construction in (86):

(88)

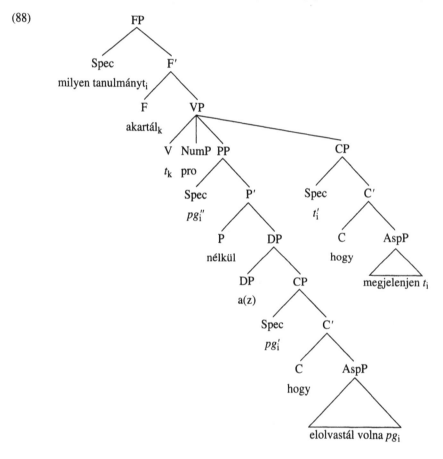

10.7   Summary

A clause can be embedded in a matrix sentence by means of a subordinating operator: the unmarked *hogy* 'that', a relative pronoun or pro-adverb, or an adverbial complementizer. Subordinate clauses functioning as arguments are associated with a pronominal or lexical head. The head associated with the subordinate clause plays a dual role: it picks up the case assigned by the matrix verb to the argument represented by the embedded clause, and, on the other hand, it represents the embedded clause in the matrix operator positions that are not available for clausal complements. So as to be able to function as a focus or a distributive phrase in the matrix sentence, even an adjunct clause may require a pronominal/pro-adverbial head to represent it in the matrix Spec,FP or Spec,DistP position. A *that*-clause cannot be internal to a lexical projection, and is also barred from Spec,AspP, Spec,DistP, and Spec,FP by independent constraints. As a consequence of these restrictions, it usually surfaces either in topic position, or extraposed to the right periphery of the matrix sentence.

Embedded questions have the unmarked *hogy* 'that' complementizer in their C position. The *wh*-phrase occupies the Spec,FP slot of the embedded clause, hence a *wh*-clause is not an island for extraction. The interrogative operator of an embedded question can assume matrix scope if the embedded question is associated with an interrogative pronoun in the matrix sentence. Alternatively, the embedded interrogative phrase can undergo long focus movement.

Complex sentences whose matrix verb is a bridge verb (a modal, a verb of saying, or a verb expressing a mental activity) can form a single domain for operator movement. A condition of long operator movement is that the pronoun associated with the subordinate clause should be a phonologically vacuous pro. Long operator movement carrying material from the embedded clause into a preverbal position of the matrix sentence may involve case reassignment to the extracted constituent by the matrix verb. Complementizer deletion blocks long operator movement. There is also a base-generated construction resembling the output of long topic movement, but exempt from its constraints.

The focus, the distributive quantifier, and the topic all license parasitic gaps, i.e., they can bind two variables in two different clauses simultaneously. Each of the variables must be linked to the operator by a legitimate chain, in which the grammatical features of the variable are properly transmitted to the antecedent.

References

Abraham, Werner and Sjaak de Meij (eds.) 1986, *Topic, Focus, and Configurationality*, Amsterdam: John Benjamins.

Ackerman, Farrel 1984, 'Verbal modifiers as argument taking predicates: complex verbs as predicate complexes in Hungarian', *Groninger Arbeiten zur Germanistischen Linguistik* 25: 23–71.

Ackerman, Farrel 1987, 'Pronominal incorporation: the case of prefixal adverbs', in Kenesei (ed.) 1987, pp. 213–260.

Ackerman, Farrel and Gert Webelhuth 1997, 'The composition of (dis)continuous predicates: lexical or syntactic?', *Acta Linguistica Hungarica* 44, 317–340.

Alberti, Gábor 1995, 'Role assignment in Hungarian possessive constructions', in Kenesei (ed.) 1995, pp. 11–28.

Alberti, Gábor 1997a, *Argument Selection*, Frankfurt am Main: Peter Lang.

Alberti, Gábor 1997b, 'Restrictions on the degree of referentiality of arguments in Hungarian sentences', *Acta Linguistica Hungarica* 44: 341–362.

Alberti, Gábor 1998, 'On passivization in Hungarian', in de Groot and Kenesei (eds.) 1998, pp. 103–122.

Alberti, Gábor 1999, 'Climbing for aspect', paper presented at the Workshop on verb clusters Dutch–Hungarian Study Center, Öttevény, Oct. 1999.

Alberti, Gábor and István Kenesei (eds.) 2000, *Approaches to Hungarian 7*, Szeged: JATE.

Alberti, Gábor and Anna Medve 2000, 'Focus constructions and the "scope-inversion puzzle" in Hungarian', in Alberti and Kenesei (eds.) 2000, pp. 93–118.

Alexiadou, Artemis and Elena Anagnostopoulou 1998, 'Parametrizing AGR: word order, V-movement and EPP-checking', *Natural Language and Linguistic Theory* 16: 491–539.

Baker, Mark 1985, 'The mirror principle and morphosyntactic explanation', *Linguistic Inquiry* 16: 373–415.

Bánréti, Zoltán 1994, 'Coordination', in Kiefer and É. Kiss (eds.) 1994, pp. 355–414.

Bartos, Huba 1997, 'On "subjective" and "objective" agreement in Hungarian', *Acta Linguistica Hungarica* 44: 363–384.

Bartos, Huba 1999a, *Morfoszintaxis és interpretáció: a magyar inflexiós jelenségek szintaktikai háttere*, Ph.D. dissertation, Budapest: ELTE.

Bartos, Huba 1999b. 'Verbal complexes and morpho-syntactic merger', paper presented at the Workshop on verb clusters Dutch–Hungarian Study Center, Öttevény, Oct. 1999.

Bartos, Huba 2000a, 'Az alanyi és a tárgyas ragozásról', in Büky and Maleczki (eds.) 2000, pp. 153–170.

Bartos, Huba 2000b, 'Topics, quantifiers, subjects: the preverbal field in Chinese and Hungarian', paper presented at the International Symposium on Topic and Focus in Chinese, June 21–22, 2000, Hong Kong Polytechnic University, to appear in Sze-Wing Tang and Dingxu Shi (eds.), *Topic and Focus in Chinese*.

Bartos, Huba 2000c, 'Affix order in Hungarian and the Mirror Principle', in Alberti and Kenesei (eds.) 2000, 53–70.

Bartos, Huba 2001, 'Mutatónévmási módosítók a magyar főnévi szerkezetekben: egyezés vagy osztozás?', in Marianne Bakró-Nagy, Zoltán Bánréti and Katalin É. Kiss (eds.), *Újabb eredmények a strukturális magyar nyelvtan és a nyelvtörténet köréből*, Budapest: Osiris.

Beghelli, Filippo and Tim Stowell 1997, 'Distributivity and negation: the syntax of *each* and *every*', in Szabolcsi (ed.) 1997b, pp. 71–108.

Bittner, Maria and Ken Hale 1996, 'The structural determination of case and agreement', *Linguistic Inquiry* 27: 1–68.

Borer, Hagit 1989, 'Anaphoric Agr', in Osvaldo Jaeggli and Ken J. Safir (eds.), *The null subject parameter*, Dordrecht: Kluwer, pp. 69–109.

Brassai, Sámuel 1860, 1863–65, 'A magyar mondat', *Magyar Akadémiai Értesítő. A Nyelv- és Széptudományi Osztály Közlönye* 1: 279–399; 3: 3–128, 173–409.

Bresnan, Joan 1982, 'Control and complementation', *Linguistic Inquiry* 13: 343–434.

Bródy, Michael 1990a, 'Remarks on the order of elements in the Hungarian focus field', in Kenesei (ed.) 1990, pp. 95–122.

Bródy, Michael 1990b, 'Some remarks on the focus field in Hungarian', *University College London Working Papers in Linguistics* 2, 201–225.

Bródy, Michael 1995, 'Focus and checking theory', in Kenesei (ed.) 1995, pp. 29–44.

Bródy, Michael 1999, 'Word order, restructuring and mirror theory', ms., University College London / Linguistic Institute of the Hungarian Academy of Sciences.

Bródy, Michael 2000, 'Mirror theory: Syntactic representation in perfect syntax', *Linguistic Inquiry* 31: 29–56.

Bródy, Michael and Anna Szabolcsi 2000, 'Overt scope: a case study in Hungarian', ms., University College London / New York University.

Büky, László and Márta Maleczki (eds.) 1995, *A mai magyar nyelv leírásának újabb módszerei* II, Szeged: JATE.

Büky, László and Márta Maleczki (eds.) 1998, *A mai magyar nyelv leírásának újabb módszerei* III, Szeged: JATE.

Büky, László and Márta Maleczki (eds.) 2000, *A mai magyar nyelv leírásának újabb módszerei* IV, Szeged: JATE.

Cardinaletti, Anna and Michal Starke 1999, 'The typology of structural deficiency: a case study of three classes of pronouns', in Henk van Riemsdijk (ed.), *Clitics in the Languages of Europe*, Berlin: Mouton de Gruyter, 145–233.

Chomsky, Noam 1976, 'Conditions on rules of grammar', *Linguistic Analysis* 2: 303–349.

Chomsky, Noam 1981, *Lectures on Government and Binding*, Dordrecht: Reidel.

Chomsky, Noam 1986, *Knowledge of Language*, New York: Praeger.

Chomsky, Noam 1995, *The Minimalist Program*, Cambridge, MA: MIT Press.

Chomsky, Noam and Morris Halle 1968, *The Sound Pattern of English*, New York: Harper and Row.

Cinque, Guglielmo 1997, *Adverbs and Functional Heads: A Crosslinguistic Perspective*, New York/Oxford: Oxford University Press.

Comorovski, Ileana 1996, *Interrogative Phrases and the Syntax–Semantics Interface*, Dordrecht: Kluwer.

Csirmaz, Anikó and Balázs Surányi 1998, 'Are there expletives in Hungarian?', paper presented at the First Conference on Linguistic Theory in Eastern European Languages, April 19–21, Szeged University.

Dalmi, Gréte 1995, *Hungarian Infinitival Constructions*, Master of philosophy Thesis, University of Sydney.

Diesing, M. 1992, 'Bare plural subjects and the derivation of logical representations', *Linguistic Inquiry* 23: 353–380.

Dikken, Marcel den 1995, *Particles: On the Syntax of Verb–Particle, Triadic, and Causative Constructions*, New York/Oxford: Oxford University Press.

Dikken, Marcel den 1999a, 'On the structural representation of possession and agreement: the case of (anti-)agreement in Hungarian possessed nominal phrases', in Kenesei (ed.) 1999, pp. 137–178.

Dikken, Marcel den 1999b, 'Agreement and clause union', ms., City University of New York.

Dikken, Marcel den 2000, 'A tárgyi személyes névmások szerkezete és az egyeztetés', in Büky and Maleczki (eds.) 2000, pp. 171–180.

Dikken, Marcel den and Anastasia Giannakidou 2000, 'What the hell?', to appear in *NELS* 31.

Dimitrova-Vulchanova, Mila 1998, 'Fragments of Balkan Nominal Structure', in Artemis Alexiadou and Chris Wilder (eds.), *Possessors, Predicates and Movement in the Determiner Phrase*, Amsterdam: John Benjamins, pp. 333–360.

Dobrovie-Sorin, Carmen 1993, *Romanian Syntax*, Berlin: Mouton de Gruyter.

É. Kiss, Katalin 1977, 'Topic and focus in Hungarian syntax', *Montreal Working Papers in Linguistics* 8, 1–42.

É. Kiss, Katalin 1981, 'Syntactic relations in Hungarian, a 'free' word order language', *Linguistic Inquiry* 12: 185–215.

É. Kiss, Katalin 1985–1986, 'Parasitic chains', *The Linguistic Review* 5: 41–74.

É. Kiss, Katalin 1987a, *Configurationality in Hungarian*, Dordrecht: Reidel.

É. Kiss, Katalin 1987b, 'Is the VP universal?' in Kenesei (ed.) 1987, pp. 13–87.

É. Kiss, Katalin 1988, 'Még egyszer a magyar mondat intonációjáról és hangsúlyozásáról', *Nyelvtudományi Közlemények* 89: 1–52.

É. Kiss, Katalin 1990, 'Why noun–complement clauses are barriers', in Joan Mascaro and Marina Nespor (eds.), *A Festschrift for Henk van Riemsdijk*, Dordrecht: Foris, pp. 265–277.

É. Kiss, Katalin 1991a, 'Logical structure in syntactic structure: the case of Hungarian', in James Huang and Robert May (eds.), *Logical Structure and Syntactic Structure*, Dordrecht: Reidel, pp. 111–148.

É. Kiss, Katalin 1991b, 'On the locality condition of anaphora and pronominal variable binding', in Jan Koster and Eric Reuland (eds.), *Long Distance Anaphora*, Cambridge University Press, pp. 245–261.

É. Kiss, Katalin 1991c, 'An argument for movement', in K. Netter and H. Haider (eds.), *Representation versus Derivation*, Dordrecht: Reidel, pp. 199–217.

É. Kiss, Katalin 1992, 'Az egyszerű mondat szerkezete', in Kiefer (ed.) 1992b, pp. 79–178.

É. Kiss, Katalin 1993, 'Wh-movement and specificity', *Natural Language and Linguistic Theory* 11: 85–120.

É. Kiss, Katalin 1994a, 'Sentence structure and word order', in Kiefer and É. Kiss (eds.) 1994, pp. 1–90.

É. Kiss, Katalin 1994b, 'Scrambling as the base generation of random complement order', in Norbert Corver and Henk van Riemsdijk (eds.), *Studies on Scrambling. Movement and Non-movement Approaches to Free-word-order Phenomena*, Berlin: Mouton de Gruyter, pp. 221–256.

É. Kiss, Katalin 1995a, 'Multiple topic, one focus?', *GLOW Newsletter* 34: 73.

É. Kiss, Katalin 1995b, 'Többszörös fókusz a magyar mondatszerkezetben', in Büky and Maleczki (eds.) 1995, pp. 47–66.

É. Kiss, Katalin 1995c, 'The definiteness effect revisited', in Kenesei (ed.) 1995, pp. 63–88.

É. Kiss, Katalin 1996, 'Two subject positions in English', *The Linguistic Review* 13: 119–142.

É. Kiss, Katalin 1998a, 'Multiple topic, one focus?' *Acta Linguistica Hungarica* 45: 3–30.

É. Kiss, Katalin 1998b, 'Identificational focus versus information focus', *Language* 74: 245–273.

É. Kiss, Katalin 1998c, 'Discourse-configurationality in the languages of Europe', in Anna Siewierska (ed.), *Constituent Order in the Languages of Europe*, Berlin: Mouton de Gruyter, pp. 681–729.

É. Kiss, Katalin 1998d, 'Mondattan', in K. É. Kiss, Ferenc Kiefer, and Péter Siptár, *Új magyar nyelvtan*, Budapest: Osiris, pp. 15–185.

É. Kiss, Katalin 1999a, 'Verbal prefixes or postpositions? Postpositional aspectualizers in Hungarian', in de Groot and Kenesei (eds.), pp. 123–148.

É. Kiss, Katalin 1999b, 'Strategies of complex predicate formation and the Hungarian Verbal Complex', in Kenesei (ed.) 1999, pp. 115–136.

É. Kiss, Katalin 2000a, 'The Hungarian noun phrase is like the English noun phrase', in Alberti and Kenesei (eds.) 2000, pp. 119–150.

É. Kiss, Katalin 2000b, 'A [+referáló] és [+specifikus] jegyek ellenőrzése a kontrasztív topik esetében', in Büky and Maleczki (eds.) 2000, pp. 85–97.

É. Kiss, Katalin 2001, 'Parasitic chains revisited', in Peter W. Culicover and Paul M. Postal (eds.), *Parasitic Gaps*, Cambridge, MA: MIT Press, pp. 99–123.

É. Kiss, Katalin to appear, 'The EPP in a topic-prominent language', in Peter Svenonius (ed.), *Subjects, Topics, and the EPP*, Oxford-New York: Oxford University Press.

É. Kiss, Katalin and Ferenc Kiefer (eds.) 1994, *The Syntactic Structure of Hungarian: Syntax and Semantics* 27, San Diego / New York: Academic Press.

É. Kiss, Katalin, Ferenc Kiefer, and Péter Siptár 1998, *Új Magyar Nyelvtan*, Budapest: Osiris.

Emonds, Joseph 1978, *A Transformational Approach to English Syntax*, New York: Academic Press.

Enç, Mürvet 1991, 'The semantics of specificity', *Linguistic Inquiry* 22: 21–25.

Farkas, Donka 1986, 'The syntactic position of focus in Hungarian', *Natural Language and Linguistic Theory* 4: 77–96.

Farkas, Donka 1987, 'Direct object pro in Hungarian', in Kenesei (ed.) 1987, pp. 191–211.

Farkas, Donka 1990, 'Two cases of underspecification in morphology', *Linguistic Inquiry* 21: 539–550.

Giannakidou, Anastasia 2000, 'Negative ... concord?' *Natural Language and Linguistic Theory* 18: 457–523.

Giannakidou, Anastasia and J. Quer 1995, 'Two mechanisms for the licensing of indefinites', in L. Gabriele et al. (eds.), *Papers from the 6th Annual Meeting of the Formal Linguistics Society of Midamerica*, Bloomington, IN: IULC Publications.

Greenberg, Joseph H. 1966, 'Some universals of grammar with particular reference to the order of meaningful elements', in Joseph Greenberg (ed.), *Universals of Language*, Cambridge, MA: MIT Press, pp. 73–113.

Grimshaw, Jane 1990, *Argument Structure*, Cambridge, MA: MIT Press.

Grimshaw, Jane 1991, 'Extended projection', ms., Brandeis University.

Groot, Casper de 1981, 'Sentence intertwining in Hungarian', in M. A. Bolkenstein et al. (eds.), *Predication and Expression in Functional Grammar*, New York: Academic Press, 41–64.

Groot, Casper de and István Kenesei (eds.) 1998, *Approaches to Hungarian* 5, Szeged: JATE.

Gyuris, Beáta 1999, 'The interpretation of adverbial quantifiers in contrastive topic in Hungarian', in Matako Hirotani and Andries Coetze (eds.), *Proceedings of NELS 30*, Amherst, MA: University of Massachusetts, pp. 259–274.

Gyuris, Beáta 2000, 'Contrastive topics crosslinguistically', paper presented at the 2nd International Conference in Contrastive Semantics and Pragmatics, Sept. 11–13, Cambridge.

Haader, Lea 1998, 'A mondatátszövődés a nyelvhasználat szemszögéből', *Magyar Nyelvőr* 122: 318–324.

Haegeman, Liliane 1995, *The Syntax of Negation*, Cambridge: Cambridge University Press.

Haegeman, Liliane and R. Zanuttini 1991, 'Negative heads and the Neg Criterion', *The Linguistic Review* 8: 233–251.

Hallman, Peter 1998, 'Reiterative syntax', in J. Black and V. Motapayane (eds.), *Clitics, Pronouns, and Movements*. Amsterdam: John Benjamins, 87–131.

Herburger, Elena 1997, 'Focus and weak noun phrases', *Natural Language Semantics* 5: 53–78.

Horvath, Julia 1986a, *Focus in the Theory of Grammar and the Syntax of Hungarian*, Dordrecht: Foris.

Horvath, Julia 1986b, 'Remarks on the configurationality issue', in Abraham and de Meij (eds.) 1986, pp. 65–87.

Horvath, Julia 1987, 'On models with a VP-less phrase structure', in Kenesei (ed.) 1987, pp. 133–165.

Horvath, Julia 1990, 'Parasitic gap constructions: an adjunct/argument asymmetry', in Kenesei (ed.) 1990, pp. 65–94.

Horvath, Julia 1992, 'Anti-c-command and case-compatibility in the licensing of parasitic chains', *The Linguistic Review* 9, 183–218.

Horvath, Julia 1995, 'Partial wh-movement and wh-scope-markers', in Kenesei (ed.) 1995, pp. 89–124.

Horvath, Julia 1997, 'The status of "Wh-expletives" and the partial Wh-movement construction in Hungarian', *Natural Language and Linguistic Theory* 15: 509–572.

Horvath, Julia 1998, 'Wh-phrases and the wh-scope-marker strategy in Hungarian interrogatives', *Acta Linguistica Hungarica* 45: 31–60.

Hunyadi, László 1986, 'The expression of logical scope in Hungarian: on its syntax and semantics', in Abraham and de Meij (eds.) 1986, pp. 89–102.

Hunyadi, László 1997, *Hungarian Sentence Prosody and Universal Grammar: Studies in Applied Linguistics* 3, Debrecen: Kossuth Lajos University.

Hunyadi, László 1999, 'The outlines of a metrical syntax of Hungarian', *Acta Linguistica Hungarica* 46, 69–94.

Jacobs, Joachim 1986, 'The syntax of focus and adverbials in German', in Abraham and de Meij (eds.) 1986, pp. 103–127.

Jakab, Edit 1998, talk presented at the Fourth International Conference on the Structure of Hungarian, Pécs: Janus Pannonius University.

Kálmán, C. György et al. 1989, A magyar segédigék rendszere. *Általános Nyelvészeti Tanulmányok* 17: 49–103.

Kálmán, László et al. 1986, 'Hocus, focus, and verb types in Hungarian infinitive constructions', in Abraham and de Meij (eds.) 1986, pp. 129–142.

Kálmán, László 1990, 'Deferred information: the semantics of commitment', in László Kálmán and László Pólos (eds.), *Papers from the Second Symposium on Logic and Language*, Budapest: Akadémiai Kiadó, pp. 125–157.

Kálmán, László 1995, 'Definiteness effect verbs in Hungarian', in Kenesei (ed.) 1995, pp. 221–242.

Kayne, Richard 1994, *The Antisymmetry of Syntax*, Cambridge, MA: MIT Press.

Kenesei, István (ed.) 1985, *Approaches to Hungarian 1*, Szeged: JATE.

Kenesei, István 1986, 'On the logic of Hungarian word order', in Abraham and de Meij (eds.) 1986, pp. 143–159.

Kenesei, István (ed.) 1987, *Approaches to Hungarian 2*, Szeged: JATE.

Kenesei, István 1989, 'On the interaction of lexical structure and logical form in pronominal binding', in László Marácz and Pietr Muysken (eds.), *Configurationality: The Typology of Asymmetries*, Dordrecht: Reidel.

Kenesei, István (ed.) 1990, *Approaches to Hungarian 3*, Szeged: JATE.

Kenesei, István 1992, 'Az alárendelt mondatok szerkezete', in Kiefer (ed.) 1992b, pp. 529–714.

Kenesei, István 1994, 'Subordinate clauses', in Kiefer and É. Kiss (eds.) 1994, pp. 275–354.

Kenesei, István (ed.) 1995, *Approaches to Hungarian 5*, Szeged: JATE.

Kenesei, István 1998, 'Adjuncts and arguments in VP-focus in Hungarian', *Acta Linguistica Hungarica* 45: 61–88.

Kenesei, István (ed.) 1999, *Crossing Boundaries*, Amsterdam: John Benjamins.

Kenesei, István 2000, 'Van-e segédige a magyarban?', in Kenesei (ed.), *Igei vonzatstruktúrák a magyarban*, Budapest: Osiris, pp. 157–196.

Kenesei, István and Csaba Pléh (eds.) 1992, *Approaches to Hungarian 4*, Szeged: JATE.

Khalaily, Shamir 1995, 'QR and the minimalist theory of syntax: the case of universally and negative quantified expressions in Palestinian Arabic', ms., University of Leiden.

Kiefer, Ferenc 1967, *On Emphasis and Word Order in Hungarian*, Bloomington, IN: Indiana University Press.

Kiefer, Ferenc 1992a, 'Az aspektus és a mondat szerkezete', in Kiefer (ed.) 1992b, pp. 797–886.

Kiefer, Ferenc (ed.) 1992b, *Strukturális magyar nyelvtan 1. Mondattan*, Budapest: Akadémiai Kiadó.

Kiefer, Ferenc 1994a, 'Aspect and syntactic structure', in Kiefer and É. Kiss (eds.) 1994, pp. 415–464.

Kiefer, Ferenc 1994b, 'Some peculiarities in the aspectual system of Hungarian', in C. Bache, H. Basbøll, and C. E. Lindberg (eds.), *Tense–Aspect–Aspectuality*, Berlin: de Gruyter.

Kiefer, Ferenc (ed.) 2000, *Strukturális magyar nyelvtan 3: Morfológia*, Budapest: Akadémiai Kiadó.

Kiefer, Ferenc and Katalin É. Kiss (eds.) 1994, *The Syntactic Structure of Hungarian: Syntax and Semantics 27*. San Diego / New York: Academic Press.

Kinyalolo, Kasangati 1990, *Syntactic Dependencies and the Spec–Head Agreement Hypothesis in KiLega*, Ph.D. dissertation, UCLA.

Komlósy, András 1985, 'Predicate complementation', in Kenesei (ed.) 1985, pp. 53–75.

Komlósy, András 1992, 'Régensek és vonzatok', in Kiefer (ed.) 1992b, pp. 299–529.

Komlósy, András 1994, 'Complements and adjuncts', in É. Kiss and Kiefer (eds.) 1994, pp. 91–178.

Koopman, Hilda and Anna Szabolcsi 2000, *Verbal Complexes*, Cambridge, MA: MIT Press.

Kratzer, Angelika 1995, 'Stage-level and individual-level predicates', in G. N. Carlson and F. J. Pelletier (eds.), *The Generic Book*, Chicago, IL: The University of Chicago Press, pp. 125–175.

Krifka, Manfred 1992, 'A framework for focus-sensitive quantification', in Ch. Barker and David Dowty (eds.), *SALT II. Proceedings from the Second Conference on Semantics and Linguistic Theory, Working Papers in Linguistics* 40, Columbus, OH: Ohio State University, pp. 215–236.

Kuno, Susumu 1973, *Japanese Grammar*, Cambridge, MA: MIT Press.

Laczkó, Tibor 1985, 'Deverbal nominals and their complements in noun phrases', in Kenesei (ed.), pp. 93–119.

Laczkó, Tibor 1990, 'On arguments and adjuncts of derived nominals: a lexical-functional approach', in Kenesei (ed.) 1990, pp. 123–147.

Laczkó, Tibor 1995a, *The Syntax of Hungarian Noun Phrases: MetaLinguistica* 2, Frankfurt am Main: Peter Lang.

Laczkó, Tibor 1995b, 'On the status of *való* in adjectivalized constituents in noun phrases', in Kenesei (ed.) 1995, pp. 125–152.

Ladusaw, William 1992. 'Expressing negation', in Ch. Barker and D. Dowty (eds.), *SALT II. Proceedings from the Second Conference on Semantics and Linguistic Theory, Working Papers in Linguistics* 40, Columbus, OH: Ohio State University, pp. 237–259.

Ladusaw, William 1994. 'Thetic and categorical, stage and individual, weak and strong', in M. Harvey and L. Santelman (eds.), *SALT 4*, Ithaca, NY: Cornell University Press, pp. 220–229.

Lipták, Anikó 1998, 'A magyar fókuszemelések egy minimalista elemzése', in Büky and Maleczki (eds.) 1998, pp. 93–116.

Lipták, Anikó 2000, 'On the difference between focus movement and wh-movement', *GLOW Newsletter* 44: 78–79.

Maleczki, Márta 1992, 'Bare common nouns and their relation to the temporal constitution of events in Hungarian', in Paul Dekker and Martin Stokhof (eds.), *Proceedings of the Eighth Amsterdam Colloquium*, Institute for Logic, Language, and Computation, Amsterdam University, pp. 347–365.

Maleczki, Márta 1995, 'On the definiteness effect in Hungarian', in Kenesei (ed.) 1995, pp. 263–284.

Maleczki, Márta 1999, 'Weak subjects in fixed space', *Acta Linguistica Hungarica* 46: 95–118.

Marácz, László 1986a, 'Dressed or naked: the case of the PP in Hungarian', in Abraham and de Meij (eds.) 1986, pp. 227–252.

Marácz, László 1986b, 'On coreferential and bound variable interpretation in non-configurational languages', *Theoretical Linguistic Research* 2: 85–172.

Marácz, László 1988, 'Locality and correspondence effects in Hungarian', in A. Cardinaletti, G. Cinque, and G. Giusti (eds.), *Annali di Ca' Foscari, Constituent Structure. Papers from the 1987 GLOW Conference*, Venezia, pp. 203–237.

Marácz, László 1989, *Asymmetries in Hungarian*, Ph.D. dissertation, University of Groningen.

May, Robert 1985, *Logical Form, Its Structure and Derivation*, Cambridge, MA: MIT Press.

Molnár, Valéria 1998, 'Topic in focus: the syntax, phonology, semantics, and pragmatics of the so-called "contrastive topic" in Hungarian and German', *Acta Linguistica Hungarica* 45: 89–166.

Olsvay, Csaba 1999, 'The Hungarian verbal complex: an alternative approach', paper presented at the workshop on verb clusters Dutch–Hungarian Study Center, Öttevény, Oct. 1999.

Olsvay, Csaba 2000a, 'Formális jegyek egyeztetése a magyar nemsemleges mondatokban', in Büky and Maleczki (eds.) 2000, pp. 119–152.

Olsvay, Csaba 2000b, *Negative Quantifiers in the Hungarian Sentence*, MA Thesis, Eötvös Loránd University, Budapest.

Payne, John and Erika Chisarik 2000, 'Demonstrative constructions in Hungarian', in Alberti and Kenesei (eds.) 2000, pp. 179–198.

Pesetsky, David 1987, 'Wh-in-situ: movement and unselective binding', in Eric Reuland and Alice ter Meulen (eds.), *The Representation of (In)definiteness*, Cambridge, MA: MIT Press, pp. 98–129.

Piñon, Christopher 1992, 'Heads in the focus field', in Kenesei and Pléh (eds.) 1992, pp. 99–122.

Piñon, Christopher 1995, 'Around the progressive in Hungarian', in Kenesei (ed.) 1995, pp. 153–191.

Puskás, Genovéva 1998, 'On the Neg Criterion in Hungarian', *Acta Linguistica Hungarica* 45: 167–213.

Puskás, Genovéva 2000, *Word Order in Hungarian: The Syntax of A' Positions*, Amsterdam: John Benjamins.

Rebrus, Péter 2000, 'Morfofonológiai jelenségek a magyarban', in Kiefer (ed.) 2000, pp. 763–949.

Reinhart, Tanya 1983, *Anaphora and Semantic Interpretation*, London: Croom Helm.

Riemsdijk, Henk van 1998, 'Categorial feature magnetism: the endocentricity and distribution of projections', *Journal of Comparative Germanic Linguistics* 2: 1–18.

Rouveret, Alain 1991, 'Functional categories and agreement', *The Linguistic Review* 8, 353–387.

Stechow, Arnim von and Susanne Uhmann 1986, 'Some remarks on focus projection', in Abraham and de Meij (eds.) 1986, pp. 295–320.

Stowell, Timothy 1981, *Origins of Phrase Structure*, Ph.D. dissertation, Cambridge, MA: MIT.

Surányi, Balázs 2000, 'Operator and head movement in Hungarian: from checking to marking', *DOXIMP 4, Research Institute for Linguistics, Hungarian Academy of Sciences, Working Papers in the Theory of Grammar* 7, 1: 35–45.

Szabolcsi, Anna 1980, 'Az aktuális mondattagolás szemantikájához', *Nyelvtudományi Közlemények* 82: 59–82.

Szabolcsi, Anna 1981a, 'The semantics of topic-focus articulation', in Jan Groenendijk et al. (eds.), *Formal Methods in the Study of Language*, Amsterdam: Matematisch Centrum.

Szabolcsi, Anna 1981b, 'The possessive construction in Hungarian: a configurational category in a non-configurational language', *Acta Linguistica Academiae Scientiarum Hungaricae* 31, 261–289.

Szabolcsi, Anna 1981c, 'Compositionality in focus', *Folia Linguistica* 15: 141–162.

Szabolcsi, Anna 1983a, 'Focussing properties, or the trap of first order', *Theoretical Linguistics* 10:125–145.

Szabolcsi, Anna 1983b, 'The possessor that ran away from home', *The Linguistic Review* 3: 89–102.

Szabolcsi, Anna 1986, 'From definiteness effect to lexical integrity', in Abraham and de Meij (eds.) 1986, pp. 321–348.

Szabolcsi, Anna 1992a, *A birtokos szerkezet és az egzisztenciális mondat*, Budapest: Akadémiai Kiadó.

Szabolcsi, Anna 1992b, 'Subject suppression or lexical PRO? The case of derived nominals in Hungarian', *Lingua* 86, 149–176.

Szabolcsi, Anna 1994a, 'The noun phrase', in Kiefer and É. Kiss (eds.) 1994, pp. 179–274.

Szabolcsi, Anna 1994b, 'All quantifiers are not equal: the case of focus', *Acta Linguistica Hungarica* 42: 171–187.

Szabolcsi, Anna 1997a, 'Strategies for scope taking', in Szabolcsi (ed.) 1997b, pp. 109–154.

Szabolcsi, Anna (ed.) 1997b, *Ways of Scope Taking*, Dordrecht: Kluwer.

Szabolcsi, Anna and Tibor Laczkó 1992, 'A főnévi csoport szerkezete', in Kiefer (ed.), pp. 179–298.

Szendrői, Kriszta 1999, 'Stress driven Focus Movement and stress avoiding verbs', paper presented at the Workshop on verb clusters Dutch–Hungarian Study Center, Öttevény, Oct. 1999.

Tóth, Ildikó 1999, 'Negative polarity item licensing in Hungarian', *Acta Linguistica Hungarica* 46: 119–142.

Tóth, Ildikó 2000a, *Inflected infinitives in Hungarian*, Ph.D. dissertation, Tilburg University.

Tóth, Ildikó 2000b, '-*va* and -*ván* participles in Hungarian', in Alberti and Kenesei (eds.) 2000, pp. 237–258.

Varga, László 1999, 'Rhythmical variation in Hungarian', *Phonology* 15, 227–266.

Vogel, Irene and István Kenesei 1987, 'The interface between phonology and other components of grammar', *Phonology* 4: 243–263.

Williams, Edwin 1987, 'Implicit arguments, the binding theory, and control', *Natural Language and Linguistic Theory* 5: 151–180.

Zanuttini, Raffaela 1997, *Negation and Clausal Structure*, Oxford: Oxford University Press.

Zolnay, Gyula 1926, 'Mondatátszövődés', *Értekezések a Magyar Tudományos Akadémia Nyelv- és Széptudományi Osztálya Köréből* 23.

Index